MASTER OF THE SACRED PAGE

Modern scholarship has examined the life and works of Robert Grosseteste (ca. 1170–1253) mainly in a philosophical or episcopal context, yet Grosseteste wrote many treatises on pastoral theology, spent some years as a regent master in theology at the University of Oxford and maintained interest in theological discourse throughout his time as Bishop of Lincoln.

This book offers the first scholarly study of Grosseteste as theologian, taking account of the whole range of his theological writing both in published and in unedited sources. Ginther reveals the central focus of Grosseteste's theology as the person and work of Christ, with the person of Christ as the interpretive key by which humanity comes to see the Trinity in the created world and the means by which humanity may participate in the divine. Surveying some of the major doctrinal issues of the thirteenth century, this book offers a thorough introduction to the theology of the period.

FOR KATYA AND NICOLA

Master of the Sacred Page

A Study of the Theology of Robert Grosseteste, ca. 1229/30–1235

JAMES R. GINTHER
St Louis University, USA

LONDON AND NEW YORK

First published 2004 by Ashgate Publishing

Published 2016 by Routledge
2 Park Square, Milton Park, Abingdon, Oxon OX14 4RN
711 Third Avenue, New York, NY 10017, USA

Routledge is an imprint of the Taylor & Francis Group, an informa business

Copyright © James R. Ginther 2004

All rights reserved. No part of this book may be reprinted or reproduced or utilised in any form or by any electronic, mechanical, or other means, now known or hereafter invented, including photocopying and recording, or in any information storage or retrieval system, without permission in writing from the publishers.

Notice:
Product or corporate names may be trademarks or registered trademarks, and are used only for identification and explanation without intent to infringe.

British Library Cataloguing in Publication Data
Ginther James R.
  Master of the sacred page: a study of the theology of
  Robert Grosseteste, ca. 1229/30–1235
  1. Grosseteste, Robert, 1175?–1253 2. Theology, Doctrinal –
  History – Middle Ages, 600–1500
  I. Title
  230'.092

US Library of Congress Cataloging-in-Publication Data
Ginther, James R.
  Master of the sacred page: a study of the theology of Robert Grosseteste, ca. 1229/30–1235 / James R. Ginther
    p. cm.
  Includes bibliographical references and index.
  ISBN 0–7546–1649–5 (alk. paper)
  1. Grosseteste, Robert, 1175?–1253. 2. Theology – England – History – Middle Ages, 600–1500. I. Title.

BX4705.G6233G56 2004
230'.2'092–dc22   2004005411

ISBN 13 : 978-0-7546-1649-8 (hbk)

Contents

Preface vii
Acknowledgments xi
Abbreviations xiii

Introduction 1

PART I   A THEOLOGIAN'S TASK

1 Grosseteste's Theological Writings 13
2 Grosseteste and the Theology of the Schools 25
3 The Subject Matter of Theology 33
4 Tools and Resources 53

PART II   A THEOLOGIAN'S VISION

5 A Triune and Infinite God 89
6 The Necessity of the Incarnation 121
7 The Church, Pastoral Care and the Deification of Humanity 151

Conclusion 189

Appendix: Transcription of Super Psalterium *100* 193
Bibliography 213
Index 229

Preface

About seven years ago, I began research for a monographic study that was to take the rather dull title of *The Exegesis of the Psalms in the Theology of Robert Grosseteste*. It was to be an extension of my doctoral thesis on Grosseteste's *Super Psalterium*, where I had examined the ecclesiological themes of his commentary. However, it soon occurred to me that the second part of the title (*in the Theology . . .*) was far more problematic than I had first realised. What exactly was Grosseteste's theology? What were his principal theological positions? Did I understand his own methods of theological discourse? What was the relationship between his philosophy (now well established in the scholarship) and his career as a professional theologian? It seemed that, if I wanted to place his commentary on the Psalms in the context of his theology, these kinds of questions needed to be answered. My putative book project, in cinematic terms, lacked a good backstory.

As I began to investigate the story of Grosseteste the theologian, I was surprised to discover that so many conclusions had been drawn, even though few had actually studied all of his theological writings (and no one had even established that corpus). While some scholars have spoken of specific theological positions that Grosseteste did hold, no one had taken the time to investigate fully the character of his theology. Perhaps the most disconcerting is the image of Grosseteste as a 'biblical theologian', a phrase used more often than not as code for 'quaint' or 'outdated'. Grosseteste somehow refused to embrace the major aims of scholastic theology. There were a number of assumptions being made here, not only about the status of Grosseteste as a theologian, but about the entire scholastic project. My interest in Grosseteste's theology was no longer for backstory purposes, but rather had been transformed into a major research agenda.

Nonetheless, even the most casual of reader will notice that the focus of this present study seems rather narrow for such a major undertaking. Why examine only five or six years of an intellectual life that appears to have lasted for more than sixty? The primary reason is that I wanted to begin my study of Grosseteste's theology within the general institutional context of scholastic theology, the medieval university. I wanted to re-examine Grosseteste's position in the narrative of scholastic theology, which means it was necessary to focus on the years in which he was a master of the sacred page at Oxford. I am the first to admit that a distinction between Grosseteste's magisterial and episcopal periods, at least in terms of his theology, is slightly subjective, as are all periodisations employed by historians. There are a number of themes and arguments that will emerge in this study that beg for further comment, and those comments are only made possible by looking to Grosseteste's theological work after 1235. Nonetheless, in the interest of pursuing the question whether

Grosseteste fully understood the scholastic project, I consider it necessary to focus on the period of time in which he was actually teaching in the schools. To make matters even more challenging, I posit a rather short career: it begins where the documentary evidence demonstrates that he was teaching at Oxford, sometime around 1229/30. It may have been a short career, but it was a robust one and there is certainly no shortage of theological works from that period.

This book thus presents a narrative of Grosseteste the scholastic theologian. Now I use the term 'narrative' in the broadest sense, for there is no attempt to tell a story in a traditional form. And yet concern for narrative has been uppermost in my mind. I have paid attention, for example, to the way in which Grosseteste has functioned within the story of the rise of scholastic theology, if only to suggest reasons why this should be changed. In addition, as I have sought to understand Grosseteste's teaching on major theological doctrines, I have tried to figure that into the larger narrative of the development of doctrine in the Latin West. Above all, since the story of Grosseteste the theologian is not well known, I have attempted to summarise some of his key arguments and texts. This has meant that the descriptive sometimes overshadows the analytical. My hope is that this study will ignite further research on Grosseteste's theology.

What I have not done consistently in composing this story is to extend the narrative beyond the confines of Grosseteste's own theology. While I attempt to account for Grosseteste's theological sources, only in rare instances do I investigate how his thought was received by his successors – and even in those cases it is only to suggest a new focus for studying Grosseteste's own arguments. It is not that I think that looking for the *nachleben* of Grosseteste's teaching is a deficient historical method; rather, I consider it my first priority to tell Grosseteste's story coherently before any epilogue can be traced. This strategy represents a considerable difference from that of many scholars who have foraged Grosseteste's writings for the background to the thought of later luminaries such as Richard Fishacre, Richard Rufus, Thomas of York and Bonaventure. My aim is to provide a more complete (or perhaps just more complex) resource for those scholars who will mine Grosseteste's theology as the source of later thinkers.

Because the story presented here is somewhat new, some arguments are contrary to current scholarship. Thankfully, this has not diminished the collegiality of scholars who have studied the life and works of this thirteenth-century scholar and bishop. I remain grateful for the generosity of many colleagues and friends. I have the privilege of still gleaning from the wise counsels of Joseph Goering and his detailed critique challenged me to present my arguments as lucidly as possible. Neil Lewis, Jim Long and James McEvoy also commented on a number of chapters and the quality improved dramatically because of their suggestions. I must also thank Fr. Servus Gieben, OFM Cap., Frank Mantello, Sr. Maura O'Carroll SND, Cecilia Panti and Elizabeth Streitz-Guez for their aid and suggestions at various stages of writing and research. All remaining errors and infelicities naturally remain my responsibility.

I completed most of the research and writing during my first professional appointment in the Department of Theology and Religious Studies, University of Leeds. I therefore owe a deep debt to my former colleagues who helped to shape this historian into a theologian. I am especially grateful to Linda Hogan (now of the Irish School of Ecumenics, Trinity College, Dublin), John McGuckin (now of Union Theological Seminary, New York), Philip Mellor and Hugh Pyper. My colleagues in the Centre for Medieval Studies at Leeds, and especially the tireless and resourceful Mary Swan, were continuously supportive of my research. I also had the privilege of working with excellent graduate students who patiently endured my monologues about Grosseteste. The joy of supervising PhD candidates is that you learn so much from the students, and I am especially grateful to Yuichi Akae, Jeff Dubberely, Eva De Visscher and Suzanne Paul, all of whom challenged me in my thinking about Grosseteste and the complex contours of scholastic theology. The last stage of writing was completed at my new institutional home, St Louis University. My departmental colleagues have warmly welcomed me, which made an otherwise overwhelming first year enjoyable. I especially need to thank Wayne Hellmann, OFM Conv. and Ken Parker for their invaluable comments and suggestions. My fellow medievalists in the Department of History, Christine Caldwell and Michael Bailey, also shaped my thinking as I completed this study. I am also grateful to the Dean of Arts and Sciences for a small research grant in 2002, which aided in the completion of one part of the book, as well as to the School of Graduate Studies for a Summer Research Fellowship in 2003, which allowed me to complete the final draft. That fellowship also supplied funds to employ Joshua Benson as my Research Assistant. Not only did he assemble the bibliography, his careful reading and attention to detail has saved me from many embarrassing infelicities. I must also thank Charity Hunter for her assistance in the preparation of the index.

As with most academic prefaces, the final word of acknowledgment goes to family: to my wife, Diana, and our children, who suffered much as this book came to fruition. While the study of medieval theology yields its own rewards, the real joy of the last few years has been the birth of our two daughters, Katya and Nicola. Without realising it themselves, they always inspired me to do my best, to see work as play, to make time for play without work, and most of all to keep my feet firmly planted on the ground. I lovingly dedicate this book to them.

J.R.G.
Feast of St Dionysius
9 October 2003
St Louis, MO

Acknowledgments

Portions of this book were first published as separate articles. The introduction contains a discussion of the date of Grosseteste's regency, which first appeared as part of 'Natural Philosophy and Theology at Oxford in the Early Thirteenth Century: An Edition and Study of Robert Grosseteste's Inception Sermon (*Dictum* 19)', *Medieval Sermon Studies* 44 (2000),108–34. Chapter 1 appeared as part of 'The *Super Psalterium* in Context', in *Editing Robert Grosseteste*, ed. J. Goering and E. Mackie (Toronto: University of Toronto Press, 2003), pp. 31–60. Parts of Chapter 4 have appeared in two articles: 'Robert Grosseteste and the Theologian's Task', *Robert Grosseteste and the Beginnings of British Theological Tradition*, ed. M. O'Carroll (Rome: Istituto Storico dei Cappuccini, 2003), pp. 239–63; and '*Laudat sensum et significationem*: Robert Grosseteste on the Four Senses of Scripture', in *For Reverence of the Word: Medieval Scriptural Exegesis in Judaism, Christianity and Islam*, ed. J. Dammen McAuliffe, B. Walfish and J.W. Goering (Oxford University Press, 2002), pp. 237–55. I am grateful to the copyright holders for permission to include this material here. I must also thank Frank Mantello for allowing me to consult his translation of Grosseteste's letters, and Joseph Goering for kindly allowing me to cite his transcription of Grosseteste's *Dicta*.

Abbreviations

Major Text Collections

CCL	Corpus Christianorum, Series Latina
CCCM	Corpus Christianorum Continuatio Mediaevalis
PL	Patrologia Latina

Published Sources

Baur	*Die Philosophischen Werke des Robert Grosseteste, Bischofs von Lincoln*, Beiträge zur Geschichte der Philosophie des Mittelalters, Texte und Untersuchungen, 9 (Münster: Aschendorffsche Verlag, 1912)
Comm. in PA	*Commentarius in Posteriorum Analyticorum libros*, ed. P. Rossi (Florence: Olschki, 1981)
DCL	*De cessatione legalium*, ed. R.C. Dales and E.B. King, Auctores Britannici Medii Aevi, 7 (London: Oxford University Press for the British Academy, 1986)
DDM	*De decem mandatis*, ed. R.C. Dales and E.B. King, Auctores Britannici Medii Aevi, 10 (London: British Academy, 1987)
De dotibus	J. Goering, 'The *De dotibus* of Robert Grosseteste', *Mediaeval Studies* 44 (1982), 83–109
Epistolae	*Roberti Grosseteste quondam episcopi Lincolniensis Epistolae*, ed. H. Luard, Rolls Series 25 (London: Longman, 1861)
Expositio	*Expositio in epistolam sancti Pauli ad Galatas*, ed. J. McEvoy, in *Opera inedita Roberti Grosseteste volumen primum*, CCCM, 130, pp. 3–175 (Turnhout: Brepols, 1995)
Hex	*Hexaëmeron*, ed. R.C. Dales and S. Gieben, Auctores Britannici Medii Aevi, 6 (London: British Academy, 1982)

McEvoy, *Grosseteste*	James McEvoy, *Robert Grosseteste* (Oxford: Oxford University Press, 2000)
McEvoy, *Philosophy*	James McEvoy, *The Philosophy of Robert Grosseteste* (Oxford: Clarendon Press, 1982)
Southern, *Grosseteste*	R.W. Southern, *Robert Grosseteste: the Growth of an English Mind in Medieval Europe*, second edition (Oxford: Clarendon Press, 1992)
ST	Thomas Aquinas, *Summa Theologiae*, Leonine Edition, 3 vols (Turin: Marietti, 1948)
Summa aurea	William of Auxerre, *Summa aurea*, ed. J. Ribaillier, 4 vols, Spicilegium Bonaventurianum, 16–20 (Rome: College of St Bonaventure, 1980–87)
Tabula	Robert Grosseteste, *Tabula*, ed. P.W. Rosemann, in *Opera inedita Roberti Grosseteste volumen primum*, CCCM, 130, pp. 235–320 (Turnhout: Brepols, 1995)
Templum Dei	Robert Grosseteste, *Templum Dei*, ed. J. Goering and F.A.C. Mantello, Medieval Latin Texts, 14 (Toronto: PIMS, 1984)
Thomson, *Writings*	S.H. Thomson, *The Writings Of Robert Grosseteste* (Cambridge: Cambridge University Press, 1940)

Unpublished Sources

Dicta/Dictum	*Dicta Lincolniensis*: a Transcription of Oxford, Bodleian Library MS Bodley 198 by J. Goering; citations will note the foliation of this ms. I have checked it against the copy of the *Dicta* in London, British Library MS Royal 6.E.v.
Dictum 19, ed. Ginther	James R. Ginther, 'Natural Philosophy and Theology at Oxford in the Early Thirteenth Century. An Edition and Study of Robert Grosseteste's Inception Sermon', *Medieval Sermon Studies* 44 (2000), 108–34
Dictum 60, ed. Gieben	S. Gieben, 'Traces of God in Nature According to Robert Grosseteste. With the Text of the Dictum, *Omnis creatura speculum est*', *Franciscan Studies* 24 (1964), 144–58
Super Psalterium	The unedited commentary survives in six manuscripts. I will make reference to the following four witnesses: B = Bologna, Biblioteca dell'Archiginnasio MS A.983

Abbreviations

> D = Durham, Dean and Chapter Library
> MS A.III.12
> E = Eton College MS 8
> O = Oxford, Bodleian Library MS e Museo 15

Editorial Sigla

<···>	In the citation of unpublished material, the brackets signal editorial additions.
[···]	In the translations found in the text, these brackets indicate glosses or interpolations; in citations of unpublished material found in the footnotes, these brackets contain the manuscript evidence for the reading printed there.

Introduction

Sometime in the year 1229/30, Robert Grosseteste, a man now in his late fifties, stood before an Oxford audience composed of all regent masters and their students and began his inaugural sermon as a new master of theology. His inception into this guild of masters – the *universitas magistrorum* – would signal the beginning to a highly productive period in his life. We may surmise that uppermost in his mind that day was the new task at hand: to be a professional theologian. His inception sermon followed the standard rhetorical requirements, namely to praise sacred Scripture, the focal point of his future theological work. At the same time, Grosseteste took this opportunity to sketch out – either for his own sake or for the sake of his future students – how he envisaged combining his past experience as a natural philosopher with this new responsibility. Grosseteste left his audience with an assurance that he was not another philosopher masquerading in theologian's clothing; rather, he demonstrated an awareness that his new tasks demanded a change in his intellectual interests.[1] That was not a difficult transition to make, as Grosseteste had been deeply involved in the literature and practice of the pastoral care for more than ten years. Now, as a master of the sacred page, as well as the first lector to the Franciscans at Oxford, Grosseteste had the privileged opportunity of developing his pastoral interests within the larger context of the theological enterprise of a university. His sermon acted as the starting pistol for five or six years of intensive work, which would see him at his most creative to date.

This study seeks to develop and explain Grosseteste as theologian. I say 'develop' since this biographical facet is the least examined in the literature. Modern readers have enjoyed a plethora of studies on Grosseteste's philosophical and scientific views, perhaps just exceeding the amount of work on Grosseteste's episcopal period (1235–53). Although students of Grosseteste have been acutely aware of the robust activity of the five or six years in between these two periods of his intellectual life, few have taken the time to study his theological works as a whole. My desire to do so is not just an attempt to fill in a lacuna in Grosseteste scholarship (although that is as good a reason as any), or even to advance and support my own field of research. This study is also a response to Grosseteste himself, who saw this brief period of his long life as highly significant. In a sermon preached just before he died in 1253, he noted that in his lifetime he had been 'a cleric, a master of theology and a priest, and then a bishop'.[2] Grosseteste issued this statement as an example for confessors to enquire into the status and responsibilities of the penitent, and so was pointing out that his own status had changed at least three times in his life. And yet, for all the ways Grosseteste could have demarcated his life – a master of arts and natural philosopher, a member of an episcopal *familia*, a judge delegate, a student of theology, all of which happened before he became a theologian – he chose to highlight his short time as a master of theology as a major period of his life. It would seem a fitting response to his own self-assessment to develop an historical narrative of Grosseteste as theologian.

At the same time, this study will endeavour to explain Grosseteste the theologian. Herein lies the greater challenge, since it is one thing to reconstruct the details of his magisterial period, but it is something wholly other to provide a meaningful explanation of his theological outlook. These two tasks are not completely separate. Any explanation of Grosseteste's theology must remain connected to the very work he completed as a master of the sacred page. While such a claim may appear stultifyingly obvious to many, it has some profound implications for the way one may approach a historical study of an individual's theology. If we pay careful attention to what Grosseteste both said and did as a theologian, we retain a stronger sense of the historical reality of theology as it unfolded in the medieval schools. In stating this, I am suggesting that we resist the negative implications of one of the strongest motivations which draws modern scholars to the history of theology: empathy and familiarity. We often look to specific events or persons from the theological past because we have discovered a voice or set of ideas with which we can empathise or find familiarity. There is nothing inherently wrong with the way we make an initial connection with the past; however, it can wreak disastrous consequences if we continue to employ it as an interpretative principle. We may find the voices of the past to be familiar, but that cannot negate the *alterity* of their existence.[3] The most common way that this plays out is that we consider the experiences which inform these past theologians to be similar to our own. Hence, when we focus on a medieval theologian, we might assume that he functioned in the same way a modern theologian does. This can lead to some erroneous assumptions about the core character of Grosseteste's theology, not to mention the character of medieval theology in general.

It is not surprising, for example, that many historians of medieval theology have on occasion failed to communicate the centrality of the Bible in theological discourse from the scholastic period; instead, the rise of speculative theology has become the mainstay of most narratives. This perspective stemmed primarily from a desire to see an affinity between scholastic and modern theology, and still today retains a powerful influence on the literature. When Grosseteste comes into the frame and fails to present the standards of this speculative theology, the inevitable conclusion is that he was hardly a man of his time; instead he was either idiosyncratic in his approach or so conservative in his outlook that he successfully resisted the innovative methods of his century.

If, however, we are willing to engage medieval theology on its own historical terms, we can envisage a different image of the medieval theologian. This has two benefits for a study of Grosseteste the theologian. First, it allows us to consider the general character of scholastic theology within its own pedagogical context. This means that the study of the Bible is not akin to the modern notion of biblical theology, but rather exegesis was posited, embraced and nurtured as a major facet of theological work. Grosseteste is not at odds with his contemporaries; rather, the modern perception of his fellow theologians is at odds with the essential character of the theology of the schools. The second benefit is that Grosseteste is allowed to speak as a master who found in 1229/30 his theological voice, which he then continued to employ until his election to the bishopric of Lincoln in 1235. He may not sound similar to Thomas Aquinas (although I shall at times posit some connection between them), but that cannot be used to strike a note of deficiency on Grosseteste's part. Rather, he must be considered in comparison to his immediate contemporaries if we are to evaluate properly both his intellectual innovation and his theological integrity. In doing so, it is very possible to consider Grosseteste as a pioneer in theological method, and one who played a role in the development of specific Christian doctrines and theological arguments.

The Date of Grosseteste's Regency in Theology

Since the aim of this study is to examine Grosseteste's theology from his days at Oxford, it is necessary first to establish the dates of his regency. There is no doubt that Grosseteste ended his magisterial period when he was elected bishop of Lincoln. The question of when he began his regency is far more vexing. In the last fifty years, there have been three dates proffered: 1214, when the University of Oxford received its charter, the *Legatine Ordinance*;[4] around 1225, when Grosseteste was supposedly ordained as a priest;[5] and 1229/30, when the Oxford Franciscans petitioned him to become the first lector in theology for their convent.[6] The arguments for each are bound up with the equally difficult issue of when (or whether) Grosseteste was chancellor of the university. As complex as these issues of chronology are, it is possible to establish a resolution, once we separate the documented evidence from the historical assumptions.

One way to resolve this would be to establish the date of the sermon Grosseteste preached at his inception into the faculty of theology. Unfortunately, this sermon is of little help in this regard. Most of the sources employed are common to all of Grosseteste's theological writings, with the exception of a citation from the *Expositio Psalmorum* of Cassiodorus.[7] The only other text in which this early medieval source emerges is the *Super Psalterium*, and indeed there is some affinity between the use of Psalm 76:12 in the sermon, and Grosseteste's comments on the same passage.[8] Since the *Super Psalterium* belongs to Grosseteste's regency period, the citation of Cassiodorus in his inception sermon may indicate that the exposition of the Psalms was the first magisterial task he undertook. There is no other feature of the sermon that can help us in determining its date of composition and delivery. We must therefore look to external evidence in order to ascertain the starting date of his regency.

The first piece of direct evidence we possess about Grosseteste's regency is that in 1229/30 the Provincial General of the English Franciscans, Agnellus of Pisa, appointed Grosseteste as the first lector in theology for the Oxford convent. His appointment was evidently a success, as the chronicler Thomas of Eccleston states: the convent 'in such a brief time made inestimable progress in subtle questions and moralities, which are congruent to preaching'.[9] The 'brief time' denotes the fact that Grosseteste left Oxford in 1235, when his fellow canons of Lincoln cathedral appointed him as the next bishop. There have been two reasons, however, why historians have believed that Grosseteste was master of theology before 1229/30. First, Daniel Callus suggested that Grosseteste was the university's first chancellor, appointed in 1214 when the *Legatine Ordinance* came into effect.[10] Traditionally, only members of the higher faculties could be chancellors in the medieval university, and so Grosseteste by this time must have been ruling in theology. In opposition, Sir Richard Southern has argued that Grosseteste was not the first chancellor, and so there was no direct evidence that Grosseteste's regency began in 1214.[11] Instead, Southern reasoned that Grosseteste became a master of the sacred page around 1225, the same year he received his first benefice with cure. Southern assumed that this procuration must have entailed priestly ordination, and since scholastic theologians were supposed to be priests, it is likely that Grosseteste began his association with the Oxford faculty of theology around the same time.[12]

Southern's argument rests on the second reason why Grosseteste must have been ruling in theology before 1229/30: Agnellus of Pisa selected Grosseteste because he was an established master with an excellent reputation.[13] However, contemporary accounts of Grosseteste's acknowledged brilliance are placed within the context of his episcopate. In other words, his fame developed as a result of his elevation to the Lincoln see, at which point his contemporaries began to realise that he was indeed one of the leading thinkers of his day.[14] In 1235, Grosseteste moved from the obscurity of the schools of Oxford – where his abilities were at least known to his fellow canons at the Lincoln cathedral – to the largest diocese in England, where he could continue to apply his seasoned intelligence to theoretical and practical problems before a larger audience. In this light, we cannot assume that Grosseteste had been the natural choice of the Franciscans when Agnellus of Pisa petitioned him to become their lector. There is no evidence that they chose him because of his well-known reputation as a regent master; historians have only inferred this fact.[15]

The notion that Grosseteste was not a well-recognised theologian, before taking charge of the Franciscan school, is supported by the unique history of the order at Oxford. When they landed on the English shore in 1224, the small band of brothers included no one qualified to be a master of theology. Nor were they – unlike the mendicant orders at Paris – able to attract any of the ruling masters in theology into their order when they finally reached Oxford that same year and established a convent.[16] Instead, they finally had to appoint an outsider, and he would not be the last. The next three lectors for their studium were all secular masters, until at last Brother Adam Marsh in 1248, twenty-four years after the Franciscans had arrived in Oxford, was ready to incept as a master in theology. More significantly, the three lectors which followed Grosseteste appear to begin their association with Oxford as lectors to the Franciscans. The details for Peter of Ramsey and Roger of Wesham are sketchy,[17] but there is no doubt that Thomas Wallensis, who was lector from 1240 to 1247, was not a master in theology before arriving at Oxford. He had been studying for his mastership at Paris, when Grosseteste enticed him away to take on a pastoral position as the archdeacon of Lincoln in 1238. He incepted in 1240 to become the fourth lector for the order.[18] Thus it would not be unreasonable to consider that earlier in 1229/30 the Provincial General selected a scholar to become the first lector, who either had just incepted or was clearly ready to incept into the *universitas magistrorum* at Oxford.

In sum, it is difficult to establish the inception of Grosseteste's regency in theology on the basis of his supposed chancellorship or even his priestly ordination. We simply lack the evidence which indicates the specific date for either of these events. What documentary evidence we do have points to a regency that began in 1229/30 – mainly because of the insight of Agnellus of Pisa – and ended in March of 1235. During this period, Grosseteste is mentioned in three other documents as a regent master: once in a letter of Jordan of Saxony during his visit to Oxford in 1229/30 and twice (1231 and 1234) in records from the royal court.[19]

Medieval 'Systematics' and the Challenge of Coherence

Perhaps a greater challenge than establishing the year Grosseteste began to lecture in theology is the apparent absence of any systematic approach on his part to the discipline. How then does one carry out a systematic study when none of the texts lend themselves to any structured account? If Grosseteste had written a *summa theologica* or had studied theology twenty years later when lecturing on the *Sentences* became mandatory for bachelors, then modern scholars would have access to a more systematic account of his theology; and such a text would have provided an immediate structure for any modern study. However, the historical record is clear: Grosseteste never composed a *summa*, nor did he, either as a student or as a master, comment on the *Sentences* of Peter Lombard. This is not to say, as so many have concluded, that Grosseteste had no interest in speculative theology; rather it simply speaks to the state of scholastic theology of the 1230s. Nonetheless, the challenge remains and the most common solution is to impose some form of modern systematics on the thirteenth-century sources. While this solution would allow some resonance between the modern reader and the medieval sources, it can obscure the nature of theological discourse from the period. We do have a possible solution, one that at least may allow the analysis to reflect, if only faintly, Grosseteste's own theological 'system'.

That solution is found in one text related to Grosseteste's magisterial period, the *Tabula distinctionum*. The *Tabula* was a theological index of grand proportions that reveals the extent of Grosseteste's reading programme as he prepared for a career as a theologian. He divided the index into nine distinctions:[20]

1   God
2   The Word
3   The Created Order
4   The Church
5   Sacred Scripture
6   Vices
7   Vices again

8 The End Times (*de futuris*)
9 The soul and its powers

Each distinction was further divided into subjects or topics, for which Grosseteste provided references to relevant biblical and patristic sources. In the first distinction concerning God, for example, Grosseteste lists thirty-four topics ranging from the doctrine of the Trinity to God's attributes to His will, and so on.[21] What made this index unique, and ultimately a project impossible to maintain, was the idea of creating an ideograph for each topic. It would appear that Grosseteste thought to insert these ideographs in the margins of books: if the reader came upon the symbol, he could look it up in the *Tabula*, and would immediately have a list of other authorities that spoke to the same topic. Grosseteste's ambition got the better of him, for he never fully marked up his own manuscript books, nor does it appear that the index was ever completed.

The *Tabula* is certainly an indicator of Grosseteste's interest in the new textual technologies that supported teaching and learning in the universities.[22] Moreover, it can be conceived as an index to Grosseteste's reading programme in theology and in fact he used it when he wrote some of his own treatises.[23] For the latter reason, the *Tabula* could be one way of investigating Grosseteste's theology. At the very least, the nine distinctions themselves point to what Grosseteste considered to be the major topics of theological discourse. The problem with using the *Tabula* as a map for his theology is that it is just a schematic. It is indicative of a *possible* framework for a theological vision, but it does not yield a full portrait of what Grosseteste actually addressed in his theological writings. I have therefore treated the *Tabula* as an index to potential issues and topics. It provided the rationale for asking opening questions of Grosseteste's theological writings: does he address the nature of God? what does he say about the person and work of Jesus Christ? what role does the created order play in his theological vision? and so on. In the end, my investigation revealed that many of the topics listed in the *Tabula* were never the objects of any disputed question nor did they become the central theme of a treatise.

How then do we establish an organising principle for Grosseteste's theology? It is Grosseteste himself who provides the solution, for he in fact provides an account of what the subject matter of theology encapsulates.[24] That description forms the rationale for the second part of this study, his theological vision. Since he broaches that description within a general analysis of the discipline's subject, it becomes essential that my account of Grosseteste as a theologian first examine what he perceived to be the essence of the theological enterprise. Most scholars have framed Grosseteste's theology as equivalent to the study of the Bible, but this is not entirely accurate. If we look at the topics found under the distinction on sacred Scripture, it becomes immediately clear that Grosseteste had a rather broad perspective on the study of the Bible:

Fifth Distinction: Concerning Sacred Scripture[25]
On the perfection of sacred Scripture
On writing

On lecturing
That the Old Testament has now ceased
That one Testament is found in the other
On prophecy
That one not dare to add or subtract anything from Scripture
How we ought to accept philosophy
That Scripture is understood in our work (*ex opere*)
How to dispute
On the method of learning and teaching
Themes related to the laity [or prelates][26]

Within the distinction on sacred Scripture, we have topics that relate to the configuration of the discipline as whole, such as lecturing and disputing, the place of philosophy within theology, and even preaching. Such a sub-division of related topics reflects a common view that the terms *theologia* and *sacra scriptura* were interchangeable. Hence it is fitting to include a section in this present study that examines Grosseteste's method in theology. I have placed this discussion at the very beginning with some hesitation. I realise that this sounds more modern than medieval, as if it were necessary to present a *prolegomena* to a theological system, in which one outlines the epistemological (and metaphysical) conditions that make the theology a possible venture. However, this is not my ultimate concern. Instead, my aim is to set the context for the reader by providing the means in which one may engage with Grosseteste as theologian. Since this part of biography remains undeveloped, I consider it vital to offer the explicit tools at the beginning which can be deployed for reading Grosseteste's theological writings. I am the first to admit that this discussion is not necessarily in its right place, for it will be immediately apparent why the distinction in the *Tabula* on the Incarnation precedes any general discussion of the discipline of theology. In response, I can only encourage readers to consider carefully the dynamic relationship between the topics broached in Chapters three and four and those examined in Chapter six.

From Master to Bishop

Having ruled his diocese for twenty-one years, Hugh of Lincoln died in February 1235. According to canon law the cathedral canons were left to appoint his successor. Matthew Paris reports that the conclave soon splintered into factions, enough to prevent any one party from gaining the majority needed for the election of their candidate. While each faction could not stomach the thought of another gaining the upper hand, what they feared even more was the election being taken out of their hands – either by royal mandate or by papal imposition. In an attempt to prevent the loss of their electoral rights, the canons sought out a compromise candidate: one who had no connection with the existing factions within the chapter and one who would also cause few problems upon his election. They soon settled on one of their own. He seemed a good choice, for he even had the administrative experience that a medieval bishop needed since he had served as an archdeacon. That canon was Robert Grosseteste.[27]

Grosseteste immediately took up his office and remained a bishop-elect until his consecration in June 1235. Grosseteste's election to the episcopal chair signals the end of the period on which this monograph focuses. This is hardly because Grosseteste stopped being a theologian in 1235; far from it, for during his reign as bishop of Lincoln he retained an interest in the faculty of theology at Oxford, and engaged in some robust theological work himself. Instead, I have not included any post-magisterial theological writings in my study simply because the context of his theologising changed so dramatically after 1235. Grosseteste was no longer developing his theological outlook as a response to his pedagogical responsibilities, or the cut and thrust of scholastic debate; rather, his theological work after 1235 grew out of his episcopal responsibilities and the cut and thrust of caring for the clergy and laity in the largest diocese in medieval England. He certainly did not abandon the theological ideals and methods developed while a master of the sacred page, but when he left Oxford he no longer functioned as a professional theologian, with his own school in a faculty of theology. The need to explain the changes to his institutional and intellectual contexts really warrants another volume.

For now, we turn to examine his magisterial period. Short as it was, that period of his life saw Grosseteste rise to some major intellectual challenges. How he responded to the currents of intellectual history of the thirteenth century and the pull and drag of his teaching responsibilities will emerge as part of the fabric of his theology. We begin by accounting for his theological writings.

Notes

1 James R. Ginther, 'Natural Philosophy and Theology at Oxford in the Early Thirteenth Century: An Edition and Study of Robert Grosseteste's Inception Sermon (*Dictum* 19)', *Medieval Sermon Studies* 44 (2000), 108–34.

2 *Sermo* 31 (London, British Library MS Royal 7.E.ii, fol. 344rb): 'fui clericus, deinde magister in theologia et presbiter; et tandem episcopus'.

3 On the role of alterity in historical analysis, see Paul Freedman and Gabriel Spiegel, 'Medievalisms Old and New: The Rediscovery of Alterity in North American Medieval Studies', *American Historical Review* 103 (1998), 677–704.

4 Daniel A. Callus, 'Robert Grosseteste as Scholar', in *Robert Grosseteste, Scholar and Bishop, Essays in Commemoration of the Seventh Centenary of his Death*, ed. D.A. Callus (Oxford: Clarendon Press, 1955), pp. 1–69, at 6–9.

5 Southern, *Grosseteste*, xvii–lxvi; pp. 70–72.

6 Joseph Goering, 'Where and When did Grosseteste study Theology?', in *Robert Grosseteste: New Perspectives on his Thought and Scholarship*, ed. J. McEvoy, Instrumenta Patristica, 27 (Turnhout: Brepols, 1995), pp. 17–51.

7 *Dictum* 19, ed. Ginther, 13 (p. 129).

8 Ibid., 4 (p. 126).

9 Thomas of Eccleston, *De adventu fratrum minorum in Angliam*, ed. A.G. Little (Manchester: Manchester University Press, 1951), p. 48.

10 On this charter and the reasons for its publication, see R.W. Southern, 'From Schools to Universities', in *The Early Oxford Schools*, ed. J.I. Catto, The History of the University of Oxford, 1 (Oxford: Clarendon Press, 1984), pp. 1–36, at 26–32.
11 Ibid., pp. 27–36.
12 Southern, *Grosseteste*, pp. 69–75, 170–72.
13 Ibid., p. 72.
14 Matthew Paris, *Chronica majora*, ed. H. Luard, Rolls Series, 5 vols (London: Longman, 1880), 3.306, 4.404–7; Roger of Wendover, *Flores historiarum*, ed. H.G. Hewlch, 3 vols, Rolls Series, 84 (London: Longman, 1889), 3.102; Salimbene, *Cronica*, ed. O. Holder-Egger, MGH Scriptores 32 (Hannover: Monumenta Germaniae Historiae, 1905–1913), p. 233; Nicholas Trivet, *Annales sex regum Angliae*, ed. T. Hog (London: Sumptibus Societatis, 1845), pp. 242–3; *Chronicon de Lanercost*, ed. J. Stevenson (Edinburgh: Maitland Club, 1839), pp. 43–6. Significantly, the only comment this chronicle makes concerning Grosseteste's position at Oxford is that he was the first person to rule the Franciscan School there. Moreover, when the convent approached Grosseteste, the *Chronicon* describes him, not as an established master, but rather as a *paedagogus* (p. 45).
15 A.G. Little, 'The Franciscan School at Oxford', *Archivum Franciscanum Historicum* 19 (1926), 803–74, at 807; John Moorman, *A History of the Franciscan Order from its Origins to the Year 1517* (Oxford: Clarendon Press, 1968), pp. 242–3.
16 Moorman states that a number of Franciscan academics were passed over in favour of Grosseteste, namely Adam of Oxford, Henry of Coventry, Vincent of Coventry and Adam Marsh: Moorman, *History of the Franciscan Order*, pp. 133–4. However, none appears to have been qualified to be a magisterial lector at that time. The first three entered the Order around the same time Grosseteste was appointed lector, and each only being a master in the arts: Eccleston, *De adventu*, ed. Little, pp. 151–61. Adam of Oxford, although a student in theology before 1229, never incepted in theology, and left Oxford in 1232 as a missionary to the Saracens. Vincent of Coventry appears not to have qualified as a master until 1236, when the provincial general, Albert of Pisa, appointed him as lector to the London Convent, and then to the Cambridge convent sometime after. We have no information about Henry of Coventry. Finally, Adam Marsh did not enter the Order until 1230, and only incepted as a master in theology eighteen years later. See *Biographical Register of the University of Oxford to AD 1500*, ed. A.B. Emden, 3 vols (Oxford: Clarendon Press, 1957–9), 1, 660 (Adam of Oxford); 2, 1225–6 (Adam Marsh); *Biographical Register of the University of Cambridge to AD 1500*, ed. A.B. Emden (Cambridge: Cambridge University Press, 1963), p. 660 (Vincent of Conventry).
17 See *Biographical Register of the University of Oxford*, ed. Emden, 3, 1545 (Peter of Ramsay); 3, 2017 (Roger of Wesham).
18 Little, 'The Franciscan School at Oxford', p. 811, assumes that Thomas was a regent master in Paris prior to coming to Oxford. See also Eccleston, *De adventu*, ed. Little, p. 49, note f. However, in a letter dated around 1238, in which he offered Thomas the archdiaconate of Lincoln, Grosseteste presents a number of reasons why Thomas should take this pastoral charge rather than become a regent master (*cathedram magistralem ut sacram Scripturam doceas non ascendere*): *Epistolae*, n. 51 (pp. 147–51, esp. p. 148). This would imply that Thomas had not yet incepted at Paris, but would do so for the first time at Oxford in 1240.
19 Cited in Callus, 'Grosseteste as Scholar', p. 10.
20 *Tabula*, pp. 245–64. For a discussion of the *Tabula*'s content and Grosseteste's intentions, see Rosemann's introduction: ibid., pp. 235–43; Southern, *Grosseteste*, pp. 188–93. See

also Richard W. Hunt, 'The Library of Robert Grosseteste', in *Robert Grosseteste, Scholar and Bishop*, pp. 121–45, esp. pp. 123–5, 144–5; and S.H. Thomson, 'Grosseteste's Concordantial Signs', *Medievalia et Humanistica* 9 (1955), 39–53.
21 *Tabula*, pp. 245–6 (list of topics), 265–72 (list with all citations).
22 See the studies of Richard and Mary Rouse, 'Concordances et index', in *Du livre manuscrit. Mise en page et mise en texte*, ed. H.J. Martin and J. Vezin (Paris: Promodis, 1990), pp. 218–28; and '*Statim invenire*: Schools, Preachers and New Attitudes to the Page', in *Renaissance and Renewal in the Twelfth Century*, ed. R.L. Benson, G. Constable and C.D. Lanham (Oxford: Clarendon Press, 1982), pp. 201–25.
23 Southern, *Grosseteste*, pp. 192–3; Neil T. Lewis, 'The First Recension of Robert Grosseteste's *De libero arbitrio*', *Mediaeval Studies* 53 (1991), 1–88, at 12–20; James McEvoy, 'Robert Grosseteste on the Ten Commandments', *Recherches de théologie ancienne et médiévale* 58 (1991), 167–205, at 190–93.
24 See below, Chapter 3, pp. 57–9.
25 *Tabula*, pp. 253–4, 310–14.
26 Ibid., p. 254, where the topic is listed as a *thema ad prelatos*; in the list with the citations, it is listed as *thema ad laycos* (p. 314)
27 McEvoy, *Grosseteste*, pp. 29–30.

PART I
A THEOLOGIAN'S TASK

PART 1
A THEOLOGIAN'S TASK

Chapter 1
Grosseteste's Theological Writings

For the last half-century, students of the life and works of Robert Grosseteste have employed the descriptor 'scholar and bishop' as a means of summarising this English thinker's long and remarkable life.[1] It has also guided modern readers through the large corpus of writings that Grosseteste penned. Grosseteste was a scholar of the natural world, who wrote treatises on cosmology, meteorology, and optics – to name but three major fields of his research.[2] He was also a philosophical scholar who committed to vellum his reflections on Aristotelian logic, mathematical theory, metaphysics and philosophical psychology.[3] His accomplishments as bishop were equally significant. He was a principal protagonist in reinvigorating episcopal visitations, much to the chagrin of his detractors.[4] Above all, he is best known for his promotion of the pastoral care. He protected the cure of souls by ensuring that all pastoral appointments in his diocese strictly fulfilled canonical requirements. As his letter collection reveals, he never shifted his position in response to a candidate's patron, be he a fellow bishop, noble or even the king.[5] He also did all that he could to improve the context of church ministry, which included the publication of an influential set of diocesan statutes that implemented the ministerial programmes of the Fourth Lateran Council.[6] In the last years of his episcopacy, he took his campaign for a more rigorous programme of pastoral care to the papal court, where he produced a *memoranda* designed to inform Innocent IV of the problems threatening pastoral ministry in the English church.[7]

Grosseteste's interest in the pastoral care emerged well before he became bishop. Prior to 1235, he had helped bridge the gap between the theory of the pastoral care expounded in the schools, and parish practice. His ability to translate complex, often obtuse, theological ideas into usable terms and practices for a literate clergy won his pastoral writings a great deal of popularity. One of his earlier works, the *Templum Dei*, has survived in over ninety manuscripts, copied throughout the thirteenth, fourteenth and fifteenth centuries.[8] Moreover, it is within these texts that one can see how the interests of a philosophical and scientific scholar merged with the concerns of a pastor, for he employed the most recent theories of the psychological make-up of humanity in his pastoral writings.[9]

This description of Grosseteste as scholar and bishop often overshadows the fact that his theological interests did not focus solely on pastoral ministry. He was also a master of theology at Oxford, and during his tenure he produced a number of biblical commentaries and theological tractates.[10] Even after he was elected bishop of Lincoln in 1235, Grosseteste continued his theological study. Despite being the bishop of the largest diocese in England, he found time to study and write, and by that time had added knowledge of Greek to his repertoire of skills. He translated the Dionysian corpus, the major works of John Damascene, and rendered for the first time in Latin the *Testament of the Twelve Patriarchs*.[11] He also produced a new translation of the *Nicomachean Ethics*, which he considered to be a good source for pastoral education.[12]

Despite writing a plethora of theological works in his lifetime, it is this biographical element, Grosseteste as theologian, that is the least developed in modern scholarship. One of the major reasons for this stems from the work of Grosseteste's most important bibliographer, S. Harrison Thomson. In cataloguing some 120 works ascribed to Grosseteste, Thomson settled on organisational categories that were to have a lasting effect on the research into this thirteenth-century thinker.[13] Thomson presented six categories of works: Translations from the Greek; Commentaries (both biblical and philosophical); Philosophical and Scientific; Pastoral and Devotional; Miscellaneous;[14] and Anglo-Norman. These were followed by a survey of Grosseteste's sermons, letters and *Dicta*. Thomson then concluded with arguments for which works must be considered spurious or doubtful, along with an outline of lost or untraced texts. It is difficult to envisage through the lens of these categories a theological career. Even though Thomson followed the idea that Grosseteste was a regent master of theology for some twenty years, and remained active in theology throughout his episcopate, our bibliographer did not consider the term *theology* to be an adequate descriptor of Grosseteste's works. Instead, Thomson helped to create an image of Grosseteste as primarily a natural philosopher, who had interests in pastoral theology and language studies. There still remains, then, the challenge of understanding Grosseteste as theologian. More to the point, if we are intent on fully understanding the nature of Grosseteste's writings, we ought to have some means by which we can relate his literary output to his theological commitments.

The category of theological writings ought to have a visible place in his corpus. The best starting point is to make an account of his writings while he was professionally involved in the theological enterprise, namely as a master of the sacred page at Oxford. This requires a strict historical approach, as we can then contextualise each nominated text, particularly in terms of theological education. An alternative methodology would be to assess each of Grosseteste's writings mainly on the basis of its subject matter or content, but this approach can yield limited success. That limitation is often due to modern theological values acting as the central guide in assessing what is theological in the medieval scholastic period. In the end, a theological corpus based on this type of analysis reflects more of modern theology than any aspect of medieval scholasticism. Even if the modern reader were able to avoid any anachronistic evaluations of the medieval sources, the analysis might still suffer slightly from a lack of precision.

Grosseteste's regency occurred in a period of robust debate concerning which topics belonged to the sacred science, and what issues were merely profane.[15] Some thinkers prescribed what type of textual production was worthy of a theologian, while others simply wished to focus on the content of any text a master of the sacred page might produce. Even if one could negotiate a consensus from the thirteenth-century debate of what is theological in terms of content, that description would not necessarily provide a precise description of what kind of texts may be classed as theological. The most sensible means of avoiding anachronistic or imprecise analysis of Grosseteste's theological writings is to connect his literary production with a historical description of theological education in the medieval university. Regardless of what was considered to be theological content by scholastic theologians, all were in agreement as to what kind of texts their institutional responsibilities demanded that they produce.[16] With this historical approach acting as the focal point for the analysis, scholars can advance towards a more accurate and comprehensive evaluation of Grosseteste as a theologian.

Still, caution needs to be exercised for we may be able to classify the principal sources of this study as 'theological', but this general term can betray the complexity of the textual resources at hand. For Grosseteste's period, theological texts were divided into three major categories, and they were related to the three-fold task of a theologian: to lecture, dispute and preach.[17] To lecture was not to expound a particular theological theme, as is often the case in the modern theology department; rather, a lecture was an exposition, a *reading*, of the sacred text. This was the foundational act of all theological work of the scholastic period. To dispute was to chew over the theological truth captured in the *lectio*: it is where one considered the implications of Christian doctrine, and where one developed the skills to refute the errors of heretics and infidels: and so disputation was the walls which protected the Christian community. Above all, there was preaching, the roof of this house of God: it was where lecturing and disputation came to fruition. These three tasks of a scholastic theologian are well known, and it behoves the historian to embrace each task in equal measure, along with their residual textual witnesses. In developing and explaining Grosseteste the theologian, we must break out beyond the standard interest in speculative theology, which draws nearly all of its data from disputed questions and the theological treatises that they spawned. In addition, we must draw upon Grosseteste's lectures on sacred Scripture and his sermons. These three genres of text form the basis of the present study.

Lectio

It is not always easy to identify the textual witnesses for all these tasks, since the texts themselves could undergo significant mutation. Texts derived from the *lectio* could survive as a student report of the classroom event (sometimes corrected by the master himself); or it may be a revised and re-edited form of the lectures, which the master himself later 'published'. A third option was that the text, or major portions, could be appropriated into another theological treatise, where biblical exposition was one of a number of methods employed to argue a case. For Grosseteste, we have no *reportationes* of his lectures. This is not surprising, since so few reports of lectures given at Oxford in the thirteenth century appear to have survived. However, we do have texts that bear the marks of re-editing, as well as other texts that have assimilated large portions from biblical commentary. The textual evidence points to Grosseteste having given lectures on the Psalms and the Pauline epistles (the staples of magisterial commentary), as well as expositions on Genesis, Ecclesiasticus, Daniel and Isaiah. Grosseteste appears to have re-edited his Psalms commentary, although it has survived in a confused state. We have two texts related to his exposition of the Pauline epistles: extracts of glosses, which were collected by Thomas Gascoigne in the fifteenth century, and the published comments on Galatians. His lectures on Ecclesiasticus have only survived as comments on chapter 43.1–5. The Genesis lectures were re-edited in part into a commentary on the creation narrative now known as the *Hexaëmeron*. Finally, the commentaries on Daniel and Isaiah were assimilated, but only in part, into his most ambitious theological tractate, *De cessatione legalium*.

At one time, the canon of Grosseteste's exegetical writings was reputed to include glosses on the books of Wisdom and Ecclesiastes, marginal notes on the *Glossa magna* of Peter Lombard, a commentary on Romans, and the *Moralitates super Evangelia*. The first two were attributed to Grosseteste on the basis of the hand in the margin; however, as the late Richard Hunt determined, these manuscripts do not contain Grosseteste's handwriting, and there is nothing else to connect these texts to Grosseteste.[18] Grosseteste's authorship of the *Lecturae in Epistolam ad Romanos* has yet to be established, and it seems unlikely that it ever will be.[19] While the single manuscript witness also contains a number of works by Grosseteste, and is certainly a manuscript produced either in a Franciscan scriptorium or for a Franciscan community,[20] the Romans commentary has two features that contradict the attribution to Grosseteste: first, the lecture is a cursory one, and so appears to be the product of lectures by a bachelor and not a master; and second, the references to the Bible are taken from the Paris Bible, where the biblical text was subdivided on each manuscript page by the letters A-G between the columns in order to provide more exact references (for example, Matt. 16D). I could conjecture that this commentary originated as a lecture while Grosseteste was in Paris (if he ever was a bachelor there), but it has no connection to his magisterial period at Oxford. Finally, the *Moralitates*, while at one time was touted as the exemplary text of Grosseteste's exegetical approach, now appears to be the work of an earlier author.[21]

Disputatio

As a master with his own school within the faculty of theology, Grosseteste, in addition to giving letures, had an obligation to lead disputations. In 1982, Joseph Goering published an edition of the *De dotibus*, demonstrating that this text was the record of Grosseteste's disputation on the marriage gifts of Christ to the Church.[22] While Goering suggested that this is the only disputed question to survive, there is evidence of other questions. The problem in identifying these works as disputed questions is that they appear to have been reworked in the format of a treatise. Still, some of Grosseteste's shorter theological works retain some identifiable features of a disputed question.

As Bernardo Bazàn has pointed out, disputed questions belong to the domain of the master and not the students. While students such as those who took the role of *opponens* and on occasion the *respondens* were involved in the process, the initial question was set by the master and it was he who produced the final resolution of the debate, known as the determination. By 1250, the process could produce two different kinds of texts: a record of the initial disputation, in which each participant's contribution was recorded, and the separate magisterial determination, in which the arguments for and against were recorded in light of the final solution to which the master had come. The latter text often retained some of the linguistic markers of the actual disputation. Questions began with markers such as *queritur, utrum, an* and so on; arguments for and against were marked by *sed contra, dicebatur quod, respondendum est* and so on. A master would also provide his overall solution (*solutio, repondeo quod, respondendum est* and so on), along with specific responses to the previous arguments against his solution (*ad obiecta dico, respondeo ad obiecta* and so on).[23]

In this light, we may consider *De veritate, De ordine emanandi causatarum a Deo* and *De libero arbitrio* to be determinations of previously disputed questions.[24] The first work contains the greatest number of textual markers from a disputed question. The last work, in both its recensions, also has a number of markers of a disputed question, and in the second recension the text ends with a list of relevant questions, which Grosseteste omitted from the determination so as not to tax the patience of the reader.[25] *De ordine emanandi causatarum a Deo* (which also circulated under the title *De aeternitate filii in divinis*) has the fewest markers, but the debate begins with *Quod primo quaeritur*, and the bulk of the work is Grosseteste's solution to the question.[26] Callus had suggested that *De veritate propositionis* and *De scientia Dei* should also be counted as records of disputed questions.[27] However, these lack any of the textual markers listed above, and have the characteristics more of *dicta* than of *quaestiones*. The first of these is closely related to *De veritate*, and the second is linked to the subject matter of *De libero arbitrio*. The same can be said of the two short works, *De statu causarum* and *De potentia et actu*, which are linked by their subject matter to the disputed question, *De ordine emanandi causatorum a Deo*.

Since the *reportationes* of the disputed question did not become an integral part of the process at Paris until after 1250, the lack of such sources for Grosseteste's disputed questions in the 1230s should not surprise us.[28] It may also be possible that Grosseteste disputed these questions within the Franciscan school (*in scholis suis*), which would have made this disputation a private affair, not part of the public activities (*disputatio ordinaria*) of the faculty as a whole.[29] This would mean that there may not have been any university official present to make an official record of the event. It is possible that Grosseteste appointed one of his students as a secretary to record the debate which he could use later in his determination, but this record would not circulate outside of the school.

This is one factor, among other things, which makes *De anima* a problematic text. For one thing, it appears to be a report of the disputation, and not necessarily a determination. Moreover, as has been pointed out, there is a close affinity between this question and the *Summa de bono* of Philip the Chancellor.[30] Two possible conclusions can be drawn from this: either Grosseteste disputed on the soul, and drew heavily from Philip's *Summa de bono*, or it is a report of some of the questions which became the basis of Philip's tome. In light of Bazàn's dictum that the material of a disputed question belongs more to a master than to the student, it would be more appropriate to draw the second conclusion. In light of the chronology of Grosseteste's education, suggested by Goering, it is quite reasonable to place Grosseteste at Paris when Philip disputed these questions.[31] We need not make a further conclusion that Grosseteste was a student in Philip's school (if indeed Philip was still head of a school in the faculty of theology at Paris in the late 1220s), since these disputations were probably ordinary, and thus argued before the whole faculty, with students from various schools participating in the debate.

At this point we can easily point to four questions disputed by Grosseteste in the Fransicans school: *De veritate, De ordine emanandi causatorum a Deo, de libero arbitrio* and *De dotibus*. There are indications of a further set of disputed questions that have not survived (or have yet to be identified). Grosseteste first mentions them in his lectures on the second chapter of Galatians. The controversy between Peter and Paul had stimulated a similar conflict of opinion between Augustine and Jerome on the the efficacy of the Jewish Law, and the point in time after which it was no longer in force. Having raised the questions, he then comments: 'But these questions will be treated much better in disputing rather than in lecturing or expounding.'[32] It would seem that these questions did take the shape of disputation, whose determinations made their way into various sections of the *De cessatione legalium*.

Praedicatio

Grosseteste fulfilled all the magisterial functions, moving from lecture to disputation, and finally to preaching. Unlike the other two textual areas of Grosseteste's theological work, his sermons remain somewhat of a *terra incognita*. While some individual sermons have been carefully edited for publication, the extant collections really require a much more strategic and holistic approach, if only to develop some sense of the transmission of these sermons and thus determine why these collections were developed and organised in the first place. The date of preaching or composition for each sermon has also yet to be established, and so it is unclear just which sermons can contribute to the larger picture of Grosseteste as a master of the sacred page. There are ways to compensate for the lack of information concerning Grosseteste's preaching, and they consist of two collections of texts. The first is the so-called *Dicta* collection, a set of texts Grosseteste himself edited after he left Oxford in 1235. He states that these are sermons and theological *notulae*, all written while he was *in scolis*. Nearly all modern scholars have taken Grosseteste at his word, and have dated the *Dicta* prior to 1235. However, there appears to be an exception in *Dictum* 51 which appears to be the sermon preached at the promulgation of the diocesan statutes for Lincoln in 1239.[33] We are left with twenty sermons in the *Dicta* collection that can be dated to Grosseteste's regency. The second resource is a set of sermons attrituted to Grosseteste in Durham, Dean and Chapter Library MS A.III.12, and it is likely that these sermons were written or preached during his magisterial period.[34] Many of these sermons, however, are less like formal sermons and are instead materials for preaching; that is, they are short notes on specific passages, skeletal outlines of sermons, and extracts from patristic sources. Since the ultimate trajectory of this study is to examine Grosseteste's theology, we may dispense with the difficult and unenviable task of determining the performative value of each of these texts.[35] The theological content remains the same regardless of whether Grosseteste actually preached a sermon or simply composed it as an aid for preaching.

Sometimes a theologian was called upon to preach in a different context, one in which the tasks of lecturing and preaching easily coalesced. These were known as *collationes*, or conferences, and Grosseteste appears to have led at least three such events while a master of the sacred page.[36] The first *collatio* attributable to Grosseteste, now designated as Sermon 6, begins with a recounting of collations in the early church.[37] The second was given at the Franciscan convent, and some manuscripts designate it as *De scala paupertatis* (Sermon 8).[38] The third has been edited as the *Prooemium* to the *Hexaëmeron*, since it focuses on Jerome's prefatory letter to the Bible.[39]

Other Theological Writings

Grosseteste's *Dicta* is a reminder that not all of his theological production can be explained by the threefold task of a theologian, for this collection also contains notes and word studies that Grosseteste probably composed as he prepared for lecturing, disputing and preaching. In addition, a theologian of the schools would sometimes produce a treatise in reply to a prominent problem or challenge, or in response to a request for an expert opinion. As we have already noted, Grosseteste's prelude to being a master of theology included some writings in pastoral theology, and in particular in the theology and practice of confession.[40] As lector to the Franciscans, it was entirely in keeping that he continue this work while teaching theology. Only two of his pastoral works can be dated to his magisterial period: his commentary on the Decalogue and a confessional treatise written for a monastic audience, *Speculum confessionis*.[41] These texts will inform principally our discussions of Grosseteste's ecclesiology and theology of pastoral care, but their assertions are based on other theological assumptions that will illuminate other topics of the study.

The final set of texts connected to Grosseteste's magisterial period is the first ten entries of his letter collection. With the exception of the first letter, all these can be dated to the period of 1229 and 1232.[42] This correspondence reminds us of the other institutional contexts of Grosseteste's theological work. In addition to being a master of theology, he was also officially an archdeacon (1229–32) and, unofficially, a counsellor to leading nobles of his day.[43] Moreover, his relationship with the Franciscans was more than just one of master and pupils. In Epistle 2, he writes to the community at Oxford to help them deal with the imminent loss of a colleague to missionary work. This text contains a heart-warming account of the joy of friendship.[44] Grosseteste's connection with the Greyfriars reached its greatest intimacy with Adam Marsh, a Franciscan who was later considered almost to be Grosseteste's *alter ego*.[45] Grosseteste felt comfortable in expressing his personal concerns to Adam, and in Epistle 9 he pours out his heart about the response to his resignation of multiple benefices. Grosseteste had thought he was doing the right thing, but ironically his colleagues accused him of abandoning the pastoral care – an accusation that must have cut him to the quick.[46] The letters are not strictly theological works, for they did not emerge from the primary responsibilities of a master of the sacred page. Nonetheless, their content is informed by the actions and outlook of a theologian, who took the time to engage his colleagues on major theological questions, offer counsel and advice, and even reprimand an opponent – even if the recipient were a powerful and influential monastery.[47]

In some ways, the letters provide a window into Grosseteste's attitudes to his own culture, and as well as supplying a way of seeing how he applied some theological precepts on which he had reflected as a master. However, they also stand in contrast to those strictly theological texts in one regard: while we can easily date these letters (or at least establish a loose sequence), the same cannot be said for the theological writings. There has been some attempt to date Grosseteste's major theological writings, but many have resisted any firm chronological fix. Some texts do speak clearly to the time of composition: it is certainly true that Grosseteste's lectures on Galatians occurred prior to the composition of *De cessatione legalium*.[48] Others give faint hints but reveal little concrete evidence: it may be the case, for example, that Grosseteste lectured on the Psalms at the beginning of his magisterial period, and then revised the commentary closer to 1235, or even after he became bishop.[49] Until all of Grosseteste's works have been edited, I see mostly folly in trying to establish a chronology for all his theological works; nor can I see the value in it for this present study. Since the book's focus is on only five or six years of Grosseteste's life, the need to trace the *development* of certain ideas is a minor one. Instead, it is my assumption that Grosseteste's short magisterial career can be treated as a coherent unit. Investigations of development are certainly worthwhile, and one of the indirect results of this study is to produce a narrative that can be used in outlining the larger developments of Grosseteste's theological thought, from master to bishop.

Notes

1 See the seminal essays in *Robert Grosseteste, Scholar and Bishop, Essays in Commemoration of the Seventh Centenary of His Death*, ed. D.A. Callus (Oxford: Clarendon Press, 1955).
2 Most of Grosseteste's philosophical and 'scientific' works are printed in Baur. An electronic version of these texts is available at http://www.grosseteste.com/.
3 McEvoy, *Philosophy*.
4 C.R. Cheney, *Episcopal Visitations of Monasteries in the Thirteenth Century* (Manchester: Manchester University Press, 1931); James R. Ginther, 'Monastic Ideals and Episcopal Visitations: the *Sermo ad religiosos* of Robert Grosseteste, Bishop of Lincoln (1235–1253)', in *Medieval Monastic Preaching*, ed. C.A. Meussig (Leiden: Brill, 1998), pp. 231–53.
5 *Epistolae*, nn.17 (pp. 63–5), 19 (68–9), 52 (151–4), 72 (203–4) and 124 (348–51). An electronic version of these letters is available at http://www.grosseteste.com/.

6   The statutes are printed in *Councils and Synods, with Other Documents Relating to the English Church*, ed. C.R. Cheney and F.M. Powicke, 2 vols (Oxford: Clarendon Press, 1964), 2.265–78; as well as in Grosseteste's letter collection: *Epistolae*, n. 52bis (pp. 154–66).

7   Servus Gieben, 'Robert Grosseteste at the Papal Curia, Lyons, 1250: Edition of the Documents', *Collectanea Franciscana* 41 (1971), 340–93. See also Joseph Goering, 'Robert Grosseteste at the Papal Curia', in *A Distinct Voice: Medieval Studies in Honor of Leonard E. Boyle, O.P.*, ed. J. Brown and W.P. Stoneman (Notre Dame, IN: University of Notre Dame Press, 1997), pp. 253–76.

8   *Templum Dei*, p. 8; See also Leonard E. Boyle, 'Robert Grosseteste and the Pastoral Care', *Medieval and Renaissance Studies* 8 (1979), 3–51; rprt. in *idem, Pastoral Care, Clerical Education and Canon Law* (Aldershot: Variorum, 1981).

9   Joseph Goering, 'When and Where did Grosseteste Study Theology?', in *Robert Grosseteste: New Perspectives on his Thought and Scholarship*, ed. J. McEvoy, Instrumenta Patristica, 27 (Turnhout: Brepols, 1995), pp. 17–52, at 29–39.

10 Beryl Smalley, 'The Biblical Scholar', in *Robert Grosseteste, Scholar and Bishop*, ed. Callus, pp. 70–97. McEvoy recognised this important facet by suggesting another binary descriptor of Grosseteste's life in a reprint of some of his articles: James McEvoy, *Robert Grosseteste, Exegete and Philosopher* (Aldershot: Variorum, 1995).

11 Daniel A. Callus, 'The Date of Grosseteste's Translations and Commentaries of Pseudo-Dionysius and the Nicomachean Ethics', *Recherches de théologie ancienne et médiévale* 14 (1947), 186–209; M. De Jonge, 'Robert Grosseteste and the Testaments of the Twelve Patriarchs', *Journal of Theological Studies* n.s. 42 (1991), 115–25.

12 F.M. Powicke, *Robert Grosseteste and the Nicomachean Ethics*, Proceedings of the British Academy, 16 (London: Milford, 1930).

13 Thomson, *Writings*, p. 1.

14 The first of these is an etymological treatise, surviving in a single manuscript. The four remaining works treat various aspects of social life in the thirteenth century, ranging from proper etiquette to the care of an estate: ibid., pp. 148–51.

15 See M.-D. Chenu, *La théologie comme science au XIIIe siècle*, third edition (Paris: Vrin, 1957); the record of sermons preached, ca.1229–31 at Paris in M.M. Davy, *Les sermons universitaires parisiens de 1230-1231*, Etudes de philosophie médiévale, 15 (Paris: Vrin, 1931); and Martin Grabmann, *I divieti ecclesiastici di Aristotele sotto Innocenzo III e Gregorio IX*, Miscellanea Historiae Pontificiae, 5 (Rome: Saler, 1941).

16 I differ slightly from the traditional account of theological texts, which often focuses on those produced by *students* of theology, rather than *masters*. Hence the traditional account places a great deal of importance on the *Sentence* commentaries. My aim is not to diminish the theological significance of these texts; rather, since they were not the responsibility of masters (and not the responsibility of students until after 1240), it is unnecessary to make any claims concerning the presence or absence of such a commentary (or any equivalent) in Grosseteste's theological corpus.

17 The first person to articulate this threefold task of a master was Peter the Chanter in his *Verbum abbreviatum*, c.1 (PL 205.25). The evidence that this description remained in force even beyond Grosseteste's mastership is found in Thomas Aquinas's inaugural lecture in 1257, where he speaks of the three duties of a master of the sacred page. The sermons are printed in Thomas Aquinas, *Opuscula theologica*, ed. R.A. Verardo *et al.*, 2 vols (Turin: Marietta, 1954), 1. 441–3. They are translated in Simon Tugwell, *Albert and Thomas: Selected Writings*, Classics of Western Spirituality (New York: Paulist Press, 1988), pp. 355–60. Using this tripartite description to examine Grosseteste's writings is

hardly novel, as Daniel Callus employed this threefold function of masters in his study of Grosseteste's intellectual career: Daniel A. Callus, 'Robert Grosseteste as Scholar', in *Robert Grosseteste Scholar and Bishop*, ed. Callus, pp. 1–70, at 28–32. See also *idem*, 'The Oxford Career of Robert Grosseteste', *Oxoniensia* 10 (1945), 45–72.

18 R.W. Hunt, 'The Library of Robert Grosseteste', in *Robert Grosseteste, Scholar and Bishop*, ed. Callus, pp. 121–45, at 140–41. For the manuscripts, see Thomson, *Writings*, pp. 73, 77.

19 See Thomson, *Writings*, pp. 74–5; Smalley, 'The Biblical Scholar', p. 76. Callus, 'Oxford Career of Grosseteste', pp. 63–4, suggested that the commentary could be ascribed to Adam Marsh. The single manuscript copy (Cambridge, Gonville and Caius College MS 439, fols 57r–70v) has been transcribed by Elwood E. Mather, '*Lecturae in Epistolam ad Romanos V–XVI Roberto Grosseteste adscriptae*', unpublished Ph.D. diss. (University of Southern California, Los Angeles, 1987). In his introduction, Mather advances some interesting arguments about the authorship, but admits that none of them is strong enough to resolve the issue fully.

20 For a description of the manuscript, see M.R. James, *A descriptive catalogue of the manuscripts in the library of Gonville and Caius College*, 2 vols (Cambridge: Cambridge University Press, 1907–8), 2.510–11.

21 Southern, *Grosseteste*, p. 31. This argument was forcefully presented in E.J. Dobson, *Moralities on the Gospels: A New Source of Ancrene Wisse* (Oxford: Clarendon Press, 1978), esp. pp. 22–34.

22 Joseph Goering, 'The *De dotibus* of Robert Grosseteste', *Mediaeval Studies* 44 (1982), 83–109.

23 Bernardo C. Bazàn, 'Les questions disputées, principalement dans la faculté de théologie,' in *Les questions disputées et les questions quodlibétiques dans les facultés de théologie, de droit, et de médecine*, Typologie des Sources du Moyen Age Occidental, 44–5 (Turnhout: Brepols, 1985), pp. 58–70, 129–36.

24 All these are edited in Baur, pp. 130–43, 147–274. The first recension of *De libero arbitrio* has been critically edited by Neil Lewis, 'The First Recension of Robert Grosseteste's *De Libero arbitrio*', *Mediaeval Studies* 53 (1991), 1–88. An abbreviated copy of the second recension exists in Durham Cathedral, Dean and Chapter Library, MS A.III.12, fols 55va–57vb. This is the earliest copy: Suzanne Paul, 'An Edition and Study of the Sermons Attributed to Robert Grosseteste in Durham MS A.III.12.' unpubl. PhD diss. 2 vols (University of Leeds, 2002), 1.159.

25 *De libero arbitrio* (second recension), ed. Baur, pp. 240–41.

26 *De ordine emanandi causatorum a Deo*, ed. Baur, pp. 147–50.

27 Callus, 'The Oxford Career of Grosseteste', 29.

28 Olga Weijers, *Terminologie des universités au XIIIe siècle*, Lessico Intellettuale Europeo, 39 (Rome: Edizioni dell' Ateneo, 1987), pp. 361–5. Earlier examples of *reportationes* deal almost exclusively with lectures and not disputed questions: Beryl Smalley, *The Study of the Bible in the Middle Ages*, second edition (Notre Dame: University of Notre Dame Press, 1964), pp. 200–209. A possible exception is the series of theological questions in Douai, Bibliothèque de la ville, MS 434. See P. Glorieux, 'Les 572 questions de Douai MS 434', *Recherches de théologie ancienne et médiévale* 10 (1938), 123–52, 255–67.

29 Bazàn, 'Les questions disputées', pp. 50, 53–7.

30 L.W. Keeler, 'The Dependence of Robert Grosseteste's *De anima* on the *Summa* of Philip the Chancellor', *New Scholasticism* 11 (1937), 197–219; Daniel A. Callus, 'Philip the Chancellor and the *De anima* ascribed to Robert Grosseteste', *Medieval and*

Renaissance Studies 1 (1941), 105–27; Thomson, *Writings*, pp. 89–90. See also McEvoy, *The Philosophy of Robert Grosseteste*, pp. 484–5.
31 Goering, 'When and Where did Grosseteste Study Theology?' pp. 40–41.
32 *Expositio*, 2.19 (p. 62).
33 Thomson, *Writings*, pp. 216–32: the sermons are *Dicta* 2, 3, 4, 6, 10, 14, 21 (which is a sermon but not sermon 68 as Thomson had supposed: see Ginther, 'Monastic Ideals and Episcopal Visitations', pp. 233–4), 35, 37, 38, 41, 50, 51, 52, 72, 87, 89, 90, 91, 101, 103, 119, 135, 137 and 138. See also Edwin J. Westermann, 'A Comparison of Some of the Sermons and the *Dicta* of Robert Grosseteste', *Medievalia et Humanistica* 3 (1945), 49–68.
34 Edward B. King, 'Durham MS A.III.12 and Grosseteste's Homiletical Works', in *Robert Grosseteste: New Perspectives on his Thought and Scholarship*, ed. McEvoy, pp. 277–88.
35 Paul, 'An Edition and Study of the Sermons', 1.24–72.
36 On *collationes* in general, see Weijers, *Terminologie des universités au XIIIe siècle*, pp. 372–8; Bert Roest, *A History of Franciscan Education (c. 1210–1517)*, Education and Society in the Middle Ages and Renaissance, 11 (Leiden: Brill, 2000), p. 135.
37 London, British Library MS Royal 6.E.v, fol. 81ra-vb; Thomson, *Writings*, p. 168.
38 Thomson, *Writings*, pp. 168–9.
39 *Hex*, prooem.112 (p. 41). If this were an evening collation, it may explain why, at one point, Grosseteste supplements his analysis *propter simpliciores*. This may point to the fact that Grosseteste's audience was the whole convent, and not just those friars who were students in his school.
40 Joseph Goering and F.A.C. Mantello, 'The Early Penitential Writings of Robert Grosseteste', *Recherches de théologie ancienne et médiévale* 54 (1987), 52–112. Grosseteste's *Templum Dei* may well have preceded his magisterial period. See *Templum Dei*, pp. 4–6, where the editors suggest a period of composition between 1220 and 1230.
41 For the date of *De decem mandatis*, see DDM, p. 1. On the dating of the *Speculum Confessionis*, see Joseph Goering and F.A.C. Mantello, 'The *Perambulavit Iudas . . . (Speculum confessionis)* Attributed to Robert Grosseteste', *Revue Bénédictine* 96 (1986), 125–68, at 131–2.
42 It would appear that, for the most part, the letter collection is ordered chronologically. Ep. 11 is the first one written by Grosseteste after he is elected bishop of Lincoln in March 1235. Epp. 2–7 indicate Grosseteste's status of archdeacon (1229–32) and Epp. 8–9 refer to his decision to resign all but one of his benefices in 1232. The only two that do not provide any explicit information about their date are Epp. 1 and 10. For the first letter, see the convincing argument by James McEvoy on why this letter was probably written in the late 1220s (and probably before Grosseteste came to Oxford as a master of the sacred page), rather than around 1210 as suggested by Henry Luard: James McEvoy, 'Der Brief des Robert Grosseteste an Magister Adam Rufus (Adam von Oxford, O.F.M.): ein Datierungsversuch', *Franziskanische Studien* 63 (1981), 221–6. Letter 10 identifies Grosseteste as a master of theology and, given its place in the collection (not the strongest of arguments), it is not unreasonable to conclude that it too belongs to the period of 1229/30–1235.
43 *Epistolae*, nn. 5–7 (pp. 33–43).
44 Ibid., n. 2 (pp. 17–21).
45 For a summary of Adam's life, see C.H. Lawrence, 'The Letters of Adam Marsh and the Franciscan School at Oxford', *Journal of Ecclesiastical History* 42 (1991), 218–38; Roger M. Haas, 'Adam Marsh (de Marisco), a Thirteenth Century English Franciscan', unpubl. PhD diss. (Rutgers University, 1989).

46 *Epistolae*, n.9 (pp. 45–7). It would appear that the only other person Grosseteste felt he could share with at this level was his sister, Yvette: ibid., n. 8 (pp. 43–5). See below, Chapter 7, pp. 163–4.
47 Ibid., n. 4 (pp. 25–33).
48 On the relationship between these two texts, see James McEvoy, 'Robert Grosseteste on the Ten Commandments', *Recherches de théologie ancienne et médiévale* 58 (1991), 167–205.
49 Southern, *Grosseteste*, pp. 118–19, suggested that the Psalms commentary was written between 1229 and 1232; but see James R. Ginther, 'The *Super Psalterium* of Robert Grosseteste: A Scholastic Psalms Commentary as a Source for Medieval Ecclesiology', unpubl. PhD diss. (University of Toronto, 1995), pp. 66–70, for a challenge to that date.

Chapter 2

Grosseteste and the Theology of the Schools

'Every syllogistic science is constructed like a net in the manner of triangular figures'; so Grosseteste begins an elaborate similitude. He appears to have had in mind the syllogistic *figurae* which Aristotle had elucidated in Book 1 of the *Prior Analytics*, where three premises come together and, based on specific rules of construction, form a properly structured argument.[1] The affinity between syllogism and triangle seemed quite natural for Grosseteste, who notes that certain philosophers consider the triangle to be the principal shape of all things.[2] Grosseteste then observes that similitudes are possible according to a twofold 'perfection' of things: one can point to the similarity between two things in terms of either form or function, and sometimes both. In comparing syllogistic sciences to a triangular net, a distinction must therefore be made: mundane sciences are such according to the first perfection, that is, the form or shape of a triangular net. Theology alone, however, is the science that is similar to a net according to both its form and its function. It both looks like a net in terms of its argumentation and it is used to capture things, namely people, from the waters of worldly mutability. This distinction is further clarified by the fact that mundane sciences either draw a person to live according to what is below him – signified by Epicurus – or according to what is equal to him, that is human reason – signified by Diogenes of Sinope. Theology, by contrast, draws a person out of the worldly waters to live according to what is above him, that is, God who is immutable.[3]

Grosseteste then takes delight in describing how theology acts as a net, which has now become the net of Peter (in contrast to the net of the Devil). While theology captures humanity, as a net captures fish, it does so only when individuals freely choose to enter the net. Naturally, they need some aid as well as some coaxing: good works illuminate the mind so they can see the net, and preaching warns them of the dangers if they do not break free from the net of the Devil and swim to Peter's net, where there is both liberty and nothing to fear.[4]

This short *dictum* captures some essential features of Grosseteste's intellectual habits. It reveals a thinker who had some exposure to the Aristotelian corpus, which at the very minimum had allowed him to become educated in syllogistic argument.[5] Moreover, it demonstrates a good understanding of the natural world on the part of its author – although it does not necessarily mean that Grosseteste was a practised fisherman! In addition, it comes as no surprise that Grosseteste would construct a complex similitude in order to make his point. He was enthusiastic, if not evangelical, about identifying the symbolic meaning of things, in both the book of nature and the book of Scripture. His use of imagination allowed him to present to his readership the kernel of the argument, so that they could reflect on the issues in light of connections between the facts, and judge what was worthy of consideration.[6] The *dictum* also speaks to the intention or trajectory of theological work. It has a soteriological end, in that it is the tool by which one may capture lost souls who are entangled in the Devil's net. Theology engenders two fundamental tools for this task: good works and preaching. His interest in theological discourse is not simply a result of curiosity, but rather a conviction that this very intellectual task would contribute to the Church's administration of salvation.[7]

At the same time, the *dictum* presents some challenges to interpreters of Grosseteste's theology. In broaching syllogistic sciences, Grosseteste states that theology must be considered as one of them. There can be no other reading of this *dictum*, otherwise the initial distinction between theology and the mundane sciences makes no sense.[8] Such a declaration would appear to render Grosseteste not only as a theologian who knew what defined an Aristotelian science, but also as one who applied that definition to Christian theology. And yet the opposite claim – that Grosseteste rejected this new approach to theologising – is part of the bedrock of modern Grosseteste scholarship. Even more curious is what is muted: the role of sacred Scripture in theology. As a discipline that embraces scientific argument, theology's intention is the care of souls. While standard accounts of Grosseteste normally connect this intention to a biblico-moral outlook, this *dictum* provides no indication of this. Clearly it is far too terse to provide, on its own, any reasonable or satisfying account of Grosseteste's theological vision. It does, however, point to a possible deficiency in the current perception of Grosseteste's theology.

The Standard Account of Grosseteste's Theology

Modern scholarship has presented a portrait of Grosseteste the theologian which focuses on three main characteristics. First, Grosseteste was a conservative theologian who was grounded in the biblico-moral theology of late twelfth-century Paris. The major indicators of his commitment to this old school of theology are his interest in biblical exegesis instead of speculative theology, and a greater attention to the spiritual sense of Scripture rather than the literal. Both factors facilitated Grosseteste's devotion to the pastoral care, particularly in terms of teaching students who were to become future preachers.[9] Secondly and more recently, Richard Southern has controversially argued that Grosseteste was almost antischolastic in his thinking, including his theologising. He showed little interest in the scholastic commitment to making distinctions and resolving contradictions in order to arrive at a definitive conclusion. Instead, Grosseteste responded to questions by quoting vast swaths of the Fathers (as opposed to the terse, epigrammatic citations of which his contemporaries were so fond). He never hesitated in venturing a *possible* solution, instead of positing a firm answer. He invited his readers not to ponder the plethora of reasons why his position was correct, but rather to consider the problem – to let it languish in their minds, to ruminate on it. Connected to this was the role of the imagination, by which, as we have already noted, Grosseteste sought to bring together philosophical or theological reasons with examples and similitudes wrought in the God-ordered world of nature.[10] Finally, the first two characteristics came together to form a third: Grosseteste's rejection of, and resistance to, the new theology of his century. Not satisfied with just promoting the traditional theological methods, Grosseteste went out of his way to limit the influence of the new methods, which apparently challenged the primacy of Scripture and gave greater priority to human reason in theological work.

It is difficult to maintain such an account of Grosseteste's theological outlook for two important reasons. In the first place, its strongest piece of evidence is a letter Grosseteste wrote to the faculty of theology sometime in the 1240s (around ten years after he had left his teaching position), in which he was supposed to have chastised his former colleagues for embracing the new theology.[11] This epistle, while it names no one in particular, may have been aimed at the Dominican theologian, Richard Fishacre. He had begun lectures on the *Sentences* sometime in the early 1240s, and Grosseteste, it would appear, responded by decrying this occurrence and admonishing the faculty to change course immediately.[12] If that were the case, then this letter would be clear and unambiguous evidence that Grosseteste conceived of the new theology as either dangerous or just misguided, and acted against its proliferation.

What has made this interpretation of the letter so attractive is that it echoes the voice of Roger Bacon. Bacon presented Grosseteste, along with the Franciscan Adam Marsh, as the two stalwarts who moved against the currents of the new theology, and lectured on no other text save the Bible. However, Bacon's view of Grosseteste is problematic because it assumes that Bacon knew and understood Grosseteste's theology well enough to present him as a counterpoint. At the very least, there is no evidence that Bacon had read any of Grosseteste's theological works – although Bacon was fairly well-acquainted with his writings on natural philosophy.[13] Hence, if we disconnect Grosseteste's letter to the Oxford theologians from Bacon's claims and instead place it within its own epistolary, institutional and intellectual contexts a very different picture emerges. Grosseteste was not objecting to someone lecturing on the *Sentences*; rather, he chastised the faculty for allowing *ordinary* or magisterial lectures on this text to take place. In other words, the central task of a theologian was to lecture on the Scriptures, which is why those lectures took place in the foundational hours of the day. Fishacre appears to have replaced his lectures on the Bible with lectures on the *Sentences*, a clear violation of university regulations, not to mention in stark contrast the standard practice for all Dominican *studia*.[14] Grosseteste pointed to the practices of the Fathers and the faculty of theology at the University of Paris – the epicentre of the new theology – as the models the Oxford theologians should follow instead. In the end, Grosseteste lost this battle when Pope Innocent IV responded to the conflict with a dispensation for Fishacre. The Pope encouraged Grosseteste to support the Dominican theologian in his ventures because he was preparing his students for the noble task of challenging and eradicating heresy.[15]

This new reading of the letter leads us to the second reason why we should jettison the standard account of Grosseteste's theology: if this letter does not present

Grosseteste as being at odds with the new theological methods of his day, then there is little other evidence to indicate that he was. In other words, the standard account is not based on any systematic or comprehensive analysis of Grosseteste's theology.[16] The initial aim of this study, then, is to provide a general account of Grosseteste's attitude towards the theological enterprise, that is, to describe his theological vision. A fuller account must allow a place for all the elements found in writings such as *Dictum* 118, and by extension should outline the rationale for *all* of his work as a theologian. This account must include Grosseteste's general view on the nature of theology as a discipline, as well as the tools and resources one employed to investigate theological ideas.

The Shape of Medieval Scholastic Theology

Two further comments need to be made before investigating Grosseteste's perception of the discipline of theology. First, it is a commonplace in the history of scholasticism to state that theological methodology revolved around the relationship between faith and reason. The genius of scholasticism, it has been asserted, was to argue successfully that Christian doctrine could withstand the critical inquiry of natural reason.[17] Moreover, that process could lead to useful and orthodox conclusions. No longer were theologians dependent upon using biblical commentary or citing church Fathers to advance an agenda; now they could position themselves in the vanguard of theological thought through debate and disputation. The natural human power to speculate – examine, categorise, define, infer difference and conclude – could make a positive contribution in Christian theology. The faith–reason dichotomy certainly reflects the medieval debate concerning effective methods in theological thought. Placing the production of reason (*scibilia*) on par with the truths legitimised by faith (*credibilia*) was a fundamental shift in medieval theology. Hence, when Aristotle's rediscovered works offered a rigorous means of securing sound argument, scholastic theologians were well prepared for it.[18]

However, by focusing primarily on the relationship between faith and reason, modern scholars have somewhat obscured a fundamental facet of medieval theology. The triumph of speculative theology did not necessarily mean the diminishment of other methodologies, such as biblical commentary. One needs only to cast an eye on the two major theological *summae* of the thirteenth century to observe this fact, namely the so-called *Summa 'fratris Alexandri'* and the *Summa theologiae* of Thomas Aquinas. In each magisterial work theological method encompasses both speculation and exegesis.[19] They were the twin pillars of theologising and were meant to work in tandem, not as competing or alternative theological tools. The compatibility of speculative and exegetical theology can be better observed if one posits not a tension between faith and reason, but rather a relationship between Scripture and reason with faith as the mutual context. This may sound like *Fideism*, but in fact it is an attempt to consider faith as both an epistemological and a metaphysical context for each theological method, as much as a reference to the cultural context of medieval theology.[20] It cannot be denied that many medieval theologians asserted that it is possible to know something about God and uncreated truth outside the confines of grace (although the degree to which this was possible was a major topic of discussion). Nonetheless, the general programme of medieval scholastic theology was not to advance a natural theology per se, but rather to investigate the content of faith with discursive argument.[21] In addition, by recognising faith as the context for these two theological methods, historians have to pay attention to the liturgical and ecclesiastical contexts of theological work. Theologians of the schools functioned as active members of a parish church or a religious order, and therefore engaged in their theology within those specific contexts. How they approached Scripture and how they constructed their arguments rested as much on their sources as it did on the communal worship experience and the acceptance (or enforcement) of ecclesiastical discipline. It is for these reasons that a historian must account for the influence of liturgy and canon law in theological thought. The standard dichotomy of faith versus reason can sometimes fail to bring these contexts to light.

Hence, from the thirteenth century onwards, theologians were challenged to develop a theological agenda that held a place for both discursive argument and the exposition of sacred Scripture. This is yet another reason why historians need to keep the pedagogical context of medieval theology in mind, for the ultimate trajectory of a professional theologian was the exposition of the Bible. Speculation (and its pedagogical context, disputation) provided ideas and approaches that enhanced – but did not supplant – the literal and spiritual readings of the sacred text.[22] This point needs to be reiterated so as to avoid the incorrect conclusion that any theologian who takes time to elucidate a hermeneutical framework for his exegesis has little or no interest in speculative forms of theologising. The reverse is also true: if a theologian fails to adumbrate his exegetical principles, it did not necessarily mean that he has abandoned this theological tool.

Having said that, we must also recognise Grosseteste's unique approach to theology. The following chapter will provide reasons to place Grosseteste within the narrative of the medieval scholasticism; however, Chapter four will demonstrate that he would not let the scholastic project obfuscate his own personal inclinations and interests. Grosseteste was indeed an idiosyncratic thinker, and there is nothing to be gained by playing down this fact. We must, however, always ensure that we do not confuse personality traits with methodological commitments. In the process, we encounter an aspect of Grosseteste's theology that is fraught with tension – between general trends in scholastic theology and his own personal interests – but in the end it is possible to preserve both Grosseteste the original thinker and Grosseteste the scholastic theologian.

Notes

1   Aristotle, *Prior Analytics*, 1.23 (40^b30–41^a18). A summary of the *Prior Analytics* is attributed to Grosseteste by Thomson, *Writings*, p. 87, entitled *Regule libri priorum analyticorum Aristotelis*. This 'commentary' is fairly pedestrian, and probably did not originate as a set of lectures on the *Prior Analytics*, but rather was written as a 'help

guide' for students new to Aristotle's text. I have consulted only one of the two extant manuscripts: Modena, Biblioteca Estense MS lat. 54, fols 1ra–48va. Most relevant is Grosseteste's summary of the syllogistic figures, on fol. 5ra: 'Figure igitur sillogistorum secundum quos recipimur diuersitatem modorum sunt tres secundum triplicem dispositionem medii. Nam medium, id est, tres bis sumptum in duabus propositionibus aut subicitur in prima et ponitur in secunda. Quod dicitur facere primam, aut ponitur in utraque quod facit secundam, aut subicitur in utraque quod facit tertiam.' For evidence that Grosseteste had studied the *Prior Analytics*, see Pietro B. Rossi, 'Robert Grosseteste and the Object of Scientific Knowledge', *Robert Grosseteste: New Perspectives on his Thought and Scholarship*, ed. J. McEvoy, Instrumenta Patristica, 18 (Steengbruge: Kluwer, 1994), pp. 53–75, at 58–60.

2   Dictum 118, quoted in James R. Ginther, 'Robert Grosseteste and the Theologian's Task', in *Robert Grosseteste and the Beginnings of a British Theological Tradition*, ed. M. O'Carroll, Bibliotheca Seraphico-Capuccina, 69 (Rome: Istituto dei Cappuccini, 2003), pp. 239–63, at 241n.

3   Ibid., p. 242n.

4   Ibid.

5   Rossi, 'Robert Grosseteste and the Object of Scientific Knowledge', pp. 53–75.

6   Southern, *Grosseteste*, pp. 40–45. It should be noted that Grosseteste's understanding of 'imagination' differs from the modern definition: the imagination was not about creating or reflecting on 'unreal' or fantastical things; rather it concerned the process by which the mind made mental images of the sensible world. For a more detailed discussion, see below, Chapter 4, pp. 61–4.

7   See the excellent summary in McEvoy, *Grosseteste*, pp. 140–45.

8   Some scholars have suggested that this Dictum makes no reference to theology as a science in the Aristotelian sense: 'The passage from Dictum 118 is neither an endorsement of the new Aristotelian texts and methods, nor an assertion that theology is syllogistic in structure. It is rather a favorable comparison of theology with secular science': Rega Wood, 'Early Oxford Theology', in *Medieval Commentaries on the* Sentences *of Peter Lombard. Current Research, Volume 1*, ed. G.R. Evans (Leiden: Brill, 2002), pp. 289–343, at 269, n.32. However, given that Grosseteste refers to theology not just as a *sciencia* but as a *sciencia syllogistica*, not to mention that the Dictum contains a direct reference to the *Prior Analytics*, Wood's interpretation seems inconsistent with the text. Moreover, this *dictum* is not the last time he would refer to theology as syllogistic in terms of method: see McEvoy, *Philosophy of Grosseteste*, p. 109, n.124.

9   McEvoy, *Philosophy*, pp. 448–9, who was drawing heavily on Beryl Smalley's work: Beryl Smalley, 'The Biblical Scholar', in *Robert Grosseteste, Scholar and Bishop. Essays in Commemoration of the Seventh Centenary of His Death*, ed. D.A. Callus (Oxford: Clarendon Press, 1955), pp. 70–97, esp. 84–8; and *idem, The Study of the Bible in the Middle Ages*, second edition (Notre Dame: University of Notre Dame Press, 1964), pp. 276–7, 279–80.

10 Southern, *Grosseteste*, pp. 26–48.

11 *Epistolae*, n.123 (pp. 346–7).

12 R. James Long, 'The Science of Theology according to Richard Fishacre: Edition of the Prologue to his Commentary on the Sentences', *Mediaeval Studies* 34 (1972), 71–98, at 72–3; and *idem*, 'The *Sentences* Commentary of Richard Fishacre, OP', in *Medieval Commentaries on the* Sentences *of Peter Lombard*, ed. Evans, pp. 345–57, at 353–4.

13 Southern, *Grosseteste*, p. 13; Stewart C. Easton, *Roger Bacon and His Search for a Universal Science: A Reconsideration of the Life and Work of Roger Bacon in the Light of his own Stated Purposes* (Oxford: Blackwell, 1952), pp. 89–91.

14　James R. Ginther, 'Theological Education at the Oxford Studium in the Thirteenth Century: A Reassessment of Robert Grosseteste's Letter to the Oxford Theologians', *Franciscan Studies* 55 (1998), 83–104. In a Dominican *studium*, lectures on the *Sentences* were scheduled in the afternoon, following the university tradition: Michèle Mulcahey, *'First the Bow is Bent': Dominican Education to 1350*, Studies and Texts, 132 (Toronto: PIMS, 1998), pp. 132–8.

15　Ginther, 'Theological Education at Oxford', pp. 102–3.

16　It is possible to see the work of Southern as the exception, as he was the first to attempt some synthesis of Grosseteste's theology: Southern, *Grosseteste*, pp. 205–32. However, I would want to qualify Southern's analysis with two observations: first, his outline of Grosseteste's theology is not a full account of his theology, but rather indicates the dominant themes, as Southern sees them, in Grosseteste's theological thought. Moreover, that assessment of those major themes is not based on the entire corpus of Grosseteste's theological writings, as Southern did not take into account some seminal pieces of Grosseteste's pastoral writings.

17　G. Fritz and A. Michel, 'Scolastique', *Dictionnaire de théologie catholique*, 14, 2.1691–728, esp. 1695–715; M.A. Hotze, 'Scholastic Theology', *New Catholic Encyclopedia*, 12.1153; I.C. Brady, J.E. Gurr and J.A. Weisheipl, 'Scholasticism', ibid., 12.1153–70; *A Scholastic Miscellany: From Anselm to Ockham*, ed. E.R. Fairweather, Library of Christian Classics (Philadelphia: Westminster Press, 1956), pp. 17–32; D. Knowles, *The Evolution of Medieval Thought* (New York: Vintage Books, 1962), pp. 79–106; A.M. Landgraf, *Introduction à l'histoire de la littérature théologique de la scolastique naissante*, trans. A.M. Landry and L.-B. Geiger, Publications de l'Institut d'Etudes Médiévales, 22 (Montreal: Institut d'Etudes Médiévales, 1973), pp. 21–41; J. Pelikan, *The Christian Tradition: a History of the Development of Doctrine, Volume 3: The Growth of Medieval Theology (600–1300)* (Chicago: University of Chicago Press, 1978); J.J.E. Gracia, 'Scholasticism and Scholastic Method', *Dictionary of the Middle Ages*, 11.55–8; B. Price, *Medieval Thought: An Introduction* (Oxford: Blackwell, 1992), pp. 119–44; and Ulrich G. Leinsle, *Einführung in die scholastische Theologie* (Paderborn: Ferdinand Schöningh, 1995), esp. pp. 111–69.

18　Edward Grant, *God and Reason in the Middle Ages* (Cambridge: Cambridge University Press, 2001), pp. 207–82.

19　*Summa fratris Alexandri*, ed. PP. Collegii S. Bonaventurae, 4 vols (Quaracchi: College of St Bonaventure, 1924–48), tract. introd. qq.1–2 (1.1–13); Thomas Aquinas, *ST*, 1.1.8–10.

20　See William of Auvergne, *De fide*, in *Opera Omnia*, 2 vols (Paris, 1674; rprt. Frankfurt A.M., 1963), prol. (1.ibBC): 'fides verae religionis fundamentum est, prima radix atque principium divinae cultus', cited in Roland J. Teske, 'William of Auvergne on the Relation between Faith and Reason', *The Modern Schoolman* 75 (1998), 279–91, at 284.

21　See the sermon of Bonaventure, *Christus omnium unus magister*, in *Opera Omnia*, ed. PP. Collegii S. Bonaventurae, 8 vols (Quaracchi: College of St Bonaventure, 1882–1902), 16 (5.571).

22　For a further discussion of this view, along with the concomitant historical methodology, see my article: 'There is a Text in this Classroom: The Bible in the Medieval University', *Essays in Medieval Theology and Philosophy in Memory of Walter Principe: Fortresses and Launching Pads*, ed. J.R. Ginther and C.N. Still (Aldershot: Ashgate Press, 2004), pp. 31–62.

Chapter 3

The Subject Matter of Theology

The opening pages of the *Hexaëmeron* provide the clearest indication of Grosseteste's understanding of theology as a discpline, making it a good place to begin.[1] Here he establishes what he considers the subject matter of theology to be, and this discussion provides a number of clues as to how Grosseteste embraced the discipline as a whole. Any careful explication of his argument must keep in mind his original aims: to explain why the Bible begins with the creation narrative. Not only does this ensure that we do not read too much into his discussion about the nature of theological discourse, but it also will keep us on a correct path towards an accurate description of his theological outlook.

Grosseteste begins by stating that every science and wisdom has a subject matter on which that discipline depends, and the most sacred wisdom, theology, is no exception. One possible identification of theology's subject matter is the 'whole Christ' (*Christus integer*), that is the union of Christ and his mystical Body, the Church. However, Grosseteste does not simply accept this term as given but rather expands on it. The whole-Christ motif highlights the relationship between Christ and his mystical Body, without explicitly stating the relationship between the Church and the other persons of the Trinity. Grosseteste's first emendation is therefore to extend the unified subject matter of theology to include the fact that Christ is a union of two natures, divine and human. At first glance, he produces a unified subject matter gathered together from three unities or unions: the union of God and humanity in Christ, the union of Christ and the Church in Christ's assumed human nature, and the reunion of Christ and the Church through the sacrament of the Eucharist, which is intimately connected to his humanity assumed from the Virgin, and which suffered, died and rose again. The three unions, bound up in one subject matter, allow Grosseteste to retain a place for the deification of humanity, for through its union with Christ, the (re-)union (or as Grosseteste puts it: humanity's conformity to the Trinity) of human nature with the Godhead becomes possible. Grosseteste's re-evaluation of the subject matter of theology does not end there. Not only is theology concerned with these three unions, it also embraces all of the created order, based on the fact that all of creation draws its essential order from the subject matter of this discipline. This does not mean that theology is the only valid domain of abstract scientific thought, for creatures are parts of other sciences, and so exist outside of the discipline of theology according to other conditions. At this point, the term 'whole Christ' disappears from view, having been replaced by a fuller definition of the subject matter of theology.

The inclusion of the created order in theology raised the question as to how one could configure theology in relation to all other domains of abstract thought. On this point, Grosseteste is unequivocal: even if one agrees to a definition of theology that envelops the created world, it does not mean that the subject is self-evident, or even received through structured knowledge (*scientia*); rather theology is taken on by faith alone. Echoing both Augustine and Anselm, Grosseteste reiterates that theology cannot be understood unless it is first believed. Such a description of theology has two immediate implications about its status as a domain of thought. First, it does not fall under any division of being that human philosophy has established. This is because theology is not just about the Creator or the created, but rather the two realities united under one subject. Moreover, since theology wanders into the territory of the uncreated, one cannot describe it as a certain nature, as one would in other sciences; instead of a nature, one must conceive of theology as 'place of wisdom' (*locus sapientiae*), a hidden place because the wise men of this world are unable to discover it on their own. Theology comes to light only through divine revelation, and this is why it is only through faith that one can perceive what the subject of theology is. The central role of faith in establishing theology's subject clarifies the appropriate point of departure for theological discourse, namely from believable things (*a credibilibus*), rather than 'knowable things without an established faith' (*a scibilibus sine fide previa*).

The distinction between *credibilia* and *scibilia* is not so clear-cut, and Grosseteste carefully explains what he means by employing these categories. He points out that one may include an element in the domain of *credibilia* for one of two reasons: either based on the likelihood of the thing itself, or based on authority. In theology, the likelihood of a thing is accidental, for what makes a thing believable in the discipline of theology is based more properly on the authority of its speaking source, that is, God. Moreover, since all of Scripture orginates from the spoken word of God, one cannot make a distinction between various passages of the sacred text; no one passage has greater authority than another, although one might argue that the words spoken by Jesus are of greater believability than any words spoken through the prophets. The consequence of this assertion is that one cannot use scriptural propositions to construct a syllogistic argument, since this method assumes that one proposition is better known than another. Nonetheless, there are identifiable differences between the elements of Scripture, for some are more imaginable than others; that is, they are immediately comprehensible even to the most misinformed or ignorant reader. It is not surprising that Grosseteste states that the species and forms of the sensible world – the heaven, earth and sea and all the sensible creatures therein – are the most easily imaginable. These elements certainly belong to the sensible world, as well as to other sciences, but the ability to imagine them with ease also makes them greatly acceptable by faith. At last, we have arrived at the explanation of why the Bible begins with creation: 'Wherefore, one should begin sacred Scripture, which is proposed in its entirety for all of humanity, with the sensible things of this world, in so far as they come under faith. The opening parts of every teaching, by which things that same teaching is proposed, ought to be the most easily grasped.'[2]

Having established the rationale for the Genesis creation narrative, Grosseteste makes one further qualification. While it is certainly true that a person can perceive the species of this world with certitude and even develop structured arguments (*scientia*) based on that sensation, the same cannot be said about the creation of sensible things: that is grasped only through faith. Thus the opening section of the Bible ought to describe the creation of the sensible world, as that very world can be apprehended through the external senses of the body. The result is that anyone, no matter how poorly educated, can easily understand the narrative, both through his or her imagination and through the images of bodily things, and can also grow stronger in faith through the authority of the speaker, that is, God.

Grosseteste's assessment of theology's subject matter has often been overlooked in the literature on scholastic theology. Even though this text has been available in some printed form since 1934, few have employed it in the history of the scholastic method.[3] M-D Chenu, in his ground-breaking work on theology as a science, focused the reader's initial attention, not on Grosseteste, but instead on a contemporary, William of Auxerre. The reason for this was Chenu's desire to explain how theology progressed from the twelfth-century methods of literary analysis of the sacred text to the concept of *sacra doctrina* as explicated by Thomas Aquinas.[4] It would appear that none of Grosseteste's writings aided Chenu in arriving at his intended destination, but William's clearly did.[5] However, without diminishing the importance of the *Summa aurea*, it is significant to note that William's prologue contains no description of the breadth or focus of theology. Instead, the reader is presented with a careful discussion of the role of *rationes naturales* in theological argument, a role that cannot usurp the primacy of faith, or reduce the articles of faith to concepts in need of proof. These articles are rather the materials for making arguments, from which one may draw conclusions; they are never the conclusions themselves.[6] Like his contemporaries Alexander of Hales and Philip the Chancellor, two other major figures in the history of early scholasticism, William shows no interest in delineating the subject matter of theology.[7]

Nonetheless, the issue of theology's subject matter was critical to the eventual adoption of theology as a science in the Aristotelian sense. Aristotle's conception of *scientia* has three requirements: that a science have a defined and unified subject; that scientific knowledge be the conclusions which resulted from syllogistic arguments; and, finally, those conclusions must be based on a set of premises that are both necessary and prior to the conclusions. These premises are the first principles of the science that are known immediately either *per se nota* or in the case of the *scientie medie* the subalternated conclusions of a higher science.[8] By the 1240s in Paris, all these conditions for *scientia* were being addressed when theologians disputed on the nature of their discipline.[9] Thus, while William and his fellow theologians made important contributions in the theological discussion of the second and third requirements of Aristotelian *scientia* to scholastic theology, it is in fact Grosseteste who made the first documented contribution in terms of theology's subject matter.

To appreciate the complexity and originality of Grosseteste's argument, it is necessary to break it down into three main components. In terms of the subject itself, Grosseteste delineates how he can maintain unity in the subject of a discipline that seems to exploit individual and changeable things in the quest to know the eternal. He also broaches the issue of necessity, in terms of the subject of the discipline, as well as of the discipline itself. The last component is a logical extension of the way he has posited the subject matter: the relationship among God's revealed wisdom, faith and human knowledge. The argument reveals a careful interweaving of both his Augustinian and Aristotelian heritage, a combination that is fraught with tension but nonetheless one that reveals a theologian on the cusp of his discipline.

Unity

In configuring theology's subject matter to the whole Christ, Grosseteste was drawing upon an ancient exegetical tradition. It would appear that Gilbert of Poitiers was the first scholastic theologian to suggest explicitly that the subject matter of the Psalms was the whole Christ (*Christus integer*), that is, Christ and his members, the Church.[10] Gilbert may have obtained this exegetical outlook from his master, Anselm of Laon, but we have no literary evidence that Anselm's Psalms exegesis advanced on a similar notion.[11] Even then, the proper roots of the whole Christ motif reached back to the patristic period. For the Latin West, it was Augustine who had the greatest influence on the exposition of the Psalms, and so he must be credited as the primary source for this approach to the Psalms. However, Augustine was hardly being innovative since his approach to the Psalms was based on the even older Greek tradition of Psalms exegesis.[12] The intention of rendering the Psalms as a dialogue between Christ and his Church was to strengthen the claim that the Psalter was originally aimed at the Church, who then had a claim on its rightful interpretation – and that interpretation focused on extracting both the christological and ecclesiological meanings from each Psalm.

While it became an integral part of Psalms exposition until the reformation of the sixteenth century, the whole-Christ motif only slowly made its influence felt on the theological enterprise in general. The next stage of its progress emerged in the writings of Robert of Melun. Born in England around 1100, Robert travelled to Paris to gain his education in both the arts and theology. There he had the privilege of studying with not just one but two of the leading lights of his age: Peter Abelard and Hugh of St.-Victor.[13] In delineating his own theological vision, Robert asserted that the subject matter of all Scripture was the relationship between Christ and his mystical body. Robert's aim was to provide a clear indication of the nature of theological work which he had inherited from Hugh. In his *De sacramentis fidei christianae*, Hugh had suggested that the Christian faith centred on the work of restoration, that is the history of human salvation. Robert, then, provided a different means of formulating this same outlook: for him all of the Scripture focused on the Incarnate Word, along with the effects and benefits of the sacraments. The last element demanded that one contextualise the Incarnation in terms of the mystical body of Christ, the Church, which his passion and resurrection established, and which was subsequently both the object and context of all sacramental activity.[14]

Grosseteste was hardly imitating Robert of Melun's configuration of theology's subject matter. His reassessment of the content of the *Christus integer* moves well beyond Robert's vision of salvation history. Instead, Grosseteste presents a subject matter for the theology that is far more complex and far more expansive than any twelfth-century theologian would have thought possible. Grosseteste's innovation was driven by his reading of Aristotle, and in particular the *Posterior Analytics*. In order to appreciate Grosseteste's indebtedness to the philosopher, we must turn momentarily to his own commentary on the *Posterior Analytics*, completed just before he became a master of the sacred page.[15]

In book 1.18 of the medieval ordering, Aristotle laid down the condition by which one organises and unifies a series of syllogistic demonstrations. That condition is not that the demonstrations were fitting or appropriate for the science in question; rather, they are brought together (*aggregrantur*) and united by the very object of scientific knowledge, the subject. Aristotle posits, as Grosseteste notes, a definition of a single science as one that has a single genus as its subject. Then Grosseteste himself posits two other examples: in arithmetic the subject genus is number and in geometry it is unchangeable magnitude. Furthermore, since all demonstrated conclusions are drawn from the first principles of a science, it is necessary that a single science has its own first principles which are united in the subject. For all this talk of unity, a single subject for a single science did not mean that the subject itself was simple; rather, a subject has parts, such as species under the genus, or integral or essential parts, or even accidents that are essential to the subject so that they are demonstrable from the subject itself or from any of the subjective parts.[16] In sum, Aristotle brings together three things which are the conditions of a science: 'unity of the subject upon which demonstration is erected, first principles unified in that subject and from which demonstration is made, and that the subject have either species or parts or essential accidents (*per se accidentia*), from which a demonstrative conclusion is grasped'.[17] These parts and essential accidents are critical in identifying the unique features of each science. This is particularly true in terms of a subalternated science, where that science receives its subject from the subalternating one. Nonetheless, those parts of the subject are not assumed from outside the science, but rather remain peculiar to it.[18] In attempting to maintain the unity of the science, one does not deny or ignore the parts which contribute or compose the subject; rather, the subject must present a means by which those parts, be they species or essential accidents, can be organised under the unity of the subject itself.

In light of this discussion, one can begin to see Aristotle's influence on Grosseteste's discussion of the subject matter of theology. In the first place, the terminology is reminiscent of his analysis in the *Posterior Analytics*: the terms *unus*, *unio* and *unitas* appear over ten times in the opening pages of the *Hexaëmeron*, the notion of *partes subiecti* twice; and the predominant verb of the argument – outside the use of the copulative – is *aggregari*, the same prominent verbal activity in his comments on Aristotle. Word usage is the minor point here, however, for the very essence of Grosseteste's identification of the subject of theology bears all the marks of Aristotle's definition. The subject of theology is one, in that all the parts inhere in the single subject, *Christus integer*. Grosseteste admits that this union is in fact composed of four different unions, but this does not negate the ultimate unity of the subject. What unites all the parts is the person of Christ. It is Christ who is at the centre of the four unions which compose his new definition of the whole Christ.[19] Christ is the union of divine and human natures; he unites with humanity through the Incarnation, and reunites with the Church in the Eucharist; and Christ as Creator is the reason why all of created reality also belongs to this domain of thought. Aristotle had demanded that the unity of a science be guaranteed by a single subject, and, while it was to be complex in nature, there must be a means of identifying an ordering principle that unified all the species, parts and essential accidents inherent in the subject.[20] In all these respects, Grosseteste's new account of the Whole Christ fulfilled Aristotle's requirements for a unified subject.

In addition to the Aristotelian elements of Grosseteste's account of theology's subject matter, there are two significant implications at work here. First, Grosseteste establishes that theology is not defined by sacred Scripture. This is not to say that theological work will not focus on the Bible, but, by positing a broader definition of the whole-Christ motif, Grosseteste was extending the theologian's territory beyond the borders of exposition. Accounting for the centrality of Christ was certainly a mandate drawn from Scripture; but, as we shall see, Grosseteste's Christ is a cosmic Christ, whose role is not limited to the passion and resurrection. As the focal point of theologising, the person of Christ leads Grosseteste the theologian to the domain of divinity as well the creative acts of the Godhead. Grosseteste will speculate on this extended role of Christ, and will conduct all his theological work within the context of all created reality, either understood by human knowledge or acquired through divine revelation.[21]

Secondly, and this follows from the first implication, since Grosseteste does not seek to work within the confines of an economic theology, he must establish methodologies that will allow him to gain access to all the necessary data. In the end, this will require some account of how theology interacts with, and exploits the findings of, the secular arts. During the period of Grosseteste's regency, it was common for theologians to acknowledge the necessity of grammar, logic and rhetoric; it was an entirely different matter, though, to have need of anything drawn from the quadrivium. Hence Jacques de Vitry could say:

> We can safely hear those secular sciences, such as grammar, dialectic and rhetoric, that prepare the listener for the science of piety. It is otherwise for the sciences of the quadrivium, which although they contain truth, do not lead to piety ... Geometry arithmetic, and music have truth in their sciences, but this is not that science of piety. The science of piety is to know and read Scripture, to understand the prophets, to believe the Gospel, and not be ignorant of the apostles.[22]

Grosseteste challenged this consensus by developing a framework in which theologians could gain access to, and then employ, the findings of natural philosophy without endangering their own piety. We shall return to this issue when the tools and resources of theology are considered. Nonetheless, this desire to coordinate all human learning with the discipline of theology was congruent with the way Grosseteste posits its subject matter.

Necessity

Theology's relationship to other forms of knowledge leads us directly to the question of necessity. In addressing it, one *observation* of Grosseteste's account can be posited, and then one *assertion* which he himself presents. The *observation* is a little-noted factor in Aristotle's configuraton of a science, namely that the subject of a science must itself be necessary. In his commentary on the *Posterior Analytics*, Grosseteste points out that Aristotle teaches that one cannot erect demonstration on things of chance, nor even sensible things. This is the logical extension to the argument that demonstration is always about incorruptible things, that is, about universals and not particulars.[23] If then the subject is that upon which a philosopher builds his demonstrations, it too must be necessary. When one considers how Aristotle had framed the *Physics*, it is clear why the subject matter of this science is not the physical realities themselves, such as rocks, trees or oceans, which are in motion, but rather the universal concept of being in motion.

It is at this point that it would be useful to consider the critique levelled by Thomas Aquinas on the subject matter of theology. In the *Summa theologiae*, Thomas makes the case that God must be considered as the proper subject of the science of theology. It is worth quoting his response in full:

> I answer that, God is the object of this science. The relation between a science and its object is the same as that between a habit or faculty and its object. Now properly speaking, the object of a faculty or habit is the thing under the aspect of which all things are referred to that faculty or habit, as man and stone are referred to the faculty of sight in that they are colored. Hence colored things are the proper objects of sight. But in sacred science, all things are treated of under the aspect of God: either because they are God Himself or because they refer to God as their beginning and end. Hence it follows that God is in very truth the object of this science. This is clear also from the principles of this science, namely, the articles of faith, for faith is about God. The object of the principles and of the whole science must be the same, since the whole science is contained virtually in its principles. Some, however, looking to what is treated of in this science, and not to the aspect under which it is treated, have asserted the object of this science to be something other than God – that is, either things and signs; or the works of salvation; or the whole Christ, as the head and members. Of all these things, in truth, we treat in this science, but so far as they are ordered to God.[24]

The argument is concise and powerful, and would appear to accuse someone like Grosseteste of envisaging a theology whose subject was not necessary, but contingent. For Thomas, the whole Christ was part of the subject of theology in as much as it was ordered to God himself. What further strengthened Thomas's rejection of the whole Christ motif was his belief that the Incarnation itself was a contingent event, the loving response of God to humanity's sinful state.[25] If Adam and Eve had not sinned, then there would have been no need of the Incarnation; and so, by its nature, it could never be considered as a subject of scientific enquiry.

However, for Grosseteste the Incarnation was necessary, not only in the Anselmian sense that the Incarnation was the only possible response to humanity's sinful need;

but additionally, the Incarnation would have happened regardless of whether man had sinned.[26] Hence one of the consequences of this 'absolute necessity' of the Incarnation is that it could qualify as a necessary subject of any structured enquiry. Moreover, if the Incarnation were necessary then so was the Church, which would have come into existence regardless of humanity's state. Grosseteste never explicitly states that he has chosen the whole Christ because of its intrinsic necessity; nonetheless, the observation stands, and it speaks to Grosseteste's careful attention to Aristotle, as well as to the internal consistency of his own theological vision.

One would expect that, if the subject of a science is necessary, so will be the science itself. In fact, this is not the case, for necessity of a domain of abstract thought was a slightly different issue. With respect to the subject of science, necessity was constructed in opposition to contingency; with respect to the science itself, necessity was constructed in relation to other sciences: namely does this science investigate an area of reality that was not examined elsewhere? In answering this, we move from observation to reporting an *assertion* of Grosseteste. To set the context, the *locus classicus* is once again the first question in Thomas's *Summa theologiae*. Here Thomas raises the question whether it is even necessary to have a discipline of theology, since what it appears to cover, namely God, is already examined under the auspices of metaphysics. This assertion is based on two factors: one that humanity's intellectual capacity for understanding the divine is already fulfilled in philosophy, and two, that in terms of subject matter God is examined under the subject of being. Thus both arguments force the reader to conclude that theology is a superfluous intellectual activity, and therefore unnecessary.[27] Thomas's solution is not our main concern here, but his formulation of the question most clearly articulates the problem.[28]

At first glance, Grosseteste appears to turn the whole issue on its head. Instead of raising the question of the necessity of theology, his assessment of theology's subject matter implies that theology is the *only* necessary science. If theology treats God, the Incarnation, the Church and human deification, as well as the whole of created reality, then what is the need for the secular sciences? Grosseteste, the good natural philosopher that he was, is readily aware that inclusion in one discipline did not exclude phenomena from another. Hence, even if creatures are part of theological discourse, 'according to other conditions they are outside of this wisdom, and part of other sciences'.[29] Still, theology is where the true meaning of all creation is discovered, even more so than in any other science.[30]

Grosseteste does not leave the issue there, but asserts that theology must be seen as necessary. In establishing the epistemological conditions for theology (a set of statements that we shall examine next), Grosseteste states that theology does not fall under, nor can it be comprehended in, any kind of division of being by which human philosophy divides the category of being. Metaphysics may embrace God *qua* being,[31] but this is not what defines or shapes Christian theology. A metaphysician may have the wisdom to ruminate on the existence of God, but without faith and ordered love, he will never penetrate the mysteries of faith, especially God's trinitarian nature.[32]

Wisdom, Faith and Human Knowledge

The discussion so far has masked a significant factor in Grosseteste's analysis of theology, namely his description of theology as a wisdom (*sapientia*). It has been suggested that Grosseteste employed this terminology 'because in wisdom belief is the presupposition to understanding'.[33] This is certainly true, for Grosseteste paraphrases the views of both Augustine and Anselm, stating that something cannot be understood unless it is first believed. At the same time, some further qualification is needed. It is the subject matter of theology that is not self-evident, nor discovered through scientific argument, but rather received and believed by faith alone.[34] Faith is therefore the precondition for knowing the subject; and it remains to be seen how exactly this precondition relates to theological work itself. It is necessary then to examine what Grosseteste understood by the terms 'wisdom' and 'faith', and what he was trying to accomplish by deploying them here.

Grosseteste never fully articulated his view on human knowledge during his regency, although he disputed on the nature and structure of the objects of human knowledge.[35] In attempting to explain the concepts of wisdom and faith, we must realise that much of Grosseteste's ideas about man's capacity to know – and how that capacity related to theological knowledge – remained inchoate during this period. It was only after he came into contact with the Dionysian corpus as both translator and commentator (ca.1239), that Grosseteste felt himself capable of providing an account of human knowledge.[36] In this light, we need not be alarmed that Grosseteste does not provide any kind of schematic account of the categories of knowledge.

It is clear, however, that for Grosseteste the term *scientia* had a precise meaning, and subsequently a limited use. In his commentary on the *Posterior Analytics*, he clarifies where he places Aristotelian science within the grand scheme of knowable things. Like nearly all ancient and medieval thinkers, Grosseteste assumed that true knowledge was about the unchangeable and incorruptible.[37] Sensory data about individual things in the world did not constitute knowledge, but rather were illusory and possibly rife with deception. While one begins with sensory data, the real focus of a person's intellect was upon the immaterial, the universal; and for Grosseteste this focus manifested itself in four ways. At the top of this great chain of immutable being are the formal exemplary causes in the divine mind of God. Plato had called them the forms, or collectively the archetypal world and they are also creative forces. Secondly, there are the created intelligences, the angels, in which one would find the universals as *cognitiones* and *descriptiones* of created things. Just below them are the powers of celestial bodies, who are the causal *rationes* of earthly species. Finally, universals exist as the formal cause of things themselves. In knowing a thing in terms of its formal cause, a person comes to know that thing as it is. One sees the *form*, to replicate Grosseteste's terminology, 'which is part of the thing'. It is within the fourth level of universal predication that Grosseteste places the activity of *science*. It is where demonstrations are composed, as they focus upon the formal cause of each thing.[38] Within this fourth category of universals, Grosseteste allows for three types of scientific knowledge, ranging from knowing based on demonstration of things as they frequently are (natural philosophy), to knowing things as they always are (mathematics), to knowing things in terms of the immutable cause of their existence.[39]

In this context, describing theology just as a science would be far too restrictive, at least in terms of Grosseteste's own reading of *scientia*. Theology must be a wisdom since it embraces a subject that brings together all that is in the sub-lunary world (the context of science), the celestial *machina* – including angelic beings – and the Creator himself. A theologian must account for creation in terms of the universals in the mind of God.[40] He must also come to understand the place and meaning of angels in the created universe.[41] These two examples reveal that the discipline of theology went far beyond the confines of sub-lunary science. This did not mean, however, that a wisdom could not have scientific features. Grosseteste has no hesitation using the wisdom of metaphysics in his examples of scientific ventures. There is no cognitive dissonance in Grosseteste's describing in one text theology as a syllogistic science, and then describing the discipline as a wisdom elsewhere. In the end, the twofold nature of theology, as a science and a wisdom, became the standard in scholastic theology.[42]

In assigning theology to the sapiential sphere, Grosseteste was also making a statement about the disposition of the human mind in theological work. Like Aristotle, he also considered the objects of knowledge in relation to specific habits and powers of the mind.[43] However, his treatment of the powers of the mind reflects more his Augustinian heritage than that of Aristotle. Above all, his views on the powers of the soul, at least for his magisterial period, are drawn almost exclusively from the pseudo-Augustinian work, *Liber de spiritu et anima*.[44] This early twelfth-century treatise certainly reflects the Augustinian tradition, which is probably why Grosseteste never came to question its authorship.[45] Not only did it teach the same threefold division of the soul (*rationalis–concupiscibilis–irascibilis*) as Augustine had; it also provided a much more detailed description of the soul's epistemic capacity, and what powers it could use to grasp knowledge. There were in fact five powers of the soul, ranging from those connected to the soul's embodiment (*sensus, imaginatio*) to its rational powers (*ratio, intellectus, intelligentia*).[46] The *Liber de spiritu et anima* clarifies at one point what each power means by comparing them to the angelic orders. The senses are like the lowest order of the angels, because they are the first messengers to the soul. Imagination is mapped onto the archangels, because it can sense more than the senses themselves.[47] Humanity's rational ability is equivalent to the angelic principalities, since it is superior and reigns over all the sensory data. Next in the order is understanding (*intellectus*), equivalent to the thrones: a throne is a seat, and a person can understand since God is seated in his heart through faith, sanctification, peace and love; and with God seated there, the intellect comes to know spiritual beings. Finally, the intelligence is linked to the Cherubim, for they know God's divinity in itself. It is the power of the mind that allows a person to gain a glimpse of the divine essence itself.[48] These powers could be, although with some difficulty, mapped onto Aristotle's notion of the soul's habits, and Grosseteste on one occasion offers a list of the soul's capabilities with just such a conflation.[49] However, for the most part he employed the terms as the author had intended them.[50]

That intention was to consider these powers in relation to a final end: wisdom. In other words, these individual powers aid the soul in its movement towards wisdom, which is to know God. While the soul's intelligence could gain glimpses of God's nature, the ultimate goal was both to know and to love God. 'Through the intelligence,' the text says, 'one merely sees the truth; through wisdom one loves it.'[51] Grosseteste echoes this sentiment, as the word 'wisdom' summed up all the goodness of the soul.[52] The result is that, by identifying theology as a wisdom, Grosseteste implied that theological work engaged all facets of the human mind, from sensory perception to imagination, to discursive and demonstrative argument, to engagement with spiritual realities, to the (occasional and rare) spiritual encounter with the uncreated light. This intellectual encounter would also produce an affective response within the soul.[53]

A final consideration of the sapiential character of theology takes us directly back to the text of the *Hexaëmeron*. In reflecting upon the subject of theology, Grosseteste states that one cannot call the subject matter a certain nature; rather 'it is a place of wisdom, which the wise men of this world cannot find'.[54] This statement is immediately followed by a citation from Job 28, where the speaker asks where one finds wisdom, to which the final answer is that it remains hidden from everyone's eyes. What at first seems to be an obtuse assertion becomes crystal clear when we consider Grosseteste's sources, for the commentary on Job by Gregory the Great was one of Grosseteste's favourite works. In the comments on this very passage, Gregory recycles an Augustinian metaphor, namely, the *locus sapientiae* is God the Father.[55] In other words, theology is grounded in the revealed Word of God, his wisdom, and so the subject of theology is found within God himself.

The hidden wisdom of God, the whole Christ, is revealed only through faith, and so now we must turn to this final concept. What Grosseteste means by faith can be clarified with recourse to *Dictum* 129. While his contemporaries would latch immediately onto the notion of the articles of faith as the first principles of theology, Grosseteste is not so forthcoming. What intially captures his interest in this *Dictum* is the use of the term *articulus*. He sees it as equivalent to describing parts of the human body as *articuli*, and so the articles form one body of faith.[56] As much as this and other similitudes fascinate him, the ultimate question he wants to raise is how one defines faith. Using a model he found successful in his commentary on the *Posterior Analytics*, Grosseteste lists what he considers to be the common definition (*communiter*), followed by a strict one (*proprie*), a stricter one (*magis proprie*) and finally the most appropriate and strictest definition (*maxime proprie*). The common definition of faith is to consent to something (*cognitio cum assensu*), a definition that he also uses to describe the basic definition of opinion and even *scientia*.[57] Here faith, opinion and science all intersect, at least in the loosest of all definitions. After this, opinion moves down the scale and further away from true knowledge, whereas stricter definitions of science rise towards knowledge of incorruptibles, as the mind penetrates into the cause of things. Faith's movement is similar to science, in that it rises up, but it first encounters, not things in themselves, but rather a medium by which those things are believed. That medium, Grosseteste states, is authority and the highest authority in which Christians believe is sacred Scripture. While that authority may be faith properly (*proprie*), in a stricter sense faith is to believe in those very things which Scripture guarantees to be true. Above all, the strictest and most appropriate definition of faith is the collection of things to be believed for justification, the articles of faith.[58] While not stated explicitly, Grosseteste seems to consider the articles of faith as first principles, as he ascribes to them properties which are the same for first principles, namely that they are the basis of complex knowledge and are unchangeable. This second property requires some qualification, for Grosseteste sees a difference between the content of the faith and its theological articulation.[59]

It is difficult to determine which definition of faith Grosseteste had in mind when he stated that the subject of theology is known by faith alone. It is doubtful that he meant simple, deliberate assent since that would sound like the common view of both science and opinion – and his intent here is to contrast faith with knowledge.[60] Moreover, Grosseteste's aim in delineating the various levels of definition was to apply the strictest definition of the term; and so it would seem to be appropriate to conclude that, for Grosseteste, the subject of theology is known by faith, that is, by the articles of faith. Such an assessment would be appropriate when one remembers that his improved rendering of the whole-Christ motif reflects the articles of faith in their entirety.[61] However, as tempting as that speculation may be, Grosseteste is not explicit enough in the *Hexaëmeron* to allow for such a conclusion. Instead, we must take into consideration his essential aim in broaching the subject of theology: to explain why the Bible begins with the creation narrative.

With faith as the precondition for knowing theology's subject – or for seeing the subject revealed – Grosseteste draws two logical conclusions. First, things belonging to the category of *credibilia* are more appropriate to the discipline's characteristics than things belonging to the category of *scibilia*. Secondly, this wisdom ought to begin with *credibilia*, rather than with *scibilia* which lack faith (*sine fide previa*).[62] It is not that the content of these categories is mutually exclusive, for in fact Grosseteste admits that the very subject of the creation narrative is composed of elements that come under the scrutiny of both sensation and knowledge. However, under the condition of faith, they are transformed into *credibilia*, especially in terms of understanding their origin and the order of their creation.[63]

Grosseteste's argument here has been much misunderstood. It has been assumed that this line of reasoning demonstrates that for Grosseteste the discipline of theology is equated solely with the Bible, and that he rejects any role for dialectical argument.[64] This is hardly the case. As already noted, Grosseteste defines the subject matter of theology as the whole Christ and not sacred Scripture; even his strictest definition of faith does not centre on Scripture, but instead goes to the articles of faith. In this context, Grosseteste presents in the *Hexaëmeron* a very precise account of what can belong to the category of *credibilia* and for what reasons. In making the distinction between credible objects that are believed because of happenstance (as with opinion), and those believed based on an authority, Grosseteste is in fact making reference to the second most strict (*magis proprie*) definition of faith: belief in those things to which sacred Scripture attests. If they are all believable according to the same authority, one cannot make any distinction among them. Moreover, this means that none of these statements can form the basis of a demonstrative argument, since that would assume a means of identifying which statement is prior and which is posterior in terms of certitude.[65]

While this description of Scripture is consistent with his description of *credibilia*, it still leaves Grosseteste in a quandary. To put it simply, if there is no difference between one credible object and another, why would it matter how the Bible began? Grosseteste's solution is to make a distinction within the category of *credibilia*: some of the objects are more easily imaginable, and others are more difficult. And what is imaginable are those things that belong to the category of *scibilia*, that is the sensible species of this world. In Scripture, especially where their origin and the order of their origin is discussed, they come under the condition of faith (*sub fidem*) and therefore are transferred into the category of *credibilia*. This condition makes the creation story the most easily grasped facet of belief.[66]

Which of Grosseteste's contemporaries would have disagreed with this rigorous description of sacred Scripture? Theologians at Oxford and Paris alike considered sacred Scripture as the foundation of all theological work: it was where theology began, and so theology began with things that were believed on the basis of authority. It is one of the reasons why scholastic theologians used the terms *sacra scriptura*, *sacra doctrina* and *theologia* interchangeably. This loose employment of these phrases did not reveal an imprecision in scholastic thought, but rather a mindset that echoed the title they took as theologians: masters of the sacred page.

The Content of Grosseteste's Theology

One final question remains: if the theological enterprise comprises an examination of the whole Christ, what does a theologian actually talk about? Is the Incarnation the only plausible object of discourse, since that is where the other unions come to be known? Or can a theologian investigate other topics without continual reference to God becoming flesh? The solution here is not so difficult, for Grosseteste obviously considered it valid for a master of the sacred page to broach a variety of topics in his lecturing, disputing and preaching. Indeed, as the visible centre, so to speak, of the theological enterprise, the whole Christ (as Grosseteste had modified it) allows for a number of theological topics to intersect. The result is that

> there can be a structured progression (*descensus ordinabilis*) from this one aggregate [that is, the subject] towards the Trinity, the unity of Trinity, the incarnate Word, and his body which is the Church, and our becoming one (*deiforme*) with the Trinity. Whence, there are wisdoms concerning these parts [of the subject] which pertain to this wisdom. Even all creatures, in as much they have an essential order to this subject (*dictum unum*) – that is, in as much as they flow from it and return to it – they belong to this wisdom.[67]

Grosseteste's theology is so encompassing, not because all theological topics collapse into his Christology, but, rather, because Christ becomes the point of departure for a theologian as he investigates the various unions that comprise the subject matter. Moreover, what Grosseteste describes is a 'structured progression', namely that the order of things has some importance. Grosseteste begins with God in himself, who is triune in nature. Then comes the second union, the Word made flesh. The implication here is that the Trinity – both in terms of essence and agency – is the proper context for examining the Incarnation. This context will become evident when we examine the broad scope that Grosseteste applies to his Christology. In turn, the Incarnation becomes the true context for any theological investigation of the Church, Christ's mystical body. Such an orientation has significant implications in terms of how he presents his own idea of the Church. As complex as any ecclesiology can be, however, the Church as an expression of temporal reality is by no means an end in itself. Rather, the ultimate end is the full union of each Christian soul with the Trinity itself.

This progression immediately raises a question: why is there no reference to the care of souls in his description of the subject matter of theology? It is not because he considers pastoral concerns to be external to theological work; and his own preaching, his literary output and, above all, his work with Franciscans testifies to this fact. Grosseteste may not articulate the pastoral care as an explicit part of the subject matter of theology, but he certainly considers it to be implicit within the subject of theology. What is the care of souls but a means to an end, namely the deification of each Christian? It was a means, furthermore, that found its context within the body of Christ. The care of souls was a form of spirituality within an ecclesiological context.

Another well-known feature of Grosseteste's thought is his fascination with the natural world. It is not surprising that he continued his work in natural philosophy after he had become a master of the sacred page, and that he exploited that research in his theologising. With this in mind, why does Grosseteste not make creation more crucial to the work of theology? It would seem that the natural world can clearly be a major resource for a theologian, but a creature's relevance is based on the fact that it can be ordered to the subject of the theology. Grosseteste's orientation of the natural world to theology does in fact accomplish several important things, including maintaining a supreme role for theological work over the tasks of the quadrivium, and at the same time reinforcing the difference between what a theologian is to do and what a natural philosopher does. In addition, it is instructive to see what Grosseteste includes in his distinction *de creaturis* from the *Tabula*. The initial topics are not very suprising, as he begins with topics such as the creation of the world, matter, form, angels, the four causes, that all creation is for the sake of humanity and so on. Then Grosseteste starts to list things that one would not necessarily connect to a creation theology: the four cardinal viritues, the three theological virtues, justification of humanity, spiritual gifts and other spiritual and ecclesiastical activities.[68] While it is dangerous to draw too many conclusions from a schematic outline, nonetheless it would be safe to say that the distinction *de creaturis* is not just about the natural world; rather, it is about the entire created order, and more importantly that created order related to salvation history. Indeed, any theological reflection on creation for Grosseteste becomes yet another context for the pastoral care, as the *Hexaëmeron* on occasion testifies. Moreover, like the care of souls, creation must be treated as a means – and this is why Grosseteste speaks of the created order existing for the sake of humanity, and why it is the context in which one can speak about the way to seek God (*quomodo querendus est Deus*).[69]

Grosseteste's examination of theology's subject matter was built upon an established theological tradition, but he also infused it with some of the concepts that he had drawn from Aristotle. For him, the focus of theology was christological, but this did not mean that the work of theology was exclusively focused on the economy of salvation. Instead, the reformulation of the whole Christ brought together the Godhead, the Incarnation, the Church and all of creation into the sphere of theological reflection. The work of a master of the sacred page was necessary and had for its object necessary things. So expansive was the subject of theology that it had to be embraced as a wisdom, but a wisdom whose initial point of departure was faith – be that defined by Scripture, the truths of Scripture or the articles of faith. This was no twelfth-century biblico-moral vision of theology; rather, it was the vision of a creative theologian, willing to engage in untested methods.

Notes

1. The following is a summary of *Hex*, 1.1.1–1.2.3 (pp. 49–52).
2. Ibid., 1.1.2 (p. 50).
3. G. Phelan, 'An Unedited Text of Robert Grosseteste on the Subject-matter of Theology', *Revue néoscolastique de philosophie* 36 (1934), 172–9; Emile Mersch, 'L'Objet de la théologie et le *christus totus*', *Recherches de science religieuse* 26 (1936), 129–57.
4. M.-D. Chenu, *La théologie comme science au XIIIe siècle*, third edition, Bibliothèque Thomiste, 33 (Paris: Vrin, 1957). See also Henry Donneaud, 'Histoire d'une histoire: M.-D. Chenu et "La théologie comme science au XIIIe siècle"', *Memoire Dominicaine* 4 (1994), 139–75; and John Jenkins, *Knowledge and Faith in Thomas Aquinas* (Cambridge: Cambridge University Press, 1997), pp. 52–77.
5. The irony is that it was Grosseteste's careful explication of subalternation in the *scientie medie* of the *Posterior Analytics* which provided a key concept for Aquinas. See W.R. Laird, 'Robert Grosseteste on the Subalternate Sciences', *Traditio* 43 (1987), 147–69.
6. *Summa Aurea*, prol.1 (1.15–16). In book 3, where he discusses the virtue of faith, William acknowledges that the articles of faith are to be considered the first principles of theology: ibid., 3.12.3 (3, 1.202–3); Chenu, *La théologie comme science*, pp. 58–9.
7. There are two exceptions to this statement. In a collection of disputed questions from the years 1229–32, there are two attempts to determine the subject matter (or end) of theology. One is by an unknown author, who makes short shrift of the task, only to draw the traditional conclusion that theology is about the *opus conditionis et opus restaurationis*: Leonardo Sileo, *Teoria della scienza teologica: Quaestio de scientia theologiae di Odo Rigaldi e altri testi inediti (1230–1250)*, 2 vols, Studia Antoniana, 27 (Rome: Pontificium Athenaeum Antonianum, 1984), 2.115–16. The second appears to be a *reportatio* of a disputation of a certain Master Willermus, and so it is difficult to follow the arguments to a finalised and certain conclusion. What is significant is that Willermus's school focused on the question in light of readings of Aristotle's *De anima* and what parts of the *Nicomachean Ethics* were available to them. There is no mention made, either implicitly or explicitly, of the teaching of the *Posterior Analytics*: ibid., 2. 119–27.

8   Aristotle, *Posterior Analytics*, 1.28 (87ᵇ1–5).
9   See for example the set of disputed questions by the Franciscan Odo Rigaldus in Sileo, *Teoria della scienza teologica*, 2, 5–74, and the *Summa 'fratris Alexandri'*, ed. PP. Collegii S. Bonaventurae, 4 vols (Quaracchi: College of St Bonaventure, 1924–1948), 1.q.1 (1.1–13).
10 James R. Ginther, 'A Scholastic Idea of the Church: Robert Grosseteste's Exposition of Psalm 86', *Archives d'histoire doctrinale et littéraire du moyen âge* 66 (1999), 49–72, at 49–50. An edition of Gilbert's commentary on the Psalms is in progress, but the prologue has already been published: Maria Fontana, 'Il commento ai Salmi di Giberto della Porrée', *Logos* 13 (1930), 283–301. For an excellent assessment of the commentary as a whole, see Theresa Gross-Diaz, *The Psalms Commentary of Gilbert of Poitiers: From lectio divina to the Lecture Room*, Brill's Studies in Intellectual History, 68 (Leiden: Brill, 1996).
11 On the Psalms commentary of Anselm, see James R. Ginther 'The *Super Psalterium* of Robert Grosseteste: A Scholastic Psalms Commentary as a Source for Medieval Ecclesiology', unpubl. PhD thesis (University of Toronto, 1995), p. 132, n. 14.
12 Ibid., pp. 139–41.
13 David Luscombe, *The School of Peter Abelard: The Influence of Abelard's Thought in the Early Scholastic Period* (Cambridge: Cambridge University Press, 1969), pp. 281–98.
14 Robert of Melun, *Sententiae*, in *Oeuvres de Robert de Melun*, ed. R. Martin, 4 vols, Spicilegium sacrum Lovaniense. Études et documents, 13, 18, 21, 25 (Louvain: Spicilegium Sacrum Lovaniense, 1932–52), 1.1.8 (3.1:181–5). Cf. Hugh of St.-Victor, *De sacramentis christianae fidei*, 1.prol.c.2 (PL 176.183–4).
15 The most relevant studies on Grosseteste's commentary are McEvoy, *Philosophy*, pp. 326–45; Laird, 'Robert Grosseteste on the Subalternate Sciences', 147–69 (see above, n. 5); Robert J. Palma, 'Grosseteste's Ordering of *Scientia*', *The New Scholasticism* 50 (1976), 447–63; and, Rossi, 'Robert Grosseteste and the Object of Scientific Knowledge', in Robert Grosseteste: *New Perspectives on his Thought and Scholarship*, ed. J. McEvoy, *Instrumenta Patristica* 18 (Turnhout: Brepols, 1995), pp. 53–75. In addition, I have consulted Stephen P. Marrone, *William of Auvergne and Robert Grosseteste: New Ideas of Truth in the Early Thirteenth Century* (Princeton: Princeton University Press, 1983), esp. pp. 157–286; and his more recent study: *The Light of Thy Countenance: Science and Knowledge of God in the Thirteenth Century*, Studies in the History of Christian Thought, 2 vols (Leiden: Brill, 2000), which mainly duplicates the findings of his 1983 study.
16 *Comm. in PA*, 1.18 (pp. 259–60, ll.17–21).
17 Ibid., p. 260, ll.31–5. For the translation of *per se* as essential, see ibid., 1.4 (p. 112, ll.70–76).
18 Ibid., 1.18 (pp. 261, ll.41–50).
19 Grosseteste uses the phrase *illud unum* to refer to his new account of this term.
20 *Comm. in PA*, 1.18 (p. 259, ll.17–18): 'incomplexorum enim non dicimus esse scientiam'.
21 See below, Chapter 6, pp. 128–37.
22 Jacques de Vitry, *Cum egredinimini*, quoted in Stephen C. Ferruolo, *The Origins of the University: The Schools of Paris and their Critics, 1100–1215* (Stanford: Stanford University Press, 1985), p. 248.
23 *Comm. in PA*, ed. Rossi, 1. 7 (p. 139, ll.88–95); McEvoy, *Philosophy of Grosseteste*, pp. 327–9; Rossi, 'Robert Grosseteste and the Object of Scientific Knowledge', pp. 68–70.

24 *ST* 1.1.7. In his *Introduction to St Thomas Aquinas* (New York: Random House, 1945), p. 13, n. 17, Anton Pegis noted Grosseteste as the source for the 'whole Christ' orientation of theology, probably based on the advice of Gerald Phelan, a colleague of Pegis (see above, n. 3). It is doubtful, however, that Thomas was responding to Grosseteste directly. Instead, he may have had his sights aimed at the Franciscan tradition, which maintained a commitment to the subject matter of theology as the whole Christ.
25 *ST* 3.1.3–4.
26 See below, Chapter 6, pp. 128–37.
27 *ST* 1.1.1.
28 The Franciscan tradition at Paris had articulated the problem in the 1240s, but only within the context of contrasting theology with other sciences, an approach that only implied that theology itself was a necessary discipline: see Odo Rigaldus, *Questio de theologia*, in Sileo, *Teoria della scienza teologica*, q.5 (2.44–9); *Summa 'fratris Alexandri'*, ed. PP. Collegii S. Bonaventurae, 4 vols (Quaracchi: College of St Bonaventure, 1924–48), n. 2 (1.4–5).
29 *Hex*, 1.1.3 (p. 50).
30 Dictum 2 (fol. 1rb): 'Unde cum omnes creature et omnes mutaciones in theologia habeant sua proporcionalia, nichil est alicuius sciencie quod in theologia plene agnita non agnoscatur, et forte melius in ea quam in propria sciencia. Quicquid ergo est propter quod expetibilis est alia sciencia, in theologia vere apprehenditur.'
31 *Comm. in PA*, 1.18 (p. 260, ll.21–4).
32 Dictum 33 (fol. 24rb-va): 'Qui eciam absit nubilo fantasmatum videt in anima superiorem trinitatem creatam secundum quam trinitatem anima est ymago summe trinitatis in ipsa trinitate anime, sicut in speculo agnoscens unam personam, agnoscit in eodem speculo ceteras. Philosophi et curiosi amatores potencie et sapiencie, et non habentes amorem ordinatum, et ideo habentes oculum cordis obscuratum, plus noverunt in se licet impure, tum noverunt memoriam gignentem intelligenciam, et intelligenciam genitam de memoria, quam amoris ordinem, et ideo in speculo anime plus cognoverunt duas personas quam terciam. Unde quidam illorum tetigerunt de duabus, nichil dicentes de tercia; quidam obscure valde aliquid intellexerunt de tercia magis limpide agnoscentes duas; quidam vero illorum qui plus accesserunt ad amorem ordinatum, et habuerunt oculum mentis puriorem, eciam trinitatem investigaverunt, sicut ille qui dixit "monas monadem genuit, et in se suum reflectit ardorem". Nullus autem habens aliquid racionis, concedens Patrem, potest negare Filium vel econverso, cum hec duo adinvicem relative dicuntur, nisi forte intellexerit Patrem ideo dictum Deum tantummodo quia creator est omnium creaturarum et nos adoptans in filios, sicut forte Iudei et illi qui negant pluralitatem personarum et concedunt Deum esse Patrem. Non tamen sequitur ita propinque ut qui concedit duas personas concedat et terciam. Potest enim habere obscuram noticiam Patris et Filii, et ignorare eos spirare amorem quo se amant adinvicem, sed non potest agnoscere Patrem et Filium esse spirantes, nisi eciam agnoverit eorum spiramen. Preterea, licet omnes magni philosophi, vel plures, qui Deo loquti sunt, noverunt ipsum esse potentem, sapientem, et bonum; et potencia attribuatur Patri, sapiencia Filio, bonitas Spiritui Sancto. Non tamen omnes noverunt Trinitatem, quia non noverunt omnes potenciam in quantum ipsa est gignens sapienciam, nec sapienciam inquantum ipsa est genita, nec bonitatem inquantum ipsa est procedens vel spirata.'
33 McEvoy, *Grosseteste*, p. 125.
34 *Hex*, 1.2.1 (p. 50).
35 Obviously, one cannot examine knowable objects without some reference to the mind's capacity for knowing; but in *De veritate* the emphasis is on the former and not the latter.

36 McEvoy, *Philosophy*, pp. 299–300. See his edition and study of the principal source of Grosseteste's account of the rational soul: James McEvoy, 'Robert Grosseteste's Theory of Human Nature. With the Text of his Conference, *Ecclesia sancta celebrat*', *Recherches de théologie ancienne et médiévale* 47 (1980), 131–87.
37 McEvoy, *Philosophy*, pp. 327–9.
38 *Comm. in PA*, 1.7 (pp. 139–41) Rossi, 'Objective Knowledge', pp. 68–70.
39 *Comm. in PA*, 1.7 (pp. 99–100).
40 *Hex*, 1.3.2 (p. 52).
41 *Epistolae*, n. 1 (pp. 8–17); *De intelligentiis*, ed. Baur, pp. 112–19.
42 See *summa 'fratris alexandri'*, n. 1 (1.1–4); *ST*, 1.1.6. See, also, Mark Johnson, 'The Sapiential Character of the First Article of the *Summa theologiae*', in *Philosophy and the God of Abraham: Essays in Memory of James A. Weisheipl, OP*, ed. R.J. Long, Papers in Medieval Studies, 12 (Toronto: PIMS, 1991), pp. 85–98.
43 Grosseteste stated that not all the powers of the mind were directed to scientific knowledge, and so some 'psychological' facets fell outside the confines of the *Comm. in PA*, 1.19 (pp. 285–6).
44 McEvoy, *Philosophy*, pp. 237, 301–2, 304–5. This text is referenced by Grosseteste as *De differencia spiritu et anime*.
45 The most recent discussion of the *Liber de spiritu et anima* is by Bernard McGinn, *Three Treatises on Man: A Cistercian Anthropology*, Cistercian Fathers Series, 24 (Kalamazoo, MI: Cistercian Publications, 1977), pp. 63–74, where there is also a translation by Erasmo Leiva and Benedicta Ward (pp. 179–288). McGinn argues convincingly that the attribution of Alcher of Clairvaux has little foundation in the textual evidence.
46 *Liber de spiritu et anima*, c.4 (PL 40.782).
47 See below, Chapter 4, pp. 61–4.
48 *Liber de spiritu et anima*, c.5 (PL 40.782–3). Mixed in with these five powers of the soul are its four *affects*: fear, grief (*dolor*), love and hope.
49 *Dictum* 15 (fol. 12ra): 'Sompnus itaque iste quo hortatur nos Apostolus surgere peccatum est. Nec immerito sompno comparatur peccatum quia sompnus est vinculum, et immobilitas sensuum. Sensus autem spirituales anime sunt memoria, et intelligencia, et dileccio Trinitatis, que supra ipsam est, et cognicio, et amor ordinatus sui et eius quod sibi par est, et cognicio regendi et administrandi ea que sub se sunt, amorque eadem recte regendi et administrandi. Hoc est, sensus spirituales anime sunt sapiencia et intellectus, sciencia, ars, et prudencia sive consilium.'
50 *Hex*, 2.9.1 (p. 96).
51 *Liber de spiritu et anima*, 11 (PL 40.786).
52 *Dictum* 2 (fol. 1vb): 'Cum itaque misericordia sit amor relevandi miserum a sua miseria, sicut multiplicatur miseria sic multiplicatur dictus amor et sic multiplicatur misericordia. Miseria vero multiplicatur sicut multiplicatur bonum hominis, quia miseria nichil aliud est quam boni defectus vel privacio. Bonum vero hominis aut est bonum anime aut bonum corporis. Bonum anime duplex est: illuminacio sive aspectus anime, et rectitudo affectus. Duplex est ergo anime miseria, scilicet tenebrositas ignorancie, et voluntatis a rectitudine deviacio. Utrumque autem bonum anime unius nominis intencione solet complecti, scilicet in hoc nomine "sapiencie", et utraque eius miseria in hoc nomine "stulticia". Unde totum bonum anime est sapiencia, et tota eius miseria est stulticia.'
53 Southern, *Grosseteste*, pp. 44–5; *Hex*, 1.8.5–6 (pp. 61–2); *Dictum* 19, ed. Ginther, 16 (p. 130).
54 *Hex*, 1.2.1 (p. 51).

55 Gregory the Great, *Moralia in Iob*, ed. M. Adriaen, 3 vols, CCL, 143; 143A-B (Turnhout: Brepols, 1979), 3.23.46 (1.144); Augustine, *Adnotationes in Iob*, PL 34.855.
56 *Dictum* 129 (fols 105vb–106va).
57 *Comm. in PA*, 1.19 (p. 278).
58 *Dictum* 129 (fol. 106rb): 'Articuli igitur fidei maxime proprie dicuntur quasi parva menbra corporis simboli, que secundum ultimitatem intencionis fidei credenda sunt. Hii, ut dictum est, per se sunt fundamentum iustificacionis. Omnia tamen que in canone scripture continentur, et que credit universalis ecclesia, extra simbolum contenta, possunt per accidens dici causa iustificacionis, quia cum contra auctoritatem scripture vel ecclesie discreduntur, sunt causa dampnacionis.'
59 See the list of the 'articles of faith' in the *Templum Dei*, 3.1–3 (pp. 32–3).
60 *Hex*, 1.2.1 (p. 50): '. . . istius sapiencie subiectum est neque per se notum, neque per scienciam acceptum, sed sola fide assumptum et creditum'.
61 *Templum Dei*, 3.1–4 (pp. 32–3), which summarise the articles of faith in terms of the Trinity, the Incarnation and its salvific benefits for the church.
62 *Hex*, 1.2.1 (p. 51).
63 Ibid., 1.2.3 (pp. 51–2).
64 Raedts, *Richard Rufus of Cornwall and the Tradition of Oxford Theology* (Oxford: Oxford University Press, 1987), pp. 126–7; Rega Wood, 'Early Oxford Theology', in *Medieval Commentaries on the* Sentences *of Peter Lombard, Current Research*, Volume 1, ed. G.R. Evans (Leiden: Brill, 2002), pp. 289–343, at 296.
65 *Hex*, 1.2.2 (p. 51).
66 Ibid.
67 *Hex*, 1.1.2–3 (p. 50, second recension).
68 *Tabula*, pp. 276–300.
69 Ibid., p. 294.

Chapter 4
Tools and Resources

With such an articulate and sophisticated understanding of the subject matter of theology, one would expect a similar presentation of a relevant theological method. However, readers of Grosseteste soon discover that he provides no complete account of how a theologian ought to investigate his subject. We have encountered some facets of a methodology that are implicit in the subject itself,[1] but there are few broader indications of how a theologian goes about his business. In one way, the absence of such an account is not surprising, for the issue of theological method did not really come to the foreground of scholastic theology until the 1240s.[2] However, given the fact that William of Auxerre had broached this very topic in his *Summa aurea* before 1225, the absence of any equivalent discussion in Grosseteste's theological writings is still somewhat glaring.

Even if Grosseteste did not provide a clear account of his methodology, there are hints regarding the various approaches he took in his theological work. Perhaps the best way to reconstruct that method is to delineate the tools and resources that he exploited. By 'tools' I mean the specific skills he employed in his writings in order to make theological assertions or develop arguments about doctrine. 'Resources' refers to the texts and textual technologies from which he drew ideas and arguments. When these two elements are brought together, they provide a good picture of Grosseteste's theological activity and its implicit methodology. This chapter will therefore outline the main tools that Grosseteste employed in theology, namely discursive argument and exegesis. Both demand a careful discussion, since the first has rarely been considered as part of Grosseteste's arsenal and the second has never received a complete account. Naturally both methods were contingent upon the resources that Grosseteste exploited, a topic with which this chapter concludes.

'It seems that one can be so persuaded': Reason as a Theological Tool [3]

When historians broach the role that human reason played in scholastic theology, they encounter a complex area of thought, one that is in fact a nexus where three major questions came together. There was first the issue of how God himself could be a knowable object, and here the primary question often focused on which aspects of God's nature can be grasped by the mind. In addition, medieval thinkers raised the question of *how* a person knows God, that is, what intellectual powers were employed in knowing God. Finally, some theologians raised the problem of how one can articulate this knowledge, or what kind of language is appropriate for describing the nature and attributes of God.[4] The first two issues were more often than not embraced as a unit of enquiry, as in the case of the writers of the *Summa fratris Alexandri*.[5] The rationale for uniting these two theological issues was twofold. First, there was the common acceptance of a symmetrical relationship between subject and object in scholastic theories of knowledge: to describe the content of knowledge was also to describe the capabilities of the mind to know it. Secondly, and perhaps more commonly in the Middle Ages, man was ontologically ordered to the knowledge of God, and thus had identifiable mental capacities in place that were adequate and appropriate for such an epistemological task. To what extent humanity had retained this ideal capacity to know God was a subject of great debate. Moreover, this debate spawned important distinctions between knowledge before the Fall of man (*ante lapsum*), the present state of humanity's knowledge (*in via*) and knowledge that would be accessible in the next life (*in patria*).[6] Nonetheless, this discussion never denied that a person could still know God to some degree in this life. Since this chapter concerns describing the tools of theological work, I shall focus here on how Grosseteste addresses the second issue.

If this area of thought was not complex enough, the historian must also make one further distinction. Scholastic theologians could easily proceed with the use of speculation in theology without feeling obliged to state the reason why or how this was possible. Not every theologian in the medieval schools considered it necessary to provide a comprehensive account of why they could introduce rational arguments to support their theological positions. This may explain why there were so few discussions of the nature of theological language prior to 1250. In these cases, one is left with providing a descriptive account of theological activity, without discovering the epistemological foundations for that work. Such an analysis may in the end be philosophically unsatisfactory, but it still behoves the historian to render the account just the same. Grosseteste, as already noted, was one who had no hesitation in embracing Aristotle's understanding of scientific argument, but was not moved to articulate all his reasons for doing so. Hence the following account may seem incomplete, but it simply reflects the recorded details of Grosseteste's thoughts and actions as a theologian. There are, however, some indications of Grosseteste's understanding of humanity's capacity to know within the context of theological activity.

Perhaps the most famous aspect of his philosophical psychology is continual use of the terms *aspectus mentis* and *affectus mentis* to describe the human mind.[7] Grosseteste did not invent these terms, for they appear in both patristic and medieval literature. Augustine is the only one to coin the term *aspectus mentis* (although he rendered it as *aspectus animae*),[8] whereas he and many others referred to the *affectus mentis* – including Cassiodorus, Paschasius Radbertus, Anselm of Canterbury, Peter Lombard and Allan of Lille.[9] Drawing upon Augustine, it is appropriate to translate *aspectus* as 'gaze', as he had used *aspectus animae* as a synonym for the mind's eye (*oculus animae*).[10] Considering the platonic origin of this metaphor, both the mind's eye and its gaze refer to a person's ability to reason (*ratio*). Even more vexing is the word *aspectus*. Lexically, it may be rendered as 'affection', 'mood', 'love', 'desire', 'inclinations', 'intentions', the state of the mind, or even the object of a person's desire. Medieval writers enhanced the usage of *affectus* by connecting it either to the virtues or to volition in general.[11] It would be most appropriate to render this word as either 'desire' or 'will'. Grosseteste's contribution to the semantic history of these two terms lies in bringing these two phrases together. He first employs them in an early treatise, *On the Liberal Arts*, completed before 1210.[12] In arguing why one should support and valorise the liberal arts, he states that these seven arts are forms of learning that can purge the mind of error. Human activity consists of knowing (*aspectus mentis*), desiring or willing (*affectus mentis*), the movement of the body and the desires related to bodily movements. The mind's gaze looks, and then it judges what it has seen to be either good or harmful: if good, the mind moves the will to embrace it; if harmful it draws the will into itself so it will avoid harmful things.[13] The mind's gaze is shaped by grammar and logic, but it is rhetoric that appeals to its desires. Grosseteste has in effect produced here a shorthand for the Augustinian tripartite definition of the soul's powers: the *aspectus mentis* maps onto the rational power (*vis rationalis*), and the *affectus mentis* onto the irascible power or force of will (*vis irascibilis*) and the soul's desires or appetites (*vis concupiscibilis*).[14]

The next significant appearance of this binary descriptor of mental activity appears in the commentary on the *Posterior Analytics*. It is part of a complex argument on why errors can still creep into the arguments of even those who embrace the syllogistic sciences. Grosseteste elegantly engages Aristotle's explanation as to why errors occur in syllogistic arguments: either because of failure to understand fully the rules of syllogisms and to follow them properly; or because of ignorance due to the lack of all the necessary sense data.[15] He brings the mind's gaze and desire into the second explanation of error and begins by providing a very pithy summary of the dictum: one less sense, one less science.[16] In other words, knowledge begins with sensory data and it is through the abstraction that a person may move towards scientific knowledge. As true as this is, it is not the whole story about knowledge. God knows things without having recourse to sense knowledge; and he is not restricted to the universal, for God also knows individuals.[17] Angels too come to know without engaging the material world, and instead are illuminated by the first light (God), and so they grasp both the universal and individuals. If the rational power of the human soul had not been darkened and subsequently weighed down by a corrupt body, through the illumination of a higher light it too could gain complete knowledge without any recourse to sensory input. Such a process will indeed be the case in the next life – and indeed in this present life it is the case for those who are freed from love of the body. Instead, for most people the mind's eye is at present prevented from such a vision, and behaves as if it were asleep. It is awoken by sensory data, which cause the mind to begin to divide and categorise that data which the senses have presented as confused and mixed. The process of division of accidents and qualities allows the mind to abstract and discover the substance of a thing, and thereby distinguish it from all its accidents. Moreover, continual experience of similar things and events allows the mind to arrive, through induction, at complex propositions about the true activities of nature.[18] Hence, while Aristotle's explanation of scientific knowledge fails to consider the whole gamut of truth, it nonetheless adequately explains the reason why knowledge for humankind must begin with the aid of the senses.

Grosseteste does not stop here, however. He feels compelled to explain why the rational powers of the mind need to be awakened in the first place. Granted, it is due to the corrupt body that was the result of the Fall of humankind; however, the deeper explanation is found by recognising that the mind's eye – its gaze – is not separated from its desires. Moreover, those desires are geared to bodily needs, and in attending to them draws the mind's gaze along with it and away from the light it needs in order to see. The result then is that the mind's gaze must seek illumination from the lesser light of sensory data, in order that it can return to the better light. Such an argument produces the observation that the more one can divert love (which Grosseteste uses here as synonym for the mind's desire) from corrruptible bodies, the more the mind's gaze will come to the light it really needs to see.[19]

Two important observations need to be made here, both of which relate to the way this descriptor has a bearing on Grosseteste's theological methods. First, the gaze of the mind embraces both a receptive and a discursive capacity. The mind not only sees, it judges.[20] In Aristotelian terms it embraces the apperception of sense data via the faculty of imagination (a process we shall return to shortly) and, through division and judgment, it verifies the truth of the object. Grosseteste goes further and even incorporates the intelligence (*intelligentia*) as part of the mind's gaze, the highest mental capacity which is necessary for obtaining wisdom.[21] Secondly, Grosseteste insists that these two features of mind are inseparable. In his work on the liberal arts, the formation of each is caused by different arts, but they in fact function together. While grammar and logic shape the mind's gaze and rhetoric shapes its desire, these arts are intimately related, for rhetoric produces arguments for proof, using both its own methods and those drawn from logic. Together these three arts shape the mind's gaze and desire and lead to perfection.[22] The mind cannot gaze upon the truth if its desires are dragging it away from the light of truth. This is what the Apostle meant when he spoke of a Christian living for God and being crucified with Christ: God illuminates the mind's gaze and forms its will so that carnal desire no longer moves the body to sinful acts.[23] This is because for Grosseteste truth and goodness cannot be separated.[24] To know truth required that both the mind's gaze and its desire be directed towards the truth and the good, that is God himself.

The unitary character of the *aspectus/affectus* distinction returns us to the sapiential temperament of theological work, and indeed why theology is the greatest human endeavour. It is the only domain of thought that embraces all human needs. Thinking theologically required a person to function both intellectually and volitionally. In theology, the mind's gaze is illuminated for true faith and knowledge and its desires are ordered to justice.[25] Discursive argument has its place, but its meaning and trajectory is realised by connecting the knowledge discovered with a human will that was in line with the divine will. Moreover, there is a reflexivity between knowledge and will. The more ordered the mind's desires are to God's will, the more opportunity a person has to gain certain knowledge of God. However, one could only order his will to divine justice by gaining knowledge of God. That knowledge would explode externally in good works which were the result of a properly ordered will.[26] In addition, the *aspectus/affectus* distinction demonstrates why preaching was so important to the theological enterprise. Grosseteste states in one of his *Dicta* that, if mercy is about love which relieves suffering, preaching is the best, most noble and most desirable of all acts of mercy. This is because preaching both illuminates the gaze of the mind and corrects its desires.[27] And since the soul is nobler than the body, any oportunity to alleviate spiritual suffering must be considered more important than the alleviation of bodily suffering.[28] Anyone who wants to alleviate suffering should consider studying theology, as they will learn how to work mercifully in the most noble and effective manner.[29]

While Grosseteste's explanation of the two parts of the mind clearly provide a place for reason in theologising, it also raises the thorny question of divine illumination. He repeatedly states that the mind gazes upon the truth because it has been illuminated by a superior light, namely God.[30] The implication of this metaphor is that Grosseteste leaves no room for any discursive knowledge, since all true knowledge requires God's direct intervention in the process of knowing. Moreover, his theological definition of truth is constructed on a similar light metaphor, which also implies that all truth requires some access to the ideas in the mind of God himself.[31] Two points need to be adumbrated here. First, Grosseteste does assert that the mind's ability to see truth is contingent upon a superior light illuminating it, but does not diminish the discursive capabilities of the mind. Rather, this illumination establishes the most effective context in which it may peform its mental duties. The mind sees, but then it must also judge. Secondly, the illumination of the mind is not a special case within the framework of God's relationship to humanity. In each case where Grosseteste speaks of the mind's gaze being illuminated, he also speaks of its desire being directed or ordained to the good by God himself. Grosseteste does not mean to say each individual therefore bears no responsibility for doing things (or desiring to do the right thing), for he maintains a coherent position on the freedom of the will.[32] Hence, if God's role in a person's ability to do good does not eliminate free will, it is equally congruent to state that God's role in the acquisition of truth does not eliminate a person's ability to come to know things by his own mental activities. Reason and action must function in harmony with God's truth and goodness, and together humanity can gain access to all truth, especially theological truth.

A Speculative Theologian at Work

As already noted, Grosseteste would wait until he was bishop of Lincoln before he provided a more extensive theory of knowledge, and so we can provide no further elaboration on the theoretical basis for the role of reason in Grosseteste's theological methods. This is somewhat disconcerting, since none of what we have outlined up to now points to Grosseteste as a *speculative* theologian. We must now turn to the way he actually functioned theologically to see if there is any evidence for nominating him as this type of theologian. In general, there are three tests we can set in order to assess whether he engaged in discursive argument in a serious way. First, a speculative theologian wanted to assess the evidence for holding a conclusion, to the point that one could ascertain the arguments for and against the held position, and even refute those arguments that appeared to undermine the correct conclusion. Secondly, he was interested in providing the necessary reasons for things believed; that is, he developed arguments that presented faith as a reasonable activity. Finally, the more daring and sometimes innovative task was to extrapolate doctrine from the established principles of the Christian faith. This was theology supposedly at its most scientific, since it relied solely upon discursive argument to advance a theological view, and became ultimately the true mark of a speculative theologian.

Grosseteste passes all three tests. As already noted, his literary remains sometimes mask the fact that a certain work began as a disputed question, and in many cases all that has survived is the magisterial determination. Of the four disputed questions we can assign to Grosseteste, the *De veritate* provides the clearest example of his desire to collate opposing arguments. The question here concerns the singularity of truth – are there truths which are distinct from the supreme truth? – which arose from Grosseteste's reading of John's Gospel.[33] Typical of a record of a disputation, the arguments for a variety of truths are presented, followed immediately by a recounting of the arguments to support the existence of only a supreme truth. Grosseteste then offers his own determination of the question, and takes the opportunity to raise some further questions, whose solutions contribute to the general position he has taken. Such a structure may appear to be uneven in its execution, particularly when placed alongside the more rarified construction which appears in later magisterial texts such as Aquinas's *Summa theologiae*. The difference in structure, however, does not indicate two opposing approaches to theological debate; rather, Grosseteste's *De veritate* has characteristics of a record of an actual disputation, whereas the later authors simplify the process for pedagogical reasons. Moreover, when compared to texts from the 1220s and the 1230s, Grosseteste's disputational method is well in keeping with general trends of his time. The same format is found in the *Summa aurea* of William of Auxerre, the *Quaestiones disputatae* of Alexander of Hales, and the disputed questions of Guy of Orchelles – all of which were composed in the 1220s – and even the *Summa fratris Alexandri*.[34] Even questions from the 1230s share an affinity in structure with Grosseteste's own disputed questions, as in the case of Hugh of St-Cher.[35] Grosseteste was not only committed to the pedagogical function of disputation; he adhered to the accepted disputational rhetoric. Where Grosseteste's own personality comes through is in the final published product: rarely did he allow a question to circulate 'as is', but either allowed his determination to be published on its own or reworked a whole question (or a series of questions) into a more treatise-like structure.

The whole point of presenting opposing arguments was not for intellectual curiosity; rather it was the first of two stages of theological argument. If all of theological thought was under the aegis of divine truth, any apparent inconsistencies within the sources for theological reflection demanded some explanation that eradicated the contradiction. Bringing those contradictions to light was therefore a necessary point of departure. The significance of the scholastic method emerged in the second stage, namely what a theologian did with these collected arguments. The *De cessatione legalium* provides a clear indication of the possibilities of discursive argument. It is worth quoting the opening statement of part 3 to this work:

> Everything which has already been demonstrated by the authority of Scripture [that is, part 2 of this treatise] can also be demonstrated by reason. And, having presented the truth of evangelical history, it can be concluded that the man, called Jesus, son of Mary (the wife of Joseph), was truly the God-man, namely the Christ promised in the law. Saint Augustine, Gregory and Anselm (most of all in his book entitled *Why the God-man*) clearly and lucidly show that it would be necessary for God and man to be united in a person, the liberator of fallen humanity from its blame and punishment, the one who leads humankind – who had wandered away by sinning – back to glory, and [he would do] this through the passion of the cross. The expositors of the sacred page constantly [*sparsim*] declare by the use of reason that the restoration of fallen humanity made it necessary that it be accomplished through the passion of the God-man.[36]

Speculative theology had a responsibility to present arguments which supported the conclusions drawn from exegesis of the sacred page. This was not a revolutionary mandate, since to do so was to follow in the footsteps of the Fathers.[37] Grosseteste's statements here encapsulate the Anselmian project of faith seeking understanding. Speculative theology, since it was connected to the biblical exegesis, did not seek to establish a separate research programme; instead, it contributed to the task of theology and provided a rational account of those things gained from the revelation of Scripture. At the same time, there was an opportunity for innovation. Grosseteste continues here by noting that his own reading had not revealed any authority who had raised the question of whether the Incarnation would have occurred if humanity had not fallen into sin. Anselm had effectively demonstrated that the Incarnation was the only reasonable (and thus necessary) solution to the fallen state of men and women; now Grosseteste raises the question as to whether that notion of necessity needed to be expanded. If the Incarnation was seen to be a necessary act in the fullest meaning of the term, it had to be presented as a non-contingent event. In other words, it could not be considered as the response to a contingent historical event, such as the Fall of humankind, even if one could argue that it was the only correct response.

There are some significant observations to be made here. First, Grosseteste is very aware that he is moving into uncharted territory. There was no biblical statement that the Incarnation would have happened if the Fall had not occurred, nor was this found explicitly in any of the articles of faith. However, Grosseteste is convinced that it does not stand in contradiction to Scripture, and sees no reason why the question cannot be investigated. Secondly, he is careful to declare his focus. The rational basis for the Incarnation as the necessary response to humanity's sinful state is not part of the question, and so it can be left to one side.[38] Grosseteste wants to make a distinction here between providing a rational account of the Incarnation itself as a salvific act and examining a far more speculative question. Finally, a careful examination of his argument reveals very few citations from authorities.[39] Grosseteste structures his arguments around the shared conclusions concerning the nature of God and his creation. It is an extremely complex piece of deductive logic (and the logic of his presentation is not always immediately clear to the reader), where patristic authority is rarely taken into account. There are citations of Scripture, but they are used to establish the premises of the argument, wherefrom Grosseteste draws his conclusion. Here we see Grosseteste acting as a speculative theologian.[40]

Nonetheless, it is important that we qualify this vignette. Since he is on unfamiliar ground, Grosseteste couches his findings in very tentative language. Perhaps someone else has made this assertion, he states, but he cannot remember having read it.[41] It is even more problematic whether he is the first person to make this case, for Grosseteste is all too aware of his limitations as a scholar: 'Regardless of whether [this assertion] is true, I know I make mistakes; and I do not suffer any mediocrity in my ignorance in this regard.'[42] This may be seen as Grosseteste backing away from the intellectual confidence of the scholastic project, or it may be another instance when his own personal inclinations bubble to the surface of his theological argument. It is worthwhile to note that he does not hesitate to continue a line of argument which assumes that the 'absolute' necessity of the Incarnation has been adequately proven.[43]

This last observation raises the question whether Grosseteste fully understood the demands of scholastic theology, for it would appear that he adopted some *unscholastic* methods in his writings. Perhaps the best way to investigate this aspect of Grosseteste's theologising is by entertaining two objections from the pen of Sir Richard Southern. They are valid objections, in need of a response if we wish to envisage Grosseteste as a scholastic theologian.

Possibilities in Theological Work

The first objection concerns Grosseteste's predilection for evoking *possible* solutions, instead of invoking one solid conclusion to an argument. This was hardly the mark of a scholastic master, notes Southern, for 'what reason had a master to speak, if not to assert truth or uncover error?'[44] There were in fact many reasons for a master to speak, and often it was not to assert a single conclusion. One of the most perplexing features of scholastic exegesis is a master given to providing more than one reading of the biblical text, multiple solutions that were *in addition* to the various senses of Scripture. Once the literal and spiritual meaning had been outlined, it was not uncommon for a master to provide afterwards alternative literal or spiritual readings of the same text. Modern scholarship is still unsure how to cope with expositions that begin with phrases like 'this can be explained in another way' (*potest aliter exponi*).[45] Do these multiple interpretations reveal the conclusions of the master himself or the opinions of his patristic sources or even his fellow masters? To suggest alternative readings seems out of step with the scholastic project, and it may explain why so few accounts of scholastic theology embrace enthusiastically the evidence of biblical commentary.[46] Nonetheless, these texts were produced by the same theologians who did not hesitate to posit one definite conclusion to a problem posed in a disputed question. It is not surprising then that most of the examples Southern employs to demonstrate Grosseteste's tentativeness come from the genre of biblical commentary. When one looks at Grosseteste's disputed questions, we see a stronger affinity for definitive solution. He is more than willing to consider possible solutions, but in the end he provides what he sees to be most logical and rigorous solutions to theological problems.

However, Grosseteste's tentativeness is evident, and there are even points in his writings when he cannot see a solution and is happy to have wiser minds tackle the problem.[47] Does this reveal an uneasiness with the scholastic method? Possibly not, for instead it may simply be a product of his personal experience rather than a statement about his methodology. Grosseteste became a master of the sacred page in his mid-fifties, and that meant that he had already been engaged in intellectual activity for more than thirty years. If his breadth of learning had taught him anything, it was that the world was often more complex than it appeared at first sight and sometimes riddled with insoluble problems. Definitive solutions were not always possible, and at times all that a theologian could do was to offer the most appropriate solution. His willingness, furthermore, to reveal openly and honestly his lack of confidence in his solution may be seen either as a personality trait (did Grosseteste struggle with self-esteem?) or as an indication of humility. On these latter points, I can hardly make any definitive statements myself, but whatever level of tentativeness we wish to assign to Grosseteste's theological solutions it is clear that his own personal inclinations were not muted in his theologising.

Imagination and Argument

Still, his interest in possible solutions did not prevent Grossteste from engaging in the standard scholastic practices of lecturing, disputing and preaching. He could speak most definitively on pastoral issues above all, and never hesitated to affirm and support a position he strongly held. How he supported his conclusions, however, also appears to be somewhat unscholastic. While Grosseteste made recourse to traditional scholastic modes of argument, he also appears to have employed some unscholastic methods. His invocation of imagination is perhaps the most significant of these. Grosseteste would often suggest examples (*imaginationes*) to support his argument or encourage his reader to engage in a thought experiment. His use of images and thought experiments is yet another reason to consider him as perhaps not just out of date with his contemporaries, but 'in a different world' altogether.[48]

Grosseteste's use of imagination is in keeping with scholastic thought, but it does betray some independence. In the standard accounts of scholastic psychology, the imagination was conceived as a processing faculty: it received the sensory data that had been coordinated by the internal common sense and created an imaginable object.[49] The imagination was a necessary faculty since neither the sense organs nor the internal common sense retained any data after the moment of impression. Instead, the imagination created a record of the sensory experience that could last well beyond the moment of sensation. Imaginary objects could be placed in memory, but their recall required they be returned to the faculty of imagination for any cognitive use.[50] Aristotle makes it quite clear that the abilities to think, perceive and judge were contingent upon imagination.[51] On this point, Grosseteste agrees with Aristotle and his commentators, and this helps to explain why the Bible begins with the creation narrative: it starts with the sensible, and therefore imaginable, world from which readers could then go on to recognise the true cause of its existence, the unimaginable creator.[52]

The imagination, however, was a double-edged sword. While foundational for rational thought, it could at the same time mislead the thinker. That is why true knowledge focused on the universal grasped only by an intellect which is both pure and separated from 'phantasms' – the products of imagination.[53] When imagination was presented as argument, the result was misinformed opinion and these 'false imaginations' led to error.[54] Metaphysically, false imagination was the pimary reason why certain philosophers failed to conceive of situations when there was an ontological distinction between a cause and its effect, as in the case of the eternity of the world. Drawing upon their imaginative conception of time as a sequence of intervals in a given place, these philosophers envisaged eternity in this way, with the only difference that the sequence was ad infinitum.[55] They failed to distinguish between time and eternity, and so this led them to posit the world as eternal, since its cause – God himself – was eternal.[56] Quite consistently, Grosseteste also asserts that these philosophers also failed to see the truth because their desires (*affectus mentis*) were not ordered to God.[57] In terms of religious belief, false imagination was at the root of idolatry, since idolaters imagine a false connection between the divine nature and the created world, which makes them think that they can legitimately worship creation in place of the Creator.[58] For these reasons, Grosseteste was explicit about the difference between imagination and argument. In his treatment of the creation of humankind in the image of the Trinity, Grosseteste includes some reasons why the Trinity is a reasonable concept. He knows that his arguments are incomplete, and so states:

> Let us be content for the time being with these reasons that prove Trinity in unity. But for imagining in a certain way that which has been proven, let us offer some other examples. The comprehension of the Trinity is absolutely necessary for us: the love of it is the salvation of the soul, and without this love there is no salvation. The love of the Trinity is in direct proportion to how much it is comprehended by faith and understanding. It is a beauty that draws the comprehension of the one believing and understanding into its own love. Therefore the examples of the supreme Trinity which are commonly offered are the following – and they are not only examples but arguments of the supreme Trinity collated in an evidentiary manner that prove efficaciously the Trinity itself. Nevertheless, we offer them now not as arguments (so as to avoid prolixity), but just as examples which aid the imagination.[59]

While there was a difference between imagination and argument, Grosseteste also saw that *true* imagination was related to good arguments. This leads us to suggest the first reason why Grosseteste was so committed to imaginative examples. They were forms of effective rhetoric that could further persuade his audience of the truth. In other words, true knowledge was bound to a will that was ordered to the divine will, and the major way in which one could properly shape the mind's desire was through rhetoric. It was one thing to assert that the Trinity was a reasonable position to hold in terms of the Christian faith, but it was far more effective to posit examples of the imprint of the Trinity in creation. It was one thing to argue that the reason why the Incarnation occurred so long after the Fall of humankind was in order to teach men and women of their inability to save themselves; but it was far more effective to create an image of a person stuck in a pit, who after numerous attempts to get himself out has to wait for somebody to come and help him.[60] It was one thing to argue that theology was the most appropriate of all sciences to be defined as syllogistic, based on the figure of a net; but it was more effective to illustrate that point by treating theology metaphorically as a net used to capture people's souls.[61] In these instances, the imagination was a bridge between the *aspectus mentis* and the *affectus mentis*. The examples of the Trinity could aid a person in believing and knowing the Trinity, and this would have a direct impact on her love of the Trinity, the kernel of the soul's salvation. The example of the person stuck in a pit reinforced the need for him to call upon God's help in salvation. Theology as a net forcefully depicted the salvific end of theological work. Grosseteste's use of imagination strengthened his arguments; they did not replace them.[62] Hence it is difficult to see his recourse to imagination and thought experiments as unscholastic. Instead, he propounded a methodology that was in keeping with the rigorous demands of scholastic arguments, but also one that allowed him to implement rhetorical strategies which spoke to both the gaze and the desire of the mind.

What drew Grosseteste to the possibilities of the imagination in theological argument? Southern suggests that it had nothing to do with the scholastic project, but rather was due to the influence of twelfth-century monastic writers, such as Anselm and Bernard, on Grosseteste's outlook.[63] However, there is a more likely explanation, and it comes from Grosseteste's work in natural philosophy. While much has been made of Grosseteste's interest in the natural world, and even his attempts to develop an 'experimental' method, few historians have focused on his formation in Euclidean geometry. And yet it was Euclid that aided Grosseteste in discerning celestial mechanics, as well as providing a means of examining cause and effect in natural phenomena.[64] Moreover, his theological explanation of the nature of light as the first form of all matter relies heavily upon geometric theory which has been subsumed (or in Aristotelian terms, subalternated) into the subject of optics.[65] Indeed, it may have been his fascination with mathematics and geometry which drew him to Aristotle's *Posterior Analytics* in the first place: until the mid-thirteenth century, this text had been considered solely within the purview of mathematicians.[66] Not surprisingly, he employed a Euclidean method in his exposition, providing summary *conclusiones* along the way. These were the general propositions or axioms which one could draw from Aristotle's arguments.[67] In this way, Grosseteste subsumed Aristotle into his own thinking, mediated through his knowledge of Euclid.

There was also a complex relationship between geometry and scholastic theology, and it was manifest in three ways.[68] In the twelfth century, some thinkers mimicked Euclid's *Elements* by presenting their theology in terms of axioms and propositions. Their aim was to establish the fundamentals of Christian theology, upon which a theologian could construct good logical arguments. Although this approach preceded the advent of the scientific theology of the thirteenth century, it gained few supporters.[69] A second, more common, influence of Euclidean geometry on thirteenth century theologians emerged in specific arguments, in which the geometric principles were entertained as ways of solving a theological problem.[70] The applicability of these principles to theological ideas was based on an assumption about the unity of truth: the content of natural philosophy could have a direct bearing on theological discussions about creation and in particular the nature of humankind. That scholastic theologians would draw from the data of geometric argument should not be surprising: they all had been trained in geometry when studying the liberal arts and, if they had been persuaded of the scientific nature of theology by reading Aristotle, they would have encountered the vitality of geometric argument in those texts as well.

Grosseteste never adopted the axiomatic method for his theological work, but he did consider that geometric principles could be of use in making certain theological arguments.[71] However, there was a third aspect of geometry that did gain Grosseteste's attention: a good geometer not only presented the logical arguments of a proposition, he also needed to visualise the argument in geometric space. That action required the use of imagination. For example, in two places in his commentary on the *Posterior Analytics*, he suggests that his reader can imagine a geometric argument that supports Aristotle's position.[72] Geometry, the original basis of scientific approach (for Aristotle considered his own work as building on Euclid's), reinforced the intimate relationship between discursive argument and imagination.[73] Recourse to the imagination did not diminish the importance of reason; rather it supported it, providing first the sensory data for analysis and then a place for one to visualise the results.[74] Grosseteste's use of imagination did indeed echo the affective theology of earlier monastic writers as it was one way to inflame the mind's desire; it also was commensurate with discursive argument.

Exegesis as a Theological Tool

The second theological tool that Grosseteste employed was the exposition of Scripture. More research has been completed on this facet of Grosseteste's theology than on his speculative interests; even here, though, there remains the challenge of rendering a full account of his attitude towards the sacred page. The clearest explanation of this relationship between the subject of theology and sacred Scripture is found in the *De cessatione legalium*. The main intent of this complex treatise was to examine in what way Christ has fulfilled the ceremonial law of the Old Testament, a query that most probably orginated in a disputed question. In part one, Grosseteste felt the need to explain why the Incarnation did not take place immediately after the Fall, and he suggests two major reasons. First, the delay allowed the human race to be taught that salvation was not possible without divine aid. The positive law of the Old Testament, as the Apostle Paul had stated, taught humanity that they were incapable of eradicating sin and its effects with their own actions or powers. Humankind needed the help of God, which then came in the form of the Incarnation.[75] To this standard explanation, Grosseteste adds a second reason: since the Incarnation itself is such a difficult and at first glance a contradictory concept, a number of testimonies were required to authenticate its truth. Grosseteste identifies four main sources of authentication: the natural world, prophetic assertions, human history – primarily the history of the Israelites – and authoritative writings – namely the Bible.[76] More importantly, the sacred text provided the interpretive key to understanding the witness of creation as well as the main gateway to the content of prophecy and human history.[77]

Drawing upon the Augustinian notion that the Bible employs both words and things as signifiers of spiritual truths, Grosseteste develops a sophisticated hermeneutic which allows him to remain attuned to the nature of the sacred text itself. At the same time, this framework provides a conduit for connecting his work as a natural philosopher to his theological tasks. Grosseteste's hermeneutical point of departure was that Scripture had both a literal and a spiritual meaning. As with many other theologians of his age, he was convinced that the literal sense ought to gain more attention than it had in previous centuries.

In a very general way, medieval exegesis oscillated between two maxims of Augustine. On one end of the exegetical spectrum, Christians were to 'meditate on what we read till an interpretation be found that tends to establish the reign of charity'.[78] Such a maxim engendered an immense amount of flexibility in exegesis: as long as charity was furthered, one could interpret the text by any means and in any direction. At the other end, an exegete was to realise that 'nothing is entirely drawn from allegorical obscurities which is not stated plainly elsewhere'.[79] According to this maxim, to expound the text literally and spiritually did not mean creating two levels of reading; rather, the basis of spiritual exegesis must be the literal rendering of Scripture. In the twelfth century, the Victorine school at Paris had launched a programme of exegesis that made new demands on theologians. A more rigorous approach to understanding the grammatical and historical meaning of the sacred text became the point of departure for exegesis. Thirteenth-century exegetes furthered this new mandate with a greater sensitivity to the nature of reading and to the role of the author in their exegesis. It would be facile, however, to argue that medieval exegesis prior to the advent of the schools aspired to follow only the first maxim, and the second became the singular catch-all for the scholastics. It is more of a question of emphasis. Monastic contemplation was given more to the consideration of the 'reign of charity', whereas the masters and students of the schools became interested in controlling spiritual exegesis through a more sophisticated understanding of the literal sense. Spiritual exegesis was never fully abandoned by the university masters, as they were the ones solely entrusted with this task.

The Literal Sense

Grosseteste embraced the Victorine exegetical programme, and provided one of the most comprehensive examples of all its hermeneutical implications. Like many other scholastics, Grosseteste considered the literal sense as having a number of components. To begin with, he often focused on the grammatical structure of the biblical text and the related problem of establishing a readable text. While Grosseteste was aware of the deficiencies of the Latin Vulgate, he rarely introduced alternative readings in the way that Peter Lombard had done in his influential commentaries. In his *Super Psalterium*, the closest Grosseteste came to producing variant Latin readings was by drawing upon the *Hebraica veritas*, Jerome's third translation of the Psalter. Grosseteste never referred directly to the Hebrew text in his expositions of Old Testament books. More commonly, he gained grammatical and textual insights from the Greek texts of Scripture. It would appear that he had access to a manuscript copy of Origen's *Hexapla* for the Psalms. He also consulted the Septuagint in the *Hexaëmeron*, and used the Greek New Testament for his commentary on Galatians. In the latter case, we know of at least one Greek manuscript that Grosseteste employed, and he had consulted a number of others.[80]

The second component of the Victorine exegetical programme was attention to biblical history. Hugh's aim was to have his students understand the relationship between various biblical books and the historical narrative which the Bible as a whole unfolded.[81] The closest inheritor of Hugh's interest in history was Peter Comestor, who provided a synoptic account of biblical history in his *Historia scholastica*. Comestor's work remained popular in the schools until the middle of the thirteenth century, when it appears to have been eclipsed by other textual resources and educational activities. Grosseteste was aware of this work and made one slight reference to it in his *Super Psalterium*, and on that occasion he reported what he did not find in this source.[82] Nonetheless, the historical context of the biblical text provided the appropriate context for a literal and spiritual reading. He is careful to delineate, for example, the relationship among the account of the Council of Jerusalem in Acts 15, Paul's memoirs in the Epistle to the Galatians and the theological teaching of that epistle.[83] In the *Super Psalterium*, Grosseteste lays out the historical context of individual Psalms, upon which he would then direct his full reading of the text. In this respect, he stands out from his contemporaries. It was not uncommon to relate specific Psalms to the events in the life of David (as the titles of certain Psalms already made the connection), but Grosseteste was of the unique opinion for his century that David was only one author of the Psalter.[84] Since the Psalter was not edited into one book until the time of Ezra, Grosseteste followed his Greek patristic sources by slotting some Psalms into the period of the Babylonian exile, or even into the post-exilic period.[85]

Had Grosseteste been satisfied with this twofold approach to the literal sense, modern scholars would be more than justified in concluding that he was solely committed to a rather dated approach to the biblical text.[86] However, as an expositor Grosseteste adopted an additional approach that expanded his hermeneutical framework. Alistair Minnis's study of the medieval theory of authorship has plotted the growing interest in the author by scholastic exegetes in the thirteenth century. Authorship of the Bible evoked two concerns: God as the ultimate author of Scripture, and the human author as the efficient cause of Scripture.[87] Grosseteste addressed both concerns, and in doing so raised some questions that had not occurred to other scholastic exegetes. In terms of God's authorship of the Bible, Grosseteste raised this point to challenge the temptation of simply 'spiritualising' a text, when it appeared to contradict Christian teaching. Specifically, in the *De cessatione legalium*, he notes that one way to deal with the mandates to keep the Sabbath and to have all male children circumcised (both of which were to be followed in perpetuity) is to read these mandates mystically: they are signs that point to a Christian truth. Grosseteste pauses to consider the implications of this approach, and finds that it is inappropriate on its own. He states that a good teacher does not say one thing and mean another:

'If something is signified in his words which is other than what he intends to teach, he is not the best teacher, but rather he is either unlearned or a deceiver.' In this case, God as the author of Scripture is the best teacher and he means what he says. Moreover, what he intended is exactly what he wishes masters in theology now to teach. Grosseteste's point is clear: spiritual interpretation must be drawn from a proper understanding of the author's original intent, which is part of the literal sense.[88]

With respect to the human author, it is David as prophet that raises another difficult point about the relationship between the literal sense of the author and any subsequent spiritual reading. In his prologue to his commentary, Grosseteste reports the standard assessment of the type of prophecy that David experienced: it was not through any medium such as dreams or visions, but rather he was directly inspired by the Holy Spirit. The implications of that line of argument pose the question, if this is the case, then how can one read his Psalms allegorically? In other words, if David's prophetic utterances were not the result of any intermediary signs, then should expositors not treat the Psalms solely *ad litteram*? Grosseteste's solution drew upon his experience with the natural world: David may have indeed received his inspiration directly, but because of the weakness of his audience it was necessary to veil the divine truth in natural objects and figures. It is akin to a person's attempt to gaze at the sun: to do so directly is not possible because human eyes are far too weak; but one can glimpse the sun through the clouds, which help to protect the eyes from the sun's powerful rays. Hence the Psalms have a theologically literal meaning (which Grosseteste considers to be the whole Christ, but this time in its traditional formulation), but readers gain access to this truth through a reading of the figures and signs that the author employed in the text. The literal intent of the author, once again, shapes the outcome of any spiritual exposition.[89]

Grosseteste's comments on the Psalm highlight two additional facets of his hermeneutic. Closely related to the issue of authorship is a form of exegesis peculiar to the Christian exposition of the Psalter, prosopological exegesis. This approach assumes that the author of the Psalms takes on a variety of voices or personae: a Psalm may be said in the person of Christ, or the person of the Church (or the collective faithful), or even both together. At first this may appear to be a form of allegorical reading, since it adds a spritual dimension to the text. Grosseteste, and others such as Thomas Aquinas, would disagree with that conclusion: taking on a voice or persona was the choice or intent of the author.[90] David was aware that prophetically he was speaking in the person of Christ or the Church. That prosopological readings functioned in the domain of prophecy did not compel Grosseteste to see them as spiritual exegesis, for he noted that prophecy could be presented either in literal readings (*in verbis nudis*) or in allegorical signification.[91]

Secondly, Grosseteste's rumination on both the Psalms and the creation narrative of Genesis brought to the forefront the problem of integrating the book of nature with the book of Scripture.[92] The sacred text exploited the natural world to describe and explain human salvation, but to what extent could a theologian draw upon the study of the natural world in his exegesis? As already noted, a number of Grosseteste's contemporaries viewed natural philosophy and its pedagogical locus, the quadrivium, with a great deal of suspicion. As one who had first been a natural philosopher,

Grosseteste would have no doubt been viewed as yet another misguided theologian who did not see the difference between philosophical and theological work. To appreciate Grosseteste's solution, it would be useful to recount how he addressed the problem, as it is a central theme in the inaugural lecture that he gave at Oxford when he became a master of the sacred page.

The Book of Scripture and the Book of Nature

Grosseteste confronts the problem by starting with a famous maxim of Augustine: 'Whatever one has learned outside of this Scripture, if it is harmful, then it is condemned in the text, if it is useful then it is found there.'[93] However, those who had completed their studies in the Arts knew that much of what they have learned appears nowhere in the sacred text. If one takes Augustine's precept to its logical conclusion, the absence of geometry and astronomy – two sciences close to Grosseteste's own heart – would seem to indicate that they have no use in the study of the Bible.[94] One could possibly argue that some secular learning is extant in Scripture, such as grammar, rhetoric and, if one pushed it hard enough, even logic. Natural philosophy, however, demanded a more complicated response. The prophets and the apostles were not given to mathematical discourse, nor were they interested in the mechanics of the universe, unless there was a need to talk about a blackened sun, a bloody moon or falling stars.

To exclude natural philosophy, however, evoked a theological conundrum. If one accepts the proposition that truth concerns the essence of creation, one runs into considerable difficulty in deeming one part of creation to be irrelevant to the study of theology. This is based on two related theological assertions. First, as Augustine noted, all creation bears the stamp of the Creator, and so has a role to play in the testimony to him. Secondly, God stated that all he had created was good. Grosseteste then draws this all together into a classic syllogism: it is through the predicate of goodness that one may deem a created thing useful, for if God can use evil for good, then clearly good things are established for a good use. This good use is the created thing's utility. Since truth is about the essence of creation, which means truth and essence are the same thing, and all essence is good, therefore all truth about creation must be useful. Since this truth is the object of the secular learning, one must conclude that this learning must be useful in the study of the sacred page.[95]

All this philosophical wrangling, however, does not transform an Ezechiel into a Euclid. Perhaps, then, some sciences are to be excluded from theological discourse. A possible solution was to speak of the misuse of learning, that is to exclude those sciences which masters abused. It would be wise, in light of these abuses, simply to withdraw this useless learning from the divine science. But if that were the case, Grosseteste notes, that could easily exclude all forms of secular learning from theology, since any form of inquiry was open to abuse. Moreover, such a solution would bring the reader of Scripture no closer to understanding Augustine's statement.[96]

Grosseteste then presents his own position, stating that Scripture does appear to contain the truth of all the sciences, and moreover approves of them. However, they act as certain elements or properties of the text, and not as the subject matter. Grosseteste's two examples illustrate that he has not only the natural world itself in mind, but also the methodologies the sciences exploit to investigate created reality. The first example is from the first epistle of John: 'no lie comes from truth'. This *lemma* points to the fact that the rules of logic are entirely valid in exegesis, for here the reader discovers a dialectical maxim, that falsehood does not follow from truth. How Scripture differs from a text on logic is that the author adds something to it, and that is the 'edification of habitual thinking' (*edificatio morum*). In addition, the rules of investigation can be used in connection with the realities of the created world. He notes a second passage, this time from the Genesis narrative: 'And God divided the light from the darkness.' He then connects this to a passage from Paul's first letter to the Corinthians, which only serves to illuminate his point. The fact that God divided light from darkness helps the Apostle to explain why Christians and pagans could not commingle. The people of light cannot conjoin with the people of darkness because contrary things cannot be connected. Here again we see a principle of logic and a reality of creation employed in the content of Scripture. However, the Apostle adds something to the biblical text, Grosseteste says, 'which pertains to the origins of creation and something which advances towards the light of faith and the fervour of love'. It is these added conditions, so to speak, which allow for the secular sciences to be employed in the exposition of Scripture.[97] When Scripture is properly expounded, Grosseteste continues, it either instructs one's faith or builds up love. This is the end of the sacred science. The only way in which the secular sciences participate in this is as a means of helping to further these goals. In this regard one may discover the truth of secular sciences in Scripture, in that they unlock the sacred page, and thus enhance the instruction of faith or the edification of love. The secular sciences are then study aids to the superior form of inquiry, the exposition of Scripture.[98] As a theologian, Grosseteste did not need to abandon his fascination with the natural world. Instead, he could plunder its riches in order to make better sense of the sacred text. Such a strategy was based on the coherence between the book of nature and the book of Scripture, and would therefore provide a stronger foundation for any spiritual exposition. Grosseteste assumed that the author of Scripture had employed created elements as signs of theological truth in relation to their true properties and attributes. Understanding those characteristics provided a fuller insight into that very meaning to which they pointed.[99]

Grosseteste adopts this specific strategy in his analysis of the creation narrative. He consistently began each section of his exposition by looking at the literal sense of the text, particularly in terms of the teaching of natural philosophy. He then moved on to the allegorical meaning of the text, which was configured in terms of his 'scientific' reading of the natural elements within the text. Finally, he ended with a moral exposition, which too was contingent upon his literal exposition. Like most scholastic theologians (and indeed many monastic theologians of earlier centuries), his treatment of the anagogical sense is uneven, for a proper anagogical interpretation demanded that the reader ultimately move beyond the text itself and confront the divine nature as the object of contemplation. The interest in spiritual exegesis is abundant in the *Hexaëmeron* and it was rooted in the logic of the literal sense.

Rules for Spiritual Exegesis

While the literal sense may have increased importance in Grosseteste's hermeneutic, he did not conclude that spiritual readings must take on a secondary role in theological discourse. Instead, he considered Scripture to be composed of four parts, related to the four authenticating witnesses to the truth of the Incarnation. One part signified the created world and another the historical narrative of the people of Israel. These two parts followed the Augustinian theory of signs: the words of Scripture firstly signified the created thing, and then secondly signified the truths of salvation. The third part of Scripture contained the Christian truths directly signified by the words themselves (*verbis nudis*), and so there was no need to seek a secondary (but no less important) signification as one would do in allegorical readings. The fourth part of Scripture was composed of prophecy, which, as already noted, could be signified by words or by things.[100] Grosseteste does not mean that these parts correspond to four divisions or sections of Scripture; instead, they constitute the four textual elements to which a theologian must be alert.

More importantly, this configuration of Scripture advances two basic rules that any student of the divine science must follow. First, where there is a literal rendering of Christian truth, the student must not seek any hidden allegorical meaning; however, where the primary signification of the words points to created reality or a historical narrative, one must seek a secondary meaning in order to gain access to the mystery of salvation. For example, the word 'fire' (*ignis*) signifies a created thing, and this species signifies 'a power of divinity consuming the blight of our vices'. Scripture demonstrates this in Deuteronomy when it states that God is a consuming fire. Moreover, Jeremiah uses fire to signify God's indignation as well as the words of God in the mouth of a preacher.[101] The collective teaching supports the general truth that fire signifies God's power consuming humanity's vices.

Grosseteste's example demonstrates the need for a second rule, namely that Scripture must be used to interpret Scripture. He states the rule this way:

> ... where the words of Scripture signify created reality or the historical facts of the prophetic conduct of the Israelites, there [the student] should seek from another place of Scripture what each and every thing signifies; and afterwards, from the many things which signify, he may seek after the connected signification in words which clearly signify the truth of love and faith.[102]

This second rule seems to reflect a late twelfth-century trend among scholastics to find ways of connecting passages of Scripture together. This trend produced a new textual technology, the *distinctio*, in which a single term could be connected to all the parts of Scripture that addressed it or defined it. These related passages or their references were then integrated into a schematic, and a set of these schematics could prove a useful resource for preachers and expositors.[103] Grosseteste himself even produces one in the preface to his Psalms commentary on the word *tuba*.[104] However, this second rule addresses the relationship between scriptural lemmata in a different way. Whereas most *distinctiones* were based on allegorical readings of texts (that is, what are all the ways Scripture uses this one term as a signifier), Grosseteste is in fact suggesting that the intertextual relationships should be coordinated along the literal–spiritual axis. One seeks to understand the signification of a thing by means of connecting it to the plain unambiguous teaching of Scripture. Once again, Grosseteste returns to the theme of a good teacher: 'A good teacher does not intend to shape the student's understanding by an oblique idea alone, but with a complete one. Nor can there be a student of any doctor or art who does not know how to separate oblique concepts from holistic ones, or who would want to comprehend fully the intention of the teacher from oblique concepts as if they were the complete and holistic ones.'[105] The correct hermeneutical approach to sacred Scripture demanded a full reading, one that embraced both the literal and the spiritual sense as well as one that allowed the initial authorial intent of the literal sense to guide the spiritual exegesis.[106]

Spiritual exegesis has further ramifications for the scholastic theologian. In his inaugural sermon, Grosseteste begins his treatment of the spiritual senses with the assertion that 'Scripture is more excellent in the human mind than on dead parchment.'[107] There is a transformative nature of sacred Scripture, in which the reader becomes the text. In this context, the human mind as a book has both an external and an internal inscription. In becoming the text, the human soul first receives the intelligible realities of the written text through gaze of the mind. The mind's gaze is not the end of comprehension, though, as the text must also be written within. It transforms the desires of the reader. The process cannot proceed in any other way, Grosseteste asserts, for we cannot love what we do not know. The process of reading and becoming the text does not end here, for this kind of reading is reflexive. The written text may transform the mind of the reader, but it will also erupt in external works of love. In this way, the book of Scripture may be read by observing the external works of the expositor of the sacred text.[108] Grosseteste, however, takes this even one step further in his inaugural sermon. If Scripture transforms the disposition of the reader, this must have an impact on the exegetical act. These works, which are the product of reading, act as a light which illuminates the mind. What begins as external writing moves to the inscription of the text internally in the human soul, which in turn bursts forth into external works. Finally, these works affect the continual act of reading Scripture. The exposition of sacred Scripture changes the state of the reader to such a great degree that the distinction between reader and text almost disappears.

Grosseteste's analysis of a spiritual exegesis moves well beyond the simplistic notion that allegory teaches what Christians believe and the moral sense teaches them what to do. In this sermon, Grosseteste began by stating that Scripture was pre-eminent among all other texts, and now the most forceful reason for this claim is stated: no other text illuminates the gaze of the mind, he says, but rather darkens it; it does not shape the will, but rather deforms it. It is Scripture alone (*sola Scriptura*) that elevates man beyond himself and towards God, causing him to live according to God's nature.[109]

For Grosseteste, Scripture was the fundamental source for his theological work: it provided the bulk of raw theological data, which was organised around his understanding of the discipline's subject matter. The connection between the reformulation of the whole Christ motif and the content of Scripture was an intimate one, and particularly in his Psalms commentary had a tremendous influence on the way he configured his exegesis. This was not to say that the Scripture was the formal object of his theological work, as Southern has suggested.[110] Rather, his approach to Scripture reflected a sophisticated hermeneutic that was drawn from his broader view of the theological enterprise. Additionally, the theologian's encounter with the sacred text was a literary, intellectual and affective experience. The act of reading, or exposition, was meant to transform the reader and by consequence the outlook and behaviour of his students. It is little wonder that the Oxford Franciscans sought after him to become their first lector: Grosseteste displayed similar commitments in thought and action to the Franciscan Order, and he would contribute to the development of the Order's mission as a teacher.

Theological Resources

As a teaching master, Grosseteste was well aware of the immense responsibility placed on his shoulders. Erudition alone did not prepare one for the task of theology,[111] but at the same time learning was necessary for good teaching. We can say very little about Grosseteste's own theological education, since the evidence is sparse to say the least. Obviously, Grosseteste received enough to allow the masters of Oxford to consider him as a viable candidate for the magisterial chair.[112] Moreover, there is an observable change in the sources Grosseteste cites, and when he began to lecture to the Oxford Franciscans he had a solid grounding in the standard resources for theology. The acquisition of these new resources does not necessarily mean that Grosseteste encountered all these texts within the confines of a university classroom. Before 1225, he had been ordained a deacon, and that meant that somewhere within the diocese of Lincoln he had liturgical responsibilities. It is possible to infer, therefore, that Grosseteste encountered some of these patristic authorities in the liturgy of the Mass.[113] Moreover, as a deacon he would have also been required to celebrate the Divine Office, and once again some of the texts which comprise the liturgy of the hours came partly from the writings of the church Fathers.[114] Texts from the liturgy, however, could not act as the sole resource for theological reflection, and so Grosseteste at one point plunged into the task of reading the main theological sources. My concern here is not to render a list of all the sources that found their way into Grosseteste's writings, a task that has already been so ably completed by others.[115] Instead, I want to focus on some salient features of his reading programme.

Grosseteste and his Contemporaries

Despite the breadth of Grosseteste's reading, much has been made of what is missing. There is no reference to any of the summist literature of the late twelfth century, not to mention recourse to any contemporary sources. It appears that Grosseteste had little interest in engaging his contemporaries and immediate predecessors in his theological work. This stands in stark contrast to other theologians, particularly those working at the University of Paris who took every opportunity to use or oppose current ideas. Once again, we are presented with evidence that points to a rather anti-scholastic feature of Grosseteste's theology. Once again, there is call for some further qualification. It is certainly true that Grosseteste makes little direct reference to the great summists of his generation, namely Philip the Chancellor, William of Auxerre and William of Auvergne – although William of Auxerre figures more prominently in Grosseteste's theology than previous scholars have recognised. It does not mean that their work had no influence at all. It is significant to note that Grosseteste's views on the nature of prophecy is commensurate with the ideas put forth by Philip, and even to some degree Alexander of Hales and Hugh of St-Cher.[116] Moreover, Grosseteste's Christology shares some commonalities with Alexander of Hales.[117] These sample affinities may simply be the result of all these scholars drawing upon similar sources (which is in itself a rather significant point), rather than Grosseteste revealing a direct influence from these other theologians. In general, Grosseteste was not always driven by the agenda of preceding generations or even by his own. The theological issues that occupy his attention as a whole reveal a theology that is unique and personal. His own concerns then became the basis for his reading, rather than his reading always acting as point of departure for his theologising.

While contemporary sources rarely appear in Grosseteste's collection of theological resources, some eleventh- and twelfth-century texts do pop up. Grosseteste did not lecture on or write a commentary on the *Sentences* of Peter Lombard, as this task had not yet become part of the curriculum during his tenure at Oxford.[118] Nonetheless, he knew of Lombard's work and made use of it in some of his disputed questions. Perhaps most revealing is the appearance of the writings of Anselm of Canterbury in Grosseteste's arsenal. In light of the modern appreciation of Anselm's genius, it is sometimes forgotten how long it took for medieval theologians to recognise his brilliance. His writings had little impact on twelfth-century thinkers, and might have remained forgotten if it were not for the work of some early thirteenth-century theologians. One of them was Alexander of Hales, who made extensive use of Anselm's writings in his gloss on the *Sentences* and disputed questions. By 1240, most Franciscan theologians were attuned to Anselm's theology, thanks to Alexander. Grosseteste must also be counted among those who brought Anselm's writings into the mainstream of scholastic thought.[119]

Latin and Greek Patristic Sources

As for patristic sources, Grosseteste was clearly enamoured with Augustine. He occupies a place on nearly every page of his writing, and many of his ideas can be roughly connected to the thought of the bishop of Hippo. The other patristic writer that captured Grosseteste's attention was Gregory the Great. Both are significant sources for Grosseteste, attested by the fact that he owned a manuscript containing Augustine's *City of God* and Gregory's *Moral Exposition of Job*, and this book contains extensive annotations in Grosseteste's own hand.[120] Since the manuscript was written around 1225, Grosseteste himself may have commissioned its execution.

The notes in his own hand reveal two important features of his reading. First, it demonstrates the strategy behind his *Tabula*: one was to place the ideographs from the *Tabula* in the margins of books, so that a later reader could go to the index and find other sources on the topic broached in the body of the text. Secondly, the notes also point to another significant aspect of Grosseteste's reading programme, for some are in Greek. In some instances, he copied out small passages from the Septuagint, but in others he used Greek letters to write out Latin words[121] – an exercise also found in the margins of Cambridge, Pembroke College MS 7, another codex that was in Grosseteste's possession at one time.[122] It would seem that Grosseteste was using these two manuscripts at the time he was learning Greek, and used their empty margins to practise his letter forms.[123]

The ability to read Greek places Grosseteste in a unique position in thirteenth-century theology, as no other scholastic theologian could lay claim to this skill. Until the critical edition of his *Hexaëmeron* was published, it was thought that Grosseteste did not learn Greek until he became bishop. This position was first suggested by Roger Bacon, and it made sense since, as a bishop, Grosseteste would have then had the resources to acquire books from abroad. However, in light of research on his works from his magisterial period, the consensus now is that he began to learn Greek much earlier. Greek sources appear not only in the *Hexaëmeron*, but also in the *De cessatione legalium*, his commentary on Galatians, and the *Super Psalterium*.[124] One would expect that access to these sources would produce a very different kind of theological reflection or at least reflection on a set of ideas that were different from Latin theology. As bishop, Grosseteste certainly did take on new ideas that he found in the Dionysian corpus (as would his contemporaries), and his knowledge of the Greek Fathers gave him an opportunity to reflect on the *filioque* controversy that had contributed to the separation of the eastern and western Churches.[125] However, Grosseteste's theology while he was at Oxford does not reveal any major divergence from the Latin tradition. A possible reason for this is that many of the concepts found in Greek patristic theology shaped the writings of John Damascene, and scholastic theologians had already been absorbing his work since the late twelfth century.[126] Instead, the Greek sources provide for Grosseteste some technical and historical details unknown to the West – most observable in how he treated some of the Psalms in his own commentary – but there was nothing that challenged Grosseteste to consider new ideas that contrasted with the accepted concepts in scholastic theology.

Extending Authorial Intent

Grosseteste's Greek sources can, however, point us to another aspect of his reading programme. In some instances, Grosseteste had the entire translated work at his disposal. For other works he relied upon the Greek source since it was found in a gloss or *catena*.[127] The way in which Grosseteste cites his sources with great prolixity implies that he read most of them *in toto*, rather than through a medium such as a gloss or a *florilegium*. Attention to a whole text rather than an excerpt is yet another reason to distinguish Grosseteste from his contemporaries, and at one point in his comments on the Psalms he sharply criticises Peter Lombard for misrepresenting Augustine because of partial quotation.[128] It would be incorrect to infer that Grosseteste had no time for glosses, for he makes use of the *Ordinary Gloss* and Lombard's own *Great Gloss* in his biblical commentaries. There are also indications that he cited the Fathers according to the way he had discovered them in other works, such as the *Decretum* of Gratian. The guiding principle here was not a distaste for glosses or florilegia; rather it was Grosseteste's desire to apply the concept of authorial intent not only to biblical authors but also to the church Fathers.

A clear example of this application of authorial intent is found in the *De cessatione legalium*.[129] In the last part of this treatise, Grosseteste raises the question of when exactly the law ceased to be efficacious. His immediate determination is that the dividing line must be the death and resurrection of Christ, for that was the fulfilment of the law and prophecy. If this were the case, it raised a significant problem related to the behaviour of the Apostles in the book of Acts. Peter, above all, appears to have continued to observe the Jewish law, a practice that came to a head in a confrontation between Peter and Paul (Acts 15; Galatians 2). Grosseteste was not the first theologian to focus on Peter's actions and the subsequent reprimand by Paul. This event had all the classic factors of interest to a theologian in the schools. It was related to a major point in the theology of salvation; it also required the exegete to render a coherent narrative in light of the evidence from the book of Acts and Paul's epistle to the Galatians[130] and, even more controversially, the disagreement between Peter and Paul was filtered through a dispute between two major authorities, Augustine and Jerome. These patristic theologians had disagreed on two major issues. First, Jerome had asserted that the validity of the Jewish law came to an abrupt halt at the passion of Christ, whereas Augustine suggested that there was a transition period that lasted during the lifetime of the Apostles. This transition, Augustine argued, was a time in which the law was dead but not yet deadly, and so the first generation of Christians continued to observe the law for the sake of the Jews among them. Each opinion had further repercussions on a second issue: how was one to evaluate Peter's behaviour? Did he in fact observe the law as a means of salvation, or did he only pretend to do so? And if the latter, could this action be classed as sinful? Jerome insisted that Peter did not sin, since he believed that the Jewish law had no salvific power and his observance was just a dissimulation. Paul's rebuke was another act of dissimulation, and was done to soothe the ire of the gentile Christians. Augustine, on the other hand, considered Peter's actions to be indiscreet – which is why Paul had to rebuke him – and so he sinned venially but not mortally.[131] This exegetical locus and its extensive patristic commentary was therefore an ideal opportunity for a scholastic theologian to impose order on what appeared to be a disordered and contradictory set of statements.

In his commentary on Galatians, Grosseteste declined to reconcile the discord between Augustine and Jerome since that would be better done in disputation.[132] The fourth part of the *De cessatione legalium* appears to be where that disputation was distilled in a more treatise-like format. In typical scholastic fashion, Grosseteste employs distinctions in order to demonstrate that the two authors are not so far apart. One distinction echoes the solution of William of Auxerre, who had suggested that one can judge Peter's actions if there is a clear understanding of the nature of his dissimulation. There is good and bad dissimulation: the latter is an attempt to deceive someone wilfully, while the former is an attempt to goad somebody to do good himself (in the way a doctor pretends to abstain from meat for the sake of his patients).[133] Grosseteste, without citing William, suggests the same, if only to clarify that Peter did not sin mortally in his observance of the law. Furthermore, if one understands the efficacy of the law within this intermediary period that Augustine posited, the difference between the two church Fathers is not so great. Drawing upon Augustine's notion of the law being dead but not deadly, Grosseteste reminds his readers of the way the dead are treated in his day. Cadavers are not immediately disposed of but, rather, many are honoured in their burial. Only when the body began to decompose and become putrid did it pose a threat to the living.[134] In the same way, the first generation of Christians were attempting to give an honourable burial for their great teacher, the Jewish law. Nonetheless, in that honouring neither Peter nor Paul claimed that the law was still alive and in effect.[135]

Still, Grosseteste recognised that these distinctions did not fully resolve the discord between the two authors. What is so extraordinary about Grosseteste's second strategy is that it incorporates a strong sense of humanity, while at the same time embracing the church Fathers as instruments of the Holy Spirit. He had begun his discussion by asking: 'But, between these two sacred writers, these two reed-pipes (*fistulae*) of the Holy Spirit, is there truly dissonance in disagreement, and not rather consonance in discord?' Grosseteste extends the music metaphor, noting that sometimes a musician can legitimately employ dissonance as it was a proper form of harmonic composition. Moreover, what appears at first to the listener to be a cacophony can actually contain hidden harmony.[136] A few paragraphs later, Grosseteste reminds his reader that Augustine and Jerome discussed each other's views as if they were only the words of a person, and not the inspired words of God; only now was it evident to Grosseteste and his contemporaries that the Spirit speaks through them. And since the Spirit of truth is one, readers of the Fathers need to seek ways of calling these two reed-pipes of the Spirit back into harmony.[137]

In a few elegant statements, Grosseteste maintains the standard view of the instrumentality of patristic authorities, for they are the pipes which the Holy Spirit breathes into; and yet simultaneously he manages to remind his readers that Augustine and Jerome were real human beings, who were engaged in a war of words. Grosseteste's call to discover the hidden harmony between these two towering figures was based on the principle of authorial intent. In terms of divine inspiration, God intended that Scripture and Christian teaching contain identifiable dissonance, which was to force readers to seek to understand not just the words, but also their deeper meaning (*sententia*). There the reader finds the necessary harmony. One ought not to shun discord, nor even to fear it, for it was the divine way of teaching. In terms of human authorship, Grosseteste focuses on the ability of each authority to discern the intention of the other, and finds it lacking. Augustine failed to understand the 'mind and intention of Jerome';[138] and Jerome was no better at discerning the full import of Augustine's argument.[139] Had they fully understood each other, they would have resolved the dissonance of their writings themselves.[140] The authoritative words of the Fathers come to life in Grosseteste's hands, both because the Holy Spirit has breathed life into them and because they were penned by two individuals who had their own intentions as well as their own foibles.

A Theologian in the Schools

If Grosseteste's sensitive reading of the Fathers betrays a humanistic strain in his outlook, it must be seen as congruent with medieval humanism, rather than a precursor to the humanism of the Italian Renaissance or its Northern successor.[141] His intellectual capacity was broad enough to appropriate a vast amount of the theological tradition of the patristic and medieval period, extant in both its Latin and Greek contexts; and at the same time to become attuned to the new discursive methods spawned by Aristotle and his commentators. He had a great deal of energy and perspicuity and a genius that enabled him to engage creatively his sources. He never slavishly followed an authority, but still maintained a reverent respect for those who had preceded him as teaching masters. He did not resist the use of reason in theological discourse, but insisted that theological knowledge have its currency in relation to a divinely ordered life. In the end, as a theologian, he taught his students to seek God with all of their mind, which for him included all that we would now classify as the heart.

Against the details presented so far, *Dictum* 118 – broached in Chapter 2 – neatly represents Grosseteste as a scholastic theologian.[142] It reveals that he not only understood the implications of Aristotle's syllogistic science, but he adopted it as a means of configuring the subject matter of the sacred science. It also points to the fact that theology focuses on truth that can only be ascertained through wisdom, for the theologian considers not what is below him (like Epicurus) or what is equal to him (as did Diogenes), but what is above him. Moreover, wisdom requires both the mind and the will to be in tune with God. Preaching, as much as lecturing and disputing, has a major role to play, for it engages both the gaze and the desire of the mind: in this respect, preaching is the ideal *praxis* of a theologian.

Now that we have outlined the theoretical concerns, it remains to see what Grosseteste did within the context of theology while teaching at Oxford. The next part of this study moves from the theory to the practice of being a theologian. Grosseteste was hardly satisfied with explaining how a theologian thinks, and we must begin to examine what he thought as a theologian, and the reasons he presents to support each doctrine.

Notes

1 See above, Chapter 3, pp. 141–5.
2 M-D Chenu, 'Maîtres et bacheliers de l'université de Paris, v. 1240', *Etudes d'histoire littéraire et doctrinale du XIIIe siècle* 1 (1932), 11–39.
3 *DCL*, 3.1.3 (p. 120): 'Quod videtur sic posse persuaderi'.
4 Perhaps the best known attempt at this third question is found in Aquinas's writings: *ST*, 1.2–13.

5   In the *Summa fratris Alexandri*, ed. PP. Collegii S. Bonaventurae, 4 vols (Quaracchi: College of St Bonaventure, 1924–48), q.1 (1.14–36), knowledge of God is treated first in terms of what is knowable with respect to God's nature (membrum 1), and then with respect to the human mind itself (membrum 2).
6   A fourth category would be added in the latter half of the thirteenth century, namely mystical knowledge (*in raptu*), in which a thinker could gain a glimpse of the beatific vision *in via*. See *Dictum* 113 (fols 93rb–95va).
7   For a general discussion of this feature of Grosseteste's thought, see McEvoy, *Philosophy*, pp. 107, 135–8, 257–8; and R.W. Southern, 'Richard Dales and the Editing of Robert Grosseteste', in *Aspectus et Affectus: Essays and Editions in Grosseteste and Medieval Intellectual Life in Honor of Richard C. Dales*, ed. G. Freibergs (New York: AMS Press, 1993), pp. 3–14, at 10–12. My account differs slightly from these two authors.
8   Augustine, *Soliloquiorum*, 1.6 (PL 32.875–6). Cf. idem, *De vera religione*, c.35 (PL 34.151). The term is used in a similar way by Hincmar of Rheims, *Quod trina Deitate est* (PL 125.579), but it is probably based on reading Augustine.
9   For example: Cassiodorus, *Expositio Psalmorum*, ed. M. Adriaen, 2 vols, CCL, 97–8 (Turnhout: Brepols, 1958), 5.3–4 (1.64); Gregory the Great, *In primum Regum expositionum libri sex*, ed. P. Verbraken, CCL, 144 (Turnhout: Brepols, 1963), 4.104 (p. 347); Paschasius Radbertus, *Expositio in evangelium Matthei*, ed. B. Paulus, 3 vols, CCL, 56, 56A-B (Turnhout: Brepols, 1984), in Matt. 26.35 (3.1304); Anselm of Canterbury, *Oratio*, in *Opera omnia*, ed. F.S. Schmitt, 6 vols (Edinburgh: T. Nelson, 1961), p. 11 (3.42).
10 See n. 8, above.
11 See for example, Hugh of St-Victor, *De sacramentis christianae fidei*, 1.6.17 (PL 172.272); Alan of Lille, *Summa de arte praedicandi*, c.1 (PL 210.112); and Peter Lombard, *Sententiae*, ed. I. Brady, 2 vols, Spicelegium Bonaventurianum, 4–5 (Quaracchi: College of St Bonaventure, 1971–81), 2.27.3 (1.482–3).
12 On the dating of this work, see James McEvoy, 'The Chronology of Robert Grosseteste's writings on Nature and Natural Philosophy', *Speculum* 58 (1983), 614–55, at 615–16.
13 *De artibus liberalibus*, ed. Baur, p. 1.
14 Ibid., p. 4; McEvoy, *Philosophy*, pp. 258–9.
15 *Comm. in PA*, 1.14 (pp. 203–16).
16 See McEvoy, *Philosophy*, pp. 329–35, for a very careful explanation of this passage.
17 Ibid., pp. 212–13. See below, Chapter 5, pp. 116–24.
18 *Comm. in PA*, 1.14 (pp. 212–15). Here Grosseteste uses a medical example in which the consuming of scammony always attracts red bile.
19 Ibid., pp. 215–16.
20 *De artibus liberalibus*, ed. Baur, p. 1.
21 *De finitate motus et temporis*, ed. Baur, p. 105. The concept of *intelligentia* is drawn from the Ps-Augustinian work, *De spiritu et anima*: McEvoy, *Philosophy*, pp. 301–6.
22 *De artibus liberalibus*, ed. Baur, p. 2.
23 *Expositio*, 2.30 (p. 67).
24 *Super Psalterium*, 100.4.33 (Appendix, p. 199).
25 *Dictum* 2 (fol. 1vb): 'per sapienciam illuminetur eius aspectus mentis ad veram fidem et scienciam, et rectificetur eius affectus ad iustitiam'.
26 *Dictum* 19, ed. Ginther, 17–19 (pp. 130–31).
27 Cf. *Glossarum in sancti Paul epistolas fragmenta*, ed. R.C. Dales, in *Opera inedita Roberti Grosseteste volumen primum*, CCCM, 130 (Turnhout: Brepols, 1995), 1 Cor. 14.3 (p. 205).

28   *Dictum* 2 (fols 1vb–24a): 'Prima ergo et precipua misericordia est amor relevandi stultum a stulticie miseria, ut per sapienciam illuminetur eius aspectus mentis ad veram fidem et scienciam, et rectificetur eius affectus ad iustitiam. Hec autem illuminacio aspectus et rectificacio affectus per verbum doctrine et predicacionis eveniunt, quapropter eximium opus misericordie est predicacio, quod non inmerito Dominus ipse in carne apparens elegit, et pastoribus ecclesie administrandis commisit. Sicut enim anima precellit corpus et bonum anime bonum corporis, sic et miseria anime deterior et miserabilior est miseria corporis, et relevacio a miseria anime, que predicacione peragitur, melior et expetibilior est relevacione a miseria corporis. Omnium ergo operum misericordie melius, nobilius, et expetibilius est predicacio.'
29   Ibid. (fol. 2ra–rb): 'Sed quem delectant hec et hiis similia admiranda addiscat theologiam, quia omnia talia ibi sciuntur melius et nobilius et expetibilius. Et omnes mutaciones quas facit natura, vel alicuius sciencie artifex, que dico mutaciones sunt a peiori in melius, faciet theologus opere predicacionis inproporcionaliter nobilius et expetibilius quam faciat illas natura vel alicuius sciencie artifex.'
30   *Dicta* 2 (fols 1va–3rb), 8 (8va–vb), 19 (16ra–18ra) and 38 (28va–29va).
31   *De veritate*, ed. Baur, pp. 137–8.
32   *De libero arbitrio*, ed. Lewis, esp. cc. 16–18 (pp. 75–88).
33   *De veritate*, ed. Baur. p. 130.
34   For the most recent discussion of William of Auxerre's theology, see Boyd Taylor Coolman, 'Spiritual Apprehension: the Spiritual Senses and the Knowledge of God in the Theology of William of Auxerre', unpubl. PhD diss. (University of Notre Dame, 2001). For the disputed questions of Guy of Orchelles, see Guy of Orchelles, *Tractatus de sacramentis ex eius Summa de sacramentis et officiis ecclesiae*, ed. D. Van den Eynde and P. Van den Eynde, Franciscan Institute Publications Text Series, 4 (Louvain: E. Nauwelaerts, 1953).
35   See the questions edited in J.P. Torrell, *Théorie de la prophétie et philosophie de la connaissance aux environs de 1230: la contribution d'Hugues de Saint-Cher*, Spicilegium Sacrum Lovaniense Etudes et Documents, 40 (Louvain: Spiciliegium Sacrum Lovaniense, 1977).
36   *DCL*, 3.1.1 (p. 119).
37   Cf. *Epistolae*, n. 123 (p. 347).
38   *DCL*, 3.1.2 (pp. 119–20).
39   We shall engage the content of this question below (Chapter 6, pp. 128–37).
40   This fact is even more striking when compared to Thomas Aquinas's response to the same question: since Scripture does not explicitly say anything about the 'absolute' necessity of the Incarnation, theologians must treat it as a contingent act: *ST*, 3.1.4.
41   *DCL*, 3.1.2 (p. 119).
42   Ibid., 3.2.1 (p. 133): 'Quod tamen an verum sit me ignorare scio, et meam in hac parte ignorantiam non mediocriter doleo.'
43   Ibid., 3.2.2–5 (pp. 135–6).
44   Southern, *Grosseteste*, pp. 35–7
45   See the comments of James O'Donnell, *Cassiodorus* (Berkeley: University of California Press, 1979), pp. 136–7.
46   I offer no revolutionary solution myself, save to note that this type of multiple reading was endorsed by scholastic theologians, and historians must therefore acknowledge that fact and embrace it. Such an exegetical strategy reveals a belief in both the pliability of the text and its multivalency, although the limits of what a text could say were clearly understood.

47 See for example *Dictum* 19, ed. Ginther, 13 (p. 129).
48 Southern, *Grosseteste*, p. 34.
49 The major source for scholastic psychology, at least for Grosseteste's regency, was the *De anima* of Avicenna. For a general account of Avicenna's doctrine, see E. Ruth Harvey, *The Inward Wits: Psychological Theory in the Middle Ages and the Renaissance* (London: Warburg Institute, 1975), esp. pp. 43–6. For Avicenna's own treatment of imagination, see Avicenna, *De anima*, ed. S. Van Riet, 2 vols (Louvain: Peeters, 1972), 4.2–3 (2.12–54). The reception of Avicenna's thought in the twelfth and thirteenth centuries has been recently examined by Dag Nikolaus Hasse, *Avicenna's* De anima *in the Latin West*, Warburg Institute Studies and Texts, 1 (London: Warburg Institute, 2000).
50 See A. Mark Smith, 'Picturing the Mind: The Representation of Thought in the Middle Ages and Renaissance', *Philosophical Topics* 20 (1992), 149–70.
51 Aristotle, *De anima*, 3.3.
52 *Hex*, 1.2.3 (pp. 51–2).
53 *Comm. in PA*, 1.7 (p. 139). Here Grosseteste is addressing the question on the relationship between incorruptible universals and corruptible singulars: 'Ad hoc dicendum quod universalia sunt principia cognoscendi et apud intellectum purum et separatum a phantasmatibus possibile comtemplari primam lucem.'
54 Ibid., 1.17 (pp. 256–7), 1.19 (283–5).
55 See a similar argument in relation to sequent neccessity and God's knowledge of future contingents: *De scientia Dei*, ed. Baur, p. 146: 'Cum autem per mensurationem aeternitatis infinitae imaginatur mensuratum a temporis totalitate, accidit nobis ab hac imaginatione deceptio, a qua non possumus absolvi, donec mentis oculus purgatus a temporis compositione ascendat ad contemplationem simplicis aeternitatis.'
56 Cf. *De ordine emanandi causatorum a Deo*, ed. Baur, p. 149.
57 *Hex*, 1.8.5–7 (pp. 61–2). See also Southern, 'Richard Dales and the Editing of Robert Grosseteste', pp. 6–9.
58 *DDM*, 1.10–11 (pp. 11–12), 1. 17 (pp. 15–16), 2.2 (p. 23).
59 *Hex*, 8.3.1–2 (p. 222).
60 *DCL*, 1.8.6–7 (pp. 41–2).
61 *Dictum* 118 (fol. 96rb–vb).
62 See below, Chapter 5, pp. 90–91.
63 Southern, *Grosseteste*, p. 44.
64 See for example Grosseteste, *De sphaera*, ed. Baur, pp. 11–32; *De lineis angulis et figuris*, ed. Baur, pp. 59–60.
65 *De luce*, ed. Baur, pp. 51–9, esp. 53–4.
66 G.R. Evans, 'The *Conclusiones* of Robert Grosseteste's Commentary on the *Posterior Analytics*', *Studi Medievali* 24 (1983), 729–34, at 729.
67 Ibid., pp. 731–2.
68 Geometry's influence on theology for this period should be seen as part of the general influence of natural philosophy in theological discourse: Edward Grant, *God and Reason in the Middle Ages* (Cambridge: Cambridge University Press, 2001), pp. 252–82.
69 G.R. Evans, 'Boethian and Euclidean Axiomatic Method in the Theology of the Later Twelfth Century', *Archives internationales d'histoire des sciences* 30 (1980), 36–52.
70 A good example of a theological use of geometry has been examined by Paul M.J.E. Tummers, 'Geometry and Theology in the XIIIth Century: An Example of their Interrelation as found in the Ms Admont 442: the Influence of William of Auxerre?', *Vivarium* 18 (1980), 112–42.

71 See for example *Super Psalterium*, 88.8 (Bologna MS 983, fol. 95rb): 'Preterea, centrum non inuenitur in circulo nisi per crucis figuram quia, vt notum est in geometria ad inueniendum centrum circuli, protrahitur linea recta vt contingit terminata utrumque ad circumferenciam quia diuisa per medium ducitur ab eodem medio linea recta ortogonaliter [origenaliter *ms.*] utrumque ad circumferenciam cuius ortogonalis sic ducte medius punctus est centrum. Sic itaque per crucis figuram quam constituunt due linee predicto modo ortogonaliter se intersecantes in circulo centrum inuenitur. Similiter verissima dietatis inuencio est Iesu Christi in ligno crucis passio. Preterea, omnis punctus extram centrum signatus, si protahitur ab ipso linea recta per centrum, ispe diuidit circulum per equalia. Ducta vero linea non per centrum non potest circulum per equalia diuidere, sic omnis virtus intellectiua create extendens se in diuinitatis simplicitatem et per illam transiens in creaturam in periodum contuendam equaliter discernit et verissime omnia diiudicat: "spiritalis enim omnia diiudicat, et a nemine iudicatur".'
72 *Comm. in PA*, 1.12 (pp. 191–2); 2.5 (pp. 400–401).
73 If Grosseteste's training in geometry encouraged him to employ imagination to support discursive reason, the dominant philosophical psychology of his day, that of Avicenna, may have reinforced it. In his attempt to declare the precise content of the faculty of imagination as well as its function, Avicenna employed a geometric example. His choice of example was judicious since geometric figures have a different form of extensibility and material existence from sensory data, and so it was an opportune example that allowed Avicenna to demonstrate conclusively that the imagination dealt exclusively with the particular and not the universal: *De anima*, ed. Van Riet, 4.3 (2.45–54). What exact impact this section of Avicenna's treatise had on Grosseteste cannot be stated. We know that he was aware of the standard elements of Avicennian psychology (Grosseteste speaks of the estimative faculty, for example, in his commentary on the *Posterior Analytics: Comm. in PA*, 1.9 [p. 166]; 2.6 [404]), but he only quotes Avicenna directly once, and this concerns the Arabic philosopher's account of bewitchment (*fascinatio*): *Expositio*, 3.3 (p. 73).
74 Later in the century, Henry of Ghent would lament that those who constantly made reference to the imagination may be the best mathematicians but it also made them the worst metaphysicians, since it led them to believe that their imaginings could encompass both the finite and the infinite: Henry of Ghent, Quod.2, q.9, cited in A.G. Molland, 'The Geometrical Background to the "Merton School"', *British Journal for the History of Science* 4 (1968), 110–25; rpt. in A.G. Molland, *Mathematics and the Medieval Ancestry of Physics*, Variorum Collected Studies Series, 481 (Aldershot: Ashgate, 1995), V. On this point, Grosseteste would have agreed.
75 *DCL*, ed. Dales and King, 1.8.1–17 (pp. 38–46).
76 Ibid., 1.8.18 (p. 47).
77 Ibid., 1.9.1–3 (pp. 47–9).
78 Augustine, *De doctrina christiana*, ed. J. Martin, CCL, 32 (Turnhout: Brepols, 1982), 3.15.23 (p. 91).
79 Ibid., 2.6.7–8 (pp. 35–6). Cf. *DCL*, 1.9.5 (p. 49).
80 *Expositio*, p. 14.
81 For the general role of history in the Victorine programme, see Hugh of St-Victor's *De tribus maximis circumstantiis gestorum*, ed. W.M. Green, 'Hugo of St-Victor *De tribus maximis circumstantiis gestorum*', *Speculum* 18 (1943), 484–93.
82 *Super Psalterium*, 86.4 (B fol. 86vb): 'Per alienigenas autem potest intelligi Ruth Moabitis et eius progenitores que fuit in recordatione cum Christus per Virginem asssumpsit carnem de eius progenie. De quo dicit Ysa. 16: Emitte agnum Domine Dominatorem terre de

petra deserti ad monem filie Syon. Set quomodo de Tiris et populis ethiopum secundum carnem natus sit Christus, non recolo modo me in Historiis legisse.'
83 *Expositio*, 2.9–19 (pp. 56–62).
84 *Super Psalterium*, praef. (B. 1ra); James R. Ginther, 'The *Super Psalterium* of Robert Grosseteste (ca.1170–1253): A Scholastic Psalms Commentary as a Source for Medieval Ecclesiology', unpubl. PhD diss. (University of Toronto, 1995), pp. 145–6.
85 For example, *Super Psalterium*, 89.4 (B. 110vb), 92.1 (B 133rb), 94.1 (B 144rb); Ginther, 'The *Super Psalterium* of Robert Grosseteste', pp. 175, 178–9.
86 Beryl Smalley, 'The Biblical Scholar', in *Robert Grosseteste, Scholar and Bishop, Essays in Commemoration of the Seventh Centenary of His Death*, ed. D.A. Callus (Oxford: Clarendon Press, 1955), pp. 70–97, at 84–8.
87 Alistair Minnis, *Medieval Theory of Authorship: Scholastic and Literary Attitudes in the Later Middle Ages*, second edition (Philadelphia: University of Pennsylvania Press, 1984), pp. 73–117.
88 *DCL*, 1.2.4 (p. 9).
89 *Super Psalterium*, prol (*B* 1vb): 'Intelligendum est quod plus quam alii sine figuris prophetauit. Vel, que [*add. DO*] sine figuris a spiritu sancto illustrante mente [*corr. ex E*, in te *B*] viderat, propter infirmitates auditorum figuris aliquando velabat [*corr. ex D*, leuabat *B*] <quia quod adiuuat irritat oculum videre. Solutio: sicut nubes clara impedit secundum oculum – ut et Deum a te – uidere solem, sed optime videt solem sine medio, nos autem non> [*add. D*].'
90 On Thomas's exegesis of the Psalms, see Thomas Ryan, *Thomas Aquinas as Reader of the Psalms*, Studies in Spirituality and Theology, 6 (Notre Dame: University of Notre Dame Press, 2000); James R. Ginther, 'The Scholastic Psalms Commentary as a Textbook for Theology: the Case of Thomas Aquinas', in *Omnia disce – Medieval Studies in Memory of Leonard Boyle, O.P.*, ed. A.J. Duggan, G. Greatrex and B. Bolton (Aldershot: Ashgate, 2004), pp. 197–216.
91 *DCL*, 1.9.4 (p. 49).
92 This is also the force of Grosseteste's exegesis of Ecclesiasticus, or at least the portion that has survived under the name *De operationibus solis*, ed. James McEvoy, 'The Sun as *res* and *signum*: Grosseteste's Commentary on Ecclesiasticus ch. 43, vv. 1–5', *Recherches de théologie ancienne et médiévale* 41 (1974), 38–91.
93 *Hex*, 1.4.1 (54); *Dictum* 19, ed. Ginther, 6 (p. 127).
94 *Dictum* 19, ed. Ginther, 7 (p. 127).
95 Ibid., 8 (pp. 127–8).
96 Ibid., 8 (p. 128).
97 Ibid., 9 (p. 128).
98 Ibid., 11 (p. 128–9).
99 *De operationibus solis*, ed. McEvoy, 9 (p. 72).
100 *DCL*, 1.9.4 (p. 49).
101 Ibid., 1.9.5 (pp. 49–50).
102 Ibid., 1.9.6 (p. 50).
103 Beryl Smalley, *The Study of the Bible in the Middle Ages*, second edition (Notre Dame: University of Notre Dame Press, 1964), pp. 246–50; Richard and Mary Rouse, 'Biblical Distinctions in the Thirteenth Century', *Archives d'histoire doctrinale et littéraire du moyen âge* 49 (1974), 27–37.
104 In MSS *BEO*, this distinction has been collapsed into a sequence of sentences; however, in *D*, the scribe made some attempt to retain the schematic nature of the distinction.
105 *DCL*, 1.9.8 (p. 51).

106 Only a few pages later, Grosseteste seems to diminish the import of the literal sense, when he states that 'the literal understanding ought to be abandoned when it is inappropriate or false': ibid., 1.10.14 (p. 57). In this case, Grosseteste is explaining why the eating of animal blood is not a mandate that Christians must follow. His reason for 'abandoning' the literal sense in this case is that the literal reading is defined by understanding that the words here signify some created reality, namely the blood of animals. The student of Scripture must therefore seek the secondary signification of the signifying element, which is drawn from other parts of Scripture, read *ad litteram*. Hence Grosseteste here is not contradicting himself, but rather consistently applying Augustine's sign theory in his exposition of the Old Testament law.

107 *Dictum* 19, ed. Ginther, 15 (p. 130): 'Excellencior enim est scriptura in mente viua quam in pelle mortua.'

108 Ibid., 17–18 (pp. 130–31).

109 Ibid., 19 (p. 131).

110 Southern, *Grosseteste*, p. 173. Southern's suggestion here – in the way that nature was the formal object of science, so the Bible is of theology – is not from Grosseteste; rather the ratio is from the pen of a nineteenth-century American theologian: Charles Hodge, *Systematic Theology*, 3 vols (Grand Rapids: Eerdmanns, 1960), 1, p. 10.

111 *Dictum* 19, ed. Ginther, 3–5 (p. 126).

112 I am working on the assumption, however, that Goering's presentation of Grosseteste's theological training is the best reading of the evidence: Joseph Goering, 'When and Where did Grosseteste Study Theology?', in *Robert Grosseteste: New Perspectives on his Thought and Scholarship*, ed. J. McEvoy, Instrumenta Patristica, 27 (Turnhout: Brepols, 1995), pp. 17–52.

113 For example, Grosseteste recommends the gospel homilies of Gregory the Great as the main resource for priests who 'know how to preach to the people': *Templum Dei*, 10.3 (p. 50).

114 On the responsibilities of parish clergy celebrating the divine office, see S.J.P. Van Dijk and J. Hazeldon Walker, *The Origins of the Modern Roman Liturgy* (London: Darton, Longman & Todd, 1960), pp. 24–5, 37–40.

115 R.W. Hunt, 'The Library of Robert Grosseteste', in *Robert Grosseteste, Scholar and Bishop. Essays in Commemoration of the Seventh Centenary of His Death*, ed. D.A. Callus (Oxford: Clarendon Press, 1955), pp. 121–45, esp. 141–5; Southern, *Grosseteste*, pp. 186–204; and Neil Lewis, 'Robert Grosseteste and the Church Fathers', in *The Reception of the Church Fathers in the West: from the Carolingian to the Maurists*, ed. I. Backus, 2 vols (Leiden: Brill, 1997), 1, pp. 198–229.

116 Ginther, 'The *Super Psalterium* of Robert Grosseteste', pp. 150–59.

117 Walter H. Principe, *Alexander of Hales's Theology of the Hypostatic Union*, Studies and Texts, 12 (Toronto: PIMS, 1967), pp. 83–5.

118 James R. Ginther, 'Theological Education at the Oxford Studium in the Thirteenth Century: A Reassessment of Robert Grosseteste's Letter to the Oxford Theologians', *Franciscan Studies* 55 (1998), 83–104, at 97–101.

119 Michael Robson, 'Saint Anselm, Robert Grosseteste and the Franciscan Tradition', in *Robert Grosseteste: New Perspectives on his Thought and Scholarship*, ed. McEvoy, pp. 233–56.

120 Hunt, 'Library of Grosseteste', p. 133; Thomson, *Writings*, pp. 27–9.

121 Thomson, *Writings*, pp. 28–9.

122 Grosseteste used this manuscript as collatoral to obtain a copy of Basil's *Hexaëmeron*, owned by the monks of Bury St Edmunds: ibid., pp. 25–6. MS 7 contained late

twelfth-century commentaries on the Psalms and the major and minor prophets. See Beryl Smalley, 'A Collection of Paris Lectures of the Later Twelfth Century in MS Pembroke College, Cambridge 7', *Cambridge Historical Journal* 6 (1938), 103–13.

123   The best study on Grosseteste's knowledge of Greek is A.C. Dionisotti, 'On the Greek Studies of Robert Grosseteste', in *The Uses of Greek and Latin: Historical Essays*, ed. A.C. Dionisotti, A. Grafton and J. Kraye (London: University of London, 1988), pp. 19–39; but see also James McEvoy, 'Robert Grosseteste's Greek Scholarship: A Survey of Present Knowledge', *Franciscan Studies* 56 (1998), 255–64.

124   For a discussion on the sources, see *Hex*, xxi–xxii; *DCL*, xxvi–xxvii; *Expositio*, pp. 8–15; and Ginther, 'The *Super Psalterium* of Robert Grosseteste', pp. 85–92.

125   James McEvoy, 'Robert Grosseteste and the Reunion of the Church', *Collectanea Franciscana* 45 (1975), 39–84.

126   Joseph de Ghellinck, *Le mouvement théologique du XIIe siècle*, second edition, Museum Lessanium, Section historique, 10 (Paris: Brouwer, 1948), pp. 374–85. Grosseteste did use the *De fide orthodoxa* of Damascene, although he referred to this work as Damascene's *Sententiae*, as did other scholastics: D.A. Callus, 'Robert Grosseteste as Scholar', in *Robert Grosseteste, Scholar and Bishop*, ed. Callus, pp. 51–2. When he came to translate this text during his episcopal period, he also included some other works of John. See Irena Backus, 'John of Damascus, *De fide orthodoxa*: translations by Burgundio (1153/4), Grosseteste (1235/40) and Lefèvre d'Etaples (1507)', *Journal of the Warburg and Courtauld Institutes*, 49 (1986), 211–17.

127   Laura Rizzerio, 'Robert Grosseteste, Jean Chrysostome et l'*expositor graecus* (=Théophylacte) dans le commentaire *Super Epistolam ad Galatas*', *Recherches de théologie ancienne et médiévale* 59 (1992), 166–209; Ginther, 'The *Super Psalterium* of Robert Grosseteste', pp. 85–7, 90–92.

128   The theological problem at issue concerned whether the humanity of Christ was deserving of worship rather than adoration: Lombard's citation implies that Augustine had answered in the affirmative, but Grosseteste points out that he in fact had concluded the opposite: see Ginther, 'Theological Education at the Oxford Studium', p. 96, n. 44.

129   For a different treatment of this example, see Smalley, 'The Biblical Scholar,' pp. 90–94.

130   Peter Comester, *Historia Scholastica*, Acta apostolorum, c.78 (PL 198.1696), provides the first attempt to reconcile the chronology of the two biblical passages, but the aim is to determine exactly when Peter left the episcopal chair of Antioch for Rome.

131   Grosseteste summarises the two opinions in his *Expositio*, 2.12–14 (pp. 58–60); see also *DCL*, 4.3.1–4.6–8 (pp. 164–79), where the analysis of the two authorities is more diffuse, mainly because Grosseteste has adopted Augustine's explanation as the point of departure for his attempt to resolve the conflict.

132   *Expositio*, 2.19 (p. 62).

133   Smalley, 'The Biblical Scholar,' pp. 91–2.

134   Cf *Dictum* 116 (fol. 95va–vb).

135   *DCL*, 4.4.3–4.4.7 (pp. 167–9).

136   Ibid., 4.3.2 (pp. 164–5). For Grosseteste's musical knowledge, see Nancy van Deusen, 'Thirteenth-century motion theories and their musical applications: Robert Grosseteste and the Anonymous IV', in *The Intellectual Climate of the Early University: Essays in Honor of Otto Gründler*, ed. Nancy Van Deusen, Studies in Medieval Culture, 39 (Kalamazoo: Medieval Institute Publications, 1997), pp. 101–24.

137   *DCL*, 4.3.7 (p. 166).

138   Ibid., 4.3.6 (p. 166).

139 Ibid., 4.6.5 (p. 177).
140 Ibid., 4.6.6–7 (pp. 177–8).
141 For the concept of 'scholastic humanism', see R.W. Southern, *Scholastic Humanism and the Unification of Europe*, 2 vols (Oxford: Blackwell, 1995–2000).
142 See above, Chapter 2, pp. 25–6.

PART II
A THEOLOGIAN'S VISION

PART II
A THEOLOGIAN'S VISION

Chapter 5
A Triune and Infinite God

Grosseteste's teaching on the doctrine of God has received little attention by scholars, leaving the impression that he had made no extensive foray here.[1] There are indications, however, that he had spent some time as a master of the sacred page reflecting on God's nature. In his *Tabula*, the thirty-four topics that comprise the first distinction (*de Deo*) betray a thorough knowledge of the general scholastic treatment of the doctrine of God. The list begins with 'Whether God exists' (*an Deus sit*), followed by the topic of God's nature (*quid Deus sit*), a sequence that became standard for scholastic theology in disputations and summit literature. Throughout the listing, Grosseteste interweaves the essential attributes that speak of God in himself (unity, trinity, eternal generation of the Son and so on), with other essential attributes that contribute to an understanding of God's agency (omnipotence, providence, will, mercy, anger and so on).[2] However, the *Tabula* is simply a list of possible topics for discussion: they do not reveal what Grosseteste said about them. For the content we must turn to his theological writings, and there his observations reveal a more limited focus in this area of theological reflection. A careful reading of Grosseteste's theological writings in fact yields three major loci. The first is a letter Grosseteste wrote just before he became a master of the sacred page, where he addresses major aspects of God's nature in response to questions posed by a former student. The second is *De libero arbitrio*, where God's knowledge forms the necessary backdrop to Grosseteste's account of free will. Finally, there is the *Hexaëmeron*, where Grosseteste discusses the doctrine of the Trinity. I shall examine these sources in sequence, and then I will conclude with a discussion of how Grosseteste perceived man's capacity to know God at all.

God as First Form

Just before coming to the magisterial chair at Oxford, Grosseteste wrote a letter to a former student and now close friend, Adam of Oxford, in response to two questions that the recipient had posed.[3] The first question focused directly on the doctrine of God, whereas the second allowed Grosseteste to formulate an answer based on that doctrine.[4] Adam first had asked Grosseteste to comment on the statement 'God is the first form and the form of all things' (*Deus est prima forma et forma omnium*). This was hardly an innocuous or idle query; instead, Adam was asking Grosseteste to pronounce on a theological *dictum* possibly taken from the *Periphyseon* of John Scottus Eriugena.[5] Just a few years earlier, Pope Honorius III had issued a public condemnation of this work, which included a command to burn all existing copies.[6]

Adam was therefore asking Grosseteste to step into dangerous territory – made even more treacherous by the fact that Grosseteste was not yet a regent master of the sacred page, but only a master of arts who was studying theology.[7] At any rate, Grosseteste proceeds cautiously first by quoting copious amounts from the most catholic of doctors, Augustine. If he were indeed advocating a position at odds with a recent papal judgment, he was in good company. Grosseteste's answer, however, is not just an Augustinian florilegium;[8] rather, he builds on the authority of Augustine to construct some important arguments concerning God's nature.[9]

The method in this letter is typical of Grosseteste: draw out the logic of the statement and then exploit the imagination to visualise the results.[10] He begins by making the case that God is form: since a form is 'that by which a thing is that which it is' (*id quod est*), God must be his own form because he is that which he is of himself, that is, he is God by means of divinity. However, Grosseteste avoids a classic 'hylomorphic heresy' with the qualification that God is divinity (*Deus est deitas*). In other words, while in other instances a form can be theoretically external to the thing in question (as *humanitas* can be distinct from an individual human), this cannot be true of God. He exists by virtue of himself alone, and not by another substance. Nonetheless, this does not yet address the heart of the matter, and Grosseteste extends this principle of God as his own form to being the form of all things through an argument drawn from predication. Everyone grants that God is beautiful both of form (*formosa*) and of appearance (*speciosa*). The conclusion is that God must therefore be both form (*forma*) and appearance (*species*) themselves, in the same way that God is both just (*iustus*) and the justice (*iustitia*) by which he is just. The predication is even more absolute, for God is not just *a certain* form or *a certain* appearance in terms of beauty, rather he is the beauty of form and appearance itself (*formositas et speciositas*).[11]

Applying this philosophical construct may appear to ignore God's own transcendence, even if the theologian accepts no distinction between God *qua* God and God *qua* divinity. Grosseteste addresses this problem in two ways. Firstly, he notes that the concept of form points to modes of perfection and completion, for a form perfects and completes matter so as to render it as an existing thing. In God's case, there is no need for any completion or perfection: 'and so he is form incapable of being formed, because he is utterly without defect and changeless'. In this way, God transcends the very nature of form, for he is 'the most perfect perfection, the most complete completion, the most beautiful of forms and appearances'. Secondly, Grosseteste emphasises God's transcendence by noting that the knowledge of God as *formositas* cannot be demonstrated. Any discursive account would be prone to rely upon corporeal images – an instance when analogical argument would only serve to obstruct the view of God as beauty. This explanation is drawn from Augustine's *De Trinitate*, where it is argued that any thought about God as truth must be immediate, since any analysis will draw the thinker away from God. Instead, 'the mind should remain in the first flash of light that dazzled you when the truth was mentioned'.[12] The same conditions apply to considering God as the most beautiful of form: it is a reality that transcends human conceptualisation and reasoning.

If the first proposition of God as first form does not diminish his transcendence, can the same be said of the second, 'God is the form of all things'? Grosseteste assures his friend that to speak of God in this manner is not once again to consider God in standard hylomorphic terms. He is not positing that God is the substantial and completive part of a created thing, that is, the form that along with matter makes a singular thing (*aliquid unum*). Instead, to make his point, Grosseteste wishes to clarify what he means by the term 'form', when referring to God as the form of all things. In this context, Grosseteste posits a twofold description of form that draws primarily on the image of a craftsman at work. The first focuses on the ontological reality of form. It is an exemplar distinct from, and outside of, the individual in question. In this instance, the form is that to which the craftsman looks when fashioning his product, just as a cobbler looks to a wooden archetype when making the sole. The second description shifts from the form itself to its relationship to matter: it is what is impressed on matter, and here the examples are a silver seal impressed on wax or the mould of a statue. With these two pithy descriptions, Grosseteste has identified the two different conceptions of the universal; how one relates these two to each other became the crux of what historians now call 'the medieval problem of universals'.[13]

Grosseteste does not address the philosophical problem embedded in the theory of universals, since in this letter his aim is to persuade Adam of God's specific role.[14] The craftsman used to exemplify the two descriptions of form is now transformed into an omnipotent maker. Adam is asked to imagine a craftsman who wants to build a house, and so he has an image of that house in his mind, from which he will fashion the material object. In addition, despite how impossible it is, Grosseteste's former student must also imagine that this builder has a strong enough will to apply that exemplar to the matter before him in order to bring the house into existence. However, one must imagine that the building materials are naturally so fluid and unstable that, without the form making its impression, the house would not remain a house. Hence this craftsman must not only apply his will initially in order to create the house; his will must also be active in maintaining its integrity. This thought experiment brings Grosseteste to his final conclusion, for it in fact describes how God is the form of all created things: this very form 'simultaneously is the exemplar, it is that which effects, shapes and conserves in the form given, when creatures are applied and called back to it'.[15] Grosseteste has therefore addressed this vexing question within the context of God's ubiquity. God's presence always has some effect. As the form of all things, God provides the exemplar of the form as it is extant in matter. In each case, the exemplar is causative in terms of the formation as well as the continued preservation of the creature.

The theme of God's ubiquity is extended as Grosseteste moves to the second question posed by Adam, namely whether Intelligences (that is, angels) occupy a distinct space or if they are in any one place at the same time.[16] Grosseteste's strategy is to place the question within the broader spectrum of spiritual or incorporeal existence. At one end, there is God who alone is 'wholly everywhere at the same time'. At the other, the soul exists, bounded within a body but yet not located in one specific region of the body, as many would believe. Angels then find themselves in the middle: like the soul, they have the power to move a body, without being situated in one physical location; but they are neither bound nor contained when they act as 'prefects' of a region in the material world. In these instances the angel inhabits that entire region of their prefecture in a way analogous to the manner in which God inhabits the whole universe.[17] It is significant to note that the strategy at work in this letter is also found in William of Auxerre and Alexander of Hales, each of whom addresses the question of God's ubiquity in comparison to the nature of angels and of human souls. They differ in that their objective is to account for God's ubiquity, whereas Grosseteste employs divine ubiquity as means of measuring the locality of an angel.[18]

God's Power to Know

If Grosseteste's first letter reveals his interest in the general relationship between God and his creation, the *De libero arbitrio* focuses more specifically on the relationship between God and humanity. The challenge is to reconcile God's knowledge of all things with free will, and Grosseteste presents the general problem this way:

> Since God knows all things, even future contingents, and his knowledge is unchangeable as it is infallible, and since whatever he knows should happen necessarily, so that what he knows would not be fallible or changeable, all things happen out of necessity, since he cannot not-know what he knows. Nothing therefore will be by the free will of a creature, because if it is by free will it is not by necessity.[19]

The manner in which he attacks this problem blends a careful use of modal logic with some traditional theological ideas. The aim in this section is not to explicate the details of Grosseteste's argument on free will per se, but rather to discuss the relevant aspects of God's nature and agency that have a bearing on this topic.[20] Even though the thrust of the text is to examine the relationship between God's knowledge and free will, Grosseteste must first engage some general precepts about God's nature. More specifically, in order to create theological space for free will, Grosseteste must account for both what God knows and what God can do in relation to his knowledge.

What God Knows

It is a given that God knows everything, which is the first problem for any theory of free will since God's knowledge implies a necessity for all the things he knows. However, one solution would be to modify the specific content of God's knowledge, that is, to argue that:

(P$_1$) God certainly knows himself;
(P$_2$) through himself God knows everything but only in terms of universals;
(C) Therefore, since he does not know singulars, contingent acts caused by free will can exist.

Grosseteste reports these claims as originating from pagan writings (*scripta ethnicorum*), but it would seem he had one particular thinker in mind, Avicenna.[21] While Avicenna's position might make sense philosophically, Grosseteste argues that it runs contrary to the testimony of Scripture, to other pagan philosophers (including oddly enough Boethius), and to the teaching of Augustine.[22] In the first recension, he also makes six arguments to support the proposition that God knows singulars, to which he adds two more in the second recension. All have direct bearing on other theological positions that he takes, but none of them appear to be necessarily original to him.[23] They are as follows:[24]

1 Since God is a just judge and justly punishes the wicked and rewards the good, he must have knowledge of the relative merits of each person to be judged.
2 God cannot be the Creator of all things, including singulars, and then be said not to know what he has made – especially since Scripture asserts the opposite.
3 If God made humanity with the capability of knowing singulars through sensation and imagination, then how could he make those faculties properly if he does not know their objects?
4 If all of human activity comes under the aegis of God's providence, how can God properly care for his creation if he does not know all of it?
5 If God loves good things and accepts good works, he knows them; for one cannot love what one does not know. To say that God is the supreme good, but does not love (and yet loves himself) is simply absurd.
6 Drawing from Cicero's assertion that God is worthy to be worshipped because of his engagement in human affairs, then there is no need to worship him if he does not know singulars.

In the second recension, Grosseteste adds these two arguments:[25]

7 If God does not know singulars, then a person knows many things which God does not know; and that is absurd.
8 St Anselm has taught us that God is greater than anything that can be thought. This statement would not be true if God does not know singulars: for if God were greater than anything that can be thought, he would know both universals and singulars. If we say he only knows universals, than we must posit someone who is greater than God.[26]

After these arguments, Grosseteste introduces a set of authorities who also argue that singulars are part of God's knowledge. This leads Grosseteste to the major conclusion that 'God knows everything for all eternity, without end, all in the same way and immutably, [and] in one, indivisible and simple gaze.'[27]

Each proposition posited by Grosseteste merits on its own a detailed explanation, but it will suffice to make the following observations. The arguments, when taken together, present a complex account of God's knowledge, especially when compared with the single topic of the small tract, *De scientia Dei*.[28] There Grosseteste struggles with divine knowledge solely in terms of future contingents, although these conclusions are eclipsed by those presented in the *De libero arbitrio* on the same issue. Even in altering his conclusions about God's knowledge and future contingents, he remains committed to providing a solution to the problem that entails a coherent account of the relevant modal principles. More importantly, the arguments are made to function within a theological framework. It is not just what God knows, but for what reasons he must know them. The very claims and promises God makes in sacred Scripture must be taken into account, or one could easily construct a logically coherent account of God that provides space for free will, but one that might also distance the Creator from his creation. Instead, the dictates of the Christian message must have a bearing here. Any account of God's knowledge must also provide an account of God's ability to engage in human history, and to acknowledge his concern for the contingent and mutable affairs of each individual Christian. In other words, the concept of free will (at least as Grosseteste has formulated it here) is a theological one.

Grosseteste connects some general claims about God's nature with his claims about his knowledge. It should not be surprising that Grosseteste would argue that God knows singulars, especially in light of his earlier defence of the dictum, *God is the form of all things*. In that case, Grosseteste had to negotiate between God's transcendence (in that the concept of form and beauty could scarcely describe him), and God's active presence in all his creation. God's transcendence is at play in the *De libero arbitrio* as well, for it has a bearing upon his knowledge. Anselm's famous argument reminded Grosseteste, not of a single argument to prove the existence of God, but rather that God's nature exceeds, transcends, any human understanding. Thus to place limits on God's knowledge violates the dictum that God is greater than anything that can be thought – a clear violation of the second commandment in Grosseteste's opinion.[29] At the same time, transcendence does not mean absence. God cares for his creation, and that demands knowledge of singulars. Finally, what brings God's providence and his transcendence together – at least from a human perspective – is his goodness and love. The supreme good necessarily embraces all good things, even those wrought by the contingency of free will. God knows his creation intimately, as is proved by the fact that he loves it.

What God Can Do

As decisive as Grosseteste is with dispelling this one solution to the initial problem posed in the *De libero arbitrio*, it remains for him to make space for free will in reality where God's knowledge makes all things necessary. His strategy is twofold: first, he presents a highly technical argument as to why the modal principle of 'necessity only follows from necessity' (*necessaria ex necessitate sequi*) may be incomplete in and of itself, and so in some cases contingency may be the result of necessary conditions.[30] Second, he suggests that God's knowledge may be necessary but not absolutely necessary. Indeed, his aim is to argue that part of his initial premise is wrong, namely that God cannot not know what he knows (*non possit quod scit non scire*). The upshot of this strategy is to argue that God has the power to not know what he knows or, as he will eventually say in a less convoluted way, God can know opposites. The first part of this strategy has been expertly analysed by Neil Lewis,[31] and so I will turn to the second part in order to extrapolate the theological features of Grosseteste's argument that relate directly to what he says about God. I make no attempt to critique whether Grosseteste effectively makes his case that free will is compatible with God's knowledge.[32]

Grosseteste's account of God's power in relation to his knowledge is presented in an undeveloped and tentative state in the first recension, but more forcefully in the second. And since the second recension also includes additional arguments, I shall use this source. In chapter 6, after demonstrating the problems that the necessity of God's knowledge presents (particularly in terms of propositions about future contingents), Grosseteste begins to present his own solution. The first thing he does is to introduce a distinction in necessity.[33] There is first of all simple or absolute necessity, in that necessary conditions will always effect necessary outcomes. His example is mathematical: it will always be the case that $2+3=5$, without end, and there is no instance in which the opposite can come to be. But there is a second kind of necessity, in which it is possible for something to be both true and false necessarily. Now this mode of necessity does not exist in time, but the power for something to be true and false exists eternally (*ab eterno, sine initio*). It is under this second modal principle that a theologian may consider God's knowledge. Such a position raises some thorny logical and philosophical problems, which Grosseteste carefully examines in chapter 7.[34] In chapter 8, he answers these objections and in the process comes to formulate his account of God's knowledge and its mode of necessity.

Grosseteste presents three major propositions that support his position of God's power to know opposites. The first one is comparative in nature. Everyone grants that God can will what he does not will and that he cannot not-will what he wills. Just because Scripture informs the reader of what God has willed does not mean that this was the only option available to him; rather he is not constrained in his choice. In fact, Grosseteste goes on to say this: 'There is in God the supreme liberty of the will. Therefore all his acts are supremely voluntary; [and] therefore they are not necessary, for what is voluntary is not necessary. Therefore, since his act is not necessary, he can act in the opposite manner (*potest ad actum oppositum*).'[35] Since the issue in question is about God's knowledge, moreover, the theologian is in fact dealing with rational powers, and not just power in general. This second proposition harkens back to an objection in the previous chapter, one that is a serious threat to God's knowledge as holding to opposites.[36] Since all power is reducible to act, God's power to know something must in some sense be reducible to an act of knowing it. Hence to suggest that God can know opposites flies in the face of the reducibility of power to act, since one cannot conceive of a power in terms of two contrary objects of that power. Grosseteste's solution is to draw upon a Boethian notion that rational powers differ in terms of their reducibility to act, and in fact can embrace opposites. The power to speak, for example, can be reduced in act to both audible speech and its opposite, silence. Now since God is wholly of reason, his power to know can embrace opposites. Grosseteste offers yet another comparative example drawn from angelic nature: in their creation, angels had the desire to be good or bad. Indeed, this very capability is why they may be judged for whatever choice each one took, since it was within their power to choose either.[37] The implication here is that, if God chooses rightly, he must know two things in order to choose one of them. Hence, if God wills that Peter will be saved, he must know that Peter will be saved *and* that Peter will not be saved.

Finally, Grosseteste clarifies what he means by the verb to know (*verbum sciendi*) when predicated of God. To know something is to describe a relation between the knower and the thing known, and that relation must be considered variable or changeable. However, God's nature is absolutely unchangeable, so we end up with an immediate contradiction, namely that 'these relations have been in God eternally and nonetheless they are variable'. Grosseteste solves this by first stating that these relations, for the very reason that they are variable, cannot be said to be God himself. Rather, these truths are relations between God and his creation. In saying so, it would appear that Grosseteste is willing to predicate eternity of creaturely things, if these truths as relations have existed *ab eterno*. But this is not the case, so he states, for even if God had not created anything there would have still been these relations in God. The eternity predicated on these truth relations is based upon the fact that God is part of the relation, and not due to some essential feature of those relations themselves. For relations, Grosseteste notes, do not have their own essence and 'this is clear to anyone who knows the nature of relations'. Hence, in ascribing what appears to be a variability in God's knowledge (he can know what he does not know, and vice versa), Grosseteste is in fact suggesting that the variability is not found in God himself but rather in the eternal relations between God and his creation.[38]

This third proposition is best understood if we look at Grosseteste's more detailed account of truth, *De veritate*. That disputed question is not about how one knows truth (although that is indeed a relevant theme); rather it concerns the nature or structure of truth, or, as Grosseteste puts it: 'what truth is'.[39] In establishing a working definition of truth, Grosseteste settles upon the correspondence theory of Avicenna, that truth is an adequation of a concept (*sermo*) and an existing thing (*res*).[40] While this is a valid theory – and one that gains a good deal of attention in the thirteenth century – Grosseteste actually modifies it in order to move his reader towards a different perspective on truth. The first phase of this modification is to argue that if an unvocalised concept is truer than a vocalised one (presumably because there is one less layer of temporal signification) then truth should be considered as adequation of an interior concept and the thing. Moreover, if the concept itself is the adequation of itself to the thing, then it would be not only a true concept, but the truth itself. It is at this point that Grosseteste moves the definition into the next phase, for he suggests that one indicates a correspondence of a concept and a thing in three ways. The first two are considered in terms of his first modification, namely in one way truth is the adequation of a vocalised concept (*sermo exterior*) and a thing; in a better way (*magis*) it is the adequation of an interior concept and the thing. However, the best definition is the adequation of the Word of the Father (*sermo patris*) and the thing.[41] In other words, truth is best defined in terms of relations between God and his creation.

However, what Grosseteste is seeking to do additionally in the *De libero arbitrio* is to place God's knowledge solely within eternity. Thus it is never tied to any form of temporality whatsoever. Within this context, he considers it possible to account for the necessity of God's knowledge, but in a mode of necessity that does not preclude contingents in the course of created reality. In effect, Grosseteste's argument arrests the standard notions of cause and effect which comprise simple or absolute necessity: God's knowledge no longer makes a thing necessary in an absolute sense. Eternity also provides Grosseteste with a way of formulating the relationship between God's power to know and what he knows. In eternity, there is certainly priority and posteriority. In the case of the Trinity, the Father is prior to the Son and the Son is therefore posterior to the Father, but that distinction is not founded upon temporal succession nor a causal relation between two natures. 'Thus, since in the divine essence, which is simpler than every simple [being], more indivisible than every indivisible [being], there is priority and posteriority, we have declared that in eternal things there is priority and posteriority.'[42] This allows Grosseteste to draw another conclusion: while it is quite orthodox to state that God's power, knowledge and will cannot be distinguished in terms of standard forms of causality, nonetheless causal priority must be given to power, in just the same way that the Father precedes the Son.[43] God's power to know what he does not know (and not to know what he knows), precedes his knowing, and this allows God to know opposites.

As he proceeds Grosseteste considers a number of theological concepts relevant to the content and causality of God's knowledge. One, however, stands out, since it is a topic to which he gives a more detailed analysis in his other writings: the necessity of the Incarnation.[44] He notes that, although God is in himself (*in se*) one and simple, there are still in him an infinite number of relations of himself (that is, truths) to the created world or even an infinite number of relations of himself to himself.[45] And so it is the case that the divine nature accepts many predications that may not exist in reality. In this context, Grosseteste raises the discrepancy between Augustine and Anselm concerning the manner in which God could save humankind. According to the former, God could have freed humanity in a way other than the passion and resurrection of Christ, whereas the latter explicitly rejects this argument.[46] Grosseteste concludes that, if one considers God in himself, Augustine is correct; but if one considers God according to his relation to creation, Anselm is right.[47] Here we have an instance of God's knowledge embracing opposites with regard to human salvation.

As much as this example clarifies his position on the status of God's knowledge, it can also yield some confusion. Grosseteste suggests that we can think about God's knowledge of human salvation in two contexts: considering God in himself absolutely (*in se absolute considerata*) and considering God according to his relationship with creation (*secundum istam habitudinem ad creata*). The first context allows for more than one solution – and the implication is that the number of solutions is infinite – whereas the second permits only one. The terminology is reminiscent of a major distinction introduced into theological discourse during the early thirteenth century concerning divine power. In its standard formulation, scholastic theologians spoke of God's power either in absolute terms (*de potentia Dei absoluta*) or in terms of a causal connection to created reality (*de potentia Dei ordinata*). God can *de potentia absoluta* make flying pigs, but the fact is that God has made *de potentia ordinata* grunting pigs.[48] The distinction between absolute and ordained power was not meant to indicate two sets of powers in God, but rather to indicate the conditions in which God could or did act in a certain manner.[49] During Grosseteste's magisterial period, theologians at Paris were coming to accept this distinction as a valid tool of theological analysis, but it would not be until a decade later that the terminology would become universally accepted, for some theologians would speak of *de potentia Dei ordinata* and *de iusticia Dei* interchangeably. The 'necessity' of the Incarnation was the classic locus for this question, since it provided one way to resolve the apparent contradiction between Augustine and Anselm. Further applications were adduced, most involving considering God's power generally in terms of its effects.

William of Auxerre was the first to broaden the debate, so that this 'Power Distinction' had a role to play firstly in the general definition of God's omnipotence, and then in theological problems other than the Incarnation. This same approach is found in William of Auvergne and Alexander of Hales and his students, and to a lesser degree in Roland of Cremona and Hugh of St-Cher.[50] There is certainly no question that Grosseteste conceived of God's power to know opposites as an indication of his omnipotence. However, that argument cannot be placed so easily within the strictly defined Power Distinction, mainly because it was used to speak about things extrinsic to God, and not about his nature per se. God's power to know opposites does not concern what God does *ad extra*, but rather it first and foremost concerns God in himself. Now Grosseteste clearly sees that it is possible to consider God's power either absolutely or in terms related to the created order (*ordinata*). His recourse to the fittingness of the Incarnation as the means of salvation is mainly to indicate an instance which proves that God knows opposites, and so further proves that the kind of necessity attached to that knowledge cannot be absolute.

My account here does not fully outline all the implications of Grosseteste's theory of God's knowledge, for he goes on to demonstrate how this mode of necessity allows for compatibility between God's predestination, grace and free will, to mention only two major issues.[51] However, the portrait I have sketched presents an expansive and all-encompassing knowledge of God. From the perspective of created reality, God knows all things, including singulars. From the perspective of eternity, God knows all things and their opposites. He knows what actually is and what may or may not come to be, including not just this world but all possible worlds.[52] Moreover, Grosseteste sought to develop his account of God's knowledge within a clear understanding of the difference between temporality and eternity. That conception of eternity is built upon a vision of the Trinity. It is to this topic we now turn, for the Trinity lies at the heart of Grosseteste's doctrine of God.

A Triune God

In the eighth part of the *Hexaëmeron*, Grosseteste focuses his expository eye on Genesis 1.26, the first account of humanity's creation. He discerns that this verse evokes two principal issues, and each requires careful explanation. The first is the nature of the Creator, which comes to the fore because of the use of the first person plural, 'Let us make man' (*faciamus hominem*). The second is the nature of humanity, since humankind is made in the image and likeness of that Creator (*ad imaginem et similitudinem nostram*). Grosseteste wants to grapple with the relationship between Creator and humanity, but he frames it by first of all exploring *how* a human being is said to be in the image and likeness of God. While he will later engage the traditional distinction between image and likeness,[53] at this point Grosseteste draws upon 'Augustine' to define image as the supreme likeness (*summa similitudo*). He states that this definition comes from Augustine's *De Trinitate*, but, as the modern editors of the *Hexaëmeron* note, it does not appear in that source. It is just as possible that the text that inspired this definition was the Ps-Augustinian work, *De spiritu et anima*. In chapter 6, while delineating the various vestiges of the Trinity in the soul, the text equates the term *imago* with the second person of the Trinity, since the Son is the image of the Father. The author then describes image as being 'beauty, harmony, equality, the first and supreme similitude, the first and supreme life, the first and supreme intellect'.[54] This source may have caused Grosseteste to think about what it means to be created in the image of God, if theologians were also speaking of the Son as the image of the Father. He follows up just such a distinction for using the terms 'image' and 'likeness': one may speak of an image of equality and parity or one of imitation – and the same must also be said of likeness. In this manner, to speak of the Son as the image and likeness of the Father is to speak of their equality: whatever the Father has, so has the Son; and whatever the Father does, so the Son also accomplishes. By contrast, therefore, a human being is the image and likeness of the Trinity in terms of imitation: 'A creation cannot be compared to his Maker, nor can it be described univocally with Him; nonetheless, he can imitate [the Creator] in a certain manner.'[55]

Grosseteste then notes a further distinction. If humanity possesses the *supreme* likeness of God, then that concept only becomes coherent if humanity somehow bears the vestiges of all that God is substantially – even if one speaks of this participation as only imitative. The implication of this assertion is that one must speak of humanity in theological terms that differ from the relationship between God and creation in general. Just as Grosseteste had argued for the sake of Adam of Oxford a few years earlier, God is indeed all things in all things (*Deus est omnia in omnibus*) – which was another way of saying that God is the first form of all things. That explanation, however, cannot fully account for the creation of humankind. If a human being is wholly in the likeness of God, somehow he too must be all things in all things. Hence understanding humanity lies not in the created world in general where one constructs an account composed of concepts such as form and species. Rather, one gains the truth of human nature by looking to the mystery of the Trinity.[56] Grosseteste certainly feels the challenge of such a demanding explanation of humanity, and it makes him feel very unlearned. Nonetheless, he will attempt to render the account just the same.[57]

Since the aim of this section is to examine Grosseteste's doctrine of God, we cannot follow him to his final trajectory in this part of the *Hexaëmeron*, namely to provide a comprehensive analysis of human nature.[58] Instead, it is the path he takes that is of immediate interest here, for Grosseteste first outlines his own Trinitarian theology as the basis for coming to terms with humanity. His explanation of the

Trinity falls into three parts, and not surprisingly they reflect his general methodology that has already been examined.[59] He first explains how the Scriptural text of Genesis provides theological space for broaching the topic of the Trinity. This is followed by his presentation of four speculative arguments (*ex ratione*) for seeing God as triune. Finally, he presents a number of *exempla* of the Trinity in the created world, and these observations allow for a transition to the ultimate example of God's triune nature, the human person. Placed within the broader context of scholastic literature, Grosseteste advances the discussion in a fairly common way. Alexander of Hales noted that the revelation of the Trinity is actually threefold: through doctrine, that is, authority; through the created world, the works of the Trinity; and finally, by the inspiration of faith. The last one remains solely within the domain of God's power, but the first two are within the grasp of the human mind. In his own gloss of the *Sentences*, he proceeds with the arguments from authority, that is Scripture, since it is prior, and then the speculative arguments follow.[60]

The Scriptural Point of Departure

Grosseteste first begins by laying out the reasons why the Genesis text is a locus for Trinitarian teaching. The use of the first person plural suggests two possible ways of understanding the text, both of which revolve around author and audience. One way would be to consider the creative act as cooperative, namely that God and a creature were responsible for the origins of humanity; hence, in this verse God is calling to his co-worker jussively to engage in a creative act. That cannot be, argues Grosseteste, for such an explanation then fails to account for how humanity would then be made in a composite image. More to the point, since one cannot speak of Creator and creation univocally, it is impossible to conceive of a condition in which divergent natures could come together to form a unified likeness in a new creation. In fact, all one can have is humanity created in two different likenesses, not one. However, the text is clear: there is only one image and likeness at work, not two.

Grosseteste adds two further proofs for rejecting this reading, one speculative and one scriptural. The speculative argument assumes for the moment that the text permits a mangled reading: humanity is to be created in the single image of God (and not a diverse one), but God is still speaking to a creaturely co-creator. This assumption, however, fails because of a contradiction. If the likeness of God instilled in human nature is the most supreme likeness possible, there is no creature superior to a human being. However, a creature who is capable of working with God to create humankind must in some way be superior to humanity, for the 'one who creates is greater than whatever is created by him'. To accept that assertion would mean there would be a creature who was both greater and lesser than humanity, a logical absurdity. In the end, Scripture rules out any non-Trinitarian reading, for in the next chapter of Genesis the claim is made that God created man in his image and likeness. Thus, with respect to humanity's creation, there is but one God at work.

The second way of reading the text is the only correct reading, namely that this verse implies a plurality of persons in the one God. There is no other logical option here, for to speak of plurality in any other category (such as essence, substance, accidents or universals) would be to deny God's simplicity. The term 'person', Grosseteste argues as he draws from Boethius, allows for identifiable individuality without compromising the unity of nature. Hence the text speaks to the mystery of the Trinity, and Grosseteste ends this first section with citations from Western and Eastern authorities to validate his own reading.[61]

Arguments for the Trinity

Having established the validity of thinking about the Trinity within the Genesis narrative, Grosseteste immediately launches into his speculative arguments that prove the doctrine of the Trinity. The first reflects some of Grosseteste's original thinking, for he draws upon his considerations about the nature of light: 'That God should be three in persons, it thus follows that God is light . . .' That Grosseteste would begin here should not surprise the modern reader, since light was the principal element of his metaphysics.[62] However, approaching the Trinity in terms of light was not exclusive to Grosseteste. The description of God as an inaccessible light was biblically based (1 Tim. 6.16), although how it was used in reference to the Trinity varied from theologian to theologian. Alexander of Hales and William of Auxerre each conclude that God as light speaks to the epistemological factors in Trinitarian theology. Alexander draws upon the invisibility of light from the sun as a metaphor for the fact that God's nature is invisible in itself to the human mind; and yet, just as one could see sunlight in the air, so the mind could see God's nature through a created similitude.[63] William draws a similar conclusion. After positing a number of metaphysical proofs of a triune God, he raises the objection that all these proofs boil down to a theologian applying created natures to the divine nature – but that is a recipe for heresy. His answer is that this is the only strategy available to humanity, for God is by nature an inaccessible light. Hence 'it is necessary for the intellect to be developed and purged in the mirror of creation, so that it may come to an understanding of the Creator through it'.[64] By way of contrast, the very properties of light were applied to the statement that God is light by William of Auvergne. While no doubt Augustine was the original source for this methodology, William found confirmation in Richard of St-Victor, who notes that light and its splendour coexist equally, and this is a concept applicable to both visible and spiritual light.[65] Even though William of Auvergne had already provided proof of the generation of the Son based on the necessary emanation of absolute being, he reiterates this point by drawing upon the reality that God as light has His own splendour that is equal to the light in every respect.[66]

Even in this context, Grosseteste still shows some originality by using the properties of light to argue for a triune God. Light certainly bears its own splendour from itself; but in addition, the generating light (*lux gignens*) and the generated splendour (*splendor genitus*) embrace one another necessarily, and they breathe forth a mutual fervour – which is another way of describing the heat (*calor*) generated by light.[67] Here light provides a clear account of the paternity of the Father, the generation of the Son and the procession of the Holy Spirit from the Father and the Son. As novel as this mode of explanation is, Grosseteste is still compelled to work through the doctrine in standard terms. Most Trinitarian theologies in the Middle Ages focused on the metaphysical issues by explaining the generation of the Son by the Father. This was partly due to historical reasons since the divinity of Christ had originally been the point of departure for the earliest accounts of Trinity.[68] Another reason was the significant challenge of moving initially from a divine essence that was both one and simple to a conception of divinity which encompassed several persons. Hence to prove the generation of the Son was in effect to prove the doctrine of the entire Trinity. In this regard, Grosseteste proceeds in the *Hexaëmeron* in a typical scholastic fashion. To understand the relation between the Generator (*gignens*) and the Generated (*genitus*), Grosseteste posits five possible explanations. They are difficult to render in English, since they are all built on subtle semantic uses of the Latin word for 'another' (*alius*). Nonetheless, it is worth noting all five options and, more importantly, why Grosseteste can dispense with four of them. They are as follows:

1 another nature and another person (*aliud et alius*),
2 not another nature but another person (*non aliud sed alius*),
3 not another person but another nature (*non alius sed aliud*),
4 neither another nature nor another person but only a second [thing] (*nec aliud nec alius, sed alterum solum*),
5 no distinction at all (*nec aliud nec alius nec alterum*).

Grosseteste's account assumes that the reader would understand that the neuter (*aliud*) points to a nature or a substance, whereas the masculine (*alius*) points to a person.[69] Moreover, it is likely that his readers would have had some familiarity with the Lateran IV declaration on the doctrine of the Trinity, where the contrast between the use of *alius* and *aliud* was central to the refutation of Joachim of Fiore's critique of Peter Lombard.[70] Grosseteste begins working his way to his own conclusion by eliminating the fifth option since it would deny any distinction at all between the Generator and the Generated. The third must also be taken away as it would introduce a second nature into the Trinitarian account, as would the first option.[71] Along the same lines, one must reject the fourth since the word *alterum* introduces the concept of accidental difference.[72] What remains is the second explanation, that the Generated is an *alius* to the Generator, that is a distinct person. Grosseteste brings his account in line with the tradition of Trinitarian literature in Latin theology by reminding his readers that 'person' means, according to Boethius, 'an individual substance of a rational nature'. Hence in God there is one, another and a third (*unus et alius et tercius*) – and all are persons.[73] Grosseteste ends this first argument by raising the possibility of a fourth person in the Trinity. His answer, since the whole argument is based on the nature of light, is pithy: it is not possible to consider a fourth person in the Godhead, for what could be said about light beyond that it is light which generates, it is splendour which is generated, and it is that which proceeds in mutual fervour from the first two?[74]

Grosseteste's second argument betrays a very careful reading of Augustine's *De trinitate*. Medieval readers had well exploited Augustine in order to speak of the Trinitarian vestige in humanity; that is, memory, understanding and will.[75] However, at this point in the argument, Grosseteste is not seeking to discover the imprint of the Godhead in human experience, but rather he argues that the similitude is coherent because each act of the mind itself points to a Trinitarian person. Memory, understanding and will (or love) form a vestige of the Trinity, because God himself is memory, understanding and love.[76] He who generates is in fact a memory who is always remembering: 'He is the retention of all knowledge, which he did not receive from elsewhere, nor does he ever forget.' Moreover, as an active memory he can only generate from himself an understanding that is wholly similar to himself. One can see the dyadic relationship here, but Grosseteste's own theological outlook allowed him to advance this proof to include a third person: memory and intelligence can only reflect one another in mutual love. How can he make this leap in logic? The answer lies in the fact that the term *intelligentia* is tied to wisdom, and as noted wisdom demands full mental activity, and that must include the faculty connected to love, namely the will (*affectus mentis*).[77]

Grosseteste then moves on to what he considers to be a central argument (*ex hoc medio*) for proof of the Trinity, and it first originates from sacred Scripture: 'If I am the one who grants the generation of children, shall I be sterile?'[78] If God is the source of humanity's capability of generating offspring then as that cause he must possess that capacity to an equal or (more appropriately in the case of God) greater degree. Grosseteste notes two aspects of this biblical claim. First, generation concerns passing one's own substance to another, but God is the only being who does so while at the same time retaining that very same substance for himself. In other words, he does not transfer a part of himself in the process, since that would indicate a change in God's nature (which Grosseteste describes here as the diminution of power). Secondly, this kind of generation speaks to the fact that God is the supreme power. Grosseteste notes that pagan philosophers had spoken of God as a creator in terms of forming the world from material that God himself had not produced. Christians differentiated the Genesis account of creation from all other ancient accounts by adding a new dimension: creation from nothing (*ex nihilo*). While creation from non-being emphasises God's incomparable power, Grosseteste suggests that the power to generate is even prior to that, for how much more incomparable is God's capability of generating, not from something else, nor even from nothing, but from his own substance. Although stated in an odd way, Grosseteste is in fact echoing his fellow scholastics who had given greater dignity to the generative power of God than to his creative power.[79]

The final argument focuses on the nature of the good. Goodness is self-diffusive, as Grosseteste will later say in his discussion of the Incarnation; or as he states here in the *Hexaëmeron*, it is by nature communicative of itself.[80] To be the supreme good God must share himself substantially, and it cannot be partially but rather entirely. These conditions severely limit the potential recipients of this sharing, since it means that those with whom the supreme goodness shares must be capable of engaging this kind of goodness in a substantial, non-temporal and non-quantitative way: that rules out any created being entirely. The only conclusion is that, if the supreme goodness is that than which no greater thing can be thought, then there must be a plurality of persons who share in this supreme goodness. There are only three persons who share in this goodness, and Grosseteste's explanation here brings his reader full circle, for the model of light once again emerges.[81] He states that three is the first perfect number, which has a beginning, middle and end; and it is the first number to produce a circle (*redit in circulum*).[82] What he means in fact is the generation of light from light, which reflects back on itself. Hence

> [The number] one expresses from itself the second; the second [number] reflects itself into the first and expresses from itself its own reflection into the first; More correctly, the first is reflected in itself through the second, and this reflection proceeds from the first and second simultaneously.[83]

Grosseteste implicitly connects the self-diffusiveness of the good with the nature of light (no doubt influenced by Ps-Dionysius), as both provide excellent models for making a rational account of the doctrine of the Trinity.[84]

Vestiges of the Trinity in Creation

At this point in the text, Grosseteste moves from speculative argument to imaginative examples, for reasons already discussed, namely that recourse to the imagination aided the mind in comprehending a reasoned argument.[85] Grosseteste outlines three universal vestiges which adorn every creature.[86] These triads were common to scholastic discussions of the Trinity: matter, form and their composition; magnitude (which Grosseteste reads for mode), species and order; and number, weight and measure. The third triad originated from Wisdom 11.21, which McEvoy notes was one of Grosseteste's favourite biblical texts.[87] The second triad was Augustine's own reflection on this pericope, where he connects measure with mode, number with species or beauty, and weight with stability and order.[88] The first triad, however, is not Augustinian but rather may have been influenced by Avicebron's *Fons vitae*.[89] Grosseteste had considered the symbolic value of the number three by describing a triad of matter and form and their composite in his treatise, *De luce*.[90] In the *Hexaëmeron*, however, he transforms this natural triad into a Trinitarian vestige. Ultimately, all three examples speak of the same reality and so Grosseteste uses specific language to communicate that: 'Matter, magnitude and measure reveal a creating, forming and sustaining power. Form, species and number reveal a creating, forming and sustaining wisdom. Composition, order and weight reveal a creating, forming and sustaining goodness.'[91]

If the three examples in the *Hexaëmeron* demonstrate Grosseteste's awareness of the theological tradition in the doctrine of the Trinity, *Dictum* 60 reveals just how original he could be.[92] Taking seriously that each and every creature reflects the Trinity,[93] Grosseteste introduces a thought experiment that reduces the universe to two creatures: a rational creature and the smallest, most worthless and least useful corporeal creature, such as 'a speck of dust, the kind that floats about in the sunlight'.[94] The rational creature will see two things. First, as he considers this speck of dust, he will discover that it is a composite, mutable and material body. Secondly, the mind will conclude that it had a maker, and most importantly it will conclude its maker produced this speck of dust from nothing (*ex nihilo*). This logical progression continues as the mind moves from maker, to the making, to the power behind the making, which leads to the inevitable conclusion that the power to create *ex nihilo* must be infinite.[95]

If considering the very existence of this speck of dust leads to positing an infinite maker, then thinking about its structure leads to something equally profound. If this small thing were a body, it must be tridimensional. Grosseteste, however, goes one step further and suggests that there is a geometric topography at the 'sub-atomic' level. Within the speck of dust is a sphere, and within that sphere an infinite number of circles as all the geometric bodies that can be inscribed in a sphere; and within each circle an infinite number of figures that one can inscribe on the circles. The rational mind, moreover, will see that it can develop a demonstrative science based on each of these infinite figures, and so each speck contains infinite knowledge. Further reflection will allow the rational mind to conclude that the infinite power which made the speck of dust has also apportioned that infinite knowledge in it. And since one cannot have infinite knowledge without infinite wisdom, the only conclusion is that the infinite power has made the speck of dust through infinite wisdom.[96]

The rational mind can go further and draw a third conclusion. The fact that the mind could have thought of such things is a remarkable achievement, or more accurately a great good. The intermediate conclusion that one can draw here is that the Creator of this speck of dust made it useful. Moreover, if this speck is useful to one rational mind, it would also be useful to an infinite number of minds, if they were created. Thus the utility of the speck is infinite, and since for Grosseteste (as with most medieval thinkers) utility and good are convertible,[97] the only conclusion available to the rational mind is that 'the power which creates the infinite through wisdom is good'. And, with that, Grosseteste has brought his reader to a reflection of the Trinity in nature: 'Behold this is how the mind can see in a speck of dust infinite power, infinite wisdom, and infinite goodness of the Creator. And to see this is to see the creative Trinity.'[98]

As tempting as it might be to do so, the modern reader cannot consider this *Dictum* as an instance of natural theology. It may sound this way, since Grosseteste suggests that a rational mind will naturally come to the conclusions he makes. Furthermore, the rational mind at work infers not only the existence of God from the speck of dust, but also some aspects of his nature, such as his power, wisdom and goodness, and all of these are categorised as infinite. At the same time, Grosseteste casts this experiment upon some rather fundamental theological assumptions. There is no attempt to argue why the rational mind would consider the creation of the speck of dust to be necessarily *ex nihilo*. Moreover, the argument which allows the mind to draw the conclusion that the Creator is infinitely good is based on the notion that all things are created for the sake of humanity, and hence its utility is established by pointing the mind towards God.[99] If this is not a case for natural theology, then what is Grosseteste's intent here? The answer takes us back once again to Grosseteste's theological method, for this thought experiment is an instance of reading the book of nature through the lens of the book of Scripture. In a general way, this thought experiment extends the Trinitarian motif of measure, number and weight from the Bible: the mind must *measure* the power that creates *ex nihilo*; the mind sees the infinite *number* of scientific arguments within one speck of dust; and the mind *ponders* the fact that the infinite power which creates also instils these infinite sciences in that speck. It is Scripture, more specifically, that informs the rational mind that all creation is *ex nihilo*, as no pagan philosopher would make this assumption.[100] Finally, the revealed doctrine of the Trinity provides the framework in which the mind can reflect on created reality and envisage the stamp of the Trinity even in the most worthless thing, a speck of dust. Pagan philosophers may have been able to realise the existence of the divine and even may in some obscure way posit a generation within the divine (without having the appropriate name for this relationship), but there is no natural reason to posit a Trinity.[101] Hence to see the Trinity in creation is first to assume it is a reality.

An Infinite God

Even if this thought experiment is just an application of medieval exemplarism, there is one innovative concept at work here: the infinite. The modern reader might consider the predicate of infinity as appropriate and even a theological standard, but in the early thirteenth century this was a controversial claim to make. The concept of infinity posed two problems for theologians in the schools. In light of its etymological link to the word 'end' (*finis*), infinity was first seen as a way of describing indeterminacy within the domain of metaphysics. Unformed matter was considered to be infinite, until a form gave it ontological shape and so ordered it to an end. Hence a perfected being had the predicate of 'finitude' since it was ordered to a proper end; and thus, if God were the most perfect being, he must have greater finitude than any creature. The second problem related to infinity as a predicate of quantity. Aristotle had granted that there could be infinite numbers, but only in terms of potency. One counted to an actual finite number, but to that number one could, potentially, always add another. The ancient Greek philosopher abhorred the notion of actual infinity for a similar reason as to why there could not be antecedent causes *ad infinitum*.[102] An infinite number of causes rendered any attempt to analyse the cause of things impossible (for there would be no limit to the scope of the investigation). In the same way, an infinite quantity would destroy any real measurement, since quantity implied a finite measure between two knowable points.[103]

These problems made it difficult to apply this predicate to God. How could one say that God was indeterminate and, even more troubling, akin (by implication at least) to unformed matter? And, how could one speak of God as infinite in quantitive terms, if that implied potency and God was a fully actualised being – not to mention that this term appeared incommensurate with God's simplicity? Scholastic theologians presented two initial solutions. The first was to use infinity as a form of 'extrinsic denomination', that is to speak only of God's power as infinite and only in terms of its effects. Since God is capable of doing whatever he wishes – which means he can do an infinite number of things – a theologian may consider God's power as infinite by extension. There was no attempt to address infinity in terms of God in himself, but rather within the context of God's agency. The second solution was to cast this predication of God in Dionysian terms, that is to say that God is both finite and infinite, in that he transcends this term: God is hyperfinite. The first solution was condemned by the faculty of Theology at Paris in 1241, and the second gained few supporters.[104] By the second half of the thirteenth century, infinity was considered to be a predicate of God's being.[105] What changed? Leo Sweeney has argued that it was the work of the English Dominican, Richard Fishacre (d.1248), who convinced his contemporaries that infinity could be a metaphysical predicate. His commentary on Lombard's *Sentences* appears to have had a profound influence on both the Oxford and the Parisian schools in this regard, and in the end theologians adopted and then developed his doctrine of God's infinity.[106] What is so interesting about Fishacre's central argument is that it is a summary of *Dictum* 60. It would appear, then, that the shift from God as possessing finitude towards God as an infinite being was begun by Grosseteste.

There is more to this narrative, since Fishacre does not report all of Grosseteste's teaching on infinity. It is useful, though, to begin with some negative comments. If we look to the *Tabula* for any evidence of new thinking about divine infinity, we find none. Moreover, like many his contemporaries, Grosseteste generally employed infinity as a predicate of indeterminacy. The concept of infinity could be used to emphasise the disordered and misdirected intentions of a human being,[107] or it could refer to an instance where there were a series of arguments that could not be fully enumerated.[108] But Grosseteste also used this term as a measurement of actions which reflect or imitate divine activity. For example, Psalm 83 teaches that, since God loves the Church (signified in the text by the tabernacle) with an infinite love, so each Christian ought to love God in the same manner, although it is unclear to Grosseteste whether this same type of love ought to be directed to fellow Christians.[109] If the written record ended here, Grosseteste could easily be counted among the theologians who had not surmounted the problems posed by the classical meaning of 'infinite'.

However, Grosseteste did use this predicate in a new way as well. The clearest instance of this different apperception of infinity emerges in his *De luce*. This text has been rightly hailed as one of the most original texts from the medieval period, and the earliest cosmogony in Western thought. Scholars have carefully examined this work for its philosophical and scientific significance, and so there is no need to examine the arguments in detail.[110] What is relevant here is the role of quantitative infinity in the cosmogonic account. The *De luce* is in part an attempt to resolve a quandary about the origins of corporeal bodies within a hylomorphic universe. If a body is that which has physical extension, that is, it exists as a three-dimensional object, how did it get that way? Matter on its own has no extension and requires a form to impress it to create a body. However, a form also has no extension, since it is simple. Hence it would appear that something else is required to create a body with form and matter – unless there was a corporeal form that has its own capabilities of generating itself and could do so in a multidimensional way. The only created thing that can do this is light. Therefore, this light 'multiplied itself by its very nature an infinite number of times on all sides and spread itself out uniformly in every direction. In this way it proceeded in the beginning of time to extend matter which it could not leave behind, by drawing it out along with itself into a mass the size of the material universe.'[111] For Grosseteste, infinity is no longer a potential quantity. In order to be effective in the formation of bodies, it must be a real quantity. He further asserts this when he argues that the infinite multiplication of light is necessary to the extension of matter. If matter and corporeity were both simple things, they would never result in physical extension. But an infinite set of numbers multiplied by a simple thing will certainly produce multidimensionality and, interestingly enough, the result will be a finite product.[112] This conception of infinity goes well beyond the potential of adding another number to a set of finite numbers.

There is a theological application of this principle. In the opening section of *De cessatione legalium*, Grosseteste argues why the law's efficacy must come to an end, and more importantly why it is incapable of making human beings happy, which is their natural desire.[113] Grosseteste presents a number of reasons why a rational creature cannot obtain the fullness of beatitude on its own power – which would be a person's mode of operation under the law. One of the reasons goes to the very nature of humankind's object of desire, and it is worth quoting the argument in full:

> Furthermore, this fullness of beatitude is a certain infinity (*infinitum quiddam*), for in it there is an understanding of infinite, uncreated reasons; and similarly also an understanding of infinite numbers and figures and through it [an understanding] of those things accidental to them (*accidentium hiis*). Also, the contuition of God (hardly a small amount of contuition, but rather a greater love of any of these things and those things understood, which, as it has been said, are infinite) is an ordered love of singulars and of everything. This love which knows, or that knowledge which loves, cannot be finite, since it would be divided into the singulars of infinite things known or loved and would continuously (*sine fine*) be dismantled.[114] But, every created power is finite, thus it cannot produce a certain infinity from itself by measure or extension. Whether a certain created and mighty power would be infinite by duration alone, anyone can doubt. Nonetheless, no one doubts that a created power is finite so that it cannot be infinite by quantity or by extension. Therefore, a finite power cannot [acquire] on its own a certain infinity. Therefore, the rational creature by itself cannot acquire the said fullness of beatitude, since this fullness in itself encompasses infinity. Thus, so that the rational creature can become fully blessed, it is necessary that it be united to an uncreated infinite power, which confers the infinite fullness of beatitude upon the same. Therefore a rational creature cannot have beatitude unless it is from a connection to God (*ex collacione Dei*), who alone is an entirely infinite power (*virtus*), from whom and through whom and in whom that same finite creature perceives the infinite act of beatitude.[115]

The last sentence leaves us with no doubt that Grosseteste considers this fullness of beatitude to be nothing other than the beatific vision. He would not fully thematise the doctrine of the beatific vision until his commentary on the *Celestial Hierarchy* of Ps-Dionysius, and so I cannot comment here on how Grosseteste, while a regent master, talks about a Christian seeing it *in patria*.[116] However, it is significant that Grosseteste maintains during his magisterial period that somehow a person can 'perceive' an infinite being. This is in direct contrast to some scholastic theologians at Paris – whose names we still do not know – who argued that, because Christians will see God in himself, he must therefore be finite in nature.[117] Instead, Grosseteste sees infinity as a predicate of God's being. God is not only infinite power in himself, but he is also infinite wisdom and infinite goodness. There is one further reason why God must be infinite according to Grosseteste, and it comes back to the existence of infinities in creation. He considers infinities a reality first of all because of their mathematical persuasiveness, as *De luce* appropriately argues. More to the point, if the created world itself reflects significant realities of its Creator, and if there are infinities in the world, then there must be an infinite mind who created them and who knows them in their entirety.

Knowing God

Ubiquitous, knowing all things (and their opposites), triune and infinite, these attributes form the foundation of Grosseteste's doctrine of God. Even then the list is not complete, for upon that foundation he added other aspects of God's nature – sometimes explicitly, other times implicitly – such as love, goodness, wisdom, omnipotence, creative and providential. The range of thought within Grosseteste's theology may appear surprising, since he is supposed to have been a theologian who was bound by the limits of salvation history. He has instead emerged in this chapter as a master of the sacred page who engaged the divine nature by exploiting reason, the imagination, patristic authority and sacred Scripture. He had mastered the theological tradition and was attuned to contemporary issues and even fresh philosophical sources. His unique outlook, fostered by his extensive work in natural philosophy, allowed him to assert some fresh and innovative ideas: light becomes a positive proof of the doctrine of the Trinity, and infinity can describe the divine nature, at a period in history when the validity of that predicate was open to question. At the same time, however, Grosseteste's brevity and sometimes cursory analysis of significant theological concepts is disappointing. For example, his discussion of the Trinity – that is, the three proofs that he presents – comprises less than a thousand words in Latin. This is rather paltry when compared to the length of William of Auvergne's *De trinitate* (just over 70 000 words). And while he had identified a number of topics *de Deo* in his *Tabula*, few of them ever emerged in complete form as part of disputations or treatises. He did indeed make contributions to the theological tradition of his century, but they were inchoate and it would be left to later theologians to realise their full potential.

While Grosseteste's doctrine of God appears inchoate within the larger context of scholastic theology, what he did say served his own needs quite adequately. He reflected on the divine nature in as much as the questions before him required him to do. Moreover, the orientation of his thought was not so much given to the vagaries of speculation as it was to the need for knowledge that would propel the mind towards a love for God. Such a trajectory may be considered a theological spirituality, since for Grosseteste any theological teaching had a role to play in the development of the human potential to move towards union with God.[118] With this in mind, it becomes necessary to complete this chapter with an examination of the way Grosseteste the theologian describes a person's capacity to know God. Now to end with the conditions for knowing the triune and infinite God appears to have things backwards. Surely it is necessary to present at the outset the conditions which make knowledge of God a possibility, and not as an afterthought. For Grosseteste, however, those very conditions were based on the fact that humankind was created in the image of God. Hence, if there is any need to describe a person's ability to know God, it must be predicated upon the doctrine of the Trinity. From our perspective this might appear as putting the epistemological cart before the horse, but for Grosseteste it was the appropriate theological sequence since it provided the correct point of departure.

In understanding the doctrine of the Trinity one can then perceive the meaning of its resulting images, especially the best one, the human mind. Because a person is made in the image of the Trinity, she does indeed have a natural capacity to know the substance of the image. But to what extent can she know the Trinity? Is it simply a case of natural knowledge, in which a person is able to remember, understand and love God because this trinity of powers is at the core of her being? Grosseteste never fully addresses this question, but a possible answer can be drawn together. To begin with, Grosseteste always wants to affirm God's transcendence and this means that man has limits imposed upon him, since he cannot fully embrace God's nature in his mind. Yet this very reality is not to be shunned, but rather embraced as an incipient value in the relationship between God and man. Consider Grosseteste's unique – and somewhat radical – reading of the second commandment of the Decalogue:

> If we are not to take the Lord's name in vain, we ought to believe and understand God, as Augustine says, in the work *On the Trinity*, 'so far as we are able, as good but without quality, as great but not quantitatively, as the Creator without need; as present but not situated; as enfolding all without relatedness; as wholly everywhere but not in a place; as everlasting but outside of time; producing changeable things but without himself changing or being affected.'[119] We should think of Him as being, not this or that true being but the *true* being itself, not this or that good but the *good* being itself; we should think of Him as that than which nothing is higher, nothing better – as not merely the best which can be thought of but also better than what can be thought of. And so, if our faith and our understanding of God is thus, and if we love Him with love that corresponds to the faith thus expressed, then we will 'take his name' intending the truth which he is, and not intending the vanity which He is not.[120]

God is not the best of what we can think, but *beyond* the best of what can be thought of. Yet, even though God's nature exceeds our ability to articulate it, that very reality forms our understanding of God, at least in a cataphatic sense. It would seem that coming to terms with God's transcendence is the beginning of wisdom in this case. Grosseteste, however, thinks human beings can move on from there. The ultimate aim of humanity is to gain the fullness of beatitude, that is to gain a vision of God. Can a person do this on his or her own, especially in the present state of human experience?

In one sense, Grosseteste would answer in the affirmative. He clearly exploited his own natural reasoning to come to terms with the divine nature. The discipline of logic energised his treatise on free will, including the preliminary issues about God's knowledge. His experience with natural philosophy influenced the way he would speak of God's ubiquity and his intimate relationship with creation, not to mention how he articulated the doctrine of Trinity and God's infinite nature. And the doctrine of God is not the only place in which the power to reason and speculate would play a definitive role.

In another sense, Grosseteste would also have to answer negatively. The reason here is not the present sinful nature of humankind, however. It would seem that, even in the pre-lapsarian state, humanity was in need of God's aid in coming to know him. In speaking of a person as being made in the image of God – which he now defines as comprising reason and free will – he introduces three ways of considering that image:

> It can be considered in the substance of the natural good which it receives from its natural creation; and it can be considered according to the way that it is elevated above the good, its creation into deification through conversion to its enjoyment of the Creator, by which conversion it is restored and glorified in the spirit of the mind. It can also be considered as moving away from the supreme good to engaging inferior things, and thus has become deformed. Hence 'image' is understood in three ways: namely the natural image, the renewed image, and the deformed image. Thus, the natural images is never lost, but the renewed image is lost through sin; and the deformed is removed through the grace of the Holy Spirit.[121]

The image of God is the natural good of a person, but even in a pre-lapsarian state it must be transformed from a natural good into deification through a conversion. The implication here is that something external to human capabilities accomplishes this. That need for an outside power becomes even more pressing now that the image has been deformed by sin. While the original image of God is never lost in a human being (for how could one's natural good be lost when goodness and being are convertible?), nonetheless humanity now needs grace to be restored to a condition in which that renewal of the image can take place. This distinction between restoration and renewal is also found in Grosseteste's description of God's providential care of humanity, which is defined by his ability and desire (*cognicio et voluntas*) to perform six tasks: 'to take away the darkness of guilt and ignorance and the defects of penalties; to direct the [mind's] desire; to illuminate the [mind's] gaze; to sustain him (who has been directed and illuminated), to promote him upwards; and to confirm him (who has been promoted to consummation) in that same perpetuity)'.[122] Humanity's progress to God, while based on natural capabilities, is always in need of powers extrinsic to a person in order to know him.

Clearly, this is an unsatisfactory answer. There is hardly any question whether it would stand up to later scrutiny, or rather whether anyone would pay attention at all to such an answer. In part, the answer lacks completion because it remains to identify that extrinsic power. That identification is bound up with the following chapter, and so the full answer to the capability of humanity to know God lies in Grosseteste's Christology.

Notes

1. James McEvoy, 'Nature as Light in Eriugena and Grosseteste', in *Man and Nature in the Middle Ages*, ed. S.J. Ridyard and R.G. Benson, Sewanee Medieval Studies, 6 (Sewanee: Sewanee University of the South Press, 1995), pp. 37–61, is an excellent start.
2. *Tabula*, pp. 265–72.
3. *Epistolae*, n.1 (pp. 1–17). On the life and works of Adam, see *Biographical Register of the University of Oxford to AD 1500*, ed. A.B. Emden, 3 vols (Oxford: Clarendon Press, 1957–59), 1.660–61; Southern, *Grosseteste*, p. 123. The date of the letter was well-established by James McEvoy, 'Der Brief des Robert Grosseteste an Magister Adam Rufus (Adam von Oxford, O.F.M.): ein Datierungsversuch', *Franziskanische Studien* 63 (1981), 221–6.
4. The two answers were later copied out as two separate treatises: *De unica forma omnium* and *De intelligenciis*, both edited by Baur, pp. 106–19; Thomson, *Writings*, p. 99.
5. John Scottus Eriugena, *De divisione naturae*, ed. E. Jeauneau, 4 vols, CCCM 161–4 (Turnhout: Brepols, 1996), 358 (versions 1–2).
6. McEvoy, 'Nature as Light in Eriugena and Grosseteste', pp. 49–52.
7. McEvoy argues that the letter supports the notion that Grosseteste was an established theologian, from whom Adam sought an opinion. But, if Grosseteste were not a master of the sacred page at the time, it helps to explain why he calls himself a 'so-called master' (*dictus magister*), perhaps a recognition that his current magisterial status did not really give him the right to entertain such questions publicly. At any rate, Grosseteste's reply puts him in good company, as Alexander of Hales had directly addressed the question as to how orthodox theologians could employ the phrase *omnia esse Deum*, without wandering into heresy: Alexander of Hales, *Glossa in quatuor libros Sententiarum Petri Lombardi*, ed. PP. Collegii S. Bonaventurae, 4 vols, Bibliotheca Franciscana Scholastica Medii Aevi, 12–15 (Quaracchi: College of St Bonaventure, 1951–57), 23. It is interesting that Alexander makes no reference to Eriugena's text either, and instead opens up the question with a citation from c.34 of Anselm's *Monologion*.
8. Southern, *Grosseteste*, pp. 33–4.
9. *Epistolae*, n.1 (p. 3): 'Ex ratione quoque formae argui potest, Deum formam esse . . .' The plays on words in the following argument are sometimes difficult to render into English. I have taken my cue from the forthcoming translation of Grosseteste's *Epistolae* by F.A.C. Mantello and Joseph Goering.
10. Although Grosseteste's method differs a great deal from William of Auxerre's, nonetheless they proceed along the same lines and come to nearly the same conclusions: William of Auxerre, *Summa aurea*, ed. J. Riballier, 4 vols, Spicilegium Bonaventurianum, 16–20 (Rome: College of St Bonaventure, 1980–1987), 1, tr.14 (1.260–269).
11. *Epistolae*, n.1 (p. 3). Cf. *Hex*, 8.1.2 (pp. 217–18).
12. Augustine, *De trinitate libri XV*, ed. W.J. Mountain, 2 vols, CCL 50–50A (Turnhout: Brepols, 1968), 8.2 (1.271).
13. For a summary of this history, see Gyula Kilma, 'The Medieval Problem of Universals', in *The Stanford Encyclopedia of Philosophy* (Winter 2001 Edition), ed. E.N. Zalta, accessed on 15 May 2003, <http://plato.stanford.edu/entries/universals-medieval/ >. See also *Five Texts on the Mediaeval Problem of Universals: Porphyry, Boethius, Abelard, Duns Scotus, Ockham*, trans. P.V. Spade (Indianapolis: Hackett, 1994); and John Marenbon, *From the Circle of Alcuin to the School of Auxerre: Logic, Theology, and Philosophy in the Early Middle Ages* (Cambridge: Cambridge University Press, 1981), esp. pp. 5–7, 12–29.

14 Grosseteste had done so in an earlier work, where incidentally he considered it a rather difficult issue to explain what the first form was exactly: *De statu causarum*, ed. Baur, pp. 120–26, esp. 125.
15 *Epistolae*, n.1, (p. 5): 'Ipsa enim simul et exemplar est, et efficiens est, et formans est, et in forma data conservans est, dum ad ipsam applicantur et revocantur creaturae.'
16 The medieval doctrine of Angels is an undeveloped area in modern scholarship, but see David Keck, *Angels and Angelology in the Middle Ages* (Oxford: Oxford University Press, 1998), whose title promises more than it delivers as Keck focuses primarily on the angelology of Bonaventure. For a broader account of the doctrine of angels in early scholastic thought, see Marcia Colish, 'Early Scholastic Angelology', *Recherche de théologe ancienne et médiévale* 62 (1995), 80–109. Also of great use is R. James Long, 'Of Angels and Pinhead: The Contribution of early Oxford Masters to the Doctrine of Spiritual Matter', *Franciscan Studies*, 56 (1998), 239–54.
17 *Epistolae*, 1, pp. 12–13; McEvoy, *Philosophy*, pp. 52–5.
18 *Summa aurea*, 1.tr.14.c.3 (1.271-3); Alexander of Hales, *Glossa*, 1.37.36 (pp. 377–87).
19 Neil Lewis, 'The First Recension of Robert Grosseteste's *De Libero arbitrio*', *Mediaeval Studies* 53 (1991), 1–88, 1.3 (p. 33). The problem is not so clearly posed in the second recension. As Lewis notes, Baur's edition is unreliable. I have used Lewis's working edition of chapters 1–8 of the second recension: Neil Lewis, 'Time and Modality in Robert Grosseteste', unpubl. PhD diss. (University of Pittsburgh, 1988), pp. 305–76. I have also consulted his translation of the same text on pp. 391–424. For the sake of clarity, I shall refer to these two texts as *Rec. 1* and *Rec. 2* respectively.
20 For a good summary of this text, see Lewis's introduction: *Rec. 1*, pp. 4–12.
21 Avicenna, *Liber De philosophia prima sive Scientia divina*, ed. S. van Reit, Avicenna Latina, 1–2 (Louvain: Peeters, 1977–83), 8.6 (2.419).
22 *Rec. 1*, 2.1–8 (pp. 33–6); *Rec. 2*, 2.1–8 (pp. 307–12).
23 Lewis, in his edition of the first recension, points to the similarity between Grosseteste's arguments and those of Alexander of Hales on a number of occasions.
24 *Rec. 1*, 2.10–16 (pp. 36–8).
25 *Rec 2*, 2.11, 2.15 (pp. 313, 314).
26 See James McEvoy, 'Robert Grosseteste's Use of the Argument of Saint Anselm', in *Robert Grosseteste: New Perspectives on his Thought and Scholarship*, ed. J. McEvoy, Instrumenta Patristica, 18 (Steenbrugge: Kluwer, 1994), pp. 257–75.
27 *Rec. 1*, 5.1 (p. 44); *Rec. 2*, 4.1 (pp. 320–21).
28 *De scientia Dei*, ed. Baur, pp. 145–7.
29 McEvoy, 'Grosseteste's Use of St Anselm's Argument', pp. 264–71. See below, p. 171.
30 *Rec. 1*, 3–6 (pp. 38–47).
31 Lewis, 'Time and Modality', pp. 129–63. See also Calvin Normore, 'Future Contingents', in the *Cambridge History of Later Medieval Philosophy*, ed. N. Kretzmann, A. Kenny, J. Pinborg and E. Stump (Cambridge: Cambridge University Press, 1982), pp. 358–81, at 364–6.
32 This is a different tactic from Peter Raedts, *Richard Rufus of Cornwall and the Tradition of Oxford Theology* (Oxford: Oxford University Press, 1987), pp. 203–7, who passes quickly over the parts of the treatise dealing with God's knowledge, in order to focus on Grosseteste's arguments about human free will. On the coherence of Grosseteste's compatibilism, see Lewis, 'Time and Modality', pp. 280–84.
33 Grosseteste is not the first to introduce this distinction: See Lewis's edition of the first recension: *Rec. 1*, p. 48.

34 *Rec. 2*, 7.1–9 (pp. 337–40).
35 Ibid., 8.3 (pp. 341–2).
36 Ibid., 7.5–9 (pp. 339–40).
37 Ibid., 8.4–5 (pp. 342–3).
38 Ibid., 8.6–7 (pp. 343–4).
39 *De veritate*, ed. Baur, p. 134.
40 *De veritate*, ed. Baur, p. 130. The definition comes from Avicenna's *Metaphysics* 1.8 (cited in Stephen Marrone, *The Light of Thy Countenance: Science and Knowledge of God in the Thirteenth Century*, Studies in the History of Christian Thought, 2 vols [Leiden: Brill, 2000], 1.40, n.7), and became a basic feature of later discussions of the correspondence theory of truth: see Marian David, 'Truth, Correspondence Theory of' in *Stanford Encyclopedia of Philosophy*, ed. E.N. Zalta, <http://plato.stanford.edu/entries/truth-correspondence/>.
41 *De veritate*, ed. Baur, p. 134.
42 *Rec. 2*, 8.11 (pp. 345–6).
43 Ibid., 8.14 (p. 347).
44 See below, Chapter 6, pp. 128–37.
45 For Grosseteste's understanding of infinity as a predicate, see below, pp. 106–9.
46 For Augustine's 'position', see *De Trinitate*, ed. Mountain, 13.10.13 (2.399), which is in fact a short parenthetical statement rather than a full-blown argument. Anselm's position was far more developed in *Cur Deus Homo*, which is to some degree an extension of the real thrust of the cited section of Augustine's *De trinitate*.
47 *Rec. 2*, 8.12 (p. 346).
48 The most recent work is Lawrence Moonan, *Divine Power: The Medieval Power Distinction up to its Adoption by Albert, Bonaventure and Aquinas* (Oxford: Clarendon Press, 1994). While Moonan provides an excellent philosophical account of the 'Power Distinction', the work suffers on occasion from too much attention being given to modern philosophical problems, as well as some ahistorical assertions. See also William J. Courtenay, *Capacity and Volition: A History of the Distinction of Absolute and Ordained Power* (Bergamo: Lubrina, 1990).
49 Moonan, *Divine Power*, pp. 16–48, resists using the English cognates to designate the two arms of this distinction. He calls *potentia absoluta* 'option-neutral power', and *potentia ordinata* 'option-tied power'. His reasoning is a good monitum for those who would read post-medieval nuances into terms like 'absolute power' and 'ordained power'. His taxonomy also allows him to engage in a freer dialogue with contemporary philosophers. However, it is possible to engage this material using the cognates (and Courtenay has done this very well), and it would seem to be far less ahistorical to use the cognates than to employ concepts drawn from modern analytical philosophy. However, this is only a minor distraction from what is otherwise Moonan's excellent account of the early history of this distinction. See the review by Francis Oakley, in *Speculum* 71 (1996), 987–8.
50 Moonan, *Divine Power*, pp. 57–147. Philip the Chancellor appears to have been the only Parisian theologian who did not fully grasp the Power Distinction, and who also did not rise above the initial incarnational context (76–86).
51 These topics are addressed in chapters 10 and 11 in the first recension: *Rec. 1*, pp. 62–7, and chapter 9 and 10 in the second: *De libero arbitrio* (*Rec. 2*), ed. Baur, pp. 196–203.
52 See *De libero arbitrio* (*Rec. 2*), ed. Baur, c.22 (pp. 206–10).
53 *Hex*, 8.7.2–8.8.3 (pp. 229–31); 8.10.1 (p. 232).

54 *De spiritu et anima*, c.6 (PL 42.783). See also, Richard of St-Victor, *De trinitate*, ed. J. Ribailler, Textes philosophiques du Moyen Age, 6 (Paris: Vrin, 1958), 3.7 (p. 141). It must be noted, however, that there is no evidence that Grosseteste consulted Richard's innovative work.
55 *Hex*, 8.1.1 (p. 217): 'Non enim potest creatura factori suo comparari, nec cum eo in aliquo univocari; potest tamen per modum aliquem imitari.' See also *Hex*, 8.9.2 (p. 231).
56 See Richard C. Dales, 'A Medieval View of Human Dignity', *Journal of the History of Ideas* 38 (1977), 557–72, at 569–71.
57 *Hex*, 8.1.2 (pp. 217–18).
58 But see below, last section of this chapter.
59 See above, Chapter 4, pp. 53–72.
60 Alexander of Hales, *Glossa*, 1.2.6 (1.29), 1.3.1 (1.37).
61 *Hex*, 8.2.1–5 (pp. 218–19).
62 The most recent account of Grosseteste's 'light-metaphysics' is Servus Gieben, 'Grosseteste and Universal Science', in *Robert Grosseteste and the Beginnings of a British Theological Tradition*, ed. M. O'Carroll (Rome: Istituto dei Cappuccini, 2003), pp. 219–38.
63 Alexander of Hales, *Glossa*, 1.1.18 (1.16).
64 *Summ aurea*, 1.3.4 (1.34): 'Ad dicendum est quod, cum Deus habitet lucem inacessibilem, opportet humanum intellectuam foveri et pugari in speculo creaturarum, ut per eas veniat <ad> cognitionem creatoris.'
65 Richard of St-Victor, *De Trinitate*, ed. Ribaillier, 1.9 (p. 94).
66 William of Auvergne, *De Trinitate*, ed. B. Switalski, Studies and Texts, 34 (Toronto: PIMS, 1976), 14–15 (pp. 82–98, esp. 96–8).
67 See *De operationibus solis*, ed. J. McEvoy, 'The Sun as *res* and *signum*: Grosseteste's Commentary on Ecclesiasticus ch. 43, vv.1–5', *Recherches de théologie ancienne et médiévale* 41 (1974), 38–91; par. 29 (pp. 86–7).
68 See R.P.C. Hanson, *The Search for the Christian Doctrine of God: the Arian controversy 318–381* (Edinburgh: T&T Clark, 1988).
69 See Richard of St-Victor, *De Trinitate*, ed. Ribaillier, 4.7 (pp. 169–70); Alexander of Hales, *Glossa*, 1.2.9 (1.31).
70 Lateran IV Council, in *The Decrees of the Ecumenical Councils*, ed. N. Tanner, 2 vols (London: Sheed and Ward, 1990), can.2 (1. 231–3). See Edmund J. Fortman, *The Triune God. A Historical Study of the Doctrine of the Trinity* (Philadelphia: Westminster Press, 1972), pp. 200–201.
71 *Hex*, 8.3.1 (p. 220, line 13), reading *genitus* for *gignens*, which as C.F.J. Martin observes must be a slip of the pen: Robert Grosseteste, *On the Six Days of Creation*, trans. C.F.J. Martin, Auctres Britannici Medii Aevi, 6(2) (London: British Academy, 1996), p. 224n.
72 That is, in the way a description of individual humans uses accidental difference between Peter and Paul (that is, one has hair, the other is bald) to identify them as persons.
73 *Hex*, 8.3.1 (p. 220).
74 Ibid.
75 Edmund Hill, in the most recent translation of Augustine's *De trinitate*, asserts that scholastic theologians – save for Thomas – completely misunderstood Augustine: *The Trinity*, trans. E. Hill (New York: New City Press, 2002), p. 25. Augustine, Hill argues, never referred to memory, understanding and will as faculties of the soul but rather as actions of the *mens*, which Hill renders as the 'inner self'. The root of this misunderstanding can be traced to Peter Lombard, *Sententiae*, 1.3.2, or so Hill insists. However, Lombard

never introduces the concept of faculty in this part of his *Sentences*, nor does he equate *mens* with *anima* – but he does invoke *animus* as a synonym of *mens*. Hill's ultimate complaint is that, by focusing on the psychological dimensions of the trinitarian image in humankind, the scholastics robbed it of any spirituality. This may be true for a neoscholastic context, but for the medieval period the construction of philosophical psychology did not necessarily muffle the spiritual dimensions of the *imago Dei* doctrine.

76 Augustine, *De trinitate*, ed. Mountain, 15.22–3 (2.520–521); but see his *Sermo* 52.10.23 (PL 38.364).
77 *Hex*, 8.3.2 (p. 220).
78 Isa 66.9: 'Numquid ego qui alios parere facio ipse non pariam dicit Dominus? Si ego qui generationem ceteris tribuo sterilis ero? ait Dominus Deus tuus.'
79 *Hex*, 8.3.3 (p. 221). This is the thrust of the remains of the disputed questions, *De ordine emanandi causatorum a Deo*, ed. Baur, pp. 147–50. See also William of Auvergne, *De Trinitate*, ed. Switalski, c.29 (pp. 166–70).
80 *DCL*, 3.1.3 (p. 120); *Hex*, 8.3.5 (p. 221). There is some resonance here with Philip the Chancellor's definition of the good, but Grosseteste aims to extend the definition in order to explain how God is the supreme good. See Philip the Chancellor, *Summa de bono*, ed. N. Wicki, 2 vols (Berne: Franke, 1985), q.1 (1.7–8).
81 McEvoy, 'Nature as Light', pp. 44–5.
82 The number three is not considered mathematically to be the first perfect number, so Grosseteste must have had in mind more a numerological explanation than a mathematical one.
83 *Hex*, 8.3.5 (p. 222).
84 See also *DCL*, 3.1.3 (p. 120).
85 See above, Chapter 4, pp. 61–3.
86 These three examples are also found at the beginning of *Dictum* 60, but in a different order: *Dictum* 60, ed. Gieben, p. 153.
87 McEvoy, *Philosophy*, p. 178. The same is said of Augustine: *The Trinity*, trans. Hill, 11.4.18 (p. 318n).
88 Augustine, *De Genesi ad litteram*, 4.3.7 (PL 34.299): 'Neque enim Deus mensura est, aut numerus, aut pondus, aut ista omnia. An secundum id quod novimus mensuram in eis quae metimur, et numerum in eis quae numeramus, et pondus in eis quae appendimus, non est Deus ista: secundum id vero quod mensura omni rei modum praefigit, et numerus omni rei speciem praebet, et pondus omnem rem ad quietem ac stabilitatem trahit, ille primitus et veraciter et singulariter ista est, qui terminat omnia et format omnia, et ordinat omnia; nihilque aliud dictum intelligitur, quomodo per cor et linguam humanam potuit, *Omnia in mensura, et numero, et pondere disposuisti*, nisi, Omnia in te disposuisti?' See also William of Auxerre, *Summa aurea*, ed. Riballier, 1.tr.8.c.8.q.4 (p. 173); Alexander of Hales, *Glossa*, 1.3.29 (pp. 50–51), where these two vestiges are part of a list of nine.
89 Avicebron, *Fons vitae*, ed. C. Beumker, Beiträge zur Geschichte der Philosophie des Mittelalters, 1, Heft 2–4 (Munster: Aschendorff, 1892–95), 5.32–4 (pp. 316–20). William of Auvergne also refers to matter and form and their composite as a trinitarian vestige. However, the configuration of his argument differs somewhat from Grosseteste's: William of Auvergne, *De trinitate*, ed. Switalski, c.25 (pp. 132–41).
90 *De luce*, ed Baur, p. 58.
91 *Hex*, 8.4.6 (p. 223).
92 See the summaries in Gieben, 'Traces of God in Nature', pp. 149–51; Southern, *Grosseteste*, pp. 216–17. See also the summary by Grosseteste, *Super Psalterium*, 88.6 (B 94ra): 'Nichil enim in creaturis tam paruum, quod oculo pure intelligencie, non sunt

manifestum continere in se infinitam pulcritudinem et sapienciam et ineffabiliem vtilitatem. In atomo enim quo nichil est vilius est infinita pulcritudo et sapiencia figurarum geometricalium et numerorum, nec est aliquod horum sine vtilitate a sapientissimo et optimo creatum. Celis itaque, hoc est defecatis mentibus, a terranis sordibus sunt omnia opera Dei mira.'

93 In addition to *Dictum* 60, see also *Super Psalterium*, 77.12 (*B* 47ra): 'Omnes species creaturarum mirabilia sunt coram illis et qui ex hiis speciebus intelligunt admirandam <esse> Dei potentiam, sapientiam et bonitatem; ex hiis relatis ad Domini Trinitatem reportant timorem, veritatem and dileccionem.'
94 *Dictum* 60, ed. Gieben, p. 154: 'utpote atomus qualis volitat in sole'. Grosseteste is not making any philosophical statement about atomic particles in the modern sense.
95 Ibid.
96 Ibid., pp. 154–5.
97 On the relationship between goodness and utility, see *Dictum* 19, ed. Ginther, 8 (pp. 127–8); and *DCL*, 3.1.14 (p. 120).
98 *Dictum* 60, ed. Gieben, p. 155.
99 *Super Psalterium*, 77.11 (*B* 49ra): '*Et obliti sunt benefactorum eius*, etc. Benefacta Dei quibus benefecit homini sunt omnes creature inquantum propter hominem facte. Agnoscit itaque beneficium Dei inquantum agnoscit creaturam propter se factam, et tamen gratias agit. Oblitus est benefacti qui et si agnoscat rem in sua natura, tamen non agnoscit eam inquantum pro se facta, inde gratias agunt. Mirabilia Dei sunt omnia inquantum ostendunt Deum mirabilem. Oblitus est mirabilium qui ex creatura non assurgit in admirandam Dei potentiam, sapientiam et benignitatem qui, inquam, non assurgit ex hiis in nomen Domini quod est mirabile. Habet itaque omnis res triplicem considerationem: unam absolute; alteram in relacione quam habet ad hominem in qua leuior fit ad benefaciendum pro hiis qui in Deum confidunt; terciam ad Deum quem innuit et insinuat omnis creature vocibus euidentie sue pulcritudinis et ordinis.'
100 See above, note 79.
101 Dictum 33, quoted in chapter 3, n. 32. Cf. *Summa area*, 3. tr.12. c.8. q.1 (3, 1. 234–7).
102 McEvoy, *Philosophy*, p. 214.
103 Leo Sweeney, *Divine Infinity in Greek and Medieval Thought* (New York: Peter Lang, 1992), is a good survey of the history of this doctrine; but see also Robert M. Burns, 'Divine Infinity in Thomas Aquinas: I. Philosophico-Theological Background', *Heythrop Journal* 39 (1998), 57–69. I was unable to incorporate into this chapter the recent work of Antoine Coté, *L'infinité dans la théologie médiévale, 1220–1255*, Etudes de Philosophie Médiévale, 84 (Paris: Vrin, 2002).
104 H.F. Dondaine, 'L'objet et le *medium* de la vision béatifique chez les théologiens du XIIIe siècle', *Recherches de théologie ancienne et médiévale* 19 (1952), 60–130; McEvoy, *Philosophy*, pp. 241–6.
105 Sweeney, *Divine Infinity*, pp. 319–36. See, for example, Bonaventure, *Quaestiones disputatae de mysterio SS. Trinitatis*, in *Opera Omnia*, ed. PP. Collegii S. Bonaventurae, 8 vols (Quaracchi: College of St Bonaventure, 1882–1902), q.4.1 (5.79–84); and Thomas Aquinas, *ST*, 1.7.
106 Sweeney, *Divine Infinity*, pp. 385–411, which was originally published as an article in *The Modern Schoolman* 35 (1958), 191–212.
107 See, for example, Sermon 34, ed. Paul, 11 (2.249).
108 Sermon 75, ed. Paul, 14 (2.394)
109 *Super Psalterium*, 83.1 (B 75ra–rb): '*Quam dilecta tabernacula tua, Dominum uirtutum. Concupiscit et deficit anima mea in atria Domini*. Quam dilecta a quo uel a quibus a te

Deus pater et a se inuicem. Sic enim a te dilecta sunt quod filio tuo unigenito non pepercisti. Set pro hiis tabernaculis illum tradidisti a seipsis quoque adinuicem dilecta pari amore quo sese diligunt, set numquid Deus diligit hec tabernacula infinito amore? Quod videtur quia nos illum infinito amore diligimus. Modus enim amandi Deum est ut sit amor sine modo sicut dicit Beatus Bernardus cuius dicti racionem subiungit dicens, 'Denique cum delectio que tenditur in Deum tendat in infinitum, tendat in inmenusm. Infinitus namque Deus est et immensus. Si igitur nos diligimus Deum amore infinito, constat autem quod ipse nos diligit maiori amore quam nos diligimus ipsum. Communis est ut ipse nos diligat amore infinito.' Set numquid proximus a proximo diligatur amore infinito? Quod iterum uidetur quia diligimus inuicem amore invincibili, quod autem inuincible est quando finitum est. Item, amor, quo diligitur a nobis creatura irracionalis in infinitum multiplicatus, non adequaret amorem quo diligimus proximos. Sequitur igitur quod amor in proximum infinitus est nisi amor quo diligit irracionalis creatura sit non proporcionalis amori quo proximus diligitur . Utrum autem finito aut infinito amore diligatur proximus a proximo congrue queritur quam dilecta cum sic diligatur proximus a proximo sicud ipse a se cum diligat immutabiliter, cum sic diligatur quod pro vita eius spirituali paratus sit qui diligit exponere morti vitam carnalem.' See also Sermon 43, ed. Paul, 23–4 (2.298).

110 The best analysis of *De luce* remains McEvoy, *Philosophy*, pp. 151–62; but see also Lucia Miccoli, 'Two Thirteenth-century Theories of Light: Robert Grosseteste and St. Bonaventure', *Semiotica*, 136.1 (2001), 69–84, esp. 73–7; and Cecilia Panti, 'L'Incorporazione della Luce secondo Roberto Grossetesta', *Medioevo e Rinascimento* 13 (1999), 45–102.

111 *De luce*, ed. Baur, pp. 51–9, at 52: 'seipsam per seipsam undique infinities multiplicans et in omnem partem aequaliter porrigens, materiam, quam relinquere non potuit, secum distrahens in tantam molem, quanta est mundi machina, in principio temporis extendebat'.

112 Ibid.; McEvoy, *Philosophy*, pp. 152–3. See especially n.12, where he presents the modern mathematical notations for Grosseteste's theory – although he is quick to point out that the mathematical argument does not stand up to modern set theory.

113 *DCL*, 1.4.1 (p. 17).

114 That is, if this relationship between love and knowledge is considered finitely, one would have to break it down into a set of infinite singulars, which would threaten its coherence. It is almost as if Grosseteste considers infinity in terms equivalent to modern set theory.

115 *DCL*, 1.4.4 (pp. 18–19)

116 But see McEvoy, *Philosophy*, pp. 246–56.

117 This position was condemned in 1241 by the faculty of theology as a whole, but its proponents were never named: Sweeney, *Divine Infinity*, 337–63; but see the corrective of Antoine Coté, 'Note sur Guerric de Saint-Quentin et la question de l'infini divin', *Recherches de théologie ancienne et médiévale* 62 (1995), 71–9.

118 On the notion of 'theological spirituality', see Walter H. Principe, 'Toward Defining Spirituality', *Studies in Religion/Sciences Religieuses* 12 (1983), 127–41, esp. 135–7. See below, Chapter 7, pp. 165–72.

119 Augustine, *De trinitate*, ed. Mountain, 5.1.1 (1. 207).

120 *DCL*, 2.5 (p. 24); the translation is from McEvoy, 'Robert Grosseteste's Use of the Argument of Saint Anselm', p. 266.

121 *Hex*, 8.6.1 (p. 227).

122 *Dictum* 8 (fol. 8va): 'Respectus Dei est eius cognicio et voluntas tollendi tenebras culpe et ignorancie et defectiones penalitatum, et dirigendi affectum, et illuminandi aspectum, directumque et illuminatum ne relabatur suscipiendi, superiusque promovendi, provectumque ad consummacionem in eadem perpetuo confirmandi.'

Chapter 6

The Necessity of the Incarnation

With this chapter, we come to the heart of Grosseteste's theological vision. While the (modified) 'whole-Christ' motif as the subject matter of theology embraced a number of essential theological topics, its very reason of existence as a subject was grounded in the historical event of the Incarnation. As I have noted, this orientation produces a tension between the subject as a universal principle (as a subject of a science was supposed to be) and the singular, contingent acts within human history.[1] Grosseteste does not consider this tension to be of any major concern (and in fact he makes no mention of it), but it is significant to note that his Christological writings attempt to present the universal and the particular as working in tandem. It is in fact the very person of Christ in which these two opposites come together, for the Incarnation has both a soteriological and cosmic role to play in his theology. Recent scholarship has carefully presented the cosmic aspect of Grosseteste's Christology under the rubric of the 'absolute predestination of Christ'.[2] My aim here is to complete the account of Grosseteste's Christology, and to explain how Christ's saving work aligns with his cosmic role.

Grosseteste's *Tabula* reveals a general awareness of the scholastic teaching on Christ. Under the rubric of *De verbo* he lists thirteen topics: the Incarnation; the hypostatic union (*de homine assumpto*); Christ's knowledge; the relationship between Christ and the Church; his merit, weakness and passion; the cross; Christ's resurrection and ascension; the mission of the Holy Spirit; the Virgin Mary; and Christ's soul.[3] Most of these same topics are also addressed by William of Auxerre in book 3 of his *Summa aurea*, save for the mission of the Holy Spirit (which is examined elsewhere) and the Virgin Mary – and the same can be said for Alexander of Hales, although in his case they are treated more diffusely as his analysis is ordered by book 3 of Lombard's *Sentences*.[4] Once again, however, Grosseteste did not slavishly follow his *Tabula* when he came to put his arguments on parchment. In fact, the *De cessatione legalium*, the main text where he divulges his Christological teaching, addresses very few of the topics from the *Tabula*, and then adds some new ones.

This treatise does not yield up its secrets so easily, and there has been some confusion in the past as to why Grosseteste wrote it. Prior to the appearance of the critical edition, some scholars had suggested that Grosseteste wrote the *De cessatione legalium* as a means of attacking the beliefs of the Jews who were living in England.[5] This interpretation assumed that the *De cessatione legalium* had a polemical function and could be linked to the conversion programme instituted by Henry III in England. While the king did institute a *domus conversorum* in Oxford for converted Jews, there is no evidence that Grosseteste had a hand in any of this. That said, the *De cessatione legalium* can be considered in one respect to be anti-judaic (but not anti-Semitic), since there is an implicit theological critique of the Jewish interpretation of their own Scriptures.[6] It is implicit because Grosseteste does not aim his comments at any specific Jewish commentator, nor even at a general class of Jewish exegetes.[7] In fact, the only opponents he names come from the early Church, such as the Manichees, the Marcionites and the Ebionites – and only the last ones were advocates of observing the Law.[8] It would be more accurate to state that there are no real opponents in the *De cessatione legalium*, and so the Jews were not the focus of the problem which Grosseteste raises.[9] Instead, Grosseteste is concerned with the theological assessment of the Mosaic Law from a Christian perspective. He opens the treatise with comments about the divergent opinions concerning the Law which had emerged in the early Church. Although apostolic decree had put an end to observance of the Law as a requirement for Christians, the arguments that supported the idea of continued observance just might be detrimental to the faith in the minds of weak Christians (*in mentibus infirmorum*). Grosseteste's modest contribution, so he says, is to rehearse these arguments and demonstrate their deficiency and confirm that the grace of Christ has voided (*evacuatam*) the Law.[10]

This 'prologue' is one instance in which we must take Grosseteste's words with a grain of salt. It is not that Grosseteste does not take the issue head on, for the first part of the treatise is a complex engagement about the temporal nature of the Law and its efficacy in terms of certain Christian principles. However, Grosseteste is not rehearsing old arguments about the efficacy of the Law. He had already done this in his commentary on Galatians. Here he has a different intention.[11] He broaches another issue and it emerges in the first objection to the Law's cessation: continuity. How can one logically claim that the Mosaic Law must cease, Grosseteste asks, if two of its central tenets – the keeping of the Sabbath and Circumcision – were commanded by God himself to be kept in perpetuity? What is lurking behind this question is the immutability of God's will, for if God had always desired that human salvation be accomplished by the passion of Christ, why then would he have made an eternal pact (*fedus eternum*) with the Jews?[12] It is one thing to assert that the Law was the teacher of humanity in which the futility of human action is demonstrated. It is an altogether different challenge to address how one fits together Christianity's claim over the Old Testament and the very claims found there. Grosseteste's final answer is not surprising, for he concludes that the Law itself was given in anticipation of Christ's advent. That answer allows Grosseteste to advance two theological principles. First, Christians are not bending the Old Testament to conform to New Testament principles, but rather the Christian message is embedded literally – not spiritually – in the Jewish Scriptures. Moreover, the continuity of message between the two Testaments is part of a larger narrative, in which the Incarnation has an essential role. The theme of continuity allows Grosseteste to address both the soteriological and the cosmic significance of the Incarnation.

Grosseteste's *Cur Deus Homo*

Grosseteste's Method

In presenting the reasons for the Incarnation, Grosseteste begins with exegesis and then moves on to natural reason in order to enlarge his teaching. This oscillation between reason and Scripture occurs throughout the work. In part one, he had begun with an examination of the reasons why the Law must cease at Christ's advent, and then moved to a more Scriptural account for the same topic.[13] The first text he draws upon at that point is from Deuteronomy 18:15, which declared: 'The Lord will raise up for you a prophet from your own people, [and] you will hear him as if [you were hearing] me' (*Prophetam suscitabit vobis Dominus de fratibus eius, ipsum tanquam me audietis*).[14] Now Grosseteste returns in part two to this same passage. He states that this verse can only have a vigorous testimony of Christ if one can demonstrate that he is the promised one from the authority of the Law and the Prophets themselves. In other words, the cessation of the Law and its true trajectory – Jesus Christ – are intimately linked. Moreover, to make this an effective demonstration from authority, Grosseteste states that he will avoid using spiritual exegesis. He considers it possible to make a case for the need of the Incarnation by engaging in a literal interpretation of the Law and the Prophets.[15]

The contrast between Grosseteste and someone like Saint Anselm could not be any clearer. What Anselm proves in *Cur Deus Homo* by reason alone, Grosseteste does by expounding the sacred text. In Anselm's case, the quasi-apologetic nature of the topic almost prohibits any direct recourse to the Christian tradition.[16] Boso, Anselm's interlocutor, reports that some 'unbelievers' (who probably were Jewish intellectuals living in England) had challenged Christians to explain (1) how it is fitting and honourable for the divine to be made flesh and experience all the oppressive realities of human life; and (2) how the Christian account of salvation does not render God less than omnipotent, for it seems that he cannot simply will to forgive humankind.[17] Anselm's initial response to the first problem illustrates the need for a *remoto Christo* condition – that is to assume that the Incarnation had not taken place – for he states that Christians should actually thank God for the willingness to save humanity in this way, and if unbelievers would 'diligently consider how appropriate that the restoration of humanity has been procured in this way, they would not make fun of our simplicity, but they would along with us praise the wise goodness of God'.[18] Boso responds that, aside from the pious truth of Anselm's explanation, it is hardly an argument. Instead, one needs to establish the firm foundation of reason for the Incarnation, before one can speak of its fittingness. Anselm clearly agrees and he eventually lays out four conditions under which the argument will proceed, and the first is to assume that the Incarnation had never taken place.[19] Instead of adopting a *remoto Christo* condition for his argument, Grosseteste assumes an almost *ante Christum* one in that he wishes to focus solely on the literal exposition of the sacred authority that pre-dated the Incarnation. In this way he aims to demonstrate the necessity and fittingness of the Incarnation as expressly present in the Jewish Scriptures. For the most part he remains true to this condition, except in his explanation of the fourth song of the suffering servant of Isaiah. There the text bleeds with references to the Gospel as he connects the description of the suffering servant to the passion of Christ. The difference in method cannot be used to demonstrate that Grosseteste once again failed to embrace the scholastic project, for he makes use of natural reason to substantiate further his teaching on the Incarnation in the third part of the *De cessatione legalium*. Moreover, Grosseteste's intention differs from Anselm's as he seeks to strengthen the shared faith of his readers.[20]

The Necessity of the Incarnation: Five Themes

The first theme in Grosseteste's presentation of the necessity of the Incarnation is a promised blessing.[21] God had said to Abraham that all nations would be blessed in him (Gen. 12:3) and that this blessing would come about because of the seed of Abraham (Gen. 18:17–18). Grosseteste establishes a number of premises from this biblical assertion, in order to draw the first conclusion about the necessity of the Incarnation. The first premise is that this promise was obviously not fulfilled in Abraham, since God promised that the blessing of all nations would be in the seed of Abraham. Secondly, God speaks of the blessing in one offspring (*in semine*) and not in many (*in seminibus*), so there will be one person who will bring the blessing of God.[22] Thirdly, the scope of the blessing is larger than any of the other blessings given in Scripture and so this will require one man of great virtue.[23] Finally, Grosseteste provides a definition of the blessing: 'Someone is not blessed unless he is part of that which is liberated from punishment and is preordained to eternal glory, otherwise he is under a curse.' But God is the only one who can liberate someone from guilt and can preordain anyone to eternal glory. All these premises then come to form the conclusion that this one offspring of Abraham through whom all nations will be blessed must be the God-man.[24]

As logical as this deduction may be, an objection can be raised. One could argue that we do not receive the blessing from Abraham's offspring himself, but rather from God on account of the merit or love of that man. In other words, one can consider the seed of Abraham to be an instrumental cause of salvation, which then does not require him to be the God-man. Grosseteste solves this by drawing upon the physical properties of light. One can speak of the air being illuminated and that this light comes from the sun since the sun illuminates the air. Now if the light of the sun in a mirror is reflected back into the air, one does not say that that air is the light in the mirror, but rather the light still comes from the sun. In other words, the medium that contains light is not an instrumental cause per se, since the true cause of illumination can only be light itself and not any medium.[25] The same is true of God illuminating a person through grace, for he is the only one who can accomplish this. Hence, if the promised offspring is the one who will bless – liberating people from punishment and preordaining them to eternal glory – then he himself must be God.[26]

Even though he thinks this light analogy completes a compelling argument that this promised offspring of Abraham has to be a God-man, Grosseteste moves to his second theme, Christ as the *optimus hominum*. He assumes that, even if one can deny (although impudently) that this promised one is not divine, but would still affirm that in him all nations will be blessed and all would agree with what that blessing would be. To uphold these two principles, Grossetest argues, means acknowledging as well that this promised man must be the very best of humanity (*optimus hominum*) and the most acceptable to God.[27] He then turns to a number of scriptural passages that describe this man, and in each case the sacred text connects the promised one, the best of humanity, to the God-man. Two examples will suffice to demonstrate Grosseteste's strategy here. The first is from Psalm 71:2, which begins 'God, give your judgement to the king, and your justice to the son of the King' (*Deus, iudicium tuum regi da, et iusticiam tuam filio regis*).[28] What has attracted Grosseteste's attention is that this Psalmist (71:2, 17) goes on to describe the son of the king as the one in whom 'all tribes of the earth will be blessed', and that 'his name remains before the sun' (*ante solem permanet nomen eius*). This rather awkward phrase refers not to a point of initiation but to eternity. This also means that one cannot predicate this verse of angels, for although they were certainly created before the sun in terms of the priority of nature (which means that they are of a greater dignity than the sun), they were not created in terms of temporal priority because God created all things at once (Eccl. 18:1). Hence the only one whose name remains before the sun is God himself. The conclusion is inevitible: the son of the king, in whom all nations will be blessed, must be the God-man.[29] The second example is Isaiah 7:14, where the prophet speaks of the two natures of the promised one. That he is described as born of a woman speaks to his human nature, but that he is given the name 'Emmanuel' – 'God with us' – speaks to his divine nature. This last descriptor requires a grammatical distinction, for this person is not called 'God' in a derivative or common manner, for the Psalmist speaks of many being called gods (Ps. 81:6), but rather by an appropriation of a name: 'He does not say "he will be called Emmanuel" but "his name," as if it has been made his own, "will be called Emmanuel".'[30]

The third theme returns Grosseteste to Genesis, where Jacob had called his twelve sons together to reveal his prophecy for each of them. When it comes to Judah, Jacob foretells that the sceptre shall not leave him until a certain person arrives and 'he shall be the expectation of the people (*expectatio gentium*)' (Gen. 49:10). Grosseteste then weaves together a number of lemmata from the major prophets which demonstrate that the one for whom the chosen people were waiting is none other than God himself. Moreover, one prophet speaks of this expected person appearing in the end, to which Grosseteste asks 'How will he appear in the end unless in the end of time he was made visible through the assumption of the flesh?' Unless one was willing to argue for two expectations of the people, the only conclusion available here was that the *expectatio gentium* was to be the God-man.[31] To reinforce his point, Grosseteste summarises the genealogical history from Jacob to David, and then even more briefly from David to Jesus to demonstrate that no one had fulfilled this expectation until Christ himself.[32]

With his fourth theme, Grosseteste begins a detailed exegesis of the fourth song of the suffering servant in the prophet Isaiah.[33] It is also where Grosseteste violates his own rule about constructing proofs for the Incarnation based on the Old Testament alone, for the chief aim of the exposition is to tie the prophet's description to the life of Christ found in the gospels.[34] One can understand why Grosseteste could not resist referring to the New Testament here, as Isaiah 53 was an integral part of the liturgy of Christ's passion on Good Friday. At the same time, Grosseteste remains committed to his literal exegesis, although there is one consideration of signification from the Isaiah pericopes.[35] For the most part, Grosseteste considers this text as a literal description of the events of the passion. He also integrates into his exegesis two supposedly countervailing explanations of Christ's saving work. The first emerges in his comments on Isaiah 53:5: 'He was wounded for our iniquities, he was bruised for our sins.' That suffering included enduring the punishment for our peace (*disciplina pacis nostre*), that is, Grosseteste writes, 'the punishment of the whips by which we can be corrected and renconciled with God the Father whom we have offended'.[36] It is through this punishment that Jesus makes satisfaction with God on our behalf. Satisfaction was necessary since each person had strayed from the correct way, failing to follow the divine will. Christ's redemption addressed the injustice of human action, which now allows Christians to commune in justice with God once again.[37] At the same time, Grosseteste also speaks of Christ's redemption as a triumph over the devil, in that Christ took sinners out of the Devil's hands in order to establish a new kingdom of believers.[38]

There can be no doubt of Anselm's influence in the first description, where sin is described as an affront to God's honour because of humanity's refusal to follow God's will in all things. That refusal meant that men and women owed a debt to God (a debt of obedience) that they could not pay. Even if a person could commit himself to perfect obedience in the future, that is what he owed to God at the very least and it would not account for the debt he had already incurred for his own personal disobedience and the general disobedience of the entire human race. That debt must be paid in light of the immutability of God's justice, for his honour must always be maintained. Since humanity could not make satisfaction, but God could, it became fitting that God became man as the only means of redemption.[39] Anselm's argument, however, included a devastating attack on the patristic doctrine of the rights of the Devil (*ius diaboli*). This theory, commonly known as the *Christus victor* model, had argued that with the fall of humankind the Devil took full control of humanity. Christ's passion was thus the price to be paid to the Devil in order to redeem humanity back from him. However, Christ also tricked the Devil into thinking that he would retain Christ as a permanent payment; instead Christ rose from the dead but not before freeing the captive faithful from the dungeons of hell (Eph. 4:8–9). Anselm's reaction to this was to reject the idea that the Devil had any rights, for God owed nothing to him. For Anselm, the only one who deserved any honour and obeisance was God alone, and that meant the debt caused by sin was owed to him, even if that produced the odd conclusion of God himself paying the debt owed to him.[40]

It was not uncommon in Grosseteste's age for both theories to be held side by side. The *Christus victor* model had a long history, and therefore a significant amount of patristic authority behind it. Moreover, it had proved to be a very effective model in preaching since it easily stirred the minds of Christians in the Middle Ages. Anselm's competing theory, as with much of his theology, took some time to gain some respectability, and even his main supporters, the Franciscans, were not concerned about the conflict between Anselm's soteriology and the soteriology of the *Christus victor* model. Grosseteste does provide a more coherent soteriology that could embrace both theories:

> imagine someone who had fraudulently and unjustly invaded a kingdom and had subjugated it. And imagine that the prince [of the kingdom] has fought against him and has even conquered him so that he is not entirely subdued, but that there is nothing he can do which cannot be overcome, with all strongly resisting. In this case all virile people may have peace in power and security if they should want, although not until all rebellion comes to an end. And so it is in this way, that through the victory of Christ, the devil, sin and concupiscence, each have been conquered and consequently the death of coporeal punishment.[41]

Here Grosseteste employs a *Christus victor* model to explain Christ's saving work, but the role of the Devil is reduced to that of an illegitimate invader. His kingdom is fraudulent and unjust, but it still needs to be conquered. It would seem that for Grosseteste the Devil has no legitimate rights to which God had to pay attention. Rather, he is the enemy of justice, and one who is eventually soundly defeated because of Christ's passion. Hence the reference to Christ taking away men and women from the Devil is not a return to the old patristic model of salvation; instead, it has been reformulated in light of Anselm's teaching.

The final theme seems hardly relevant to making a case for the necessity of the Incarnation: the time of Christ's advent. Nonetheless, Grosseteste considers it essential for two exegetical reasons. First, it gives greater weight to his messianic reading of Jacob's prophecy in Genesis 49: the *expectatio gentium* would come when Judah lost its regal sceptre, and so the fact that Christ arrived at a time when the nation of Israel was being ruled by a non-Jew (Herod) is not insignificant.[42] Secondly, the same connection between the decline in Jewish political power and the advent of the promised one is found in the prophecies of Daniel, and so Grosseteste devotes the bulk of this section to unlocking the meaning of 'seventy weeks' in the angel Gabriel's speech in Daniel 9. His main source is the work of Bede, *De temporum ratione*, but he does not hesitate to add his own arithmetical observations to demonstrate that Christ accurately fulfilled this prophecy by living on the earth at the time he did.[43]

Grosseteste breaks no new ground in his account of the necessity of the Incarnation, although there is some exegetical inventiveness. He completes his intended task, namely to present the biblical evidence which demonstrates the continuity of God's plan. The Mosaic Law was not expected to be the means of salvation, for at the core of the Jewish Scriptures was the promise of the one who would bless all nations. Grosseteste has no interest in how medieval Jewish expositors would respond to this, nor does he feel the need to pay attention to what they are saying about the same passages. Instead, he is convinced that these sacred texts relate directly to the person of Jesus Christ, a conviction he shared with every other theologian of his era. And yet there is a flicker of originality in his comments and it lies in his definition of the promised blessing. Grosseteste initially describes it as liberation from punishment and preordination to eternal glory, but he later provides equivalent definitions. The blessing is God illuminating through grace and purging believers from the darkness of punishment, or it is a purgation from punishment and an intersection (*collacio*) of grace and glory.[44] In this blessing, the *expectatio gentium* will loosen the bonds of sin and confer grace and glory.[45] Once again, there is no novelty found in these descriptions and they all ably encapsulate the twofold intention of Christ's saving work, namely to delete the punishment due to humankind and to restore humanity to its original state. However, as Grosseteste pursues the reasons why the Incarnate God can be the only one who can give this blessing, he introduces an additional function: justification. A person is both reconciled (blessed) and justified in Christ.[46] It is certainly possible to see this phrasing as a form of apposition, for to be reconciled is to be justified. That interpretation is difficult to maintain when the reader moves into part three of *De cessatione legalium*, where Grosseteste articulates a more specific distinction between reconciliation (or sanctification) and justification. This distinction refers to the double intention for the Incarnation, which also embraces the larger, cosmic reasons for God becoming man.

The Cosmic Necessity of Christ

When we turn to the third part of *De cessatione legalium* we encounter Grosseteste at his most original. He begins by noting that the great theologians of the past – notably Augustine, Gregory and Anselm – had declared that the restoration of the human race could only be realised through the passion of the God-man. However, it had not occurred to these sacred expositors to ask whether the Incarnation would have taken place if Adam and Eve had not sinned. The question had been posed before, but Grosseteste is the first to address this problem with such intensity that it created a new topic for scholastic theologians to examine for the rest of the century. It attracted the attention of almost every major theologian of the period, including Richard Fishacre, Richard Rufus, Alexander of Hales, Guerric of St Quentin, Albert the Great, Bonaventure, Thomas Aquinas and John Duns Scotus – and this is by no means an exhaustive list. While most of these theologians would disagree with Grosseteste's putative solution, the question still retained a strong force in the Christology of the Schools.

It seems to be a rather odd question for a medieval theologian to ask, especially one like Grosseteste who had already devoted a great deal of speculative and exegetical energy to presenting the Incarnation within the narrative of salvation history. It has been remarked that the formation of the question borders on the impossible, the theological equivalent of trying to square the circle. In other words, as interesting as the topic might be, it will always remain insoluble, which raises questions about the wisdom of even engaging in this type of enquiry.[47] Grosseteste's query is in fact akin to a 'counterfactual'. The aim of counterfactual analysis is to explore the structure of causality, by positing a probable condition (normally a negation) that has no real truth value in order to establish the difference between the real and apparent causes of something.[48] One can ask, for example, if Frederick the Elector had not ruled Saxony during the time of Martin Luther, would the Protestant

Reformation have occurred? Such a counterfactual question seeks to establish a real cause of the Reformation, in this case Martin Luther, in contrast to an apparent cause, the political machinations of Frederick, who ended up protecting Luther in the process. While the philosophical rationale for counterfactual analysis is relevatively recent (and still the subject of great debate), positing counterfactuals had been part of theological discourse long before Grosseteste. For Christian thinkers, there was an ideal opportunity for this kind of argument and it was found within the short account of humanity's pre-lapsarian state in the book of Genesis. The most prominent counterfactual assertion was that, if Adam and Eve had not sinned, the human race would not have experienced death, but would have remained immortal.[49] This was a more than probable counterfactual claim, since it drew from the Apostle Paul's assertion about Adam in Romans 5:12 : 'Just as sin entered in the world by one man, and death through sin'. One early medieval thinker, Claudius of Turin (d.827), raises two points about the relationship between men and women, if Adam had not sinned: man would have rational control of his genitals and so would not need to rely upon a sinful libido to have sexual relations. Claudius also wonders whether Eve would have remained under Adam's power if there had been no sin. He answers in a casual patriarchical way that nothing would have changed, although her submission would not have been out of fear, but rather out of love.[50] Rabanus Maurus (ca.776–856), a favourite author of Grosseteste, notes in his gloss of the word *reges* that, if humanity had not sinned, each person would be at rest with the angels, who rule in heaven with God.[51] And, a century prior to Grosseteste, Richard of St-Victor argued that, if man had not sinned, he would have been able to ascend to heavenly beatitude with the help of justice.[52] Grosseteste's question may appear odd to the modern reader, but it was well within the line of reasoning available to a medieval theologian.

Two important points need to be made here, however. First, most of these counterfactual claims were made as a point of contrast between the actual and a putatively possible set of events; and the main intention was to highlight specific *true* conditions of the world as it is now. Secondly, and this follows from the first, the counterfactual argument was meant to emphasise discontinuity, not continuity. These theologians employed counterfactual arguments as a means of focusing on the disastrous *consequences* of sin, but there was no interest in questioning whether the Fall could properly act as the cause of the most significant event in human history, the Incarnation. Grosseteste is therefore attempting something slightly more complex, for he is suggesting a course of investigation that attempts to establish that sin cannot have any causal role for the Incarnation without denying Christ's saving work. That means he must establish reasons for the Incarnation that not only function in a world where the counterfactual holds true (that is, there is no sin), but also in the world as it is now, which is mired in sin. Grosseteste's aim is not to separate the Incarnation from Christ's saving work, but rather to elucidate its twofold role. Previous studies on this part of the *De cessatione legalium* have explained the philosophical features.[53] My aim here is to integrate this section with Grosseteste's teaching on the Incarnation elsewhere.

God's Goodness and the Incarnation as a Good

Grosseteste begins: 'God is the supreme power, wisdom and goodness', an assertion that is an integral part of his doctrine of the Trinity.[54] In this case, he focuses on God as goodness and explicitly makes reference to Anselm's argument of the *Proslogion*, namely that God is a 'greater good than can even be thought'. To this he adds the Ps-Dionysian concept of goodness as being self-diffusive,[55] which means that God made the universe in such a way that it was capable of receiving his goodness. God fills the universe with his goodness (which is the cause of the utility of all creation) and, since that is true of the present, the universe's reception of God's goodness must include the Incarnation. Moreover, it is difficult to make the case that somehow the universe was made capable of receiving that specific good of the Incarnation through the advent of sin. If the divine nature can unite with human nature, and the reality of sin does not prevent that from happening, would not the conditions for that union (its unitability, as Grosseteste calls it) be greater without sin?

The neo-Platonic concepts are easily identified in this argument as Grosseteste latches onto goodness as the primary description of God's relationship with his creation. He had argued elsewhere that, because God saw all of his creation as good (Gen. 1.31), there was a link between essence, goodness and utility.[56] Hence, as the Creator of all reality, who imbued all things with essence, God was also the source of their goodness. But Grosseteste wants to transform this metaphysical statement into a Christological one, for the Incarnation becomes a primary example of the reception of goodness in creation, as it is the divine uniting with the human. Moreover, the existence of sin cannot prevent creation from receiving its goodness, and that must include the Incarnation. What in fact Grosseteste is arguing against is the notion that somehow sin created the potential within creation to receive this good, the Incarnation – as if humanity could ever be united with the divine unless humanity had sinned. If one looks at the mode of union within the Incarnation, Grosseteste argues, one could only argue the opposite. His major proof comes from Peter Lombard, or rather the way that Lombard brought together citations from Augustine and John Damascene: 'The Son of God assumed flesh and soul, but the flesh with the soul mediating. The Word of God was united to the flesh through a medium, the intellect (*per medium intellectum*).'[57] There then exist two possible modes of explanation: either the sinful condition has no effect on the unitibility of the *homo assumptus* or, if it does, the only logical conclusion to draw is that in the sinful state the strength of the union is diminished. This is because, in a sinful state, a person has less of a union between mind and flesh, and indeed the difference between the two is so stark that it is equivalent between dying and not dying.[58] It is therefore impossible that sin made human nature more capable of being united to the Word of God, and thus could not be the cause of such a good as the Incarnation. Grosseteste then offers additional arguments concerning the nature of sin as a privation of being, which can in no way be the cause of anything good.[59]

The Glory of Creation and the Adoration of Christ's Flesh

The reasons that sin could not be the cause of the Incarnation become even stronger when one considers the effects of the Incarnation in creation. Grosseteste does not move far from the unitability of human nature in this next argument, for it is at the centre of his position. Let us suppose, Grosseteste writes, that humanity had not sinned and the Incarnation had not taken place, which supposes that sin is the cause of the Incarnation. Would the universe have the same attributes it has now? Could this sinless world be considered as perfect, as beautiful and as glorious? It is the last attribute with which Grosseteste advances his argument. He first connects *gloriositas* with being worthy of worship (*adorabilis*), and no creature can lay claim to this attribute. In this present world, there is one creature that is worthy of worship, and that is the flesh of Christ. Grosseteste had broached this topic in his Galatians commentary as a proof that Christ's passion was not accomplished in vain. If nature does nothing in vain, how can one say that the Creator of all nature would do something in vain. Moreover, God is the most powerful, most wise and the best in all things (*optimus*), which further indicates that he does nothing in vain. Given Christ's divinity, the same must be be said of the Incarnate Son, and so, if he gave himself over to death as a sufficient cause for justification, it would not be necessary for something else to be needed to achieve that justification. Christ exceeds all creation, and so does not need a co-justifier such as the Law. It is his very role as justifier that is the basis for the adoration of the flesh of Christ. Grosseteste cites John Damascene as the authority who advocates the worship of Christ's human body. It can be worshipped because it is united to the Word of God, a union that remained intact even after the passion. This unique status is a further reason why connecting the Law to salvation is unnecessary (since Christ's sacrifice is sufficient) and incoherent (as no created thing can equal even Christ's flesh).[60]

Christ's human body is the only way that glory can be brought to bear on creation. Grosseteste inserts an analogy from nature to demonstrate the type of change that occurs to the human nature united to the Divine. A piece of wood cannot be considered untouchable, but put in the fire, and when it becomes fuel (*carbo*), it has also become untouchable (or rather as Grosseteste states, inaccessible). In the same way, the divine nature transformed human nature in the Incarnation. Furthermore, since a burning piece of wood has a greater brightness (*splendor*) and heat than an unlit piece, so the whole universe experiences a greater glory because of the union of the divine and human in the Incarnation than if the Incarnation had not taken place.[61] It would seem to make little sense that humanity's Fall increased the quality of creation. If anything, the state of creation would be better without sin, so the Incarnation cannot be contingent upon sin. Grosseteste then puts it another way: all creation is loved by God, and in some way participates with God, and so each is also good according to its creation. Now if included in this panoply of goodness is the lowliest worm, why would God exclude the person of Jesus Christ, who is of a higher goodness than reptiles and worms? Grosseteste is quick to reject any Arian reading of this argument: he is not saying that the God-man is a creation in that sense, but the fact is that the human nature of Jesus is indeed part of creation. Hence it makes little sense that, if God's communication with creation includes reviled creatures (like worms and reptiles), he would exclude the most perfect of all creation, Jesus.[62]

Justification, Sanctification and the Incarnation

Grosseteste appears then to jump to a theme that has little connection to the prior one, namely that, if there had been no Incarnation, the Church would be headless, not to mention all of humanity, as the Apostle Paul seems to imply (Eph. 5:23). I can only infer, based on study of Grosseteste's ecclesiology, that God's communication with all creation reminds Grosseteste of God's special communion with humanity in terms of the Church. The absurdity of this statement – a headless church – would not have been lost on Grosseteste's contemporaries, for an institution cannot exist without its leadership, the source of authority. This argument is certainly tautological, but this mention of the Church turns Grosseteste's attention immediately to the salvific work of Jesus, the means by which sinful humanity can become members of Christ's mystical body and be united to its Head. Drawing upon his long experience with propositional logic, Grosseteste parses a common assertion about Christ's saving work: 'The *suffering* God-man alone justifies *fallen* humanity.'[63] Now this statement contains a cause that is precisely proportionate to its effect. If one removes both the accidental conditions (*suffering* and *fallen*), the relation between cause and effect is not altered, for what remains is that the God-man alone justifies humanity. Grosseteste goes on to make the case that there must be a distinction between justification and sanctification, and that humanity is in need of justification regardless of whether Adam and Eve had sinned; and that justification is achieved through the Incarnation.

Grosseteste raises a possible objection which could defeat his argument by a similar use of logic. One might say that God alone justifies man, that is, not the God-man. Whereas Grosseteste wants to make the predicates 'suffering' and 'fallen' correspond, in this case there must also be corresponding subjects; that is, one must link 'suffering man' with 'fallen man'. In a sinless world, the proposition would be 'God justifies man', but in the actual sinful world it must be 'the suffering man justifies the fallen man, in as much as he is fallen'. This argument reduces the necessity of the Incarnation to the redemption of humanity alone: if Adam and Eve had not sinned, the Incarnation would not have been needed. This condition introduces two distinct processes: one is justified by the God-man in this present world so that he is raised from his fallen state and purged of all filth. If humankind were sinless, God alone would shape (*informat*) humanity by means of justice, and this requires no Incarnation.[64] Grosseteste's solution to this objection is not to undermine the logic used in the objection, but rather to turn to authorities that demonstrate that his own argument is consistent with biblical and patristic teaching. In the first place, the Apostle Paul describes Christ becoming many things for Christians: wisdom from God, justice, sanctification and redemption.[65] Christ accomplishes these things, not on the basis of his divinity, but rather though the assumption of humanity, which allows him to be the mediator between God and man. In other words, 'the form of justice flows into us through Christ, the man who is just and is obedient to the Father'. Ps-Dionysius also reinforces this point, as he speaks of the highest angelic orders drawing their capability to contemplate the divine essence from their communion with Jesus himself.[66]

Grosseteste is averring here a unique notion of justification. For most medieval theologians, justification was the term ascribed to the process of salvation – and Grosseteste himself sometimes uses it in this manner. One was justified by the grace of God and by the merit of Christ's passion. In other words, justification concerned the sinful state of humankind and the means by which the punishment due to each sinful person was deleted.[67] In the *De cessatione legalium*, Grosseteste places the process of salvation under the rubric of sanctification, and claims that justification has nothing to do with sin. Even in their prelapsarian status, Adam and Eve would have needed justification, which in turn required the Incarnation. In a sinless state, however, the Son of God did not need to endure the suffering of the Cross, but only needed to be Incarnate in order to justify humankind. What then is justification? Before we examine Grosseteste's additional arguments in the *De cessatione legalium*, it would be useful to address what he thinks justice is in general. Grosseteste provides no indication here, but fortunately the topic is addressed in his *Dicta*. He discusses the nature of justice in three discourses, two of which seem to be *notulae* while the third is a sermon addressed to priests.

In one *notula*, he begins with the standard Ciceronian definition: 'justice renders to each one what is due to him'.[68] Grosseteste finds this definition problematic for it assumes that each just person will have it in his power to distribute what is owed to each one, and that is not always the case. Should justice rather not be located in the will rather than in human action? More importantly, the definition of justice should be applicable to the next life where the generous actions that such distribution demands will not be necessary. Instead, justice concerns receiving a glorius grace for one's good merits and a just penalty for evil deeds.[69] The upshot here is that distributive justice functions solely within a social context, and so does not fully communicate all aspects of what justice is. In the second *notula*, Grosseteste further differentiates between social justice and a theological account of justice. In this multivalent definition, he begins with justice that comprises the 'doctrine of morals and observations invented by human reason and wisdom'. And, since human justice rarely relates to divine justice, one must think of this first definition as wholly contrary to God's justice. However, in the second definition one is a little closer to God's justice, in that it comprises the 'exterior observance of God's commandments'. Even here Grosseteste adds a rider that this is the justice of the Scribes and Pharisees, and this observance will not bring about entry into the kingdom of heaven. The third definition of justice, and implicitly the best kind, is that which 'proceeds from the root of love with action (*opus*) that is both correct and regulated by sacred Scripture, and has the supreme good as its end'. This is a justice that justifies and comes from a faith that works through love.[70]

In the sermon, Grosseteste echoes some of the same ideas, although the definitions are far more refined. The sermon's theme comes from Psalm 131:9: 'May your priests be clothed with justice' (*Sacerdotes tui induantur iusticiam*). It is fairly clear that the intended audience is composed of priests, but in what circumstances they would have gathered it is difficult to say. Even then, Grosseteste is aware that the charge to be clothed in justice is applicable even to the laity, for the whole Church is called a royal priesthood (1 Pet. 2:9). He then lays out three definitions of justice with the eventual aim of aligning justice with beauty (*pulcritudo*). The first is the Ciceronian definition, but Grosseteste has modified it somewhat so as to lay emphasis on its voluntary nature: 'Justice is the desire (*voluntas*) to render to each one what he is due.' Here Grosseteste is extremely practical in his explication, for this kind of justice concerns a variety of social relationships that demand certain behaviours which ensure that each is given his due.[71] As useful as this definition is (and Grosseteste provides clear guidelines as to how priests should behave in this mode of justice), it does not fully capture the relationship between justice and beauty, and so he moves to a second definition, the one penned by Anselm of Canterbury, 'Justice is the rectitude of the will kept for its own sake', where Grosseteste glosses the last prepositional phrase as 'for its own rectitude'. In this definition, justice encapsulates not only the correct social and legal behaviour, but also the will of the actors involved. In sum, justice comprises an upright will, work and intention.[72] This form of justice is commensurate with beauty, Grosseteste notes, for beauty is defined by Augustine as that which consists in equality and rectitude. In other words, justice is beauty because it is concerned with the correct order of things.[73] This alignment is reinforced in the last definition, which Grosseteste draws from Boethius: 'Justice is a likeness with the celestial and divine substances', that is, angels. If priests can imitate the angels, they would ensure that they wore the habit of justice in their vocation. What makes angels such an ideal model was not only their intellectual, non-corporeal nature but also that they were oriented to God in their contemplation of the Trinity. Even if men and women could not contemplate the Trinity in this life as the angels do, they were nonetheless the prime example of justice.[74] Grosseteste is more concerned about making a concrete account of justice in this sermon, an account that priests could understand and employ in their own lives. And yet his definitions also provide a glimpse into his general understanding of justice, one that has Anselmian influences as justice is defined in terms of beauty and order.[75]

It is not inappropriate then to speak of the justification of both men and angels, for justice descends into every rational creation from God through Christ. It is through justification that men and angels are ordered to God.[76] Whether he means the 'original justice' that Adam possessed before the Fall or some other form of justice, Grosseteste does not say. From the fact that Grosseteste speaks of the justification, as opposed to being in a state of justice (as most theologians would describe humanity's prelapsarian status), it would appear that he is thinking of something that operates outside the initial conditions of Adam's creation. Hence, if Adam had not sinned, there still would have been justification. Grosseteste then connects the Pauline notion of the adoption of sons to this justification, for this aspect of humanity's final trajectory cannot be a result of sin: how could a person receive the greater good of being a son of God by adoption through sinning? 'If the son of God would not become man unless man had sinned, then a man could not become a son of God by adoption unless God became a man by nature, [and] in sinning man gained the possibility to become the son of God by adoption.'[77]

There are two implications in this argument. First, Grosseteste is envisaging a Church that originates with Adam, and not with Abel, as his contemporaries would suggest. This means that the Church is not framed in terms of the work of restoration, but rather as a natural aspect of creation. Adoption highlights the kind of union between God and humanity; it is about participation in the divine. Moreover, adoption is about filiation which is not the same as the friendship of community, as the latter originates in a conformity of wills.[78] Instead adoption, which leads to deification, is a sacramental mystery. To underline this point, Grosseteste asks: if the Incarnation did not need to happen if man had not sinned, then what of Adam's prelapsarian prophecies about the the unity of Christ and his Church? Grosseteste is referring to the proclamation of Genesis 2:24 concerning the nature of marriage, that a man and woman become one flesh. Grosseteste makes two assumptions here about Adam's knowledge in order to render an effective argument. First, Adam was cognisant of his own prophecy: he knew that he was speaking not only of the institution of marriage, but also of its sacramental signification. Secondly, this spiritual insight did not allow him foresight of his own imminent descent into sin, and its consequences for the whole human race. The only conclusion to draw is that Adam's prophecy is only coherent if the Incarnation was not a response to the Fall of humanity.[79]

Sensing Beauty

The next argument at first seems to represent a disjuncture in the overall flow of the case Grosseteste is building, but there is in fact a logical progression: he moves from speaking of the source of justification, the Incarnation, to what justification actually does. Since justice concerns order and therefore beauty, a justified person gains the capability of sensing true beauty through the Incarnation. This argument is driven by a citation from the *De spiritu et anima*. The author of this text states that in a person there are two senses, one interior and one exterior. While the interior is fed by its contemplation of the divine, the exterior is nourished by its contemplation of humanity. This is yet another convincing reason for arguing that God would have become man even if humanity had not sinned. God became man so that the whole person could be beatified, so that the soul and body could be nourished equally, that is the bodily senses would feed upon the flesh of the Saviour as means towards beatitude.[80] This configuration can raise an objection, since it would appear that a person can obtain beatitude with the mind contemplating one thing, and sensing through the flesh of another. Grosseteste grants that this in fact is representative of general cognition, namely that the intention of the soul can be divided into many things, and thus can become lost in singulars (*in singulos minorata*). However, dividing up the soul cannot be the condition of beatitude for this state of perfection requires a conversion of the whole intention of the soul into the supreme good. We are left then with two alternatives: either the exterior sense is never perfected for beatitude, or it is perfected in something other than God – and with either solution there would be no beatitude.[81]

Grosseteste's solution rests on two important assumptions. The first is the glory of Christ's flesh and the reasons that it is worthy of worship. The Incarnation was a union of the uncreated with a created nature, humanity. The divine touching the human in such an intimate way transformed the assumed man in the hypostatic union and, as we have seen, Grosseteste used the image of a piece of wood transformed into fuel that burned with the splendour of fire as a way of demonstrating that relationship. The second assumption is that, in the last resurrection, each faithful Christian will receive a glorified body. Embodiment remained a central feature of being human in medieval Christianity. Despite the profound influence of neoplatonic thought – where the movement of the soul away from the prison of the body and towards the Good is the essential feature of perfection – medieval Christianity stuck doggedly to the precept that the last resurrection was a physical one. This doctrine therefore required some account of what the glorified body would be like, and not surprisingly some of that teaching was influenced by monastic perspectives on the body.[82] By the time Grosseteste came to teach at Oxford, the glorified body doctrine had also taken on a marital theme. Christ as the bridegroom endowed his bride, the Church, with certain marriage gifts (*dotes*), and some of them concerned the nature of the glorified body. Grosseteste recognised that in the life to come there would be a physical aspect to humanity's glorification.[83]

In this context, Grosseteste's solution is compelling. He notes that in the final resurrection Christ's own body will be manifested as more splendid and beautiful than any created body, including the sun. Indeed, the sun will be barely visible, so bright will Christ's flesh be. Now the carnal eye has the capacity (*possibilis est*) to see this beauty but only when it will be glorified. If God had not become man, it would mean that there would be no object for the glorified carnal eye to envisage, since nothing can come close to the beauty of Christ's glorified flesh. The result would not be beatitude but misery since this absence of a worthy object for the glorified eye would be a perpetual imperfection. In other words, the divine nature assuming the flesh is the only way in which the embodied soul may be brought wholly into the supreme Good. The interior sense will behold the Trinity, as will the exterior sense, but through the glorious flesh of Christ.[84]

The Unity of Creation

Grosseteste's final argument reminds us why the Incarnation is at the centre of theological discourse. He begins with an assertion that all creation is one. To be a unified entity requires a unifying principle. Christ can qualify as that unifying principle because he can relate to all the various forms of created reality according to his humanity. Moreover, a unifying principle must be greater than the parts that compose that unity, and so this rules out either an angel or a human being as the unifying factor since they are equal to one another in dignity. Nor can it be another creature, since all are of lesser dignity than humanity. The Incarnation, as Grosseteste has stated already, introduced a greater sense of worth and dignity into created nature within that union. This allows the hypostatic union to qualify as the most worthy, and thus be the unifying principle. However, that union must be with a nature that has something in common with all creation, which means it cannot be a God-angel, for that union would not touch upon corporeal creatures. The only conclusion is that the unifying principle must be the God-man. This conclusion is further strengthened if God enters the picture. The only way in which God may realise union with his creation is through a unifying principle that provides a point of intersection between the uncreated and the created. That, of course, is the Incarnation. None of this requires the fall of humanity, and so the Incarnation would have happened, even if Adam and Eve had not sinned.[85]

James McEvoy has quite rightly pointed out the Eriugenist ideas that permeate this final argument. He notes that, 'in the thought of both men [Grosseteste and Eriugena], all things stand together, in unity, in the Word before creation, and that that unity of origin is also the unity of the return, mediated by the Word incarnate who leads all natures and all creation back in a circle towards their primal origin, and who unites human nature to the divine (*deficatio*)'.[86] There are also echoes of the whole-Christ motif, which Grosseteste had amended in the opening pages of the *Hexaëmeron*. As the unifying principle of all reality, and as the intersection of the divine and the mundane, the Incarnation became a valid focal point for a theologian's vision. In Christ, one found not only the means by which one gained the eventual vision of God (as both a spiritual and a physical phenomenon), but one could engage all of created reality. The Incarnation was the way to the hidden place of wisdom, for Christ as the God-man unveiled all the secrets of the world and outlined the intimate relationship between God and his creation. Grosseteste had developed a powerful and all-encompassing Christology.

The Uniqueness of the Incarnation

Such a Christology obviously had to lay claim to Christ's unique status in both human history and the universal created order. Most of the remaining sections of the third part of the *De cessatione legalium* focus on providing further indications of the Incarnation's uniqueness.[87] The place and timing of Christ's nativity are presented as indications of the importance of the Incarnation and also extend the notion of fittingness. It is fitting, for example, that Christ was born in the middle of the Earth.[88] It is also fitting that the first advent took place six thousand years after creation, and thus in the sixth age of man.[89] Above all, it was fitting that the Incarnation be a unique event, and that Christians ought not to expect another Christ. It is this last argument to which I will turn, since it is the closest Grosseteste comes to any sustained discussion of the hypostatic union.[90]

If one accepts that Jesus the son of Mary is the Christ, that is, the God-man, there are reasons why it would be futile to expect another Christ. If there were to be many Christs, so Grosseteste begins the hypothetical argument, that would only happen if other persons in the Trinity assumed human flesh. The reason for this was due to two principles of the hypostatic union. First, the Master of the *Sentences* had taught that a person cannot assume a person, nor a nature assume a person, but only a person (the Son) can assume a nature (humanity).[91] Lombard had raised this question as a means of testing whether one could speak of the divine nature becoming incarnate, just as one could say that God became incarnate, or the Word became flesh.[92] This concern was more than just scholastic pedantry, for Lombard himself wanted to ensure that there was a consistent use of philosophical terms like 'person' and 'nature' between his Christology and his trinitarian theology. Since Scripture spoke of only the Son taking on the form of a servant (Phil. 2:7), any suggestion that this was equivalent to the divine nature becoming incarnate would undermine the distinction of persons within the Godhead. The authority of both the sacred text and the Fathers (in this case, Augustine is the main source for this position), required Lombard to conclude that it must be a trinitarian person who alone took on human flesh.[93] As to why it is human nature assumed and not a human person, Lombard is less forthcoming. He insists that theologians must speak about the Son being united to a human soul and body, rather than to a person composed of a soul and body, but provides no supporting reasons.[94]

Later commentators felt compelled to provide those reasons. Someone like William of Auxerre would connect this problem to the way that the term 'person' within the hypostatic union points to the mode of union.[95] If one talks about a divine person assuming a human person – each being an individual substance of a rational nature – it would be difficult to maintain any sense of unity within the Incarnation. Rather, there would be a duality in Christ, that is two subjects or supposits, each identified as a separate person. William's own solution is to speak of the human nature as accidental of the divine person, so that the personal identity of Jesus is more the result of the presence of the divine nature than of the human nature. William clarifies this assertion further when he poses the question: if the Son had assumed two different bodies and souls at two different times, where one would be called Jesus and the other Peter, would it be correct to say that Jesus is Peter? William's answer is in the affirmative, as long as one kept in mind that Peter and Paul as men were still individuals. Nonetheless, in terms of personal identity, which was dependent primarily upon the divine nature in the union, they were the same.[96] Ultimately what is driving William's Christology, particularly in relation to the way a theologian should deploy concepts like 'person' and 'nature', is his commitment to one specific theory about the Incarnation and his resulting rejection of two others.[97]

The adopted theory is now known as the *Subsistence* theory, which argued that the Incarnation was a union of the Son with a human body and soul, and these two separate acts of union came to form one person, Christ. In other words, the Son assumed human nature and not a human person. William himself considered the *Subsistence* theory to be more reasonable since it allowed for a more intimate unity within the Incarnation.[98] As a result, he completely rejected a second opinion, known as the *Homo-assumptus* theory, a position that considered the Incarnation to be a union of the Son with a fully composed human being. While this theory appeared to be consistent with the patristic emphasis of asserting the complete humanity of Christ united to the Son, it raised serious problems about the unity of Christ and perhaps even more seriously it raised the possibility of a complete separation between the divine and human natures, since there was no way in which personal properties would be shared within that union. Hence a proponent of this theory might have a difficult time asserting that the Son truly suffered and died on the cross, since there was no sharing of properties between the two natures in the union. That could lead to a damning charge that the *Homo-assumptus* theory was semi-Nestorian.[99] William was also quite dismissive of the third opinion, the *Habitus* theory. This opinion suggested that the relationship between the divine and human natures was the same as the one between a person and his clothes: the Son took on human nature, or he cloaked himself in humanity. Whereas the *Homo-assumptus* theory asserted a fully concrete human person, this last opinion asserted the opposite. Theologians like William gave this third opinion short shrift since it had become identified with two condemnations of Pope Alexander III in the 1170s.[100] From William onward, most theologians followed his lead by advancing the Subsistence theory as the orthodox opinion.

It would appear that Grosseteste also advocated the Subsistence theory. We may place him alongside William and others not only because he adopts the person-assuming-a-nature principle, but also because of how he considers that principle affection the union between the person and nature. It is necessary, he writes, to speak of 'person' in the Incarnation as from two natures, not one. Like William, Grosseteste considers the notion of personal identity to be more appropriate to the Son than to the assumed human nature. For this reason he can draw his first conclusion about the uniqueness of the Incarnation: even if the same Son assumed the same nature on a number of occasions, there would be still one union in terms of personhood (*unicus in persona*) since it would be the same God and the same human nature assumed.[101]

While these few short sentences reveal Grosseteste's awareness of some standard scholastic arguments in Christology, the direction in which he moves the argument next reveals once again his independent streak. The contrast is striking when we consider another question from William's *Summa aurea*. In advancing his support of the Subsistence theory, he asks: if the Father assumes the same body and soul with the Son, would they be the same person? In other words, how does the presence of a trinitarian person affect the mode of union? William's answer is that it would make things somewhat awkward, for one could not speak of multiple unions within the Incarnation (that is, a union between the Son and the assumed human nature and the Father and the same assumed human nature) since there is only one human nature being assumed, but theoretically one could speak of the existence of two persons within the Incarnation, primarily because of the presence of two divine persons.[102] Grosseteste, however, posits a situation in which the Son and the Father each assumes human nature, but his query diverges from William in that he is speaking of two historically different individuations of the assumed nature.[103] The first observation that one must make from this hypothetical case is that one can still speak of one God but many men since there would be a multiplication of persons and individuals. Grosseteste then goes on to describe what these two incarnations would produce. If the Incarnate Son has two wills (that is, the uncreated and created will), and in the same way two kinds of knowledge and two powers, one would have to the say the same of the Father if he were incarnated. Grosseteste does not wish to deny the unity of will in the Trinity, and so he quickly affirms that the will, knowledge and power of the Father and the Son are all indivisible, and in fact one must speak of the one God willing, knowing and doing. However, given the reality of two trinitarian persons becoming incarnate, one must also acknowledge two wills, two forms of knowledge and two powers, in that the Son-man and the Father-man (as Grosseteste delineates them) are each united to a created will, knowledge and power in their respective hypostatic unions. In the end, the theologian is confronted with a perplexing statement that there is one God who wills, and knows and does, but many men who also will, know and do. Scripture assigns omnipotence to the Son-man ('all power in heaven and earth is given to me'), and so by extension he is all-willing and all-knowing, which means that these three attributes are also applicable to the Father-man.[104]

For all the intermediate conclusions that Grosseteste draws concerning the nature of two incarnations by two persons of the Godhead, he makes no general conclusion whatsoever. The probable intent in making the argument is to demonstrate its unsuitability or inappropriateness (*inconveniens*).[105] Indeed, this becomes the recurring theme for the rest of this section. If both the Father and the Son were incarnated, Christians would need to offer adoration (*latria*) to both glorified bodies. That state of affairs would apparently undermine the unity of worship, which the reader must infer to be an inappropriate outcome. Moreover, with more than one Incarnation the body of Christ, the Church, would have more than one head and here Grosseteste explicitly calls this a monstrous thought. Another inappropriate outcome of two Incarnations would be the sacramental relationship between the institution of marriage and the mystical relationship between God and humanity. There is a direct relationship, Grosseteste argues, between the social construction of marriage and its sacramental meaning. Two incarnations would establish the most repulsive model of marriage, he states. It is true that at certain times one man could take many wives, and the reason for this (so he continues) is that one man can impregnate many women. However, Grosseteste cannot bring to mind any social or biological reason for one woman having many husbands, and so this model of marriage can only produce lust.[106] Grosseteste offers further examples of the absurdity of multiple incarnations. How would Christians maintain their adoption as sons of God, for example, since through the incarnated Father Christians would also be fathers? Such a condition would become even more confusing if the Holy Spirit assumed human nature, since it would mean that Christians would have a trinity of adoption. All this multiple adoption is simply inappropriate.[107] A multiplicity of incarnations would also have consequences for the modes of prayer available to the Church, and it is clear that Grosseteste has Christ's specific role as the mediator in mind here.[108] The ultimate conclusion that all these absurd conditions evokes is: 'Thus, another Christ would be entirely superfluous.'[109]

Even with this final conclusion, the reasons for the supposed absurdities and the superfluousness of multiple incarnations remains unspoken. However, if this short section of the *De cessatione legalium* is read within the context of the whole work, it is possible to see the coherence of Grosseteste's arguments. One must remember the centrality that Grosseteste gives to the Incarnation, not only as a central Christian belief, but also as the very unifying principle of all reality. The Incarnation, the union of the divine and the human, was what united all of created reality, and it was what reunited creation with its Creator. In Christ, one found the truth of the Trinity, the *rationes* of creation, the kernel of salvation, the social and spiritual unity of humankind, and the means by which each person could be reunited with the Trinity. To then establish a set of conditions that would dislodge the Incarnate Son from the central role would threaten the very order, and thus the beauty, of the created world. To suggest a second Incarnation was to suggest an unordered and thus *inappropriate* event. Another Christ, while theoretically possible (Grosseteste does not want to deny that the other trinitarian persons are capable of assuming human nature), it must remain outside the actual created order. Moreover, another Christ cannot be reconciled with the witness of Scripture. Jesus, the son of Mary, the Incarnate Son of God, was the promised offspring of Abraham, the best of humanity, the expectation of the nations and the suffering servant who would bring salvation and destroy the Devil's fraudulent kingdom. Through his passion and resurrection, humankind could be sanctified from sin so that they could also be justified. For Grosseteste, this unique, historical and contingent event, the Incarnation, allowed humanity to engage with the universal and the unchanging. Christ brought truth back into a sinful world, because in him one found all truth.[110] Grosseteste treated the person of Christ as if he were the visible centre of everything.

Notes

1 See above, Chapter 3, pp. 39–40.
2 James McEvoy, 'The Absolute Predestination of Christ in the Theology of Robert Grosseteste', in *Sapientiae Doctrinae: Mélanges de théologie et de littérature médiévales offerts à Dom Hildebrand Bascour O.S.B.* (Louvain: Abbaye du Mont César, 1980), pp. 212–30. But see also, idem, 'Ioannes Scottus Eriugena and Robert Grosseteste: An Ambiguous Influence', in *Eriugena redivivus. Zur Wirkungsgeschichte seines Denkens im Mittelalter und im Übergang zur Neuzeit*, ed. W. Beierwaltes (Heidelberg: Carl Winter Universitätsverlag, 1987), pp. 192–223, at 214–23.
3 *Tabula*, pp. 246–7, 273–6.
4 *Summa Aurea*, 3.tr.1–tr.9 (3.11–112); Alexander of Hales, *Glossa In Quatuor Libros Sententiarum*, 4 vols, ed. PP. Collegii S. Bonaventurae (Quaracchi: Collegium S. Bonaventurae, 1951–57), *divisio textus* (3.1–9).
5 The first to suggest this was Samuel Pegge in his putative biography of Grosseteste. His claim was accepted by most medieval historians of the early twentieth century. For a summary of the historiography, see the introduction to the critical edition: *DCL*, ix–xv; and James McEvoy, 'Grossatesta: An Essay in Historiography', in *Robert Grosseteste and the Beginnings of a British Theological Tradition*, ed. M. O'Carroll, Bibliotheca Seraphico-Capuccina, 69 (Rome: Istituto dei Cappuccini, 2003), pp. 21–99, at 91–2.
6 Dominic Baker-Smith, in his introduction to the translation of Erasmus's exegesis of the Psalter, suggested that, though Erasmus was certainly critical of Jewish theology and of those Christian exegetes who employed Jewish scholarship in their commentaries, he did not necessarily have anti-Semitic sentiments: Desiderius Erasmus of Rotterdam, *Expositions of the Psalms*, ed. Dominic Baker-Smith, trans. Michael J. Heath, *Collected Works of Erasmus*, 63 (Toronto: University of Toronto Press, 1997), xliv–lvi. This assessment seems appropriate for Grosseteste as well.

7. The editors suggest an implicit reference to the Jewish scholar of medicine, Isaac Israeli, but that reference was probably mediated through the works of Constantine the African: *DCL*, 1.6.12 (p. 31).
8. Ibid., 1.3.1 (pp. 14–15); 4.6.2 (p. 175).
9. Grosseteste's views on the Jews (particularly those living in England) has received some contrary intepretations. Southern, *Grosseteste*, pp. 247–8, has suggested that Grosseteste acted brutally at least in one instance towards the Jews (evidenced, Southern asserts, in *Epistola*, n.5, pp. 33–8), while others have suggested that he was far more favourable to Jews and Jewish learning: L.M. Friedman, *Robert Grosseteste and the Jews* (Cambridge, MA: Harvard University Press, 1934). Joseph Goering's recent study of Letter 5 would seem to confirm Friedman's reading over Southern's: J. Goering, 'Robert Grosseteste and the Jews of Leicester', in *Robert Grosseteste and the Beginnings of a British Theological Tradition*, ed. O'Carroll, pp. 181–200; although another recent study follows the same line of argument as Southern: J.A. Watt, 'Grosseteste and the Jews: A Commentary on Letter V', in ibid., pp. 201–16. In contrast, David J. Wasserstein has argued that Grosseteste showed little interest in the 'Jewish question' of his day: 'Grosseteste, the Jews and Medieval Christian Hebraism', in *Robert Grosseteste: New Perspectives on his Thought and Scholarship*, ed. J. McEvoy, Instrumenta Patristica 18 (Turnhout: Brepols, 1995), pp. 357–76. See also the comments of Gilbert Dahan, *Les Intellectuels chrétiens et les juifs au moyen âge* (Paris: Cerfs, 1990), pp. 575–8.
10. *DCL*, 1.1.1 (p. 7).
11. Ibid., 1.11.1 (p. 68): 'Ad ostension autem cessacionis legalium per Christum alie plures et efficaces possunt adduci rations quarum quasdam pro facultate nostra scripsimus in explanacione super apostolum ad Galatas, et ideo in presenti ab earum scriptione desistimus.' This is an instance in which we can say with assurance which text follows another. See *Expositio*, pp. 17–19.
12. Ibid., 1.2.1–1.2.6 (pp. 7–10). See Nancy van Deusen, *Theology and Music at the Early University. The Case of Robert Grosseteste and Anonymous IV*, Brill's Studies in Intellectual History, 57 (Leiden: Brill, 1994), pp. 19–36.
13. Ibid., 1.11.2 (p. 68): 'Quod autem nunc ostensum est de veteris legis abolicione per rationem, potest confirmari per eiusdem veteris legis auctoritatem, cui etiam concinit et nove legis auctoritas et sacrorum expositorum concors et uniformis veritas.'
14. Ibid.
15. Ibid., 2.1.2 (p. 76).
16. I say 'quasi-apologetic', since Anselm's intended audience was to be Christians, not Jews. However, he appears to be keen to aid those in contact with non-Christians, so that they could respond to their challenges.
17. Anselm of Canterbury, *Cur Deus Homo*, in *Opera omnia*, ed. F.S. Schmitt, 6 vols (Edinburgh: T. Nelson, 1961), 1.3 (2.50); 1.6 (2.53–4). On the identification of the 'unbelievers', see Richard W. Southern, *Saint Anselm: a Portrait in a Landscape* (Cambridge: Cambridge University Press, 1990), pp. 167–202; and Dahan, *Les Intellectuels chrétiens et les juifs*, pp. 427–31.
18. *Cur Deus homo*, ed. Schmitt, 1.3 (2.51): 'Si enim diligenter considerarent quam convenienter hoc modo procurata sit humana restauratio, non deriderent nostram simplicitatem, sed dei nobiscum laudarent sapientem benignitatem.'
19. Ibid., 1.10 (2.67): 'Ponamus ergo dei incarnationem et quae de illos dicimus hominie numquam fuisse . . .' Cf. also ibid., 1.20 (2.88). One cannot see this condition as an implication of natural reason that is prior to Christian revelation – a sort of *intelligam ut credo*. Anselm is not suggesting that one can come to know the salvific work of Christ

by reason alone. Rather, he is proposing that recourse to the reality of the Incarnation cannot be used to prove its own necessity. Instead, one needs to see the problems that Christ's saving work sought to remedy, so that his necessity becomes clear – and that means detaching the Incarnation from the theological arsenal in the *Cur Deus Homo*. See Jasper Hopkins, *A Companion to the Study of Saint Anselm* (Minnesota: University of Minneapolis Press, 1972), pp. 63–5.

20 *DCL*, 2.1.1 (p. 76).
21 Grosseteste touches briefly on this theme in his commentary on Galatians: *Expositio*, 3.19–20 (pp. 88–9).
22 *DCL*, 2.1.2 (pp. 76–7).
23 Ibid., 2.1.3 (p. 77).
24 Ibid., 2.1.4 (p. 77); see also 2.1.6 (p. 78), for the scriptural basis of this definition.
25 See *Comm. in PA*, 1.14 (p. 213); cited in Cecilia Panti, 'L'Incorporazione della Luce secondo Roberto Grossetesta', *Medioevo e Rinascimento* 13 (1999), 45–102, at 48.
26 *DCL*, 2.1.5 (pp. 77–8).
27 Ibid., 2.2.1 (p. 78)
28 There survives no record of Grosseteste's exegesis in his *Super Psaltierium* of the verses broached in the *De cessatione legalium*.
29 *DCL*, 2.2.1 (pp. 78–9).
30 Ibid., 2.2.2 (p. 79).
31 Ibid., 2.3.1–3 (pp. 82–3).
32 Ibid., 2.3.5–12 (pp. 84–8).
33 Isa. 52:13–53:12; *DCL*, 2.4.1–2.6.5 (pp. 90–102).
34 See especially *DCL*, 2.4.2 (p. 91).
35 In ibid., 2.5.1–2 (p. 93), Grosseteste does raise one form of signification on the sprinkling mentioned in the Isaiah text. He immediately connects this action with baptism, which (drawing from 1 Pet. 1:2) is a 'sacrament of the blood of the Lord Jesus Christ' (*Est enim baptismus sacramentum sanguinis Domini Ihesu Christi*). That *sacramentum* was also signified in Numbers 19, where the text describes the water of expiation that was mixed with ashes from the sacrifice of a red heifer.
36 Ibid., 2.6.8 (p. 98): 'disciplina videlicet verberum qu corrigi possumus et cum Deo Patre nobis offenso reconciliari'.
37 Ibid., 2.6.9 (p. 98).
38 Ibid., 2.6.15 (pp. 101–2).
39 See the outlines of Anselm's argument in Southern, *Saint Anselm*, pp. 206–7; Alistair McGrath, *Iustitia Dei: A History of the Christian Doctrine of Justification*, second edition (Cambridge: Cambridge University Press, 1998), pp. 59–60.
40 *Cur Deus Homo*, ed. Schmitt, 1.5,7 (2.52–3, 55–9).
41 *Dictum* 38 (fol. 28vb): 'ymaginemur aliquem qui regnum alterius fraudulenter et iniuste invasisset et sibi subiugasset. Et ymaginemur heredem contra eum dimicasse, eumque sic vicisse non ut omnino nullus sit in eo motus rebelligerans, sed ut nullus sit eius motus quem superare non possit, omnis viriliter resistens. In hoc ergo casu omnis virilis in potestate et in securitate si vellet pacem haberet, licet nondum omnis motus rebellans quiesceret. Sic itaque per Christi victoriam in passione mors est triumphata, id est diabolus, peccatum, et peccati fomes, ac per consequens mors corporis penalis'.
42 *DCL*, 7.1.1 (pp. 102–3).
43 Ibid., 2.7.2–2.9.1 (pp. 103–15). See also ibid., 3.4.1–8 (pp. 138–42), where Grosseteste also proves that Christ's advent was at the fitting time in relation to the beginning of the world.

44 Ibid., 2.1.5 (p. 78); 2.2.1 (p. 78).
45 Ibid., 2.3.2 (p. 82).
46 Ibid., 2.3.5, 2.3.8 (pp. 84, 86).
47 J.-F. Bonnefoy, 'La Question hypothétique *Utrum si Adam non peccesset* . . . au XIIIe siècle', *Revista Espanola de Teologi* 14 (1954), 327–68, at 327. See also Rudolf Haubst, *Vom Sinn der Menschwerdung: Cur Deus Homo* (Munich: Hueber, 1969).
48 The seminal work is David Lewis, *Counterfactuals* (Cambridge, MA: Harvard University Press, 1973); but see also Igal Kvart, *A Theory of Counterfactuals* (Indianapolis: Hackett, 1986). See Neal J. Roese and James M. Olson, 'Counterfactual Thinkings: A Critical Overview', in *What Might Have Been: the Social Psychology of Counterfactual Thinking*, ed. N.J. Roese and J.M. Olson (Mahwah: Lawrence Erlbaum Associates, 1995), pp. 1–56, for a good summary of the literature since Lewis's study. It should be noted that, in contemporary modal logic, counterfactuals are often connected to the 'possible worlds' strategy, in that counterfactuals suggest an alternative reality, even if the variation in the stream(s) of cause and effect is only slight. Grosseteste does not construct his counterfactual hypothesis here in order to consider a possible world (although he is certainly aware of this philosophical construct), but rather as a means of identifying the true cause of the Incarnation in the actual world.
49 See, for example, Boethius, *De persona et duabus naturis*, 8 (PL 64.1353); and Fulgentius Ruspensis, *De trinitate liber unus*, 9 (PL. 65.505).
50 Claudius of Turin, *In Genesim*, PL 50.901, 913. For a recent analysis of this commentary, see Michael M. Gorman, 'The Commentary on Genesis of Claudius of Turin and Biblical Studies under Louis the Pious', *Speculum* 72 (1997), 279–329.
51 Rabanus Maurus, *De universo*, R (PL 112.1038).
52 Richard of St-Victor, *De verbo incarnato*, 8 (PL 196.1002–3).
53 See n.2 above.
54 See above, Chapter 5, pp. 104–5.
55 Cf. *The Divine names*, in *Dionysiaca*, ed. P. Chevallier, 2 vols (Paris: Descleé de Brouwer, 1937), 4.1 (1–145–172).
56 *Dictum* 19, ed. Ginther 8 (pp. 127–9).
57 Peter Lombard, *Sententiae*, ed. I. Brady, 2 vols, Spicilegium Bonaventurianum, 4–5 (Quaracchi: College of St Bonaventure, 1971–81), 3.2.2 (2.29).
58 *DCL*, 3.1.5 (pp. 120–21).
59 Ibid., 3.1.6–7 (p. 121).
60 *Expositio*, 2.33 (pp. 69–70); and *Super Psalterium*, 88.8 (*B* 94vb): 'Quis igitur *in nubibus equalis Domino aut similis in filiis Dei*? nullus videlicet qui ipse est *Deus qui glorificatur in consilio sanctorum magnus et terribilis super omnes qui in circuiti eius sunt*. Glorificatur Deus cum intelligitur siue creditur immensitas, sapiencia, bonitas, summum gaudium, summa quod iocunditas ab intelligentibus seu credentibus talis diligatur, predicatur et laudatur. Consilium sanctorum est vnanimus consensus et concordia in glorificacione predicta et hec concordia siue consilium est ecclesia primitiuorum conscriptorum in celis vel est fidelium vnanimus conuocacio in terris. Et cum consilium proprie sit in rebus dubiis non tamen sancti de gloria Dei quo ipse sit glorificandum dubitant, potest tamen per nomen consilii exprimi esset consensu vnanimus sanctorum et dubietas que est aput mentes impiorum. Non enim credunt impii ipsum hominem esse Deum glorificandum neque eius humanitatem diuinitati vnitam esse adorandam indiuisa adoracione cum diuinitate. Ideo dicit in consilio sanctorum, quod dicit, in congregacione impiorum non glorificatur, sed videntes eum in forma serui et audientes ipsum dicentem "Ego sum veritas" et "antequam Habraham fieret

ego sum" scandalizati sunt et Christo detraxerunt dicentes eum filium fabri et demonium habentem.'
61 *DCL*, 3.1.8 (p. 122).
62 Ibid., 3.1.9 (pp. 122–3).
63 Ibid., 3.1.11 (p. 123): 'Deus-homo passus per se iustificat hominem lapsum'.
64 Ibid., 3.1.12 (pp. 123–4).
65 1 Cor. 1:30, quoted in ibid., 3.1.13, but not noted in the editorial apparatus.
66 Ibid.
67 McGrath, *Iustitia Dei*, esp. pp. 40–70, 158–63.
68 *Dictum* 70 (fol. 51va): 'Iusticia reddit unicuique quod suum est.' Cf. McGrath, *Iustitia Dei*, p. 35.
69 Ibid. (fol. 51va): 'Sed numquid in potestate cuiuslibet iusti est unicuique quod suum est reddere, non equidem ut hoc faciat actu et opere, sed ut vel actu et opere, vel voluntate et beneplacito? Qui enim vere iustus est vult unicuique tribui quod suum est, et si hoc esset in eius potestate tribueret. Beneplacet autem iusto quod unicuique quod suum est tribuitur, et quod unusquisque quod suum est possidet, displicetque contrarium. Unde qui voluntate et beneplacito quod suum est alii aufert, licet non actu, iniustus est. Perpetua itaque est iusticia creature et immortalis non quo ad actum largiendi et tribuendi unicuique quod suum est, quia talis actus non erit in patria, sed quo ad beneplacitum quo bene placebit iustis quod unusquisque quod suum est habebit et possidebit, sive pro bene meritis gloriam graciosam, sive pro male meritis penam iustam.'
70 *Dictum* 74 (fol. 55va): 'Est iusticia triplex: Prima est que consistit in doctrina moralium et observacionum ab humana racione et sapiencia inventorum. Et quia humana sapiencia ad divinam non potest attingere, necesse est ut alicubi dissonet a iusticia divina, et ita in alico repugnet iusticie Dei, et ita simpliciter iusticie Dei, quia: "Qui in uno offendit factus est omnium reus", et "qui non est mecum contra me est". De sic iustis dicit Apostolus: "Ignorantes iusticiam Dei et suam volentes statuere iusticie Dei non sunt subiecti." Et Dominus ait: "Frustra colunt me servantes doctrinam et mandata hominum." Est quoque secunda iusticia que consistit in observancia exteriori mandatorum Dei. Hec est iusticia legis et factorum, et iusticia scribarum et phariseorum, supra quam iusticiam nisi nostra habundaverit, non intrabimus in regnum celorum. Hec est iusticia quam "qui facit homo vivet in ea", hoc est, temporaliter pro transgressione a iudice homine non punietur. Tercia iusticia est cum opus rectum et a sacra scriptura regulatum a radice caritatis procedit, et finem habet summum bonum. Hec itaque iusticia habundat a iusticia scribarum et phariseorum in radice et fine, communicat autem in opere. Ipsi enim faciebant opera ex amore terreno, sive terreni comodi consequendi et incomodi vitandi. Idem itaque in quo vestra iusticia ab illorum iusticia habundat per se meretur regnum celorum, quia ex operibus non iustificatur omnis caro coram ipso, sed ex fide per dilectionem operante.' Cf. *Expositio*, 2.16 (pp. 63–4).
71 *Dictum* 3 (fols 3vb–4ra): 'Solet autem iusticia hoc modo diffiniri: Iusticia est voluntas reddendi unicuique quod suum est, utpote superioribus filialem timorem, reverenciam, et obedienciam; paribus fidem, societatem, et honoris adinvicem prevencionem; inferioribus regimen, et disciplinam, et protectionem. Sed hec diffinicio, licet in veste hac illud explicet quod sacerdotibus cum reliquis est commune, debent tamen sacer in participacione huius vestis cum reliquis a reliquis sic differre, quemadmodum accidit in magna domo magni patrisfamilias quod plurimi servientes veste unius coloris communiter induuntur. In ipsa tamen multitudine sic indutorum sunt quidam in quorum veste color communis omnibus relucet preciosior, factura figuratur pulcrior, et corpori aptacior, cultus habetur decencior. Sic sacerdotum obediencia debet esse humilior,

reverencia devocior, timor amancior, societas fidelior, honoris adinvicem prevencio a simulacione remocior, gubernacio moderancior, disciplina sapiencior et prudencior, protectio invincibilis fortitudinis constancia strenuior. Hoc ergo modo quod in veste iusticie cum reliquis vobis est commune universalis nature participacione, debet sacerdotibus esse proprium superhabundanti intencione, et hec licet prerogativa intencionis in veste vestra sacerdotali non parvam explicet pulcritudinem et preciositatem.'

72 Ibid. (fol. 4ra): 'Potest tamen adhuc eius pulcritudo magis explicari illa diffinicione qua Anselmus illam diffinit, dicens quod: "Iusticia est rectitudo voluntatis servata propter se", hoc est propter ipsam rectitudinem. Multociens enim servatur a multis voluntas recta, non tamen servatur amore rectitudinis. Utpote quandoque aliquis iudex aliquem qui deli<n>quit et meruit puniri vult punire, et rectum et iustum est ut is qui deliquit puniatur, et ut iudex velit eum punire. Servat itaque iudex quo ad hoc rectitudinem voluntatis. Sed si velit punire delinquentem plus amore alicuius lucri quam zelo iusticie, servat rectitudinem voluntatis non propter rectitudinem sed propter lucrum, et ita non est vere iustus, quia non recte rectitudinem, nec iuste iusticiam, servat aut exequitur, contra hoc quod precipit legislator dicens, "Quod iustum est iuste exequamini", ut scilicet sit voluntas recta, opus rectum, et intencio recta.' Cf. *Expositio*, 3.15 (pp. 84–5).

73 *Dictum* 3 (fol. 4ra–rb): 'Hec est ergo integra iusticia, ut servetur rectitudo voluntatis non alterius gracia aut amore nisi ipsius rectitudinis. Et dixi hanc diffinicionem evidenter explicare vestis vestre pulcritudinem quia, ut ostendit beatus Augustinus, omnis pulcritudo equalitate et rectitudine consistit, nec est aliud pulcritudo quam ipsa equalitas et rectitudo. Igitur et voluntas et intencio conformes rectitudini, conformes sunt ipsi pulcritudini. Ergo cum ipsa pulcritudo sit in se pulcherima, quid magis potest ornare animam aut decorare et pulcram facere quam integra et plena conformitas ipsi pulcritudini, hoc est ipsi rectitudini? Pulcherimus ergo ornatus anime pulcherimumque indumentum eius est conformitas voluntatis et intencionis sue ipsi rectitudini. Hec autem conformitas voluntatis et intencionis sue rectitudini iusticia est.'

74 Ibid. (fol. 4va–vb): 'Licet autem predicta diffinicio iusticie eius pulcritudinem et preciositatem simul evidenter et eleganter depromat, excellencius tamen eas videtur explicare diffinicio qua diffinivit iusticiam philosophus ille idemque catholicus, dicens quod iusticia est similitudo cum supernis divinisque substanciis supernas divinasque substancias angelos vocans. Est igitur iusticia similitudo cum angelis. Et hec diffinicio precipue convenit vobis sacerdotibus, qui propter similitudinem vite vestre cum vita angelica eciam angeli vocamini, dicente Malachia propheta, "Labia sacerdotis custodiunt scienciam, et legem requirunt ex ore eius, quia angelus Domini exercituum est." Et Iohannes in Apocalypsis per septem angelos septem ecclesiarum quibus scribit universitatem prelatorum designat. Similitudo itaque cum angelis est iusticia qua oportet nos nominatos angelos vestiri et ornari. Et ut huius indumenti nostri pulcritudo et preciositas planius explicentur aspectui vestro, consideretis attencius [autencius MS] quales sunt angeli, et in quibus oportet nos et vos assimilari eis. Sunt itaque angeli substancie incorporie intellective, irrepercussa acie intelligencie ineffabilem pulcritudinem Trinitatis contemplantes. Ipsaque sapiencia et verbum Patris est eis liber vite et speculum eternitatis in quo intelligibiliter legunt et limpide conspiciunt inmensam Patris potenciam per quam venerantur, innumerabilem Filii sapienciam qua illustrantur, suavissimam Spiritus bonitatem quam amplexantur. Ibidemque conspiciunt quid ad Deum superiorem illis, quid ad sibi pares, quid ad inferiores illis sit agendum. In illum a quo ad hec videnda illustrantur, superfervido amore rapiuntur, et in eius visione dilectione suavissima delectantur omnes operaciones suas secundum regulas quas in

libro vite legunt, regulariter dirigunt, tranquillissimam pacem servantes adinvicem, de bonis alterius fraterne congratulantur, nostram curam dum in hac misera peregrinacione sumus solicite, prudenter et fortiter agunt, tenebras ignorancie nostre illustrando, et sic nos occulte interius instruendo, affectiones nostras ad bonum excitando, opera nostra dirigendo, insidias et insultus aeriarum potestatum et malignorum hominum a nobis propellendo, profectui nostro congaudent, defectui vero nostra non modicum condolent. Hee et alie quamplurime istis similes sunt proprietates angelice in quibus oportet nos illis assimilari si voluerimus eorum societati uniri. Verumptamen cum non possumus in hac vita fragili eis assimilari similitudine perfectionis, oportet tamen assimilari similitudine imitacionis. Dum enim in hac vita mortali seu morte vitali detinemur, minores sumus angelis, nec cum eis possumus a pari contendere, sed multum a longe vestigia imitari. "Cum ergo mortale hoc induerit immortalitatem et corruptibile incorrupcionem", equalis angelis efficiemur. In hac autem mortalitate, dum "corpus quod corrumpitur aggravat animam", et carnis affectus obnubilat mentis aspectum, non possumus revelata facie, sicut faciunt angeli, ineffabilem pulcritudinem Trinitatis contemplari. Nec possumus in libro vite, sicut ipsi aperte legunt, legere quicquid perficit mentis nostre contemplacionem, et quicquid regit nostram actionem. Oportet enim nos angelos a longe imitando nichil avidius appetere, nichil dulcius habere, quam Trinitatis potenciam, sapienciam, bonitatem, licet in enigmate, contemplari.'

75 On the relationship between beauty and justice in Anselm's thought, see Stephen R. Holmes, 'The Upholding of Beauty: a Reading of Anselm's *Cur Deus Homo*', *Scottish Journal of Theology* 54 (2001), 189–203.
76 *DCL*, 3.1.14 (pp. 124–5).
77 Ibid,. 3.1.17 (p. 126).
78 Ibid., 3.1.17 (p. 126).
79 Ibid,, 3.1.18–19 (pp. 126–7).
80 Ibid., 3.1.22 (p. 128); *De spiritu et anima*, 9 (PL 40.785). Cf. Alexander of Hales, *Quaestiones disputatae antequam esset frater*, ed. PP. Collegii S. Bonaventurae, 3 vols, Bibliotheca Franciscana Scholastica Medii Aevi, 19–21 (Quaracchi: College of St Bonaventure, 1960), q.15, disp.2.1.33 (1.202–3).
81 *DCL*, 3.1.23 (pp. 128–9).
82 The most recent study on the doctrine of the last resurrection is Carol Walter Bynum, *The Resurrection of the Body in Western Christianity, 200–1336* (New York: Columbia University Press, 1995).
83 *De dotibus*. See below, Chapter 7, pp. 172–3.
84 *DCL*, 3.1.24 (p. 129).
85 Ibid., 3.1.25–30 (pp. 129–32).
86 McEvoy, 'Scottus and Grosseteste', pp. 220–21.
87 The exception is *DCL*, 3.2.2–5 (pp. 133–6), where Grosseteste broaches Christ's headship of the Church and the ecclesiological implications of the Cosmic Christ.
88 Ibid., 3.3.1 (p. 136).
89 Ibid., 3.4.1 (p. 138).
90 Grosseteste does broach the hypostatic union elsewhere, but mostly in comments made in passing, providing little indication of his general theology of the hypostatic union. See, for example, *Expositio*, 4.4 (p. 100), 4.7 (p. 102).
91 Peter Lombard, *Sententiae*, ed. Brady, 3.5.1 (2.41–6).
92 Ibid. (2.41): 'Et an ita conveniat dici divinam naturam esse incarnatum, sicut Deus incarnatus, et Verbum incarnatum sane dicitur.'
93 Ibid. (2.43): 'His insinuari videtur quod persona tantum, non natura naturam assumpserit.'

94 Ibid., 3.5.3 (2.47): 'Ideo vero non personam hominis assumpsit, quia caro illa et anima illa non erant in unam personam, quam assumpserit; quia non ex illa constabat persona, quando illis unitum Verbum est. Nam sibi invicem unita sunt simul cum Verbo.'

95 The best account of William's Christology is still Walter H. Principe, *William of Auxerre's Theology of the Hypostatic Union*, Studies and Texts, 7 (Toronto: PIMS, 1963).

96 *Summa aurea*, 3.tr.1.c.3.q.5 (3, 1.25–6). William had argued earlier that the personal identity of the God-man was more dependent upon the divine nature than upon the assumed human nature, which 'degenerates into an accident' of the union; that is, it does not remain a subject of identity since that would undermine the unity of the Incarnation: ibid., 3.tr.1.c.9 (3, 1.19–20).

97 For a good summary of the three opinions, and their history in twelfth- and early thirteenth-century theology, see Principe, *William of Auxerre's Theology*, pp. 64–70; Richard Cross, *The Metaphysics of the Incarnation: Thomas Aquinas to Duns Scotus* (Oxford: Oxford University Press, 2002), pp. 29–33.

98 *Summa aurea*, 3.tr.1.c.2 (3, 1.13); Principe, *William of Auxerre's Theology*, pp. 74–5.

99 Principe, *William of Auxerre's Theology*, p. 73.

100 Ibid., pp. 67–8, 71–2. See also Cross, *Metaphysics of the Incarnation*, pp. 32, 240–41.

101 *DCL*, 3.5.2 (p. 143): '[S]i enim essent plures Christi, id es plures quorum quilibet existens unus in persona esset Deus et homo, hoc fieret pluribus personis in Trinitate assumentibus hominem. Unica enim persona non posset assumere plures homines quia, ut ostensum est in libro *Sententiarum*, persona non potest assumere personam, nece natura personam, sed persona naturam. Persona vero unica assumente unicam naturam non provenit nisi unica persona in duabus et ex duabus naturis, et etiam si bis vel ter vel pluries assumeret eadem persona eandem naturam, semper unicus in persona, ille idem Deus, et ille idem homo [referring to the universal and not a individual] qui prius nec esset alius homo nunc et prius, cum semper esset unus in persona et unus in natura qui prius.' Compare this with William's reporting of a similar argument in the *Summa aurea*, 3.tr.1.c.3.q.6 (3, 1.28): 'Item si Filius Dei assumpisset infinita corpora et infinitas animas, et ita infinitas humanitaes, tamen propter ydemptitatem assumentis non esset nisi unicus homo, ut probatum est supra [=question 5].'

102 *Summa aurea*, 3.tr.1.c.3.q.6 (3, 1.27–8).

103 *DCL*, 3.5.3 (pp. 143–4): 'Ponamus enim quod Pater esset homo, et Filius esset homo, sicut Petrus et Paulus sunt do homines quia due persone in quibus multiplicatur humanitas; sic Pater et Filius essent due homines quia due persone in quibus esset multiplicata humanitas.'

104 Ibid, 3.5.4 (p. 144). Grosseteste seems to be following the teaching of Hugh of St-Victor that there were no limits to Christ's knowledge: *De sacramentis christianae fidei*, 2.1.6 (PL 176.384).

105 *DCL*, 3.5.3 (p. 143): 'Plures vero personas in Trinitate assumere humanam naturam est inconveniens'.

106 Ibid., 3.5.6–7 (pp. 145–6).

107 Ibid., 3.5.6.9 (p. 146).

108 Ibid., 3.5.11 (p. 147).

109 Ibid., 3.5.12 (p. 147): 'Ergo alius Christus superflueret omnino.'

110 *Dictum* 21 (fol. 18rb–va): 'Hec itaque terra veritate est vacua, quia veritas est adequacio sermonis et rei. Cum scilicet res est sicut dicitur, precipua itaque veritas est adequacio sive correspondencia vel conformitas rerum summo sermoni, hoc est Verbo Patris eterno, verbo, inquam, quod Pater eternaliter dicit, et verbo scripture, quod dicit per ora eorum

qui scripturam ediderunt. Hec veritas in supradicta terra, id est in anima perversa, non est, quia cogitacio eius et voluntas verbo scripture et Verbo beneplaciti Dei conformis et adequata non est. Ac per hoc nec sermo eius exterior, nec opus exterius Dei Verbo adequatur, ac per hoc totus homo interior et exterior veritate, hoc est a Verbi Dei conformitate, vacuus est. Totus est terra in quo veritas non est. Licet enim malus quandoque cogitet et velit, dicat et faciat quod rectum est, non tamen hoc recte facit, et ideo Verbo Dei, quod dicit quod rectum est debere recte fieri, conformis non est, unde plene veritate vacuus est. Veritas autem ante lapsum parentis primi fuit in terra. Eo autem labente recessit a terra, nec potuisset reverti in terram nisi veritas orta esset de terra. Ideoque ut rediret veritas in terram veritas de terra orta est, id est Verbum Patris de carne Virginis. In sola autem veritate, hoc est in conformitate ad eternum verbum, est pulcritudo, bonitas, perpetuitas, et si quid aliud nominari potest verum bonum vere desiderabile.'

Chapter 7

The Church, Pastoral Care and the Deification of Humanity

If Grosseteste considers Christ to be the visible centre of all reality, where the uncreated and created come to be united as one, it might seem odd to suggest that his theological vision still remains incomplete. And yet Grosseteste also states that any mention of Christ must make reference to his mystical body, the Church.[1] Owing to the way in which Grosseteste describes the subject matter of theology, the Church becomes the proper context for any reflection on humanity's deification, that is its ultimate union with the Trinity.[2] There is no doubt that Christ is the sole means by which this deification happens as it is the trajectory of justification through the Incarnation. It remains then to examine how this final return to God takes place within an ecclesiological context. We must begin, however, by posing a very basic question: what does Grosseteste mean by 'Church' (*ecclesia*)? As with previous chapters, it is useful to glance at Grosseteste's *Tabula*, where *ecclesia* is one of the index's nine distinctions. That distinction is composed of biblical and patristic citations organised under forty-three subjects headings:[3]

1 Concerning the mission (*ordinatio*) of the Church
2 Concerning the spiritual edifice
3 Why the law (*legislacio*) or the incarnation was delayed
4 Concerning the liberty of the Church
5 Concerning the persecution of the Church
6 That there is no salvation outside the Church
7 Concerning the martyrs who suffered for justice
8 Concerning the calling of the gentiles
9 Concerning ultimate rejection (*abiectione*) of the Jews [by God?]
10 Concerning the feast days in both testaments
11 Concerning the offerings in both testaments
12 Concerning dispensation
13 Concerning electing prelates
14 How subordinates are related to prelates
15 Concerning priests
16 Concerning preaching and preachers
17 Concerning the good king
18 Concerning the laws of war
19 That prayers are far more effective for war than weapons and power
20 Concerning the good judge

21 Concerning just judges
22 Concerning the tithe
23 Concerning excommunication
24 Concerning appeals
25 Concerning witnesses
26 Concerning testimony
27 Concerning sacrament
28 Concerning circumcision
29 Concerning baptism
30 Concerning confirmation
31 Concerning marriage
32 Concerning bigamy
33 Concerning consanguinity
34 Concerning relations by marriage
35 Concerning spiritual relationships
36 Concerning penance
37 Concerning scrutinising yourself
38 Concerning confession
39 Concerning fasting
40 Concerning orders
41 Concerning irregular orders
42 Concerning the sacrament of the altar
43 Concerning last rites

This distinction reveals a detailed conception of what constitutes a theological analysis of the Church. Grosseteste's idea of *ecclesia* includes an account of its mission (1), its spiritual nature (2) and soteriological role (6) – elements that one could describe as strictly theological – but also some description of its institutional structure (13–16) and juridical functions (20–26). He also considers temporal authority as an integral part of this area of theological thought, as the conduct of a king and the waging of war contribute to an understanding of *ecclesia* (17–19). And, not surprisingly, an idea of the Church embraced the sacraments, each of which had both theological and juridical features (27–43). In sum, for Grosseteste ecclesiology is an account of the nature, function and structure of the Church.

Grosseteste's skeletal idea of the Church is far grander than most scholars would attribute to a medieval ecclesiology. Historians have commonly described this category of medieval thought as solely juridic in nature and papal in orientation.[4] It was juridic in nature because it mainly concerned institutional structures and how they functioned in Christian communities that had simultaneously local, national and trans-national identities. Hence, most medieval ideas of the Church addressed principally the question of where temporal authority fitted into the Church, that is how the relationship between 'priesthood and kingdom' (*sacerdotium et regnum*) could be constituted.[5] Medieval ecclesiology was papal in orientation because the papacy was at the apex of the ecclesiastical hierarchy. Nearly every medieval discussion of the idea of the Church seems to examine in some form or another the role and authority of the papacy, either in terms of the pope's relationship with temporal authority or in terms of his relationship with other members of the hierarchy.[6] In accepting these two characteristics as fundamental to its definition, most historians have subsequently contended that medieval ecclesiology did not come into its own until the last third of the thirteenth century. Only then did a fully developed ecclesiology emerge in theological writing.[7] Many of the themes raised by the reforms of the eleventh century did not receive a complete analysis until the late thirteenth century, an analysis that was heralded by the appearance of a new kind of treatise, the *tractatus de ecclesia*.[8] As a result, medieval ecclesiology has been divided into two phases: a 'pre-history' from circa 400 to circa 1260 and the history of medieval ecclesiology, fully developed, from about 1260 to the end of the Middle Ages.[9]

Grosseteste would seem to demonstrate that this standard account is not wholly accurate. More importantly, his schematic description of ecclesiology raises another point about the subject area. It is tempting to consider the juridical definition of ecclesiology as a form of *Gesellschaft* analysis, in that its primary focus is on the Church as institution. Consequently, one might conclude that those medieval thinkers who showed little or no interest in the juridical analysis of the Church were more attuned to the Church as community (*Gemeinschaft*). Some twelfth-century theologians focused, for example, on how one may identify a member of the Church, and whether one could be a member in a sinful state.[10] The model of mystical embodiment (*corpus Christi*) also attracted attention in the twelfth and thirteenth centuries, and theologians examined the relationship between Christ as head and believers as members of the body.[11] These types of analyses do not fit well into a juridical ecclesiology proper, nor do they necessitate a focus on the apex of ecclesiastical authority, the papacy, but instead on the Christian community as a whole. Giving in to this temptation, however, would result in a bifurcation of medieval ecclesiology which may be more reflective of tensions in modern ecclesiology rather than any accurate account of medieval ideas of the Church.[12] In Grosseteste's case, this temptation must be fully resisted. All the elements of a *Gemeinschaft* ecclesiology are present, such as a focus on the Church as a spiritual entity or the sacramental experience. These elements are likewise mingled with a *Gesellschaft* analysis, such as the role of prelates and kings, the relationship between clergy and laity and the function of judges.

In Grosseteste's case, the ability to think of the Church as both a communion of the faithful and an institution that requires modes of regulation is found in the continual use of two metaphors. His principal one is the Church as Christ's mystical body, a metaphor grounded in Scripture and well developed by the Fathers.[13] This metaphor is certainly a more ephemeral conception of the Church where institutional activities do not necessarily contribute to any understanding of the constitution of the Church, but it does not exclude any consideration of ecclesial functions. In the body of Christ, Grosseteste argues in one *Dictum*, church leaders are like the eyes of Christ's body as they provide insight for the rest of the members.[14] Furthermore, pastors can be described as the mouth of the spiritual body for two reasons: first, they are God's spokesmen who must take care in what they say and how they say it; and second, they are the ones who masticate Scripture in order to nourish the whole body.[15] Grosseteste is hardly being innovative by mapping ecclesiastical roles onto body parts and bodily functions, but his use demonstrates a greater flexibility for this metaphor than some modern scholars have acknowledged.[16] At the same time, Grosseteste is able to consider ecclesial functions with a second metaphor of the Church as flock. Grounded in Scripture as well, this metaphor gave natural support to a topic close to Grosseteste's own heart, the care of souls as the pastor's main task. This metaphor naturally highlighted pastoral functions, but not to the exclusion of the ultimate trajectory of shepherding a flock, that is union with God. Hence Grosseteste uses the shepherd–sheep model to examine the spirituality of the laity.[17]

If Grosseteste's theological vision addresses both the theoretical and practical realities of the Church, one might expect to discover a treatise among his works entitled *De ecclesia*. There is none, of course, but this does not mean that Grosseteste's ecclesiology has no textual locus. Rather, much of his ecclesiology resonates in his commentary on the Psalms. As noted in the account of his exegetical tools, Grosseteste's approach to the Psalms was typical of scholastic exegesis: the subject matter of the Psalter is the whole Christ, that is, the relationship between Christ and his mystical body, the Church. Moreover, that subject unfolds in the biblical text by means of the author (and even the reader) taking on the persona of Christ or of the Church. In the case of the latter, Grosseteste notes at one point, to read the text in the person of the faithful is for the Church to talk about itself as if it were speaking about another person.[18] And yet, to assert that Grosseteste's *Super Psalterium* is his ecclesiological treatise is slightly problematic. Whereas most scholastic expositors took the time to elucidate clearly what they considered the subject of the Psalms to be, Grosseteste is less than forthcoming. It is possible, though, to infer that Grosseteste is in agreement with other scholastic expositors. The subject matter of a text (*materia*) was closely connected with the exegetical method one was expected to employ in interpreting the text (*modus agendi*), because the exegetical strategy was connected to the text's structure (*forma tractatus*).[19] If one accepts that the whole Christ is the subject matter of the Psalms, that position has a bearing on the method of exposition. In the *Super Psalterium*, the preface ends with a summary of the Tyconian rules. These are a set of seven rules that Augustine borrowed from the Donatist Tyconius. While Augustine obviously rejected Tyconius's general theology, he still believed that Tyconius's exegetical method was worthy of consideration and so he incorporated it into the third book of *De doctrina christiana*.[20] The first two rules are the most relevant to the exegesis of the Psalms. The first rule advocates a communication of idioms between Christ and his Church, head and body. The second rule points out that the Church is a bipartite body, composed of both good and evil people; hence Scripture may refer to both in the same breath. Grosseteste reminds his reader that this is because these two disparate groups are temporarily joined together by their mutual participation in the Sacraments. These two rules would have aided Grosseteste in the development of an ecclesiological mindset as he expounded the Psalms.[21] In fact, these rules could act as the *modus agendi* for the exposition of the Psalms.[22]

We have more than inference to conclude that Grosseteste considered the whole Christ to be the subject matter of the Psalter. In his comments on Psalm 87, for example, he begins by pointing out that in the past expositors have interpreted this

Psalm as if it were Christ speaking. While this is possible, Grosseteste states that it is more appropriate if one explains the Psalm as if it were the Church speaking.[23] He then works his way through the text, verse by verse, with this distinction in mind. He notes that the verse which reads: 'For my soul is filled with evils and my life has drawn nigh to hell' is scarcely applicable to Christ. How could the sinless Word be filled with evils? Instead, this is about Christ's body: the Psalmist says this in the 'person of a faithful Christian'. Such an interpretation is a bold position to take, considering that the weight of tradition was against him. At the very least, it provides a further indication that for Grosseteste the subject matter of the Psalms was the whole Christ.[24] Grosseteste's comments on Psalm 93 also reinforce the notion that he considered the whole Christ as the subject of the Psalms. He first points out the historical context of the Psalm: the condemnation of the Babylonians for their treatment of God's people. Historically, this Psalm concerns God's promise to avenge his own people, but it also speaks of the mystery of Christ's passion, which is itself an avenging of God's people since Christ triumphed over the Devil. In the same way that the Psalm was historically written to console the Jews concerning the harsh treatment by their enemies, so too the Psalm contains a consolation for the people of God. Christ provides victory and liberty to his own spiritual people.[25]

In this chapter, Grosseteste's *Super Psalterium* will be the textual anchor as we explore his ecclesiology. However, since this commentary is Grosseteste's largest (more than 300 000 words in length) it would be far too difficult to account for its exposition in a solitary chapter.[26] Instead, I will focus on the exposition of Psalm 100 as representative of an ecclesiological reading. There will certainly be a need to call upon other sections of the commentary and Grosseteste's other theological writings, so that his main premise is understood. That premise is that the Church is the context of humanity's deification, where progress towards union with the Trinity occurs. As the context of each Christian's spiritual development, Grosseteste theorises the Church as a place for 'the perfect conduct of life' (*perfectam vite conuersationem*). Such a conception has implications for the way one speaks about the nature of the Church as corporate reality. Moreover, the focus on conduct certainly has juridical and pastoral implications, and so Grosseteste's ecclesiology will become the natural context for examining his views on the pastoral care.

Conduct and Community

Misericordiam et iudicium cantabo tibi Domine: to sing about mercy and discernment to the Lord, as the first verse of Psalm 100 states, means, for Grosseteste, to focus on the proper conduct of a Christian. 'According to Cyril [of Alexandria],' he writes, 'this Psalm describes the perfect conduct of life and teaches the form of perfect holiness, which consists not only in fleeing evil and doing good, but also in pursuing and destroying evil, both in oneself and in others; and in promoting good, not only in oneself, but, as much as it is possible, in all others.'[27] If the entire Psalm unfolds to define the terms 'mercy' and 'discernment' in the context of a person's behaviour, how does one read this Psalm ecclesiologically? Grosseteste presents two basic reasons in his exposition. In the first place, he explicitly states that this Psalm is to be read in the person of the collective faithful (*in persona fidelium*), and that is because the first principle of perfect conduct is loving knowledge, or knowing love, of divine things.[28] Secondly, all the features of perfect conduct which are present in this Psalm relate, not just to the individual Christian, but to the Church as a whole. The foundation for Christian behaviour is a community that is united in a common faith and shares a love for God and for one another.

Grosseteste's discussion of mercy and discernment illustrates the ecclesiological orientation of this perfect conduct. To begin with, members are to express their mutual love by showing mercy to one another. Grosseteste notes, for example, that judges are especially to be merciful in fulfilling their judicial office. The careful blending of mercy and discernment produces a tempered approach to rendering justice, where one does not judge too harshly, but still exercises the rigours of justice.[29] Careful discernment identifies the crime and decides the punishment, but it is the merciful judge who realises that punishment is meant to draw the accused to penance and eventually reconciliation.[30] Grosseteste then expands the role that mercy may play in rendering justice. Not only should the judge exhibit mercy, but the whole community should demonstrate mercy to the accused person. The judge should turn to other members of the Church for merciful acts of intervention. 'Because a punishment for the most part is remissible by the intervention and merits of others,' Grosseteste argues, 'which nonetheless cannot be remitted justly through oneself, the judge ought to desire that the merits and interventions of others aid accused people in the alleviation of the punishment.'[31] Members of the Church should show mercy to one another, because it was God who showed mercy to them when he infused them with saving grace.[32] Furthermore, Grosseteste has in mind the discernment made possible by the grace given by Christ in the marriage gifts to his spiritual bride, the Church. He connects discernment with the virtue of faith, since this gift is the practical instantiation of the knowledge which Christ has bestowed upon each of the members of his body.[33] That it is a function of the community Grosseteste makes clear elsewhere in his commentary. He notes that discernment is often connected with the seat of the Lord. In Psalm 88, the Psalmist describes justice and discernment as the preparation of the Lord's throne. Grosseteste states that the seat of the Lord is not only the just person alone, but also the congregation of all just souls, the Church.[34] It is justice and discernment which prepare the Church to become the seat of the Lord, his throne, in which they attain full conformity to God.[35]

This conformity is the act of restoration in which the Creator transforms his creation. In all the works of God one should see God's mercy when he moves his creation from non-being to being, from privation to habit, from defect to healing, from a qualitatively lesser existence to the greater, from the state of diminishment to perfection.[36] The abstract nouns used in each of the five couplets indicate that Grosseteste has the act of redemption in mind: it is the salvific work of Christ that draws man from the region of sin into the region of full being;[37] it is also the redemption of humanity which moves the Christian from a predisposition of the sinful nature (often described as the absence of original justice, a privation) to the grace-infused habit of justice, to name but two of Grosseteste's examples. Discernment, then, moves the Christian, who remains in the grace received and does not decline from it, to a greater good and a greater perfection.[38] What makes this possible is the Incarnate Word of God, who also displays the attributes of mercy and discernment in the two natures of the hypostatic union. Christ shows mercy in his divine nature, for as the divine person of the Trinity he leads the members of his mystical body from non-being to being. He displays discernment according to his human nature, since Christ received the power to judge as the Son of man. 'Since we therefore believe in the dual nature of Christ with a loving and rejoicing faith,' Grosseteste concludes, 'let us sing to him mercy and discernment.'[39]

Grosseteste then moves on to the next verse, where he lays out his interpretative strategy for the rest of the Psalm. The two verbs of this verse – 'I sing' (*psallam*) and 'I understand' (*intelligam*) – become the launching point of the major features of the holy life. In singing, the Psalmist points to the active life, doing what is required of the Christian materially and physically (*per organum carnis*). In understanding, the Psalmist points to the contemplative life. These two 'movements' (*motio actionis, motio contemplationis*) remain pure and undefiled if they take place on the immaculate way, which Grosseteste identifies with Christ.[40] Grosseteste parallels these two movements of Christians with the two natures of Christ: 'He who walks in the footsteps of the man Christ in his actions and contemplates the excellence of his divinity, walks in the way which is not defiled.'[41] While Grosseteste is aware of the fundamental differences between the active and the contemplative life,[42] he treats them as two parts of perfect conduct. Nowhere does he dismiss one and elevate the other. Perfect conduct, however, is more than a commingling of action and contemplation. Perfect conduct has three parts to it: knowledge of one's own conduct, knowledge of conduct with respect to one's family and knowledge of conduct with one's fellow citizens. Drawing these two assumptions together, Grosseteste states that the Psalmist composed this Psalm with three parallel parts.[43] This tripartite division of conduct reflects the common description of what, since the time of Boethius, was known as practical philosophy. Boethius had based his bifurcation of philosophy into speculative and practical on Aristotle's *Metaphysics* and *Nichomachean Ethics*. Since these two works were not fully recovered until the thirteenth century, Boethius's work became the main transmitter of this classification of intellectual inquiry.[44] Practical philosophy, sometimes called moral philosophy, encompassed three related arenas, as it were: the solitary, private and public life. Or, in more common parlance, these areas focused on the individual in terms of ethics, the family in terms of economics and the society at large in terms of politics.[45] Grosseteste's comments on Psalm 100 are more than a disquisition on practical or political philosophy dressed up in theological language. He has in mind here a form of citizenship that is based on membership in the body of Christ, not the body politic. Naturally, the distinction between these two was minimal and often blurred in Grosseteste's lifetime, but the society or republic upon which Grosseteste is reflecting is founded upon the salvific work of Christ, not any governmental structure or political affiliation. One may easily build upon the idea of the Church such types of associations, but they cannot substitute for the rationale of the Church's existence.[46]

Since each Christian is a member of the body of Christ, as Grosseteste works through the proper conduct one has with oneself and with one's family, it is the community on which he has set his sights. If each individual would embrace mercy and discernment, as well as the active and contemplative life, in the end this would produce perfect conduct in family life and in the life of the Church. We need to retrace Grosseteste's exegetical steps to see how he arrives at this position.

Active Faith: 'I Will Walk in the Innocence of my Heart'

At the foundation of perfect conduct is loving faith. Grosseteste sees this implicitly expressed in the opening words of the first verse, because the full meaning of mercy and discernment is drawn from an understanding of the two natures of Christ, which is wholly an object of faith. What the Psalmist has in mind is not just *fides*, but *fides diligens*, the kind of faith that unites one believer to another.[47] This communal character of faith is not simply a question of consensus, in that a corporate assent to the articles of faith constitutes a unified body of Christians. Grosseteste would not reject this description, but he would certainly consider it to be incomplete. There are two facets of faith by which it is the principle of unity in the Church. First, it is through faith, Grosseteste argues in his exposition of Galatians 3:27–8, that Christians become the sons of God. Through baptism, traditionally called the sacrament of faith, all Christians become one in Christ.[48] One reason for this is that we 'put on' Christ as if he were a piece of clothing. The Apostle's terminology probably referred to the fact that early Christians were baptised in the nude, and so being clothed after immersion in water became a symbol of the new Christian life, that is being clothed in Christ.[49] Grosseteste's comment on this imagery is that this type of clothing transforms the soul and body, as if the person is configured for this clothing, rather than tailoring the clothes for the person. This being clothed in Christ is the very means by which Christians become the sons of God. However, Grosseteste also wants to point out that, if the process of spiritual filiation is unique and miraculous, its effects are equally so. The type of unity and conformity that filiation achieves transcends the standard accounts of how human beings associate with one another. This union in Christ is not configured in terms of bodily affinities since there is neither male nor female in Christ; nor is it constructed in terms of political relationships (*relationes actuales*) since there is neither slave nor free in Christ; nor is it established on the basis of ethnic kinship (*relationes naturales*) since there is neither Jew nor Greek in Christ.

What then is the basis of this union? It is twofold, Grosseteste explains, for the body of Christ is conceived as one person (*unus in Christo*) and as one nature (*unum in Christo*). The first description focuses on the grace of headship, that is, the means by which members of the Body are united to Christ as the Head of the Church.[50] The second spoke to a common nature among all believers, in that Christians participate in the divine nature of Christ. Faith produces a unified Church, and it is a union that is not just voluntary (in terms of both common assent to the articles of faith and of obedience to God)[51] but also an ontological reality.[52]

Secondly, faith has immediate social consequences. Faith without love, Grosseteste declares, is like a dried-out and dead tree. A tree that has no foliage and bears no fruit is surely dead. So too with faith: if there are no good words and works within a Christian, then there is no active faith.[53] Within the text of Psalm 100, this type of faith expresses love in four actions: compassion, examination, penitential discipline and contemplation. To be merciful the Christian must first show compassion to himself. The gift of discernment entails a rigorous self-examination. Connected to this is penance, which 'softens' the soul, and this is the active life of penance. The believer must also contemplate celestial things, for in this action one finds the immaculate way by which God comes to man.[54] Grosseteste then connects active faith with another disposition of perfect conduct, innocence of the heart. This also defines the immaculate way to God. Innocence is the opposite of doing harm (*nocere*), Grosseteste observes, whence innocence may be understood as not causing misery, or deserting it when one comes across it. Causing misery is doing violence to another, by stealing, oppressing the poor, and such like. Deserting those suffering is to avoid giving aid to the weak. All these actions are contrary to the last seven commandments of the Decalogue. In contrast, those who walk in the innocence of the heart display mercy to all those who suffer. This is possible, because they have first shown mercy to themselves. Merciful and innocent Christians know what it means to be merciful and not to harm anyone. 'Innocence therefore,' Grosseteste concludes in agreement with Augustine, 'is full justice.'[55]

The communal focus of Grosseteste's discussion of an active faith and an innocent heart is readily apparent already in this description. For the family, he continues, it is the head of the household who should be an example of an active faith and an innocent heart. If innocence embraces the act of not causing misery nor deserting those suffering, then the master of the household must demonstrate the full meaning of the term. The master, because he has power over them, may do harm to the members of his household, both servant and offspring, and not fear any form of retribution. If he should choose not to do any harm, then he demonstrates a truly innocent heart, choosing the path of mercy rather than the path of harm, even when the latter would be licit.[56] Innocence of the heart also demands that the master of the household take special care of the family needs and never jeopardise the family fortune upon which they rely for sustenance.

Taking care of his family also requires that the master investigate and understand what is happening in the lives of the family members, who are more important than any of his material possessions. No matter how pleasing those possessions may be to the master, no amount of care or concern will keep his holdings intact if his family is corrupt in its behaviour.[57] Finally, the innocent master realises that the examination of his own family (which is a loving act) assumes that, although by all rights he is lord of the family, he is also part of that family, and in some respects draws his authority from the rest of the family. He also recognises that ultimately he and his servants are equal. Grosseteste has carefully drawn out that leadership really means taking the position of a servant. In the family, if the master is much like the heart in the body, all the necessary nutrients will flow from him. He may have the dignity of being the one who supplies the spiritual and material necessities, but that act is one of service.[58]

It is this very same idea of servanthood through which Grosseteste connects the active faith and innocence of the heart found in the individual with the congregation of all believers. In his exposition of Psalm 83, Grosseteste notes that innocence means not to harm any one. Here he notes that being innocent includes both avoiding evil and doing good. If one does not do good, Grosseteste reasons, he first does harm to himself because he deprives himself of receiving merit for a good work. He likewise does harm to one whom he could have helped. There is a mutual need at work here, for all those who are part of the body of Christ share in a mutual debt of love. The proof of love is in the exhibition of a good work. Walking in innocence entails a mutual service among the members.[59] In Psalm 100, Grosseteste presents a specific situation where an active faith in collusion with an innocent heart produces an air of mutual servanthood in the community. Grosseteste considers the third verse to direct the reader's attention to the Church's response to apostates. The phrase found in the third verse, 'I did not lay before my eyes an unjust thing' (*Non proponebam ante oculos meos rem iniustam*), indicates that the faithful do not grasp by either internal or exterior sense anything which would lead them away from God. Grosseteste notes that the Psalmist is speaking of intellectual grasping, for he uses the verb *proponere* and not *facere*. There are many times in which a Christian has offended Christ without doing any injustice, and hence the Psalmist has a cognitive situation in mind.[60] Grosseteste moves his audience to consider a circumstance which normally prompted a harsh, physical response. He suggests, instead, an entirely different course for members of the Church to take. The Psalmist states that he has hated those who transgress, which through Augustine, Grosseteste identifies with those who know the Law of God and transgress it nonetheless.[61] Grosseteste exhorts his audience in these cases to hate the sin, not the sinner. His reasons are based on speculative grammar and his strong commitment to the role of penance in Christian life. Grosseteste first states that, if a person hates another sinful human being, then in effect the former hates himself, since he is also a human being. Moreover, he also hates Christ who became a man in the Incarnation and, by extension, that person hates the whole human race. The Christian's hatred has further ramifications: since humanity is a creation, it shares a common attribute with all that is created. Therefore the hatred of apostate men is extended to include all creation and, ultimately, the Creator himself.[62] What concerns Grosseteste even more than what hatred of one apostate implies is that this hatred often leads to killing. This is the entirely wrong response. Even if one concedes that the death of an apostate is due to the hatred of the vice and not the man, still nothing has been accomplished since it does not eradicate the vice, and in fact causes even more evil. 'The true destruction of a vice,' Grosseteste concludes, 'is to preserve the man in this life and direct him to a life of virtue which opposes the vice. Only in this way is the vice which one hates truly destroyed.'[63]

An Upright Heart

The concept of an upright heart (*cor rectum*) is another principle that Grosseteste first develops concerning perfect conduct with oneself, and then applies to the familial and communal context. He contrasts it with the term 'crooked heart' of the third verse in Psalm 100 (*Non adhesit mihi cor prauum*). The way of perfect conduct with oneself does not allow for association with a crooked heart, for it is not pleasing, nor does it share any common attribute with the upright heart. In contrast to the distorted and crooked heart, the upright heart of perfect conduct is in perfect alignment with the will of God: 'The upright heart does not decline to the right of prosperity nor to the left of adversity,' but keeps on the straight path designated by the will of God. The upright heart follows the example of Christ, who at his greatest time of need stated that he desired what the Father willed. With this mindset, the believer knows that all things happen (other than sin) under the control of the divine will.[64] The crooked heart, in contrast, does not conform itself to the will of God, but rather moves away in the opposite direction. Grosseteste describes this spiritual declination as composed of three actions. First, in declining, those with crooked hearts defile their image of God (*deiformitas*) and degenerate into a skewed and misshapen creature. They then lower themselves to the love of material and corporeal things, becoming subject to the finite things of this world, and in the end hand their faculty of reason over to the control of their bodily desires. Ultimately, they decline so far into the desire for only external things that they cannot be reclaimed.[65]

By contrast, if the upright heart conforms to the will of God then it has no room for pride. Grosseteste uses the image of the house from the seventh verse of Psalm 100 to illustrate this point. What a person loves inhabits his heart metaphorically, as a lover will often say about the one he loves, and two contraries cannot cohabit in the heart of the just person. However, if one hates pride and its related vices and loves only what is in conformity to God, this does not entail any abandonment of the corporeal world. The Psalm states that pride does not dwell in the middle part of the house (*in medio domus*), which signifies the tabernacle of the human body. Grosseteste then relates this love to three relationships. God inhabits the superior part of this house and, since he is above man, the just person is to love him more than he loves himself. Below man is his own body and the rest of creation, which although inferior in dignity the just man nevertheless loves with an ordered love. Finally, sharing the middle part of the house, the just man encounters his fellow citizens whom he is to love just as much as he loves himself. Nowhere will one find evil, because the just person hates it. Once again, Grosseteste clarifies that this cannot mean that a person with an upright heart can hate people engrossed in evil. He is not to honour them, but rather he is to desire that they destroy the evil within by entering the life of grace.[66]

In applying the principles of an upright heart to the two other parts of perfect conduct, Grosseteste first focuses on the make-up of a family. He has noted in his explanation of the previous verse of this Psalm that an evil person cannot both be unjust and be the servant of a just man. Because the just man is part of the body of Christ, the servant would end up serving two contrary masters, the Devil and his just earthly master, and by extension Christ himself.[67] In this verse, Grosseteste connects these two principles to conclude that a man who wishes to be perfect in his conduct among his fellow citizens should receive into his family only those who walk in the immaculate way and those who will not be the cause of pride. Grosseteste states that the Psalmist has servants in mind here (*Hic vero agit non de proximo et pari, set de seruo superbiente*), the members of the household who, although they are not bound by blood relation, are intimately connected with the moral health of the family. If their moral disposition is opposed to that of the family, then they threaten to introduce the vice of pride into the household. Servants, who do not share the same spiritual head with their masters, should not be part of the household.[68]

The principle also applies to the Church as a whole, for pride has no place there either: 'Although the proud man may participate in the sacraments of the Church, he is not part of the unity of the body of Christ.'[69] Grosseteste cannot exclude individuals, since only God knows who is truly part of the unified body and who is not.[70] Moreover, the standard scholastic teaching concerning eucharistic reception, which symbolised the Church's unity, taught that a priest could not refuse the host to any communicant (save for those who had been publicly excommunicated), for fear of causing scandal. If a person should wish to eat and drink unworthily and risk harsh punishment by God (so the Apostle Paul warned in 1 Cor. 11:27–32), he should be allowed to do so; the celebrant should not intervene.[71] Thus, when Grosseteste speaks of excluding pride from the Church, he speaks not of persons but of behaviour: he wishes to exclude from the body of Christ a specific activity of members towards one another, injurious speech (*iniqua locutio*). Grosseteste follows the text here, as the same verse which introduced the image of a house also contains the phrase: 'He who speaks unjust things did not prosper before my eyes' (*Qui loquitur iniqua non direxit in conspectu oculorum meorum*). Members of the Church abuse the faculty of speech when they use language for another end than for what it was intended. Speech is intended either to bring the hearer closer to the truth, or instil a loving desire, or do both, or even resonate with praise for God. Speech must at all times be kept immaculate and should not be abused. The requirements become even more stringent for those in positions of authority. Grosseteste includes a lengthy quotation from Gregory the Great's *Moralia in Iob*, which advocates careful use of speech. Grosseteste concurs, especially when it comes to jocularity. A frivolous word can become pernicious, and he notes Bernard of Clairvaux's pronouncement: 'Among the laity a joke is a joke; but in the mouth of a priest, it is blasphemy.'[72] The driving force behind Grosseteste's desire to eradicate injurious speech in both lay and sacerdotal members of the body is not just his commitment to purity in life and obedience to God's commands, though these weigh heavily in his mind in all his theological writings.[73] Rather, Grosseteste's idea is that the Church as a unified community is in preparation for eternity, that it is mercy and discernment, the active life of confession and the contemplative life, which shape the Church into the refined and recreated bride of Christ. This is the very reason that the Christian faith produces a community, a congregation of the faithful, who unite to form what Grosseteste calls a 'society of people which lives under one law of God' (*de societate hominum sub vna Dei lege viuente*).[74] In that process, the people of God become refined and are made ready to become part of the Church triumphant.

Community and Pastoral Care

Grosseteste's Own Pastoral Experience

This desire for mutual ministry which innocence produces must be taught, and not surprisingly Grosseteste lays that responsibility on the shoulders of pastors. It was a duty that Grosseteste himself had experienced, although somewhat unevenly. While he became interested in the pastoral care long before he began to teach the Franciscans at Oxford, it is difficult to ascertain the precise institutional context for his earliest penitential writings.[75] One or both texts may have been inspired by Grosseteste's appointment to the diaconate, which took place before 1225, the year in which the bishop of Lincoln gave him a benefice with cure in the village of Abbotsley.[76] The only mention he makes of this parish is in a letter he wrote to the Cluniac monastery at Reading: they once had the right to collect the annate from Abbotsley and they were pressing Grosseteste to resume that financial responsibility. The letter's sole aim is to take the monks to task for their false claims.[77] In addition to his appointment at Abbotsley, Grosseteste also became archdeacon of Leicester in 1229, as well as taking a benefice with cure at St Margaret's parish church in that same town. As archdeacon, Grosseteste was certainly engaged in the care of souls but in a more juridical fashion. That may have been balanced by a more personal engagement at St Margaret, but just as with Abbotsley we know next to nothing about his involvement in that parish.

We do know that this state of affairs ended in an admission of failure within three years of his becoming archdeacon. Grosseteste seems to have been aware that, although holding multiple benefices was common, it had recently become a point of controversy. The attack on pluralists had been spearheaded by the mendicant orders at Paris as they fired vociferous condemnations from the university pulpit.[78] The Dominican Jordan of Saxony took the battle to England when he came to preach at Oxford in 1229.[79] When taken seriously ill in 1231, Grosseteste thus came to the conclusion that God was punishing him for this transgression. He sought advice from the papal court through an intermediary and, although he could not obtain any written decision, he later claimed his plurality of benefices was contrary to the constitutions of the apostolic see.[80] After his recovery he resigned all the benefices, except for a prebend at St Margaret by which he remained a cathedral canon.

Grosseteste wrote two letters to explain his decision. In light of the fact that no medieval correspondence was ever private in the modern sense – but rather was written with the expectation that it would be read by more than just the recipient – these epistles may have been Grosseteste's attempt to explain his decision publicly.[81] To his sister Yvette, Grosseteste writes of the conflict between spirituality and the burden of wealth, a theme that she as a nun would appreciate. He may have cut himself off from a comfortable life by his resignation, he notes, but 'I have freely become poorer so that I may be richer in virtue'. The wealth generated by his pastoral benefices had prevented him from attaining even a faint form of the religious life, and this seems to have been a genuine concern for Grosseteste.[82] As noble and admirable as this reason was, it did not protect him from the more serious charge that he was shirking his responsibility. Those close to him probably saw his resignations as rather ironic: Grosseteste, the author of at least two treatises (and perhaps three) related to the pastoral care,[83] had done nothing but abandon his pastoral charges.

In his letter to Adam Marsh, the only close friend who had not attacked him, he presents three reasons for his resignations. The first echoes his line of defence from the previous letter, but this time he connects the burden of income to the perils of high office. Power and wealth are a deadly combination and he knows this from first-hand experience. They yielded a false sense of reality as they did not provide Grosseteste with any of the promised security and enjoyment, but rather impoverished him spiritually. Secondly, the burdens of all these pastoral responsibilities were so demanding that he realised he could not discharge any of those duties properly. Whatever he accomplished, he notes, it was done with too little thought and hardly enough boldness. Finally, he was compelled to resign in order to remain obedient to the apostolic constitutions. That argument was a difficult one to maintain as canon law had made no provision for resigning a benefice because the holder had more than one to his name. Grosseteste, in fact, lists the canonical reasons for resignation and then claims that, even though his own falls outside this list, he had acted out of fear of God.[84]

Grosseteste's failure to discharge his pastoral duties does not necessarily mean that he was somehow ill-equipped for the care of souls.[85] His pastoral works had already demonstrated a thorough knowledge of pastoral theology as well as the very practical issues of hearing confession. The *Templum Dei* is an excellent example of how to 'popularise' the complexities of Christian theology.[86] But is this a case of a man who knew all the theory but was unable (or lacked the desire) to function as a pastor himself? After all, there was more than one option before Grosseteste in late 1231: he could have resigned Abbotsley and St Margaret, Leicester and devoted all his energy to being a thoughtful and bold archdeacon; or, he could have receded from the prestige of an archdeacon and the comfort of an urban parish and instead dedicated his acumen and time to being a simple priest of the rural parish of Abbotsley. Grosseteste did not need to resign all his positions, and could have easily chosen to stick with only one of them. However, there was clearly a non-negotiable element of Grosseteste's life and one that remains unmentioned in his correspondence: his position as master of the sacred page at Oxford. His decision to resign all his benefices revealed the priority he gave to teaching at Oxford. It was not negotiable, though, because of any financial consideration. It was unlikely that he was receiving a substantial income from his mendicant charges (as masters collected their fees directly from their students) and it may explain why he retained the prebendary. Even if we could assert that Grosseteste himself had a capacity for pastoral ministry, it would still seem correct to conclude that he was more comfortable in the master's chair than the confessor's seat.

That may very well be true. Sometime after 1230, Grosseteste finally fulfilled a promise to a monastic acquaintance and wrote a treatise on confession. This work shares some similiarities with the *Templum Dei* in that Grosseteste discusses the type of topics and questions that one can use to structure a confessional enquiry. At the same time, this text is unique among Grosseteste's pastoral works, for it is imbued with a number of personal reflections. The reason for the delay, in fact, is the result of a personal struggle with confession in his own Christian practice. As he had lost interest in prayer, meditation, fasting, keeping vigils and other kinds of spiritual and corporeal exercises, confession perished as well. But the living, according to the prophet Isaiah, confess to God, that is those who not only are the living in terms of their own nature, but also in terms of the life of grace. In the latter, the heart pours itself out entirely before the sight of God, as if it were water. Hence, if he were to confess honestly, Grosseteste writes, it would be equivalent to encountering himself in prayer; that is, he would find himself in the true light from the sun of Grace.[87] In other words, Grosseteste found it difficult to write about the practice of Confession when he was not availing himself of this very spiritual exercise. It is thus possible to consider that generally he may have found the burdens of the pastoral care too heavy because it demanded more from his spiritual life than it did of his own talents. It had become so serious that those positions themselves became an impediment. The wealth and power of the benefices threatened the fabric of his Christian life and so he fled the pastoral care for the safer haven of the Franciscan convent, where the simple life was constantly valorised. For Grosseteste, the pastoral care was more than just a collection of responsibilties; instead, to be a pastor was to embrace a specific form of spirituality.

The spirituality of pastoral care continued to weigh upon Grosseteste's mind throughout his academic career. At one point, he was invited to give a series of sermons on the pastoral office. He complied by preaching first on the good pastor followed by an account of a bad pastor, a sequence built on the assumption that often something good is better understood when compared to its opposite. The last sermon focused on what he called the root of the pastoral office. Only the last two sermons have survived as Grosseteste included his own version of these sermons in the *Dicta* collection.[88] The exact context of these sermons eludes the modern reader. There is a reference to a principal auditor (*caritate vestri*), which may refer to the fact that Grosseteste was preaching in the court of someone who had pastoral responsibilities, like a bishop or an archbishop; but other than that, the texts make no reference to the circumstances. In the last sermon, Grosseteste employs an elaborate similitude of pastoral care being like a tree, and the principal auditor is akin to the fertile earth in which it is planted. That comparison assumes that this person is someone who is responsible for pastors, and so it cannot refer to someone like an archdeacon or a papal legate. Regardless of their original context, these sermons spell out clearly what Grosseteste considered to be the two essential elements of the pastoral care.[89] One element is that the pastor has a clear understanding of how to nurture the laity in their own spiritual growth. The second concerns the spiritual life of the pastor himself, since spirituality and ministry could never be divorced. We shall consider his discussion of these two elements in reverse.

A Pastor Rooted in Love

If the care of souls is like a tree planted in fertile ground, its only root is love. Grosseteste then begins an elaborate account of what he means by love. Augustine's notion of an ordered love (*amor ordinatus*) is at work here, and Grosseteste combines a number of Augustinian themes as he proceeds towards a complete account of love. To love, as Augustine described, is to bring together (*copulare*) the lover and the loved as one, but in the case of humanity that coming together crystalises in an eventual conformity to God himself. This is a conformity that comprises a transformation in terms of beauty, truth, goodness and strength. God does not inscribe in the soul a partial beauty as he deifies humanity, but rather he inscribes all beauty in the soul. The same may be said of truth, although Grosseteste pauses to admit that this does not mean that pastors who love God will know all things in this life. Rather the transformation in the soul towards full knowledge is developmental. Just as a master will not divulge all the principles of a certain art to his students, but rather take them step by step from the beginning; so the Holy Spirit is said to teach us all truth (John 16:12), but he does not divulge all of it at once. Instead, as a pastor increases in love, so he will increase in the knowledge of this great art of the Christian life.

Knowledge and beauty easily lead the author to consider goodness, that is the truest description of ordered love. Love completes the transformation by making the person strong. 'Therefore,' Grosseteste summarises, 'since love is the consummated beauty of beauty (*speciei consummata pulcritudo*), the fullness of wisdom, the sweetness of goodness and the unconquered, most victorious strength of power, it is clear that, beyond the Creator, there is nothing as great, desirable or precious as the love of the Creator – but all things in comparison to love are reckoned as dirt.'[90] This love ought to be boundless (*sine modo*) because God is the object of the love. Since he is without mode or measure, so humanity's love for him should be the same. Furthermore, he is the creator of all things: 'In creating, he elevated us from nothing to something, and between those two (that is between nothing and something), is an infinite distance. All being infinitely exceeds that which is nothing.'[91] God's creative act must be reflected in the love humanity owes to him, and so that love ought in some way to be infinite.[92] Finally, the link between loving God and the pastoral care is found in the person of Christ. He is the way in which the pouring out of this rooted love can emerge in the care of souls. This is because to love Christ is to love both his natures, human and divine. Thus to love Christ is first of all to love both God and humanity, and secondly to love him as the way, the truth and the life: 'He who says he remains in Christ, that is through love, ought to walk as he walked, that is to follow Christ through the imitation of his actions and sufferings.'[93]

A love which transforms the pastor, is boundless, embraces the person of Christ and imitates him will be the exact requirement for the care of souls. It allows the pastor to endure any kind of opposition (without fleeing it), to fear no adversity and most of all to inform, promote and confirm the same kind of love in those under his charge. Secondly, it is a love that will move him to nourish his flock, a consequence that Christ himself highlighted when he questioned Peter about his love for him.[94] The effectiveness of the pastoral care is not based on the talents of the leader or even in his personal desire to care for the laity, but rather is based solely on the transformative love, a love that deifies the person.

Grosseteste's account of the root of the pastoral care here stands in stark contrast to other contemporary analyses. During his lifetime, the expectations concerning parish priests were fairly mild. For the most part, both patrons of benefices and the laity were happy with a parish priest who was literate enough to perform his liturgical duties and generally was of a good character.[95] In raising those expectations, the primary emphasis in the literature of pastoral care or *pastoralia* was on the essential *tools* of the office. Driven mainly by the reforms of the Fourth Lateran Council (1215), this burgeoning literature focused the attention of bishops on the need to ensure that parish priests knew not only how to celebrate the mass, but how to hear confession properly and instruct the laity in the fundamentals of the Christian faith.[96] Little, if any, of these texts cultivated a specific form of spirituality, where love predisposes the priest for the care of souls. That is not to say that Grosseteste's assertion of love as the root of the pastorate is in opposition to the more functional concerns of other theologians who shared his interest in pastoral theology. Rather, in this sermon Grosseteste is raising the expectations somewhat higher. While possessing all the correct tools for the care of souls is necessary, they alone do not ensure success. More importantly, Grosseteste sees the spiritual disposition of the pastor in a twofold way: first, it is one way in which the laity may be instructed, for he presents clerical example as a fundamental source of education; and second, this disposition is not unique to priests, but rather describes the general progress of all Christians. This transformative love, ordered to God, is the root of the pastoral care because ultimately it is the root of the entire Christian life. The pastor's task is to aid in the transformation of his subordinates.

A Judicious and Nurturing Pastor

The variety of pastoral tasks used in effecting this transformation could be distilled into two basic ones: to judge and to nourish. Grosseteste opens his sketch of a bad pastor with a distinction about commandments. There are those, he says, that are to be followed by prelate and subordinate alike, such as the decalogue. Then there are those mandates that bind leaders alone, and these concern the responsibility of ensuring that the leader's flock follows the first kind of commandments. When a pastor's flock disobeys those commandments, the pastor will be held responsible. This does not limit or negate the responsibility of every individual Christian, but it does underline the serious task of caring for the souls of Christians.[97] The judgment of Christians occurs in two related fora: the internal forum or the individual's conscience (which was examined in the sacrament of penance) and the external forum, the ecclesiastical court. For most of the scholastic period these two fora shared an intimate relationship, since both regulated the behaviour of Christians and both drew upon canon law for that regulation. As an archdeacon and ordained priest, Grosseteste would have experienced both fora, although his pastoral writings clearly favour the internal forum. The only confessional treatise we can be sure that Grosseteste wrote while a master of the sacred page is the one devoted to penance in a monastic context.[98] Because of the intended recipients, we might think that this text cannot be representative of Grosseteste's general views on the role of confession in his pastoral theology. To draw such a conclusion would be a mistake, for its general principles (if not the actual mode of inquiry that Grosseteste suggests) are equally applicable to the world outside the monastery gate.

It was difficult for confession to be effective unless the penitent understood the questions being asked of her.[99] A good confessor instructed as well as enquired. Hearing confession about moral turpitude – defined mainly by failing to keep the ten commandments and committing one of the seven deadly sins – meant that the penitent had to learn the ten commandments and had to have some understanding about virtues and vices. Hearing confession about doubts and faithlessness clearly implied that the penitent could recite, and to some degree understand, the creed of the Church.[100] Moreover, Grosseteste considered that penitential discipline had a role to play in teaching the laity to ruminate on sacred Scripture. In his comments on Psalm 94, Grosseteste capitalises on the sheep imagery within the text. Pastors were to show the laity not only how to gnaw at the shoots of scriptural history, but how to pull at the deep roots, that is, to delve into the spiritual understanding of Scripture. All that feeding meant that the flock would have to drink and shepherds often ensured that their flocks would inadvertently eat salt so as to ensure they would seek water. So too with the care of souls, for the salt of penitential discipline ensured a balanced diet in lay education.[101]

To nourish was to teach the laity, or in the metaphor of shepherd and sheep, the pastor had to ensure that his charges grazed in the correct fields. Those fields included Scripture, creation, the person of Christ and the divine ideas in the mind of God.[102] In another *Dictum*, Grosseteste adds a fifth field for feeding, the pastor himself.[103] In his commentary on the Psalms, Grosseteste speaks of the pastoral example as the catalyst to the feeding of the flock: God's people must see in the words, examples and prayers of their teaching master an innocence of the heart which will encourage them to duplicate it in their own lives. Teachers must bring the Church into the fields of Scripture, creation and celestial contemplation so that they may feed on the elements which produce an upright, innocent heart.[104] A bad pastor, by contrast, shows little concern for the hunger of his flock. His charges may hunger after all those things in which salvation consists – the Word of God, doctrine and moral precepts – but they do not receive it. And the reason is not surprising: 'because many [pastors] do not know how to expound one article of faith, nor one precept of the decalogue . . . indeed, many despise doctrine and spurn knowledge.'[105] Such a negative attitude towards doctrine and a love of ignorance, Grosseteste argues, can threaten the health of a community of the faithful. Teachers and pastors are the mouth of the body of Christ. Their oratorial tasks are initially defined as being spokesman for God himself, but he extends this to include chewing on Scripture so that the rest of the body may benefit from the digestion. If leaders do not masticate, the rest of the body deteriorates.[106]

Peter the Chanter had stated that preaching was to be the result of chewing over Scripture, and so it was also part of the pedagogical profile of both masters and pastors.[107] Since the Fourth Lateran Council, and the advent of the mendicant orders, preaching had taken on a larger profile in ecclesiastical ministry. Once limited to the episcopal brief, now clergy and even laity could take on the role of preacher. There were specific guidelines set in place to monitor and control the burgeoning group of itinerant preachers in Western Europe, and the cathedral schools and universities began to develop literary guidelines that educated preachers could imitate. By the time Grosseteste had come to teach at Oxford a new form of sermonising had taken hold: the modern or thematic sermon, as it was called, provided for a tighter structure which drew from the classical arts of persuasion and gave a prominent place to stories and similitudes as vehicles for communicating any abstract truth of Christian doctrine.[108] Even with this change in the rhetoric, however, the aim of preaching had remained the same: to invoke a transformation in the listener. Grosseteste strongly believed in the evangelical character of preaching, for in his mind the preaching of the gospel was a catalyst to unity of the Church.[109] The task of the preacher did not end there, for once he enticed people to enter the Church he must then begin to open their ears to hear fully his voice.[110] That could only be accomplished with tears and prayers, which is why Grosseteste has no hesitation in adopting Gregory the Great's assertion that it is the contemplative life that must drive the preacher.[111]

Tears, moreover, indicate that compassion must also motivate pastors to instruct, especially those in need of hope. There are those broken Christians (*confracti*), Grosseteste notes in his sermon about bad pastors, who are so overwhelmed by the magnitude of their own sin that all they can do is despair. They have not been taught properly about God's justice and mercy:

> There are many who focus on the unchangeable foreknowledge of God, and so fall into despair. There are others who focus on the immutability of predestination and so have far too much confidence. Whence for the sake of rooting up each danger, it is necessary to show to both the concord between God's foreknowledge and predestination, between grace and free will (*liberi arbitrii*). There are few church leaders, however, who know how to explain the greatness of God's mercy and justice, and know how to demonstrate the concord between them. And perhaps they are even fewer whose interior eyes are not blinded when reflecting upon the concord of free will, foreknowledge, predestination and grace. Whence there are few who are to be found capable of binding the fracture of despair.[112]

The kind of compassion required in good pastoral ministry was bound up with an intimate relationship between pastor and laity. An integral part of the pastoral office, Grosseteste argues, is being able to call the sheep by name. That can only happen if the pastor is attentive to his charges both inside and outside confession. He must observe their activities, and once he has connected their actions to their confessions he can make the claim that he calls his subordinates by name. Moreover, even if the laity are his subordinates the effectiveness of confession is contingent upon the laity knowing their pastor well. Not that any layperson is to hear his confession, but rather they know him to be honourable, discreet and compassionate, and one who seeks to minister to the suffering.[113]

The high expectations of the pastor find similar echoes in those for the laity. Pastors were to bring their flock to the field of Scripture. That was a fairly easy thing to do, as the Bible was well ensconced in the liturgy of the Mass, and biblical themes adorned churches in interior wall paintings and as relief sculptures on the exterior walls. At the same time it was no mean feat to have the laity come to a spiritual understanding of the sacred page. A lay person may find the field of creation (laid out in similitudes and exemplary stories) and even the field of the moral example of priests to be accessible to some degree, but to graze in the field of the Incarnate Word was hardly on the same level. Finally, the whole trajectory of this metaphorical feasting was to encounter the solid food of the divine vision, or what Grosseteste calls feeding upon the divine ideas in the mind of God.[114] Was this a realistic expection in a society where literacy levels were extremely low, and where many of Grosseteste's clerical contemporaries referred to the laity as 'simple' and 'unlearned' (*ydiote*)? Two points are worth keeping in mind here. First, most preaching from the late twelfth century onwards to the laity drew upon a non-literal form of exegesis, namely reading the text tropologically or morally. As already noted, this was often supported by biblical histories, exemplar and similitudes drawn from nature, but preachers nonetheless considered it possible to use this form of exegesis as a means of instructing the laity. Secondly, there is no necessary corrrelation between literacy and an increasing sophistication in lay religious education after 1100. As Brian Stock has argued, oral and literary cultures were intertwined during this period. A community may begin with a text as means of shaping and identifying itself, but this did not require every member of that community to possess the knowledge of letter forms.[115] Indeed, in Grosseteste's account of the various fields available to the Christian, a text appears only in the first one, that is, Scripture. After that the Christian encounters the truth in other semiotic systems. It remains for the pastor to act as the interpreter, but the fields of creation, clerical example, the Incarnate Word and the divine ideas themselves do not necessarily require literary form.

Nonetheless, this kind of spiritual growth for both clergy and laity was a tall order. While Grosseteste could envision practical solutions to common problems in confession, he remained almost entirely theoretical about the final trajectory of the pastoral care: a maturity in doctrine and life that culminated in contemplation of the divine ideas in the mind of God. This configuration suggests that Grosseteste had a theological spirituality, in that his theological reflection was wholly integrated into a practice of Christian life.[116] The text that best exemplifies this is his commentary on the Decalogue, since it combines a practical account of how to obey the commandments with a discussion of the theological and spiritual ramifications.[117] Grosseteste summarises the ten mandates with one exhortation: love. That love, however, is well informed with knowledge so that the reader does not confuse love with unbridled desire (*libido*), but love rather as an affect of the mind that embraces all the right things and rejects the wrong things.[118] It is an ordered love that moves Christians to desire the true good for themselves: 'Our true good is eternal life,' Grosseteste writes in the preface, 'namely, to know the true God and whom he has sent, Jesus Christ. It is also the catholic faith, which operates through love, that leads us without error through this pilgrimage to our homeland.'[119] In other words, those who seek to obey the commands will experience that same love that motivates the pastoral care.

Grosseteste evokes another tree image in the *De decem mandatis*. Once again, love is the root, but at the base this tree splits into two large trunks: one of love for God, the other of love for neighbour.[120] Grosseteste describes both 'trunks' at a depth that is unusual for pastoral commentaries on the Decalogue. Having no other gods is to believe that God is the highest good (which Grosseteste calls the *diffinicio Dei*).[121] I have already noted that taking God's name in vain includes failing to recognise that God is greater than anything which can be thought.[122] This second commandment also has Christological implications, for to follow the teaching of Arius is to speak incorrectly about the divine nature.[123] As important, to diminish something God has made is also to take his name in vain. This assertion is another way of reiterating the usefulness (and necessity) of feeding in the field of creation. Even the most vile of creatures will reveal its Creator. Its measure will display the Creator's power, its beauty his wisdom and its order his goodness, and 'thus from any creature one may ascend into the Trinity as Creator'.[124] The seven commandments that concern love of neighbour contain some very practical explanations. Honouring one's father and mother, for example, must include caring for them in their old age and ensuring that a child's speech has a deferential tone and is at all times peppered with respectful language.[125] Conversely, the honour due to parents means that they have a tremendous responsibility in raising their children in a loving manner.[126] The mandate against theft becomes an opportunity to speak about restitution of stolen goods, and to point out that those in positions of power and merchants often steal from their customers or clients.[127] These practical comments fall alongside more sophisticated assessments. The prohibition against killing, for example, leads Grosseteste to explain why the slaughter of animals is not wrong (based on humanity's dominion over nature) but hating someone is the same as murder.[128]

All these details might make it seem that Grosseteste is supplying too much information. If this text were meant to act as a manual for pastors as they educated the laity, it would seem to focus on the wrong things. The result is that Grosseteste was writing for no other than himself.[129] That is an accurate assessment, in so far as any writer composes mainly for himself, especially when the topic concerns religious practice. The intention of the work is that, while the Decalogue may easily breed a functional notion of Christian practice (what to do, what not to do), it cannot be viewed solely in functional terms. Instead, behind the commandments, or more correctly behind the keeping of the commandments, lies the true motivation for these actions – love. It is not that Grosseteste is minimising the importance of obeying the commandments, but rather that obedience is the means to an end. The Ten Commandments are like the ten strings of the Psalterium or cithara: striking the chord is like performing the work, and so hearing the sound is equivalent to understanding the commandment in the same way as one comes to understand a philosophical proposition. That is because a proposition is like a line or string between two points, the subject and predicate. Its understanding comes when the signified proposition is sounded out in the mind. So too with the commandments. In working them out – that is, sounding them out in one's actions – the Christian comes to rejoice in both the commandment's action and its meaning.[130]

In other words, fulfilling the Ten Commandments is only part of a larger perspective of which Grosseteste wants his readers to gain a view. Obeying the first commandment did not just mean rejecting polytheism, but rather it is a context for considering God's nature. Taking God's name in vain was not about the misuse of God's name in the swearing of oaths, but rather it concerns how we speak of both God's nature and the Incarnation. The prohibition against killing certainly forbade taking the life of another human, but that also required some reflection on how hatred is murder, and that is based on a theological account of human nature and its place in the universe. Grosseteste certainly wrote for himself, but the *De decem mandatis* was an invitation to look over his shoulder and consider the kind of spirituality that obeying the commandments demanded. This is why he considered the Decalogue to be a special kind of Scripture: 'Because in their keeping there is salvation and eternal life, and in their transgression there is perpetual death. They are the supreme works of God which effect principally and specially human salvation and they direct the spiritual advance of humanity into the life of salvation and peace.'[131] In his commentary, Grosseteste aimed to provide a way for the pastor to seek and acquire that transformative love that would ignite his pastoral office, and consequently ignite the lives of all his pastoral charges. Grosseteste was personally aware of how demanding this outlook was, as he himself found it dificult to attain it; and yet he was convinced it was the only route available to pastor and layperson alike.

The End of History

Where is the ecclesiological context for this transformative love? In one way, it is implicit in that very configuration of love since there is both a theological and a social element at work. A more obvious answer is that, by connecting a theological spirituality with the care of souls, Grosseteste ensured that the context of this spirituality would be the corporate reality of Christianity. There is, however, a further theological explanation of the ecclesial nature of the spirituality of the pastoral care. If the aim of pastors is to be deified themselves and contribute to the deification of the laity, we once again find ourselves in an ecclesiological context. The union of humanity with God, in Grosseteste's mind, was not the union of individuals with the divine; rather, it was the union of God within the universal and triumphant Church.

Ecclesia triumphans is the kind of descriptor that does not sit well in modern theological analysis. It evokes, quite correctly, a triumphalist attitude that emerged from the early days of the Latin Crusades. The church militant (*ecclesia militans*) became an effective image, for just as Christian knights raised arms against a supposedly threatening infidel, so too the Church as a whole should take up arms against a spiritual opposition. Moreover, just as those knights triumphed over the Muslims (at least in the First Crusade) so too the Church as a whole would triumph – and that triumph would be over all the enemies of Christendom, spiritual and corporeal alike.[132] By the time Grosseteste began to lecture at Oxford, the image of Crusade had been seriously tarnished, and so the theological terms *ecclesia militans*, *ecclesia triumphans* had taken on a life of their own. They soon became shorthand for the Church in the present life (*ecclesia militans = in via*) which was composed of baptised persons, and the Church in the life to come (*ecclesia triumphans = in patria*), composed of both humans and angels.[133]

The reunion of humanity with God, that conformity to the divine nature, was to occur at the end of history and within the context of the Church triumphant. Angels had no reason to embark on a movement towards God, for they were already bound to him by the love that humanity would discover in Christ through faith.[134] Humanity within the Church militant, however, is bound to God in faith in a mystical marriage between Bridegroom and Bride. It is a bond of faith because there is a mediating factor, namely the Incarnation, where human nature finds union with the divine. Because of these two reasons, faith and the Incarnation, humanity enjoys a different kind of union with God in the mystical body. More importantly, because humanity is composed of both body and soul, it warrants special dowry gifts (*dotes*) in order to prepare the body for that final reunion with the Trinity.[135] These gifts are realised through the cardinal virtues. In this present life, the body should be ruled by these virtues because they are the path to the glorification of the body. Through a perpetual and immortal justice, the Christian acquires an unchanging glorified body (*inpassibilitas*); through prudence – which enlightens the soul – one gains clarity; through fortitude by which adversity is rebuffed and terrible things are attacked, the Christian becomes agile; and through temperance which attenuates the body itself, one obtains a spiritual simplicity (*subtilitas*).[136] In one respect, these are gifts to the individual Christian, but they are received solely by virtue of the corporate relationship between Christ and his Bride, the Church.[137] All the work of pastors, the feeding of the flock of Christ, comes together in the fruition of the sanctified soul and the glorified body. The whole Christ will find its completion in the final reunion between Christ's mystical body and the Trinity. Grosseteste's ecclesiology may be one that embraces both the theological and juridical elements of the Church as mystical body and flock, but its real efficacy is found in the fact that it is the place in which the progress towards deification both begins and ends.

Notes

1 The consistent capitalization of the word 'church' is not an act of piety here, but rather an attempt (albeit a weak one) to distinguish the abstract notion of Church from any reference to a specific, localised community of Christians or a physical building.
2 See above, Chapter 3, pp. 45–7.
3 *Tabula*, pp. 251–3.
4 The standard surveys of medieval ecclesiology are still Yves Congar, *L'Eglise de Saint Augustin à l'époque moderne* (Paris: Cerf, 1970) pp. 12–268 (chs 1–8); Edward J. Gratsch, *Where Peter Is: A Survey of Ecclesiology* (New York: Alba House, 1975), pp. 53–107; Eric Jay, *The Church: Its Changing Image Through Twenty Centuries*, 2 vols (Atlanta: Knox Press, 1978), 1.97–141.
5 See, for example, Ernst H. Kantorowicz, *The King's Two Bodies. A Study in Mediaeval Political Theology* (Princeton: Princeton University Press, 1957); Karl F. Morrison, *The Two Kingdoms: Ecclesiology in Carolingian Political Thought* (Princeton: Princeton University Press, 1964).
6 See the seminal studies of Walter Ullmann, *The Growth of Papal Government in the Middle Ages. A Study of the Ideological Relation of Clerical to Lay Power*, third edition

(London: Methuen, 1970) and Michael Wilks, *The Problem of Sovereignty in the Later Middle Ages. The Papal Monarchy with Augustinus Triumphus and the Publicists* (Cambridge: Cambridge University Press, 1963), esp. pp. 15–64.

7   Yves Congar, 'Ecclesia ab Abel', in *Abhandlung über Theologie und Kirche. Feschrift für Karl Adam*, ed. M. Reding (Düsseldorf: Patmos, 1952), pp. 79–108, at 93; reprinted in idem, *Etudes d'ecclésiologie médiévale* (London: Variorum Reprints, 1983), II; idem, *L'Eglise*, pp. 217–18.

8   Francis Oakley, *The Western Church in the Later Middle Ages* (Ithaca: Cornell University Press, 1979), pp. 157–74; Scott H. Hendrix, 'In Quest of the *Vera Ecclesia*: the Crisis of Late Medieval Ecclesiology', *Viator* 7 (1976), 347–78, at 347–8.

9   Yves Congar, 'Aspects ecclésiologiques de la querelle entre mendiants et séculiers dans la seconde montié du XIIIe siècle et le début du XIVe', *Archives d'histoire doctrinale et littéraire du moyen âge* 28 (1961), 35–151, at 99–104. Others have argued for a later date for the beginning of ecclesiology proper: R. James Long, 'The Question "Whether the Church Could Better Be Ruled by a Good Canonist than by a Theologian" and the Origins of Ecclesiology', *Proceedings of the PMR Conference* 10 (1985), 99–112, who argues that Godfrey of Fontaine's Quodlibetal question of 1293 was the first formally and exclusively ecclesiological treatise of the Middle Ages; and Henri Arquillière who argues that the first ecclesiological treatise was James of Viterbo's *De regimine christiano* (ca.1301–02): Henri X. Arquillière, *Le plus ancien traité de l'église: Jacques de Vitèrbe, De regimine Christiano (1301–1302). Etude des sources et édition critique* (Paris: Beauchesne, 1926).

10 Artur Landgraf, 'Sünde und Trennung von der Kirche in der Frühscholastik', *Scholastik* 5 (1930), 210–27; Johannes Beumer, 'Zur Ekklesiologie der Frühscholastik', *Scholastik* 26 (1951), 364–89; 27 (1952), 183–209.

11 Artur Landgraf, 'Die Lehre von geheimnisvollen Leib Christi in dem fruhen Paulinenkommentaren und in der Frühscholastik', *Divus Thomas* 24 (1946), 217–48, 393–428; 25 (1947), 365–94; 26 (1948), 160–80, 291–323, 395–434; partially reprinted in Landgraf, *Dogmengeschichte der Frühscholastik*, 4 vols (Regensburg: Pusset, 1952–56), 4.2.48–99. See also Walter H. Principe, 'Quaestiones Concerning Christ from the First Half of the Thirteenth Century: IV. Quaestiones from Douai 434: Christ as Head of the Church: The Unity of the Mystical Body', *Mediaeval Studies* 44 (1982), 1–82; Emile Mersch, *Le Corps mystique du Christ*, 2 vols, Museum Lessianum – Section théologique, 28–9 (Louvain: Museum Lessianum, 1933), esp. 2.157–60. For the eucharistic background of this idea, see Henri de Lubac, *Corpus mysticum: L'eucharistie et l'église au moyen âge. Etude historique* (Paris: Aubier, 1944).

12 See the classic but general analysis of Avery Dulles, *Models of the Church* (New York: Doubleday, 1974); rprt. Image Books, 1978), pp. 51–66.

13 See, for example, Stanislaus Grabowski, *The Church: An Introduction to the Theology of St. Augustine* (London: Herder, 1957), pp. 3–92.

14 *Dictum* 41 (fols 29vb–30ra): 'Prelati et doctores ecclesie in corpore Christi comparantur oculis, ut in Psalmo "Conturbatus est in ira oculus meus", et in Canticis: "Oculi tui columbarum." Primo, quia viam morum ceteris ostendunt menbris, suntque sicut dux itineris. Unde Petrus: "Pascite gregem Domini qui in vobis est, providentes non coacte sed spontanee secundum Deum, neque turpis lucri gracia sed voluntarie, neque ut dominantes in clero, sed forma facti gregi ex animo." Sic oculus providet ceteris menbris spontanee, nec sui comodi, sed comodi illorum gracia, nec sicut dominans, sed sicut ministrans. De hoc eodem spirituali oculi officio idem Petrus ait: "Parati ad satisfactionem omni poscenti racionem de ea que in vobis est spe et fide."'

15 James R. Ginther, 'A Scholastic Idea of the Church: Robert Grosseteste's Exposition of Psalm 86', *Archives d'histoire doctrinale et littéraire du moyen âge* 66 (1999), 49–72, at 65–6.
16 See the extensive mapping of ecclesiastical functions onto the body parts (even to the point where the mucus expelled from the nose signifies heretics!) in Wolfgang Beinert, *Die Kirche, Gottes Heil in der Welt: die Lehre von der Kirche nach den Schriften des Rupert von Deutz, Honorius Augustodunensis und Gerhoch von Reichersburg. Ein Beitrag zur Ekklesiologie des 12. Jahrhunderts*, Beiträge zur Geschichte des Philosohie und Theologie des Mittelalters, neu Folge, 13 (Münster: Aschendorff, 1973).
17 *Dictum* 101 (fol. 251vb): 'Ad hoc enim venit in carnem ut nos oves pascue eius pasceret herbis seminalibus doctrine scripture sacre; ut nos pasceret floribus specierum creature; ut nos pasceret exemplorum fruge; ut nos pasceret carnis sue lacte; ut nos pasceret divinitatis soliditate. Et ad hoc prefecit prelatos simplici plebi sue velud gregi ovium ut similiter pascant gregem Domini moralibus preceptis scripture, moralibusque institutis assumptis ex similitudinibus cum speciebus creatura, quia omnis creature species habet aliquod exemplar honesti et invisibilia Dei per ea que facta sunt intellecta conspiciuntur. Item, ut pascant gregem operum fruge exemplari; ut pascant sacramentum corporis et sanguinis Domini nostri Iesu Christi administrando, ut pascant eciam visionem divinitatis per speciem promittendo.'
18 *Super Psalterium*, 86.5 (fol. 87ra): '*Numquid Sion* (hoc est ecclesia loquens de se quasi de altera) *dicet homo et homo natus est in ea* quasi dicat: vere hoc dicet.'
19 Alistair Minnis, *The Medieval Theory of Authorship*, second edition (Philadelphia: University of Pennsylvania Press, 1984), p. 118.
20 Augustine, *De Doctrina Christiana*, ed. J. Martin, CCL 32 (Turnhout: Brepols, 1962), 3.32.45–3.37.56 (pp. 104–16). See Pamela Bright, *The Book of Rules of Tyconius. Its Purpose and Inner Logic* (Notre Dame: University of Notre Dame Press, 1988).
21 *Super Psaltierum*, praef. (*D* 2rb): 'Hec est prima regula de domino et eius corpore, quando a capite ad corpus aut a corpore transitur ad capud, et tamen ab una eademque persona non receditur. Una est persona. Subiungit Isaias dicens, *Sicut sponsa imposuit mihi mitram et sicut sponsam ornauit me ornamento*. Et tamen quid horum capiti quid corpori id est quid Christo quod ecclesie conueniat, utique intelligendum est. Secunda est de corpore Christi bipartito, uel potius "de Domini corpore uero atque simulato", ut sancto Augustino appellari placuit. Appellauit autem tantumodo corpus Christi bipartitum pro malis qui suscipiunt sacramenta ecclesie, et pro bonis. Augustinus uero corripit illam regulam quia non concedit aliquod malum esse membrum Christi uerum, sed solum simulanti eius membrum. Dicit enim ecclesia, *Fusca sum speciosa ut tabernacula cedar ut pelles Solomonis*. Non enim ait, "Fusca sum et speciosa sum", sed utrumque se esse dixit propter communionem sacramentorum et propter temporaneam conmixtionem intra una et eadem retia piscium bonorum et malorum. Tabernacula cedar ad Ysmaelem pertinent qui non erit heres cum filio libere.'
22 In the margin of *O* 1rb, the scribe has written *modus tractandi* beside the Tyconian rules.
23 *Super Psalterium*, 87.1 (*B* 87va): '*Domine Deus salutis mee in die clamaui coram te*. Licet iste Psalmus legitur ex persona <Christi> secundum formam serui orantis patrem, potest tamen fortasse non in commune vel in toto vel in parte legi ex persona membrorum. Est itaque ista vox primi vel generalis iusti vel cuiuslibet fidelis clamantis ad Dominum.'
24 Ibid., 87.5 (*B* 88rb): 'Licet autem hic versus expressime conueniat Christo, potest tamen fortasse non incongrue exponi de eius corpore vt sit vox generalis iusti dicentis, *Estimatus sum*, etc., quia iniqui vt scriptum est in libro Sapientie: *Vitam iustorum estimant*

infamam et finem illorum sine honore, ac per communis descensiuos cum malis in lacum miserie.'

25 Ibid., 93.1 (*B* 136ra–rb): '*Deus vltionum Dominus, Deus vltionum libere egit*. Psalmus iste historialiter legitur contra babilonios predicens eis retributionem vltionis quia Dei populum inique oppresserant et per tipum eorum designat vltionem omnium iniquorum iustos tribulantium. Continet etiam psalmus iste misterium passionis Christi, qua morte superauit mortem et diabolum triumphauit et continet insuper doctrinam patientie sanantis morbum murmuris contra Deum. De eoque prosperant mali et tribulantur boni. Et continet etiam consolationem iustorum a malis afflictorum, docens ne deficiant vel murmurent cum vident malos prosp<er>ari, se autem affligi. Ait ergo ex persona populi, Iudeorum captiuati seu populi fidelis afflicti, O vos iniqui oppressores ne gloriemini in malitia qui potentes estis in iniquitate quia Deus vltor existit... Subiit ex persona quoque fidelium tribulatorum contra murmurantes per impatientiam contra Deum. Legitur istud quasi dicerent ne putetis malos impune prosperari et impune iustos affligere quia Deus ulcisceret in eos. Ipse enim est *Deus ultionum et libere seu fidenter aget*, sicut habet alia translatio.'

26 See James R. Ginther, 'The *Super Psalterium* in Context', in *Editing Robert Grosseteste*, Proceedings of the Annual Editorial Conference, held at University College, University of Toronto, 2–5 November 2000, ed. J. Goering and E. Mackie (Toronto: University of Toronto Press, 2003), pp. 31–60 at 40–46, for a discussion of the commentary's content and structure.

27 *Super Psalterium*, 100.1.2 (Appendix, p. 193). For an account of Grosseteste's sources used in the *Super Psalterium* (especially the Greek texts), see James R. Ginther, 'The *Super Psalterium* of Robert Grosseteste: A Scholastic Psalms Commentary as a Source for Medieval Ecclesiology', unpubl. PhD diss. (University of Toronto, 1995), pp. 84–92.

28 *Super Psalterium*, 100.1.4 (Appendix, p. 194). Cf. *DCL*, 1.4.4 (pp. 18–19).

29 See *Dictum* 103 (fols 85va–86va), for another discussion of judges. This dictum also appears in two of the manuscripts of the *Super Psalterium*: *B* 33vb–34ra and *E* 38va–39rb.

30 *Super Psalterium*, 100.1.15 (Appendix, p. 195).

31 Ibid.

32 Ibid., 84.12 (*B* 77vb–78ra): 'Misericordiam et gratiam dat Dominus in presenti, veritatem et gloriam in futuro. Misericordia namque est qua nos auertit ab amore temporalium. Gratia vero est qua nos conuertit in amore sui. Veritas autem est qua in futuro, sicut promisit, liberat a pena. Gloria autem est qua in futuro conferetur gemina glorificationis stola... Vel diligit Dominus in nobis misericordiam qua dimmittimus nostris debitoribus et veritatem qua retribuimus nostris benefactoribus, quibus duobus ipse rependit gratiam dimittentem et gloriam beatificantem. Hanc misericordiam habere debemus quia nosmetipsos debitores per peccati obligationem esse cognoscimus, neque iustum est nobis dimitti nisi et dimittemus. Hanc misericordiam voluit Christus commonere iudeos, cum dixit: *Qui vestrum sine peccato primus in illam lapidem mittat*.'

33 Cf. *Templum Dei*, 6.5 (p. 38).

34 *Super Psalterium*, 88.15 (*B* 97va): 'Sequitur, *iustitia et iudicium preparatio sedis mee*. Sedes Dei celum est, sicut ipse ait: *Celum mihi sedes est*, et in Psalmo dicitur: *Dominus in celo sedes eius*. Et iterum: *Dominus in celo preparauit sedem suam*. Hoc autem celum est anima iusti. Anima namque iusti sedes est sapientie. Preparatio itaque sedis Dei est preparatio anime iusti, tam igitur unaqueque anima iusta quam tota congregatio animarum iustarum.'

35 Ibid. (*B* 97vb): 'Iustitia namque est rectitudo voluntatis; iudicium [*E*; id est iudicium *B*] vero est discretio veritatis. Recta autem voluntas, qua verum amatur, et discretio iudicii qua verum amandum dinoscitur, <pre>parant animam ad Dei conformitatem et ita ad hoc ut sit Dei sedes. Vel, potest dici iustitia habitus animi nostri ex quo bene agimus; iudicium vero quo vitam nostram discutimus et mala nostra condemnamus et persequimur. Iudicium itaque ad penitentiam, iustitia ad bonam pertinet actionem. Hec preparant animam ad Dei comformitatem et Dei sedem et hec sunt omnis boni fundamentum et firmamentum. Vnde Aquila transtulit: "Iustitia et iudicium basis sedis tue." Hebraica veritas habet "firmamentum sedis tue".'
36 Ibid., 100.1.5 (Appendix, p. 194).
37 On the theological conception of being in terms of salvation, see Walter H. Principe, *Alexander of Hales's Theology of the Hypostatic Union*, Studies and Texts 12 (Toronto: PIMS, 1967), pp. 30–40.
38 *Super Psalterium*, 100.1.5 (Appendix, p. 194). Cf. Peter Lombard, *Collectanea in Epistolas S. Pauli*, ad Eph. 1 (PL 192.70); 'Recte illa duo posuit; tunc enim prodest ac creditur bona vita, si fides est in Christo Jesu; tunc vere sancti sunt, si fideles in Christo. Vel distingue inter sanctos et fideles, ut sanctos intelligas majores et perfectiores, fideles minus perfectos. Scribit ergo sanctis, id est perfectis, et non solum eis, sed etiam fidelibus, qui, si non sancti sunt, vel in fide sani.' See also, Artur Landgraf, *Dogmengeschichte*, 4, 2.57.
39 *Super Psalterium*, 100.1.7 (Appendix, p. 194).
40 Ibid., 100.2.17 (Appendix, p. 196).
41 Ibid., 100.2.18 (Appendix, p. 196).
42 Ibid., 100.2.19 (Appendix, p. 196).
43 Ibid., 100.2.20 (Appendix, p. 196).
44 Grosseteste completed his translation of the Nicomachean Ethics around 1242, well after he had left the schools for the episcopal chair at Lincoln. When he had lectured on the Psalms, the only extant translation of the Ethics did not contain book 6, where Aristotle discusses the division of the sciences. See Daniel A. Callus, 'The Date of Grosseteste's Translations and Commentaries of Pseudo-Dionysius and the Nicomachean Ethics', *Recherches de théologie ancienne et médiévale* 14 (1947), 186–209, at 200–207.
45 Hugh of St Victor, *Didascalion*, ed. C.H. Buttimer, Studies in Medieval and Renaissance Latin, 10 (Washington: Catholic University of America, 1939), 2.19 (pp. 37–8); James A. Weisheipl, 'The Nature, Scope and Classification of the Sciences', in *Science in the Middle Ages*, ed. D.C. Lindberg (Chicago: University of Chicago Press, 1978), pp. 461–82, at 467–9, 473–4.
46 *Super Psalterium*, 100.6.56 (Appendix, pp. 204–5).
47 Ginther, 'A Scholastic Idea of the Church', pp. 57–61.
48 Ibid., pp. 61–2.
49 Wayne A. Meeks, *The First Urban Christian: the Social World of the Apostle Paul* (New Haven: Yale University Press, 1983), p. 151.
50 See Ginther, 'A Scholastic Idea of the Church', p. 59n, for the relevant literature on the doctrine of grace of headship (*gratia capitis*).
51 On the voluntary aspect of ecclesial unity, see *Super Psalterium*, 95.10 (*B* 153ra): 'Duplex est enim Christi regnum: vnum naturale secundum quod vt omnipotens regnat eternaliter super voluntarios et super inuoluntarios. De quo regno dicitur in Ezech. quod *in manu forti et brachio extento et in furore effuso regnabo super nos*. Alterum est regnum quod est secundum fidem et voluntariam obedientiam hominum. De qua dicitur: *Dicite in gentibus quia Dominus regnauit*.'

52 *Expositio*, 3.28–29 (pp. 94–96).
53 Ibid, 2.24 (p. 64).
54 *Super Psalterium*, 100.2.20 (Appendix, p. 196). The connection of penitential acts with Psalmody is also found in Grosseteste's exposition of Psalm 91: ibid., 91.1 (*B* 128vb–129ra): '*Bonum est confiteri Domino et psallere nomini tuo, Altissime*. Confiteri est veritatem dicere de tuis malis ut te factorem accuses et de tuis bonis in Dei largitoris laudem et gratiarum actionem, ut quod nostrum est nobis tribuamus, et quod Dei est Deo.'
55 Ibid., 100.2.22 (Appendix, p. 197). Cf. Augustine, *Enarrationes in Psalmos*, 100.4 (CCL 39.1409).
56 *Super Psalterium*, 100.2.25 (Appendix, p. 197).
57 Ibid., 100.2.26 (Appendix, p. 197).
58 Ibid., 100.2.27 (Appendix, p. 198). For a brief discussion of fatherhood (although based mainly on fourteenth-century English sources) see David Herlihy, *Medieval Households* (Cambridge, MA: Harvard University Press, 1985), pp. 127–30.
59 *Super Psalterium*, 83.13 (*B* 78ra–rb): 'Vnde subiungit: *Non priuabit bonis eos qui ambulant in innocentia. Ebraica veritas* habet "non prohibebit bonum ab eis qui ambulant in perfectione". Vnde manifestum est quod innocentia est vite pefectio. Non enim vere innocens est qui solummodo declinat a malo nisi insuper faciat bonum. Qui enim omittit bonum facere cum possit primo sibi ipsi nocet quia seipsum priuat primo quod mereri potuit ex opere bono. Secundo nocet alii cui suo bono prodesse potuit. Non enim solummodo ille nocens est qui alii aufert bonum quod iam possidet, set etiam qui cum possit non tribuit bonum, quod dicit: "Sumus autem adinuicem debitoris mutue dilectionis ac per communem mutue bone actionis quia probatio dilectionis exhibitio est operis." <In> innocentia igitur ambulat qui quantum potest non solum sibi, set et aliis prodest . . . Cum igitur innocens non sit qui debitum retinet cum soluere possit, manifestum est quod non est innocens qui debitum non soluit beneficentie. Omnes enim sumus vnius corporis menbra, et menbra ex debito nature pro se inuicem sunt solicita propter hoc debitum soluendi. Dicit Apostolus ad Galath. 6.: *Alter alterius onera portate*. Et ad Eph. iiii.: *Cum patientia supportantes inuicem et caritate*. Et ad Col. iii.: *Supportantes inuicem et donantes vobismetipsis.*'
60 Ibid., 100.3.29 (Appendix, p. 198).
61 Ibid., 100.3.30 (Appendix, pp. 198–9). Cf. Augustine, *Enarrationes in Psalmos*, ed. D.E. Dekkers and J. Fraipont, 3 vols, CCL, 38–40 (Turnhout: Brepols, 1956), 100.5 (2.1410).
62 *Super Psalterium*, 100.3.30 (Appendix, pp. 198–9). Cf. *DDM*, 5.9 (p. 63).
63 *Super Psalterium*, 100.3.30 (Appendix, pp. 198–9).
64 Ibid., 100.3.31 (Appendix, p. 199).
65 Ibid., 100.4.34 (Appendix, pp. 199–200).
66 Ibid., 100.7.59 (Appendix, pp. 205–6).
67 Ibid., 100.6.57 (Appendix, p. 205).
68 Ibid., 100.7.60 (Appendix, p. 206). In most mercantile households, servants would have been hired on a yearly basis: Peter Fleming, *Family and Households in Medieval England* (Basingstoke: Palgrave, 2001), pp. 72–6.
69 *Super Psalterium*, 100.7.58 (Appendix, p. 205).
70 On the history of this 'inner circle' of members of the Church, see Scott H. Hendrix, *Ecclesia in Via: Ecclesiological Developments in the Medieval Psalms and the Dictata Super Psalterium (1513–1515) of Martin Luther*, Studies in Medieval and Reformation Thought, 10 (Leiden: E.J. Brill, 1974), pp. 15–74; Landgraf, *Dogmengeschichte*, 4.2.48–99.

71 So far, no one has uncovered any explicit discussion on eucharastic reception by Grosseteste. For early thirteenth-century teaching, see Alexander of Hales, *Glossa In Quatuor Libros Sententiarum*, 4 vols, ed. PP. Collegii S. Bonaventurae (Quaracchi: Collegium S. Bonaventurae, 1951–57), 4.10.1–3 (4.152–4); William de Melitona, *Quaestiones de sacramentis*, ed. PP. Collegii S. Bonaventurae, 2 vols, Bibliotheca Franciscana Scholastica Medii Aevi, 22–23 (Quaracchi: College of St Bonaventure, 1961), 4.10, q. 64 (2.749–55). For the social implications, see Gary Macy, *The Theologies of the Eucharist in the Early Scholastic Period. A Study of the Salvific Function of the Sacrament according to the Theologians, c.1080–c.1220* (Oxford: Clarendon Press, 1984), pp. 118–21.
72 *Super Psalterium*, 100.7.63 (Appendix, p. 207).
73 *Dictum* 35 (fol. 25rb–va): 'Os Dei es. Numquid igitur loqueris opera hominum, qui "ut non loquatur os meum opera hominum", ait per Psalmistam? Perpende eciam diligenter quod idem instrumentum est quo sapis et quo loqueris. Quare, putas, sic ordinavit Deus ut eodem instrumento quo loqueris sapores discernas, nisi ut per hoc intelligeres quod omnis sermo tuus condiri debet sapore salis sapiencie, ut "os tuum loquatur sapienciam, et meditacio cordis tui prudenciam?" Item, cur ponitur lingua tua sub palato, quod figuram habet celi, unde et a polo palatum dicitur, nisi ut intelligas omnia verba tua debere esse celestia, omniaque formanda percussione interioris lingue cum celo spirituali, nilque extra huius celi ambitum debere figurari, ut agnoscatur in lingua tua, sicut docet Ecclesiasticus: "Firmamentum in operibus iusticie."'
74 *Super Psalterium*, 100.8.74 (Appendix, p. 210).
75 See Joseph Goering and F.A.C. Mantello, 'The Early Penitential Writings of Robert Grosseteste', *Recherches de théologie ancienne et médiévale* 54 (1987), 52–112, where they edit a complex set of texts about penance datable to ca.1219. The same editors date Grosseteste's most famous work, the *Templum Dei*, to sometime between 1220 and 1230. Grosseteste was given the benefice at Abbotsley on 25 April 1225: Leonard E. Boyle, 'Robert Grosseteste and the Pastoral Care', *Medieval and Renaissance Studies* 9 (1979), 3–51 at 4.
76 *Rotuli Hugonis de Welles episcopi Lincolniensis*, ed. F.N. Davis and W.P.W. Phillimore, 3 vols, Lincoln Record Society, 3, 6, 9 (Lincoln: Morton and Sons, 1912–14), 3.48.
77 *Episotolae*, n.4 (pp. 25–33). The Convent of Reading Abbey had lost their claim to the annates since they had not presented a new candidate to the bishop of Lincoln within six months of its becoming vacant. According to the Council of Oxford (1222), the bishop could reclaim a benefice if this situation occurred, which explains why Grosseteste was not given Abbotsley until April 1225, even though it fell vacant in the Autumn of 1224. Grosseteste therefore quite rightly makes the claim that his bishop had prevented him from sending a payment to the monastery. Ironically, the monks' claim that they had control of Abbotsley since 'time immemorial' may be an indicator that they lacked any documentary evidence, as this parish does not appear in the convent's cartularies: *Reading Abbey Cartularies*, ed. B.R. Kemp, 2 vols, Camden Fourth Series, 31 and 33 (London: Royal Historical Society, 1986). The rest of the letter focuses on the monks' attempt to proceed with a lawsuit against Grosseteste, even though they had originally agreed to a continuance so he could go on pilgrimage to Rome.
78 On the controversy over the plurality of benefices at Paris, see M.M. Davy, *Les sermons universitaires parisiens de 1230–1231*, Etudes de philosophie médiévale, 15 (Paris: Vrin, 1931), esp. pp. 90–93.
79 On the preaching of Jordan of Saxony at Oxford, see A.G. Little and D.L. Douie, 'Three Sermons of Friar Jordan of Saxony, the Successor of St Dominic, Preaching in England, A.D. 1229', *English Historical Review* 54 (1939), 1–19.

80 In a letter written not long after 1237 to the papal legate to England, he describes how he sought advice from the papal court on this matter: *Epistolae* 74 (pp. 241–3).
81 For a dicussion of Grosseteste's letter collection, see Thomson, *Writings*, pp. 192–213; and Ginther, 'Theological Education at the Oxford Studium in the Thirteenth Century: A Reassessment of Robert Grosseteste's Letter to the Oxford Theologians', *Franciscan Studies* 55 (1998), 83–104, at 87–93. The best guides to the medieval art of letter-writing (*ars dictaminis*) are Giles Constable, *Letters and Letter Collections*, Typologie des sources du moyen âge, 17 (Turnhout: Brepols, 1976); and Martin Camargo, *Ars dictaminis, ars dictandi*, Typologie des sources du moyen âge, 60 (Turnhout: Brepols, 1991).
82 *Epistolae*, 8 (pp. 43–4).
83 In addition to the works mentioned in n.75 above, Grosseteste also penned a work about confession for a monastic audience. There is no evidence to indicate a precise date for its composition (save for the fact that the rubric describes Grosseteste as *magister*) and so he may have (or may have not) completed it before his resignations in 1231: Joseph Goering and F.A.C. Mantello, 'The *Perambulavit Iudas . . .* (*Speculum confessionis*) Attributed to Robert Grosseteste', *Revue Bénédictine* 96 (1986), 125–68.
84 *Epistolae*, 9 (pp. 45–7).
85 So argues Southern, *Grosseteste*, pp. 74–5.
86 *Templum Dei*, pp. 6–9.
87 *Speculum Confessionis*, ed. Goering and Mantello, 4 (pp. 148–9).
88 *Dicta* 90–91 (fols 66va–72rb). By the phrase 'his own version', I mean that they are not *reportationes* of the sermon. Rather, Grosseteste refers to the sermons in the past tense in his prefatory comments for each of them, and so I infer that these texts represent his own record of preaching. It could be conjectured that *Dictum* 101 may be the missing sermon (*Sermo ad pastores de hoc verbo, 'Ego sum pastor bonus'*), but Grosseteste makes no connection between *Dicta* 90–91 and 101. That Grosseteste may have preached these sermons before Hugh de Welles is plausible, but lacks any supporting evidence.
89 The following will seem to be a rather cursory account of Grosseteste's thought on the care of souls. For obvious reasons, Grosseteste gave greater attention to this subject as bishop of Lincoln, and so this is one topic that demonstrates the weakness of focusing solely on Grosseteste's magisterial career. For more comprehensive accounts of the pastoral care, which take account of his writings after 1235, see Boyle, 'Robert Grosseteste and the Pastoral Care', *passim*; the introductory comments to the edition of *Deus est*: S. Wenzel, 'Robert Grosseteste's Treatise on Confession, *Deus est*', *Franciscan Studies* 30 (1970), 218–93; and the introduction to the *Templum Dei*, pp. 1–14.
90 *Dictum* 91 (fol. 70rb): 'Cum igitur amor sit et speciei consummata pulcritudo, et sapiencie plenitudo, et bonitatis dulcedo, et potencie invictissime victoriosissima fortitudo, patet quod citra creatorem ut amor creatoris nil magnum, aut appetibile, aut preciosum, sed omnia amore comparacione computantur ut lutum.'
91 Ibid. (fol. 70rb): 'Creando enim nos elevavit a nichilo ad aliquid, inter que duo, scilicet inter nichilum et aliquid, est distancia infinita. Omne enim ens id quod nichil est infiniter excedit.'
92 See above, Chapter 5, n. 109, p. 117.
93 *Dictum* 91 (fol. 71va): 'Qui enim dicit se in Christo manere, per dilectionem videlicet, debet sicut ille ambulavit et ipse ambulare, hoc est per actionum et passionum ipsius imitacionem ipsum sequi.'
94 Ibid. (fol. 71va–vb): 'Hec est igitur pars dilectionis que vera radix est cure pastoralis, ut diligat invincibiliter omnium adversorum tolleranciam pro fide et veritate non deserendis,

sed observandis in se, et pro eisdem informandis et promovendis et confirmandis in subditis, et ut invincibiliter pro eisdem diligat omnium prosperorum contemptum, adversa nulla timeat, prospera nulla concupiscat, in adversis si accidant non deprematur, immo pocius in eorum tollerancia pro Christo vehementer letetur, "omne gaudium", secundum Apostoli doctrinam, *existimans in temptaciones varias incidere*. In prosperis si accidant non elevetur, sed magis timeat eorum blandam fallaciam quam adversorum torrentem seviciam. Ex hac tali dilectionis radice crescere potest in altum robur pastoralis cure. Hoc est enim oves vere pascere, omnia sustinere adversa, omnia recusare prospera, pro veritatis confessione ut oves vos imitentur. Et hec talis ovium pastio est retribucio quam retribuere possumus Domino pro omnibus que retribuit nobis. Hec est calicis salutaris accepcio. Unde et Augustinus super hoc verbo ait: "Quid illi poterat retribuere Petrus qui amabat illum? Audi quid: pasce oves meas, id est fac pro fratribus quod pro te feci. Omnes sanguine meo redemi. Nolite dubitare mori pro veritatis confessione ut ceteri vos imitentur." Et ut noveris quia sic ab eo pasci volebat oves suas ut animam suam pro ovibus poneret, hec illi continuo dixit: *Cum esses iunior, cingebas te et ambulabas ubi volebas. Cum autem senueris, extendes manus tuas et alius te cinget et ducet quo tu non vis. Hec autem dixit*, ut ait Evangelista, *signans qua morte esse clarificaturus Deum*, ut cui dixerat, pasce oves meas, doceret eum ponere animam pro fratribus suis.'

95 Joseph Goering, *William de Montibus (c.1140–1213). The Schools and the Literature of the Pastoral Care*, Studies and Texts 108 (Toronto: PIMS, 1992), pp. 60–62.
96 Leonard E. Boyle, 'The Fourth Lateran Council and Manuals of Popular Theology', in *The Popular Literature of Medieval England*, ed. T.J. Heffernan (Knoxville: University of Tennessee Press, 1985), pp. 30–43.
97 *Dictum 90* (fol. 66vb): 'Duplex enim genus mandatorum proponitur in scriptura: Unum quod precipit agendum et prohibet omittendum, ut *honora patrem et matrem, non occides, non mechaberis*, etc. Et hoc genus mandadorum astringit communiter subditos et prelatos. Alterum est genus preceptorum, quod precipit punire dictorum mandatorum transgressores, et premiare observatores, ut *qui maledixerit patri vel matri, morte moriatur*, et *qui occiderit hominem occidatur*, et *morte moriantur ambo et mechus et adultera*. Et hoc genus preceptorum non astringit ad agendum ea plebem subiectam, sed prepositos. Ad punicionem vero transgressorum et premiacionem bonorum tenentur prepositi soli, quorum solummodo est confessos vel rite convictos ex sentencia iudiciaria condempnare vel bonos premiare. Itaque prepositi duplici precepto mandatorum sunt constricti, sicut dicit Apostolus: *Qui bene presunt, duplici honore digni sunt*, quia premiacione pro utriusque generis mandatorum observacione. Et similiter qui male presunt, a contrario duplici dampnacione digni sunt, pro utriusque scilicet generis mandatorum transgressione. Ad hec pastor malus pro suis et pro gregis punietur delictis. Licet enim unusquisque proprium onus portabit, nichilominus tamen verum est quod pastor punietur pro delictis gregis, quia quicquid peccat grex per omissionem doctrine, exempli, et oracionis pastoris, per omissionem videlicet eius quod non, sicut precipit Apostolus, *predicat verbum, instat oportune, inoportune, arguit, obsecrat, increpat in omni paciencia et doctrina*, in pastoris culpam et necgligenciam redundat, sicut econtra quicquid bene facit grex per pastorum, in predictis que numerat Apostolus, diligenciam, in pastorum gloriam et meritum habundat. Recte igitur qui bene presunt, duplici honore, aut qui male, duplici condempnacione, sunt digni.' Compare this to Grosseteste's opening statement at his audience with Pope Innocent IV in 1250, quoted in Southern, *Grosseteste*, p. 258.
98 See above, n. 83.

99 For a general account of the literature of the pastoral care, see Boyle, 'The Fourth Lateran Council and Manuals of Popular Theology', pp. 30–43; Goering, *William de Montibus*, pp. 58–99.

100 See the schematic account of how to use the decalogue, the virtues and vices, and the Creed in the *Templum Dei*, 3.1–5.6 (pp. 32–6).

101 *Super Psalterium*, 94.7 (*B* 147rb–vb): 'Sequitur, *Et nos populus eius et oues manus eius*, quasi dicet: ipse est Dominus nos possidens, Deus nos creans videtur participatione nostre nature et ideo securi ante illum procedamus quia sumus *populus pascue eius et oues manus eius*. Exaudiet enim quos pascit et fecit et sicut notat Augustinus super hunc locum: "Psalmista eleganter verborum ordinem commutauit et tanquam non propria reddidit vt ipsos intelligamus oues qui sunt populi. Non dixit *oues pascue et populus manuum eius*, quod magis putabat posse congruere quia oues ad pascua pertinent, set ait *populus pascue*. Ergo populus oues sunt quia dicit *populus pascue eius*" . . . Oues iste pascuntur in agro scripture et in agro creature ex apicibus literarum et speciebus rerum . . . Hec oues multum morantur pascentes in vno loco quia carpunt herbas vsque ad radices non contente extremitatibus sicut capre. Quia cum versantur circa aliquem scripture locum vt illum intelligant et intelligendo proficiant, non contenti sunt sola literali superficie, sicut vage et statuendo a sinistris capre, set vsque ad radicem perscrutantur vt intelligant et memorantur vt faciant. Non solum enim egrediuntur ad litere superficiem set et ingrediuntur ad spiritualis intelligentie radicem, vt pascua inueniant . . . Ideo sapientes pastores dant hiis ouibus plerumque salem, hoc est asperam [*corr. ex E*, aspersam *B*] et amaram reprehensionem et penitentialem asperitatem, vt has aquas magis sitiant et spiritali gaudio plenius inpinguantur. Cauent tamen pastores ne nimium pinguescant oues circa renes, hoc est circa sensuales voluptates que pinguendo multiplicantur propter bona pascua, hoc est propter multiplicata bona temporalia.' See Ginther, 'A Scholastic Idea of the Church', p. 67.

102 *Dictum* 90 (fol. 67ra–rb): 'Nonne greges pascuntur a pastoribus? Et quid est semetipsos pascere, nisi de bonis temporalibus que a subditis vi vel fraude extorquent, vel secundum legem oblata recipiunt, sua carnalia desideria complere, et nichil spiritualis profectus in subditis curare vel querere, cum e contra pastoralis cure officium sit, non que sua sunt, sed que Iesu Christi querere, et spiritualem profectum subditorum non solum carnalibus suis desideriis, sed eciam vite proprie carnali preferre, subditos verbo, exemplo, et oracione reficere in agro scripture, in agro creature, in agro latitudinis operum et passionum que Christus homo gessit et passus est in carne, in agro eciam latissimo racionum eternarum descriptarum, in divina mente.'

103 *Dictum* 101 (fol. 82ra–rb): 'Unde patet quod quinquefaria est pascua gregis Domini. Prima pascua gregis est ager scripture, in quo agro singula precepta moralia sunt sicut singule herbe virides et seminales quas oves plebium simplicium prelatorum exposicione intelligendo velud deglutiunt et in ventrem memorie trahiciunt, et recordando ruminant, et amando sibi incorporant. De quo agro dicitur, "Simile est regnum celorum thesauro abscondito in agro," quia in latitudine scripture sub sensus historici superficie latet thezaurus desiderabilis spiritualis intelligencie. Secunda pascua est ager latitudinis creature, in quo agro singularum specierum pulcritudines sunt sicut flores singuli quibus pascuntur plebium greges cum pastorum doctrina et erudicione ex similitudinibus specierum creature informantur aliqua morum honestate. Tertia pascua est ipsius prelati respectu plebium simplicium vita et conversacio bona secundum exemplum eiusdem, et Christus homo respectu prelatorum, quia prelatorum imitatores sunt plebes sicut ipsi prelati Christi, secundum vocem Pauli, dicentis, "Imitatores mei estote sicut et ego Christi." In hoc agro de semine verbi erumpunt fruges bonorum operum, quorum exemplo

pascuntur subditi velud quadam fruge sicut prelati pascuntur fruge exemplorum Christi. De hoc agro dicit Ysaac, "Ecce odor filii mei sicut odor agri pleni." Christi enim bonus odor sumus Deo, aliis vite in vitam, aliis mortis in mortem. Sed quia sumus adhuc agni novelli et tenelli, egemus adhuc lactis confortacione. Unde quartum quo pascendus est grex Domini verbum est incarnatum. Ipsa enim verbi divinitas, ut docet Augustinus, per carnem assumptam et lactescebat. Hoc autem lacte roboratus grex, et in tribus prescriptis agris pastus, tandem perveniet ad pascuam soliditatis divine visionis, ut dicat cum Psalmista, "Satiabis me cum vultu tuo". Hec pascua est ager amplissimus, quia magestas divinitatis immensa. In hoc agro est flos inmarcessibilis pulcritudinis universe. Ipse quoque flos est eterna Dei sapiencia, in qua descripta est pulcritudo universa, in qua sunt omnium rerum mortalium et corruptibilium et irracionabilium viventes et eterne raciones. Huius agri flores habent in se robur universe potencie et suavitatem universe bonitatis. De huius agri pulcritudine ait Psalmista, "Et pulcritudo agri mecum est." Ab eo igitur quod in hiis quinque pascuis gregem Domini pascimus, in nostro capite pastore Christo pastores sumus. Ymmo magis, omnes in illo unus pastor sumus, sicut omnes fideles in illo cum illo sunt unus Christus.'

104 *Super Psalterium*, 77.72 (*B* 57vb): '*Et pauit eos in innocentia cordis sui* – in cordis recta intentione et munditia, in recta predicationis intelligentia, que dirigit secundum sui intellectum recta opera in hiis, in quam tribus pascendus est Domini grex: in cordis immunditia recta, <in> predicationis intelligentia, in operum efficacia, propter hoc forte dixit Dominus Petro ter "Pasce." Vnde noueris in operum efficacia trinitatis illius sacramentum in nullo frustratum a te, si pascas verbo, pascas exemplo, pascas et sanctorum fructibus orationum. Manent itaque tria hec: verbum, exemplum <et> [*add. E*] oratio. Maior autem hiis est oratio, nam et operis et uoti gratiam efficaciamque promeretur oratio. Pascendi itaque sunt magistri in [in magistri *B*] innocentia et orationis puritate ut hii innocentes sint in affectu pascendi eius: verbo vt sint illuminati in aspectu pascendi; exemplo vt sint perfecti in opere. Pascat in agro scripture, in agro creature et in agro contemplatiue puritatis pulcritudinis eterne.'

105 *Dictum* 90 (fols 67vb–68ra): 'Cum enim assumunt officium pastorale, obligant se ad pascendam turbam populi subiecti, fame verbi Dei periclitantis, pane doctrine vere fidei et moralium preceptorum, in quibus consistit salus, et sine quibus salus non est. Et inopes sunt cibi, quia multi nec unicum fidei articulum, nec unicum de preceptis decalogi, populo sciunt exponere. Et velud tot panum indigentes sunt quot sunt articuli fidei et precepta moralia saluti necessaria, que exponere nesciunt, et cum hos panes non habeant, obligati tamen ad pastum ex hiis panibus populi subiecti, discere ea que nesciunt necgligunt. Ymmo et multi eorum sapienciam atque doctrinam despiciunt, scienciamque repellunt.'

106 *Super Psalterium*, 70.15 (*B* 38vb): '*Os meum anunciabit laudem tuam*. Prelati sunt os [omnes *B*] Christi et ecclesie. Isa: *Qui separauit pretiosum a vili quasi os meum erit*. Et in canticis: *Osculetur me osculo*, etc. Hii enim sunt Christi et ecclesie per locutores sicud dicit Apostolus: *Si quis loquitur quasi sermones Dei*. Ieremias: *Ecce dedi verba mea*, etc. Si igitur sunt os Christi et ecclesie, nu<m>quid loquuntur verba scurilitatis, otiositatis lasciuie et immunditie, vel detractionis vel proditionis, vel huiusmodi? Os equi non mugit, os bouis non hinnit et sic de ceteris. Merito fortius os Christi non loquetur verba dyaboli, os iustitie non verba iniustitie, os veritatis non verba falsitatis, os munditie non verba inmunditie, os misericordie non verba crudelitatis, et sic de ceteris. Item, sunt prelati os ecclesie quia cibum toti corpori ministrant. Precindunt enim cibum, cum aliquam exponendam de corpore scripture assumunt; masticant cum subtiliter discutiunt, exponunt et spiritum a litera diuidunt per affectum trahendi cibum in corpus

ecclesie, quasi cibum deglutiunt.' Cited in Ginther, 'A Scholastic Idea of the Church', p. 66n.
107 See Peter the Chanter, *Verbum Abbreviatum*, PL 205.25.
108 The most recent discussion of the scholastic sermon is Suzanne Paul, 'An Edition and Study of Selected Sermons of Robert Grosseteste', unpubl. PhD diss., 2 vols (University of Leeds, 2002), 1.73–123. See also J. Longère, *La prédication médiévale* (Paris: Etudes Augustiniennes, 1983); David D'Avray, *The Preaching of the Friars: Sermons Diffused from Paris before 1300* (Oxford: Clarendon, 1985); *The Sermon*, ed. B. Mayne Keinzle, Typologie des Sources du Moyen Age occidental, fasc. 81–3 (Turnhout: Brepols, 2000).
109 Ginther, 'A Scholastic Idea of the Church', pp. 63–4.
110 *Dictum* 101 (fol. 82va): 'Cum itaque prima pars officii pastoralis sit per Christum predicatum intrare, congrue secunda pars est ut, quantum in se est, vocem predicatam faciat oves audire, quia predicationem sequi debet audicio. Audient autem si habeant aures perfectos. Est autem auris perfecta cum verbi sonantis in aure corporis significacio hauritur ab intelligencia, et intellecta reponitur in memoria, et memoria imprimitur in affectum beneplaciti, ut sit memoria mandatorum Dei ad faciendum ea. De hiis auribus dicitur, "Aures autem perfecisti mihi", et "Quibus aures audiendi audiat." Si autem desit vel in affectu beneplaciti impressio, vel intellecti memoria, vel auditi aure corporis interior intelligencia, non est auris perfecta et integra set abscisa. Non est autem in loquentis exterius potestate ut veritatem quam loquitur ostendat audientis intelligencie, vel infigat memorie, vel imprimat affectui. "Unus enim est magister, Christus", qui hec operatur interius. Quomodo igitur qui loquitur exterius efficiet ut vox eius audiatur interius? Forte is est modus, ut oracione moveat interius loquens verbum Christum ad imprimendum interiori auditui quod ipse exterius loquitur auditui exteriori. Cum enim attendit predicator quod sue potestatis non est nisi exterius sonare ad aurem corporis, et ob desiderium inscripcionis eorum que loquitur in aure mentis, gemitibus et oracionibus efficit ut Christus verbum loquatur in aure mentis ut audiat auditor quid in se loquatur Deus, eciam ipse predicator non immerito ob hoc dicetur efficere quod oves eius vocem dicantur audire.'
111 *Super Psalterium*, 86.2 (*B* 85vb): 'Vel sic *fundamenta Syon*, id est, vite contemplatiue cuius conuersatio est in celis, sicut in montibus sanctis, id est in angelis. Et *Dominus diligit portas Syon*, id est vitam contemplatiuam, qualis est dum adhuc viuitur in hac carne corruptibili que introducit in illam contemplationem que erit in patria. *Super omnia tabernacula Iacob*, id est super opera vite actiue que euacuabuntur cum venerit quod perfectum est. *Maria enim optimam partem elegit que non auferetur ab ea*. Gregorius quoque *Super Ezech.* in omelia 3 ait: "Due autem sunt sanctorum predicatorum vite, actiua scilicet et contemplatiua. Set actiua prior est tempore quam contemplatiua quia ex bono opere tenditur ad contemplationem. Contemplatiua autem maior est merito quam actiua quia hoc in vsu presentis operis laborat. Illa vero sapore intimo venturam iam requiem degustat."'
112 *Dictum* 90 (fol. 68va): 'Multi autem, considerantes Dei prescienciam inmutabilem, incidunt in desperacionem. Alii ex considerata inmutabilitate predestinacionis nimium confidunt. Unde ad tales eruendos ab utroque periculo, oportet ostendere eis concordiam presciencie et predestinacionis, et gracie et liberi arbitrii. Pauci autem sunt prelati qui magnitudinem misericordie et iusticie Dei sciunt explanare, et harum adinvicem concordiam monstrare. Et pauciores forte, quorum oculi interiores non multum caligant in contuendo concordiam liberi arbitrii et presciencie et predestinacionis et gracie. Unde et pauci inveniuntur ydonei sufficientes ad fracturam desperacionis alligandum.' Does

Grosseteste have in mind here Anselm's *De concordia praescientiae et praedestinationis et gratiae Dei cum libero arbitrio*?

113   *Dictum* 101 (fols 82vb–83ra): 'Tercia pars officii pastoralis est ut proprias oves vocet nominatim. Sed eas sic vocare non potest nisi noscat et nomina. Hec autem nomina sunt illa quibus scribuntur in libro vite. Et est cuiusque nomen quo scribitur in libro vite colletio virtutum interiorum quam non est in alio reperire. Propter quam eciam de quovis dici potest, "Non est inventus similis illi, qui conservaret legem excelsi." Hec itaque nomina propriam ovium debet pastor agnoscere. Et sunt duo modi veniendi in talium nominum noticiam. Quia sicut medicus agnoscit in cura sua suscepti occulta, partim ex signorum consideracione, partim vero ex ipsius suscepti relacione, sic et pastor, qui idem est medicus animarum susceptarum, in cura sua secreta et occulta debet agnoscere, partim per signa, partim per relata, maxime in confessione. Debet enim pastor omnia sensibilia opera subditorum suorum diligenter notare, et ex quo affectu procedant prudenter conjicere, [convicere MS] quia sicut ait Salomon, "Quomodo in aquis resplendent vultus prospiciencium, sic corda hominum manifesta sunt prudentibus." Et alibi, "Cor hominis immutat faciem illius, sive in bonum, sive in malum." Eciam in Ecclesiastico, 19o capitulo, "Ex visu cognoscitur vir, et ab occursu faciei sensatus. Amictus corporis, et risus dencium, et ingressus hominis annunciant de illo." Ex huiusmodi itaque signis cum hiis que audit ex narracione proprie confessionis, debet pastor animam subditi sui plene agnoscere, ut conveniat illi quod alibi dictum est, "Novit iustus animas iumentorum suorum." Et sic agnoscens illum secundum propriam nominacionem qua scriptus est in libro vite, vocet, id est a torpore excitet, et ad bonorum exercicium stimulet. Hoc est quod post dicitur, "Cognosco oves meas." Sed nota quod sequitur, "Et cognoscunt me mee." Non enim pastor agnoscet suas per ipsam confessionem nisi et ipse cognoscant pastorem. Cognoscant, inquam, non eius similiter confessionem audiendo, sed ex signis operum cognoscant illum hominem veracem, secretarium fidelem et occultorum racione nulla revelatorem, miserie agnite compacientem et eiusdem pro viribus relevatorem. Tali namque et vix vel nullo modo alii plene revelant subditi occulta interioris morbi.'

114   See above, n. 95.
115   Brian Stock, *Listening for the Text: On the Uses of the Past* (Baltimore: Johns Hopkins University Press, 1991), pp. 16–51, 149–58.
116   Walter H. Principe, 'Toward Defining Spirituality', *Studies in Religion/Sciences religieuses* 12 (1983), 127–41; idem, *Thomas Aquinas' Spirituality*, Etienne Gilson Series, 7 (Toronto: PIMS, 1984).
117   The most recent studies on this text are Lesley Smith, 'The *De decem mandatis* of Robert Grosseteste', in *Robert Grosseteste and the Beginnings of a British Theological Tradition*, ed. M. O'Carroll, Bibliotheca Seraphico-Capuccina, 69 (Rome: Istituto Storico dei Cappuccini, 2003), pp. 265–88, and James McEvoy, 'Robert Grosseteste on the Ten Commandments', *Recherches de théologie ancienne et médiévale* 58 (1991), 167–205.
118   See *Templum Dei*, 21.3 (p. 66), where loving God describes one form of affective contemplation.
119   *DDM*. prol.3 (p. 3).
120   Cf. *Templum Dei*, 5.3 (p. 35), where Grosseteste had divided the Decalogue into commandments concerning God (1–3), oneself (4–6) and one's neighbour (7–10).
121   Ibid., 1.2 (p. 6).
122   See above, Chapter 5, p. 110.

123 *DDM*, 2.6 (pp. 24–5).
124 Ibid., 2.7 (p. 25). See above, Chapter 5, pp. 110–11.
125 Ibid., 4.11–22 (pp. 42–7).
126 Ibid., 4.25–39 (pp. 48–52).
127 Ibid., 7.1–10 (pp. 75–9).
128 Ibid., 5.1–9 (pp. 58–63).
129 Smith, 'The *De decem mandatis* of Grosseteste', p. 287.
130 *Super Psalterium*, prol. (*B* 1rb–va): 'Tria autem latera psalterii in quo tu quisquis es debes psalmos canere sunt: dilectio Dei qua diliget te et tuum proximum; et dilectio qua tu diligis Deum et proximum; et dilectio qua proximus diligit te et Deum. Hec enim singularium trium dilectionis singule tres extensiones ad duas ceteras sunt summa latera in figura psalterii. Tria latera quorum latus supremum est dilectio qua diligat Deus te et proximum et hec dilectio ipse Deus. Hoc latus supremum per humilitatis excellentiam concauum est quia concauitas in typo humilitatis est secundum quod precipitur in Exodo xxvii, altare concauum fieri in humilitatis typum. Ab hoc supremo latere sonus in psalterio redditur, quia iocundatio anime de operum recto regimine a Deo incipit et in Deo terminatur. Sicut autem in psalterio vnus terminus corde fingitur in vno latere deorsum et reliquus terminus in reliquo latere resonante sursum protenditur quia lateraliter quelibet corda iuxta tercium latus. Sic in te diligentem Deum et proximum quasi in latere deorsum primo fingitur quodlibet x. mandatorum. Tu enim subiectus termino es cuiuslibet mandatorum. Tibi enim dicitur: tu non adorabis deum alienum; tu non accipies nomen Domini in vanum; tu seruabis diem sabbati. Quodlibet autem trium mandatorum primorum ad dilectionem pertinens qua a te Deus est diligendus in ipsa dilectione a te in Deum protensa expresse est quasi corda ab inferiori latere ad latus superius extensa. Cum autem proximi dilectio non sistat in ipso scilicet proximo, sed per proximum tendatur ad Deum quia proximus non in se sed in Deo diligendus est. Et reliqua .vii. mandata que pertinent ad dilectionem proximi in ipsa dilectione proximi in Deum tendente, quia ab inferiori latere ad latus superius iuxta latus tertium protenduntur. Hoc itaque psalterium spirituale quod non debemus solum vt honus portare, sed ad honeris et laboris leuamen in eo canare. Quelibet enim propositio secundum philosophum interuallo et linee comparatur, in qua subiectus et predicatus sunt duo puncta lineam terminantia. Copula autem est [vt *add. ms.*] extensio linee medie inter [in *ms.*] puncta. Intelligentia veritatis complexe per enunciationem significate in anima est intelligibilis et spiritualis linea in qua, si intelligentia delectetur et iocundetur est, velud linea aut corda sonatina. Ipsa mentis iocunditas tantum est spiritualis [spirituale *ms.*]. Si autem propositio intellecta sit propositio practica iocundeturque anima non tam in eius speculatione quam in operis quod regit executione, tunc enim intelligentia est quasi corda ad pulsum manus soni redditiua. .X. autem mandata decalogi sunt velud propositiones practice operum nostrorum regitiue. In earum itaque intelligentia amata in quantum regunt et ordinant nostra opera anime iocundatio quasi .x. cordarum est ad pulsum manus sonatio.'
131 *DDM*, prol.6 (pp. 4–5).
132 Christine Thouzellier, '*Ecclesia militans*', in *Etudes d'histoire du droit Canonique dédiées à Gabriel Le Bras*, 2 vols (Paris: Sirey, 1965), 2.1407–23.
133 *Super Psalterium*, 83.5 (*B* fol. 86va–vb): '*Beatus qui habitant*, etc. Peregrini et transitores summus per ecclesiam militantem, sed in triumphantem erimus habitatores. Unde et ista proprie signabatur per tabernaculum Moysi quod portabatur; illa vero per templum Salomonis quod stabiliter figebatur.'
134 *De dotibus*, 2 (p. 102); *DCL*, 3.2.2–3 (pp. 133–4).

135 Grosseteste acknowledges that there are three dowry gifts for the soul, but he does not broach them in this text: *De dotibus*, 3.1 (p. 106).
136 Ibid., 3.2 (p. 106).
137 Ibid., 1.2–5 (pp. 102–3).

Conclusion

Fui clericus, deinde magister in theologia: what kind of theologian was Robert Grosseteste? The most common answer has been a 'biblical theologian' because he used no other text in his lectures save the Bible – or so Roger Bacon has told us. There is an element of truth in Bacon's assertion, for Grosseteste adhered to the standards of university education and lectured on the principal text of his discipline. He did not lecture on the *Sentences* of Peter Lombard because as a rule that text was not in the purview of regent masters. But to take Bacon's statement as a declaration that Grosseteste solely defined theology as biblical exegesis is surely a misunderstanding of both the nature of medieval theological education and Grosseteste's own theological disposition. Like every other master of the sacred page, Grosseteste followed the dictates of his discipline in the way he ruled his school in the faculty of theology. He lectured on Scripture, disputed theological questions and preached. Solely on the basis of this type of historical narrative, it would seem reasonable to describe Grosseteste as a scholastic theologian.

Was there more to being a scholastic than just lecturing, disputing and preaching? Grosseteste may have indeed been a theologian in the schools – and hence a scholastic in a loose sense – but one might argue that his conservatism prevented him from embracing the 'scholastic project'. The adjective 'conservative', however, can pose as many problems as it purports to solve. If we mean conservative in a classical sense, then there is no doubt that Grosseteste was a *conservator* of a particular tradition. His theology was well ensconced in the Augustinian tradition; and he drew heavily from it as he wove together his views on the nature of God, the Incarnation and the idea of the Church. His general perception of reality as a composite of exemplars of God's nature bears the indelible mark of the bishop of Hippo. His metaphysics of light and its epistemological implications also find their origin in Augustine's works. However, if we mean conservative in the sense that Grosseteste *resisted* new ideas and methods in his lifetime, the grounds for this claim are less than firm. Even as biblical exegete, Grosseteste commingled the methods of twelfth-century scholasticism with newer techniques of his own century. His spiritual reading of the text was certainly based on a theory of signification that had resonated in earlier centuries, but it was also driven by a keen interest in literal exposition. Scripture must interpret Scripture, he argued, which means that what Scripture stated literally must have a bearing when one engages the spiritual meaning of another lemma. Moreover, he took into consideration the developing ideas of authorship and authorial intent, which he then combined with the ancient method of prosopological reading. As a speculative theologian, he advanced ideas based on rational argument, including God's as the first form and the form of all things, the relationship between God's knowledge and human freedom, God as an infinite being, and the cosmic role of the Incarnation. In light of these theological positions, the word that comes immediately to mind is not 'conservative', but rather 'innovative'.

For every innovation, however, one could point to a standard, traditional theological assertion. Grosseteste may have been fascinated by Aristotle's logic of scientific discovery, but he did not fully embrace the philosophical psychology which underpinned the *Posterior Analytics*; rather, he stuck to many Augustinian epistemological themes, even if that led to some tension in his theology. Grosseteste may have modelled his account of the subject matter of theology on Aristotle's description of the subject of a science, but he did not feel compelled to state explicitly that he had adopted the Stagirite's method of argument in his theological work, much less indicate unequivocally what the first principles of theology are. Grosseteste may have speculated on the cosmic role of the Incarnation, but his own explanation of its salvific necessity was drawn solely from the exposition of the Old Testament. The innovative stands side by side with the traditional, and yet Grosseteste never seemed conscious that he was drawing from two systems of thought that were not completely compatible.

If 'innovative' does not fully capture Grosseteste's theology, we are left with only one other adjective: 'transitional'. One can see similarities between Hugh of St-Victor and Grosseteste, but in no way did Grosseteste simply mimic the Victorine approach to the theological enterprise. One can also see continuities between Grosseteste and Aquinas, but in no way could one make the argument that these two theologians were cut from the same methodological cloth. Instead, Grosseteste brought to his theological teaching the influence of Augustine, Bernard of Clairveaux and the Victorines, but also newer sources such as Aristotle and Avicenna. He leapt upon current ideas of the Incarnation in terms of the role of 'person' in the hypostatic union, but in the course of that analysis he did not consider more recent arguments about the status of Christ's knowledge, adopting instead the older position championed by Hugh of St-Victor. He was certainly convinced of the Trinitarian nature of God, which had implications for the structure and inherent meaning of all creation; but he did not take the time to write any text called *De trinitate*. Grosseteste sketched a schematic structure for theological work – the *Tabula* – but that index yielded no *summa theologiae*. The result is that, within his theological writings, the modern reader can observe a theologian who experimented with many new ideas and methods, but in the end left it for later thinkers to develop a more systematic understanding and usage of those novelties.

A state of transition explains the eclectic nature of Grosseteste's theology, but only in part. The additional factor is the *personal* nature of his theological work. Grosseteste never let the rhetoric of scholastic thought hide his personal commitments to theology. Rarely did he let a textual witness to his teaching tasks escape that had not first undergone a major transformation in its structure. Disputed questions became treatises that bore faint traces of their original context. Sections of scriptural commentaries were excised so as to become parts of a larger work. In other words, unlike other scholastic theologians who often sacrificed their own personality at the altar of rhetorical uniformity, Grosseteste often allowed his personality to shine through at the cost of rhetorical confusion. This meant that a line of argument sometimes wobbled from side to side instead of proceeding in a clear and linear fashion. Even when marshalling all his rhetorical skills to construct a persuasive argument, Grosseteste could cut the rug from under himself by admitting to intellectual weakness. 'I leave it for wise men to examine this further,' he concludes, after offering a coherent argument as to how one might integrate natural philosophy with biblical exegesis. The complexity of his reasoning for a cosmic role of the Incarnation is also partially undermined by his admission that his theologising can suffer from mediocrity. All this hesitation can sound incongruous, for any modern reader can immediately recognise Grosseteste's command of logic, his vast knowledge of the Fathers, his linguistic skills unique for his century, his intimate and abiding knowledge of the sacred text, his ability to exploit successfully the natural world for theological gain, and the creativity of his writing. Nonetheless, these are indicators that Grosseteste had a strong personality that the standard guidelines for textual production could never mute.

Grosseteste as a *personal* theologian accounts for more than idiosyncratic writing. It also points to a central characteristic of his theologising: the study of the sacred page must engage the master and student in every aspect. His modification of the whole-Christ motif not only ensured that the Trinity was included in the subject matter of theology, but also guaranteed that the trajectory of history and individual human experience became part of the theological narrative. The whole Christ embraces not only the union of the mystical body, but also the final deification of humanity, that final union with the Trinity. For Grosseteste this assertion was more than just eschatological desire; instead, it demanded that the experience of the mystical body itself be part of that movement towards that final union. The Church itself, as both a theological and a juridical expression, became the context of each Christian's journey to deification. That journey required guidance and support, tasks that in Grosseteste's mind were clearly the responsibility of pastors. On the one hand, that responsibility had to be fostered and shaped in very practical ways, such as developing guidelines to confession. On the other hand, the success of caring for souls lay not so much in the functions of the pastorate as it did with the spirituality of the pastor himself. Grosseteste's teaching on the Church and the care of souls – summed up in the modern term 'ecclesiology' – had at its heart a notion that theological teaching must transform both pastor and layperson. It was a demanding and exhausting task, one at which Grosseteste himself failed. Even reflecting on the work of pastoral care could be a difficult task for him. Nonetheless, he persevered and eventually would re-enter the pastoral care at an even more demanding level: bishop of Lincoln.

Finally, we must never forget that Grosseteste was a *teaching* theologian. His writings came out of a school in a faculty of theology. That points not only to specific rhetorical forms for textual production, but also to a pedagogical context. He had a responsibility to instruct and guide his students. The Franciscans were pleased with their first lector, for he found a way to provide the kind of educational resource they needed in order to prepare for a future ministry of preaching and pastoral care. His own interest in a life of simplicity cohered easily with the Franciscan ethos of mendicancy. Under Grosseteste's tutelage, students excelled (so Thomas of Eccleston tells us) which is the highest praise anyone can lavish upon a teacher. However, this aspect of Grosseteste's theology highlights a significant historical problem: Grosseteste may have ruled a school, but did he found a school of thought? There is no indication that the succeeding lectors necessarily built upon Grosseteste's work. Adam Marsh, some eighteen years later, as the fourth lector for the convent, may have returned to some of Grosseteste's theological themes, but the absence of any textual evidence allows us to make mainly suppositions rather than documented descriptions about Marsh as a theologian.[1] At one time, modern historians claimed that Grosseteste was wholly ignored by his contemporaries and that he only gained the attention of a few fourteenth-century thinkers. That conclusion is now open to question, since his influence can now be traced in some thirteenth-century theologians, such as Richard Fishacre, Richard Rufus and Bonaventure. The question of Grosseteste's influence rests primarily on knowing what to look for. In this study, I have sought to detail Grosseteste's theology in both method and content, a theology that was part of the scholastic narrative. It may now be possible to begin to write an epilogue of theological influence for this one-time master of the sacred page.

Notes

1 See the attempt by Servus Gieben to fill in the documentary lacunae: Servus Gieben, 'Robert Grosseteste and Adam Marsh on Light in a Summary Attributed to St Bonaventure', in *Aspectus et Affectus: Essays and Editions in Grosseteste and Medieval Intellectual Life in Honor of Richard C. Dales*, ed. G. Freibergs (New York: AMS Press, 1993), pp. 17–33.

Appendix: Transcription of *Super Psalterium* 100

The following is a transcription of Grosseteste's comments on Psalm 100 from Bologna, Biblioteca dell' Archiginnasio MS 983, fols 168vb–173vb. It has been checked against another witness, Eton College MS 8, but the text has not been established critically. With the exception of biblical references noted within the text in square brackets, the sources have not been identified. This transcription supports mainly the discussion found in Chapter 7, but also provides another example of Grosseteste's exegetical skills and theological interests.

<100.1>

/168vb/
1   Misericordiam et iudicium cantabo tibi Domine. Psallam et intelligam in via immaculata quando venies ad me. Materia huius Psalmi est misericordia et iudicium quia vt dicit Augustinus: /169ra/Quod habet iste Psalmus in primo versu hoc in toto eius corpore querere debemus.
2   Et secundum Cirillum iste Psalmus describit perfectam vite conuersationem et docet formam perfecte sanctitatis que consistit non solum in fugere malum et facere bonum, set etiam in prosequi et destruere malum tam in se quam in aliis; et promouere bonum non solum in se set, quantum valet, in omnibus aliis. Et propter hanc perfectionem est iste Psalmus centesimus quia centenarius numerus perfectus est, productus videlicet ex ductu denarii in se, qui denarius est numerorum perfectio. Vnde centenarius est quasi perfecta perfectio, hoc est perfectio in perfectione ducta. Perfectio enim in hoc Psalmo descripta ducit decalogum descriptum in cognitione diligente in eundem decalogum perfectum in exteriori opere. Vnitas quoque caritatis multiplicatur in mente in denarium decalogi cogniti et amati, et iste denarius ducitur in operis exterioris perfectionem et sit perfecta conuersatio que in hoc Psalmo describitur. Producitur ex vnitate in decies decem quia ex caritate in decem mandata prius congnita et deinde operata.
3   Inducit autem Psalmus <historice>[1] Iosiam regem et eius coram Deo perfectam conuersationem, vt in ipso quasi in caritate et exemplo habeatur forma perfecte conuersationis. Iste Iosias docendo et operando ex mentis hilaritate cecinit misericordiam liberans populum de seruitute ydolatrie, et cecinit iudicium occidens sacerdotes Baal et ydola subuertens et excelsa auferens. In eius igitur persona dicit Dauid, Misericordiam et iudicium cantabo tibi Domine, hoc est hilariter operabor. Et

193

prefiguratur in ipso Christus faciens misericordiam, eripiens humanum genus de seruitute peccati, et faciens iudicium, conuertens aereas potestates et tirannidem diaboli.

4   In persona fidelium legitur sic quia primum perfecte conuersationis est diligens cognitio siue cognoscens dilectio diuinorum.

5   Incipit sic describere conuersationem perfectam: MISERICORDIAM ET IUDICIUM CANTABO TIBI DOMINE, id est ex diligente et per hoc gaudente cognitione predicabo ad tuam laudem Domine, misericordiam tuam et iudicium tuum. In omnibus enim operibus Dei est considerare hec duo, sicilicet misericordiam et iudicium: misericordiam scilicet cum prouehit a non-esse ad esse, a priuatione ad habitum, a defectu ad perfectum, a minori ad melius, a diminuto ad perfectum; iudicium vero cum perstante et permanenti in accepto, et non declinanti quantum est de se ab accepto, adicit prouectionem ad maius bonum et maiorem perfectionem. Vel cum rem accepto bono reluctantem et illud excutientem relinquit sibi ad corruptionem, non tamen ad omnimodam vt omnino nichil sit, set relinquit ei esse corruptum vt iusto iudicio penale sit.

6   Set sic videtur quod res perstantes prouheat semper et quod proficiunt in infinitum. Set ad hoc dicendum est quod licet res consummatas non promoneat semper in perfectionem maiorem secundum magnitudinem, non definit tamen ea semper prouehere per hoc quod prestat eis durationis perpetuitatem. Et si bonum quod diuturnius est melius est quanto quelibet /169rb/res plus durat, licet non ex intentione bonitatis, tamen ex eiusdem duratione diuturniori non inmerito dicetur melior.

7   Intelligitur quoque per MISERICORDIAM ET IUDICIUM vtraque Christi natura, per misericordiam videlicet diuina natura cuius est a non-esse ad esse ducere; per iudicium vero humana natura quia potestatem dedit pater Christo iudicium facere quia filius hominis est. Cum igitur vtramque Christi naturam fide diligente et gaudente credimus, misericordiam et iudicium eidem decantamus.

8   Possimus etiam temporibus MISERICORDIAM ET IUDICIUM distinguere, quia sicut dicit Augustinus, non sine causa isto ordine posita sunt, non tamen diceret iudicium et misericordiam, set misericordiam et iudicium. Tempus igitur misericordie nunc est, cum Deus 'solem suum oriri facit super bonos et malos, et pluit super iustos et iniustos' [Matt. 5:45], et equaliter dat ista bona transitoria vtrisque. Nec in hoc Deus iniustus est qui equaliter dat ista nunc iustis; et iniustis misericordie enim tempus adhuc est et nondum iudicii. Cum venerit autem iudicare tunc 'reddet vnicuique secundum opera sua' [Rom. 2:6], differenter tribuens iustis bona et iniustis mala.

9   Qui igitur Deum laudant bonos remunerantem et malos punientem in iudicio – murmurant vero quia hic equaliter omnia proueniunt bonis et malis – iudicium cantant Domino, set non misericordiam. Qui vero e conuerso laudant Deum quia etiam malis tribuit hic bona, displicet eis tamen quia in iudicio reddet malis mala, misericordiam Deo cantant et non iudicium.

10   Item, nunc est tempus misericordie dum pacientia Dei ad pentitentiam nos adducit, dum expectat nos longanimiter, dum parcit per misericordiam, vt inueniat quos coronet per iudicium. Sicut enim dicit Augustinus, nisi primo Deus per misericordiam parceret non inueniret quos per iudicium coronaret. Tempus iudicii erit cum inpenitentibus reddet iram quam sibi thesaurizauerunt secundum cordis sui duritiam. Hec duo tempora distinguit Apostolus ad Rom.[2] [Rom. 2:4–6]: 'Ignora<n>s',

inquit, 'quoniam benignitas Dei ad penitentiam te adducit ecce tempus misericordie, tu autem secundum duritiam cordis tui et cor inpenitens thesaurizas tibi iram in die ire et reuelationis iusti iudicii Dei qui reddet vnicuique secundum opera sua'. Ecce tempus iudicii, ecce MISERICORDIAM ET IUDICIUM CANTABO TIBI, DOMINE.

11   Item misericordia est in remittendo peccata, iudicium in reddendo secundum opera que duo distinxit. Item, apostolus dicens [I Tim. 1:13]: 'Blasfemus sui et persecutor et contumelosius,[3] set misericordiam consecutus.' Ecce misericordia. Audi de iudicio de cetere 'reposita est mihi corona iustitie quam[4] reddet mihi in illo die iustus iudex' [II Tim. 4:8]. Non dixit 'donat' set 'reddet'. Quando donabit misericors erat; quando reddet iudex erit.

12   Item, Psalmista distinguit hec duo tempora dicens [Ps. 49:21], 'Hec fecisti et tacui' – inde tempus misericordie – 'arguam te et statuam te illa faciem te' – ecce tempus iudicii. Augustinus autem in libro *Enchiridion* intelligit hunc cantum perficere cantandum in patriam. Ait enim: Remanentibus itaque angelis et hominibus reprobis in eterna pena, tunc sancti scient plenius quid boni eis contulerit gratia. Tunc rebus ipsis euidentius apparebit quod in psalmo scriptum est: 'Misericordiam et iudicium cantabo tibi domine', quia nisi per indebitam misericordiam nemo liberatur, et nisi per debitum iudicium nemo dampnatur.

13   Item, *Super Iohannem* dicit: Si primo venisset iudicaturus, neminem inuenisset cui premia iustitie redderet. Qui /169va/ergo vidit omnes peccatores, et omnino neminem esse immunem a morte peccati, prius erat misericordia preroganda, et post excerendum iudicium; quia <de illo>[5] cantibat <psalmus>:[6] 'Misericordiam et iudicium cantabo tibi, domine.' Non enim ait iudicium et misericordiam; nam si primo esset iudicium, nulla esset misericordia; set primo misericordia, postea iudicium. Quid est primo misericordia? Creator hominis, homo esse dignatus est; factus est quod fecerat, ne periret quem fecerat.

14   Intelligitur quoque quod iustus cantat Deo non solum misericoridam et iudicium Dei, set etiam misericordiam et iudicium sui, id est misericordiam et iudicium que ipse iustus facit. Cum enim ex mentis hilaritate in caritate misericordiam facit et iudicium quasi per corporis organum cantat misericordiam et iudicium, misericordiam autem facit donando et conando secundum illud Euangelii [Lk. 6:38]: 'Date et dabitur vobis dimmitte et dimittetur vobis.' Iudicium facit seipsum diiudicando vt si iudicetur <recordans>[7] illud apud: 'Si nosmetipsos diiudicaremus non vitque iudicaremur' [I Cor. 11:31]; misericordiam in proximum, iudicium in seipsum.

15   Ad potestates quoque iudiciarias pertinet specialiter hoc verbum, quibus congruit ne remissum sit iudicium velut per misericordiam, nec minus fit rigidum velut per iustitiam, set sit ex vtrisque temperatura medie carens crudelitatem et remissionem. Misericordie oportet iudicem esse reis ex affectu animi compaciendo, iudicii tamen rigorem exercere oportet modis quibus legittime potest ueritatem inquirendo et secundum probata sententiando, nec aliud de pena contra leges remmittendo, quantum tamen potest secundum leges penam debet temperare et cum animi compassione penam infligere, dolens videlicet quod legis coactio vrget eum ad penam. Et quia plerumque fit pena remissibilis aliorum interuentu et aliorum meritis, que tamen per se iuste non potest remitti, debet iudex desiderare vt reis subueniant ad alleuiationem pene aliorum merita et interuentiones.

16 Vnde Augustinus ad Macedonium iudicem ait: Prodest seueritas vestra cuius ministerio quies adiuuatur et nostra prodest et intercessio nostra cuius ministerio seueritas temperatur et vestra. Non vobis displiceat quod rogamini a bonis quia nec vobis displicet quod timemini a malis. Sicut dilectionem iussi sunt terentibus debere, qui timent, ita dilectionem iussi sunt timentibus debere qui terrent. Nichil nocendi cupiditate fiat, set omnia consulendi caritate et nichil fiat inmmantor nichil inhumaniter ita formidabitur vltio cognitorum vt nec religio intercessoris contempnatur quia et plectendo et ignoscende hoc solum, Vnde agitur vt vita hominum corrigatur. Et hiis verbis Augustini patet quod cum ex remissione pene speratur rei correctio optanda est a vidce vt fiat vero intercessio qua iuste valeat impetrari pene remissio.

<100.2>

17 Sequitur: PSALLAM ET INTELLIGAM IN VIA IMMACULATA QUANDO VENIES AD ME. PSALLAM ex hillaritate animi bene operans per organum carnis ex virtute actionis et intelligentia per virtutem contemplatiuam. Vtrumque autem faciam /169vb/IN VIA IMMACULATA quia tam motio actionis quam motio contemplationis munda erit et non coinquinata, videlicet aliqua circumstantia inconuenienti.
18 Vel VIA IMMACULATA est Christus qui peccatum non fecit, 'nec inuentus est dolus in ore eius' [I Pt. 2:22]. Qui igitur imitatur operando vestigia Christi hominis et contemplatur excelsa diuinitatis, ambulat in via que nichil habet commaculationis. Qui autem imitantur regulas morales philosophorum in opere et secuntur in contemplatione doctrinas quas tradiderunt de diuinis preter fidem Iesu Christi et summe Trinitatis IN VIA ambulant IMMACULATA.
19 Vel potest hic particula IN VIA IMMACULATA referri solum ad hoc verbum 'intelligam', et secundum hoc insumatur differentia vite contemplatiue ad actiuam quia actiua vita circa plurima turbata plerumque maculas incurrit. Contemplatiua vero vni intenta purior est a macula quod designatur in Rachele et Lya, quarum altera lippis erat oculis, altera vero pulcra facei et aspectu decora. Intelligitur autem contemplatiuus sursum in Deum directus est VIA IMMACULATA per quam Deus venit in animam. Vnde quando est intellectus contemplatio, venit Deus ad conte<m>plantem per contemplationem vite in contemplantem, et ipsa contemplatio intelligit eum venientum et hoc totum insumatur cum dicitur, INTELLIGAM IN VIA IMMACULATA QUANDO VENIES AD ME.
20 Et quia iste Psalmus describit perfectam conuersationem que tres habet partes – scientiam videlicet conuersandi secum et scientiam conuersandi cum familia et scientiam cum conciuibus – possimus in hoc Psalmo has tres partes considerare, et in hoc versu partem primam que pars prima integratur ex fide diligente, sicut fundamento; deinde ex compassione sui de se cum incipit se dolore; tertio ex iudicio sui cum se subtiliter diiudicat et discernit; quarto ex punitione et maceratione sui per opera penitentialia; quinto ex contemplatione celestium in qua est via immaculata qua Deus venit ad hominem.
21 Fides itaque diligens exprimitur in primo verbo secundum illam supradictam expositionem qua per misericordiam et iudicium intelligitur vtraque Christi natura.

Et conitetur cum hoc in misericordia et iudicio, compassio hominis de se, et sui ipsius discussio. Per 'psallere' vero intelligitur carnis maceratio per penitentiam, per 'intelligere' vero ipsa contemplatio. In hiis autem est sui ad se perfecta conuersatio.

22   Sequitur, PERAMBULABAM IN INNOCENTIA CORDIS MEI. Augustinus habet, Deambulabam in innocentia cordis mee. Et secundum ipsum Augustinum exponitur hic que sit VIA IMMACULATA. Ipsa enim est deambulatio in cordis innocentia. Innocentia autem duas habet partes, sicut et nocere duas habet partes, que sunt facere miserum et deserere miserum quarum opposita sunt non facere miserum et non deserere miserum. Facit autem miserum qui infert violentas vel /170ra/insidias, qui rapit res alienas, opprimit pauperes, furatur, coniugia aliena sollicitat, calumpniosus est, vult inferre hominibus quod doleant studio maluolentie. Deserit vero miseras qui videt inopem aliquo auxilio agentem et cum habeat quomodo prestet, contempuit, despicit, alienat cor suis; despicit lacrimis. Miserum ergo facit per transgressionem mandatorum decalogi scriptorum in secunda tabula, miseros vero deserto torpens ab operibus. Misericordie igitur a contrario innocens est qui nullum ledit et insuper, per quantum potest, per opera misericordie cuiuslibet miserie subuenit. Ad innocentiam igitur pertinet sibi ipsi non nocere set primo sibi misereri, quia non potest misereri alii qui sibi prius non miseretur. Sicut non potest nocere alii nisi prius sibi ipsi noceat. Innocentia igitur plena iusticia est. Vnde Augustinus ait: Tota iusticia ad verbum vnum innocentia redigitur.

23   Cor autem conscientia intelligitur et idem per DOMUM signatur. Vnde ambulare in CORDIS INNOCENTIA et in MEDIO DOMUS sue est late spatiari in propria conscientia quod non possunt mali facere quia angustias patitur omnis malitia. Trahit enim malitia cor ad imum vbi est angustia, et coartat semper inter opposita que similis non potest optimere. Cum tamen vtrumque cupiat, bonitas autem et innocentia appetit celestia in quibus est latitudo et dilatatur spe et gaudio et quocumque appetit simul potest optimere, et hanc latitudinem denotat verbum DEAMBULATIONIS.

24   Vel allegorice legitur de Christo, qui deambulat in medio ecclesie in plenitudine innocentie quia 'ipse peccatum non fecit nec inuentus est dolus in ore eius' [I Pt. 2:22].

25   Refertur etiam versus iste ad instructionem conuersationis patrisfamilias cum propria familia. Est autem magna virtus Domini, domus et patrisfamilias vt nulli noceat de sibi subiectis quantamcumque super eos habuerit potestatem et ibi elucet precipue virtus innocentie cum ille non nocet qui posset maxime impune nocere et plenum irritatur ab hiis quos posset maxime impune ledere. Quis autem sic impune potest ledere alium ut dominus seruum vt paterfamilias familiam? Et quis tam prouocat alium vt plerumque seruus dominum, et famulus patremfamilias? In patre ergo familias precipue fulget virtus innocentie.

26   Et quia multiplex est innocentia ad distinguendam veram innocentiam ab innocentia falsa, adicit hoc nomen CORDIS. Est enim quedem innocentia impotentie, et quedam ignorantie, et quedam innocentia timoris, et quedam cupiditatis et quedam bone voluntatis siue caritatis. Quidam qui nesciunt vt moriones quidam quia non audent timentes penam consecuturam; quidam vero non ledunt quia credunt aliquid assequi quod cupiunt /170rb/eo quod a lesione se continent. Quidam vero, licet possunt ledere et sciant et audeant, amore tamen virtutis a ledendo se continent et hec sola est vera innocentia et innocentia cordis, hoc est bone voluntatis.

27 Item ad innocentiam patrisfamilias pertinet vt ex cura rei familiaris seipsum non ledat, vt videlicet ex rei familiaris integritate et augmento non eleuetur in superbiam aut gestiat inani et effuso gaudio neque ex rei familiaris detrimento perturbetur aut decidatur animo. PERAMBULATIO autem patrisfamilias IN MEDIO DOMUS sue est perscrutatio et agnitio eorum que sunt in moribus familie sue. Non enim tantum eget cognoscere que et quanta habet in possessionibus, quantum cognoscere qualis sit sua familia in moribus quia si sit familia, bene morigerata erit sua possessio, bene conuersata licet ignorauerit que et qanta in bonis habuit. Nulla autem patrisfamilias sollicitudo conseruabit possessionem suam integram, si sit familia moribus corrupta. Vnde et Putifar cognoscens domum esse cum Ioseph proposuit eum domui sue et vniuersis possessionibus ignorans ipsemet quid haberet in domo sua, hoc est enim domui sue, bene esse propositum, vt videlicet docet Bernardus: Paterfamilias per se prouideat qui pro se de suis rebus prouideat. Qui sit fidelis et prudens, fidelis videlicet ne fraudet, prudens vero ne fraudetur. Hoc est igitur patrisfamilias perambulatio IN MEDIO DOMUS sue.

28 Moraliter familie sue diligens et perfecta perscrutatio per hoc autem quod dicit IN MEDIO DOMUS sue, insumat quod licet sit constitutus super familiam est tamen in illis quasi virtus ex illis. Insumatur etiam quod, licet sit demonii potestate prolatus, agnoscit se tamen secundum nature cognitionem seruis suis coequalem. In medio etiam consistit cum admodum cordis in medio corporis collocati omnibus. Vnde influit regimen et doctrinam et morum informationem, cum omnibus etiam influit sensum et motum, id est scientiam operandi et actum operis scientie conformem. In medio autem est cum vnuscuiusque ministerio tradit de bonis suis administrandis secundum propriam virtutem. In medio etiam est quia paucos sibi iungit immediate. Qui sibi reddant rationem, illis autem paucis plures subiicit qui non sibi immediate, set per medium propositorum rationem reddant. Quemadmodum de medio stipite arboris immediate prodeunt maiores rami per quorum medium prodeunt, de eodem stipite rami immitiores immiteri.

<100.3>

29 *NON PROPONEBAM ANTE OCULOS MEOS REM INIUSTAM.* Secundum Augustinum exposuit Psalmum in hoc loco vsque ad illum versum *OCULI MEI AD FIDELES TERRE*, partes innocentie et congruunt ea que dicuntur ad illum locum ad rectum conuersationem tam sui ad se quam ad familiam et ad conciues. Primum itaque est non proponere ante oculos rem iniustam, hoc est non apprehendere aliquo sensu interiori vel exteriori rem iniustam /170va/ ad amandum, vel ad condelectandum, vel ad eligendum, vel ad inclinandum, vel ad faciendum. Et non dicit quod non fecit rem iniustam. In multis enim offendimus omnes et solius Christi est nichil iniustum fecisse, set dicit *NON PROPONEBAM*, hoc est 'non intendebam', 'non deliberabam', 'non eligabam' vt facerem.

30 Insuper quoque facienti malum non consensi set *FACIENTES PREUARICATIONES ODIUI*. Preuaricatores autem sunt, vt dicit Augustinus, qui oderunt legem Dei, qui audiunt illam et non faciunt. Illi igitur proprie dicuntur preuaricatores qui legem acceptam transgrediuntur. Preuaricatores igitur odire debes non homines, vicium non naturam,

et hoc satagere vt moriatur vicium et viueficetur natura. Si enim homines odis, teipsum odis cum sis homo, et Christum odis cum ipse sit homo, et totum humanum genus odis. Et cum homo dicatur omnis creatura propter communem quam habet cum omni creatura, in homine odito etiam omnis creatura cum qua communicat homo, odio habetur et per communes creator et conseruator omnis nature Deus. Non igitur odiendus homo, set vt dictum est, hominis vicium. Quod si vere odis illud in terris destruere, non autem destruitur vicium necessario interfecto[8] homine quia male affectiones possunt etiam remanere post mortem. Et cum post mortem non sit locus penitentie fructuose ubi meruerit homo in vita vt purgetur post mortem, mors hominis est male affectionis et vicii confirmatio. Igitur qui interfecit hominem quia odit hominis vicium, non illud quod odit persequitur, set magis forcitan inesse confirmat. Vera igitur destructio vicii est conseruare hominem in hac vita et in viuentem inducere virtutem vitio oppositam. Solum enim sic veraciter destruitur vicium quod oditur.

31   Sequitur *Non adhesit mihi cor prauum*, quod dicit *odiui preuaricatores* et insuper cor prauum, id est voluntas distorta et non recta. *Non adhesit mihi*, id est non placuit mihi; neque concordabit mihi; nec etiam in meipso permansit et si forte aliquando surrepsit, est autem cor prauum tortum et recto contrarium. Vnde ex cordis rectitudine intelligi potest quid sit cor prauum, vt autem dicit Augustinus: Rectum cor dicitur hominis quia omina que vult Deus ipse vult. Rectum est cor quod dicit cum Christo, non quod 'ego volo, pater' set quod 'tu vis' [Cf. Lc. 22:42]. Rectum est cor quod extra se non deflectitur quod nec declinat ad dextram prosperitatis nec ad sinistram aduersitatis. Rectum est cor quod non exit a medio vel huc per superfluitatem, vel illuc per diminutione. Rectum est cor quod non exit ab extrinsicis, id est quod semper habet in memoria nouissima sua quia vt dicit Salomon [Ecli. 7:40]: 'Memorare nouissima tua et in eternum non peccabis.'

32   Cor autem quod habet primo dictam rectitudinem, id est, ad voluntatem Dei in omnibus conformitatem, non potest de aliquo contristari. Scit enim quod omnia que eueniunt preter peccatum, quod nichil est sunt et eueniunt secundum dispensationem voluntatis diuine. Quapropter omnia sunt quemadmodum et ipse vult cum vult, sicut Dominus vult et per hoc ipse vere Dominus est omni cum omnia sunt ad libitum voluntatis sue.

<100.4>

33   Quid est enim aliud alicui dominari /*170vb*/nisi habere illud sub rectu[9] et potestate voluntatis sue? Declinantem vero a rectitudine non cognoscit qui rectus est, ideo sequitur *Declinantem a me maligno non cognoscebam*. Que enim conuentio lucis ad tenebras que coniunctio tortuosi cum recto, quod autem dicit *non cognoscebam*, dupliciter intelligitur. Malicia enim sicut tenebras et ideo malitia non habet cognitionem nisi sicut tenebras visionem. Item, malitia aput bonos non habet cognitionem, id est non habet approbationem non tangit illam affectio<nem> caritatis, nec aspectus veritatis quia essentie defectio est vt lucis priuatio.

34   Declinatur autem a recto per dissimilitudinem cum recto. Declinatur quoque a recto, hoc est conformitate cum Deo primo ad se, ad sui videlicet propriam potestatem

amandam. Et sic deformat se a deiformitate et generat se degenerem et qui, per genituram ex Deo erat rectus per propriam genituram qua degenerat se, fit obliquus et curuus. Deinde declinat inferius ad amandum libidinose corpus naturaliter sibi subiectum et in hac declinatione suam dominationem, qua prefuit, ratio corpori tradit et donat et subicit ipsi corpori, et sic fit seruus serui sui. Tertio declinat vltra in ambitionem rerum exteriorum et effundit se in ista exteriora, et quia non potest ista adipisci non rapiat. Aliena declinat tandem in ablatione violentiam. Sic igitur a rectitudine in qua sola est vera nominatio secundum quam nominatur et scribuntur iusti in libro vite.

35 Fit flexio et casus primo in degenerationem quas in genitiuum. Secundo in dationem qua spiritu se donat carni quasi in datiuum. Tertio monetur ad exteriora que motio partium ad accusatum. Quatro flectitur in ablationem quasi in casum ablatum.

36 Vel secundum Eusebium per MALIGNUM intelligitur hec dyabolus qui non inuenit loqui in corde recto, quod plenum est Deo in quod, cum ingredi, non potest declinat. Iustus tamen eius declinationem non sentit quia eius potentiam non accepit. Si autem scisisset potentiam concendendo, sentiret et declinationem. Potest etiam in hiis duobus versibus denotari primo quia non ex se intendebat in aliquid iustum, set illud odio habebat. Secundo quod malum ingerens se non admisit in se, nec mouit cum consensu et cum delectatione, et ideo nec recessum malitie sensit per tristitiam cuius non admisit potentiam.

<100.5>

37. Sequitur, DETRAHENTEM SECRETO PROXIMO SUO HUNC PERSEQUEBAR. Detrahare est alterius bonum locutione imminuere vel malum augere. Nascitur autem detractio de inuidia. Inuidia namque est amor depressionis aliene et odium aliene felicitatis. Quando igitur non potest alienam felicitatem ipsa re subuertere sermonibus, /171ra/ vult eam imminuere in epimone. Est igitur detractio filia inuidie, neptis superbie, soror facinoris. Hanc pestem prohibet Dominus per Moysen in Leuitico [Lev. 19:16] dicens: 'Non eris criminator vel susurro in populis' et in libro Sapientie ait [Sap. 1:11]: 'Custodite vos a murmuratione que nichil prodest et a detractione parcite lingue quoniam sermo obscurus in vacuum non obit.'

38 Quod autem hic dicitur SECRETO, detractio hoc ibi sermo obscurus qui sermo non vadit in vacuum, hoc est non euadit impune. Vadit enim primo in odium Dei. Vnde Apostolus ad Rom. ait [Rom. 1:30]: 'Detractores Deo odibiles.' Et merito detractio dicitur spiritualiter odibiles Deo, quia euideintissime contraria est Deo. Dominus enim verbo suo omnia facit. Detractor autem ex parte ea qua destractor est verbo suo destruit. Factio autem per verbum et eiusdem rei per verbum destructio euidentissimam habent contrarietatem. Quapropter proprissime habent adinuicem inimicitiam et odium. Vadit etiam detractio in sui ipsius consumptionem. Sicut ostendit Apostolus ad Gal. [Gal. 5:15], dicens: 'Quod si inuicem mordetis et comedetis, videte ne ab inuicem consummamini.' Detractio enim mordendo consumit illum quantum est in se cui detrahit et ideo iusta pena est consumptio propria quia

quod iniuste facit in alterium hoc iuste pacietur in penam. Non[10] igitur in vacuum vadit obscurus sermo detractionis, set vt dictum est in odium Dei et proprii subiecti iustam consumptionem.

39 Item, sicut dicit Iacobus [Ja. 4:11]: 'Qui detrahit fratri, detrahit legi.' Ex quo consequitur quod detrahit etiam latori legis. Qui enim detrahit fratri plerumque immunit bonum eius quod ipse facit secundum legem et ita detrahit legi per quam frater operatur bonum. Quod ipse detrahendo immunit persona qui[11] detrahit fratri, contra legem facit quam supradiximus in Leuitico scriptam, 'Non eris criminator et susurro in populis.' Est autem detractor similis mordenti, tamen illud quod morsu decorpsit sibi non corporanti. Ideo detractores propter morsum et delacerationem canibus sunt similes qui carnes dilarerant et eis plerumque subiecta sibi non incorporant. Bona namque aliorum que quasi mordendo auellunt ab aliis sibi non vniunt et quia detractores sic delacerant. Merito monet Salamon cum detractoribus ne commisceris.[12] Propter hunc morsum dicit Salamon [Ecc. 10:11] quod 'si mordeat serpens in silentio sic qui fratri tuo occulte detrahit'. Item dicit Ieronimus: Parce detractioni lingue custodi sermones tuos et scito quia cuncta que de aliis loquitur tua sententia iudicaris et in hiis ipse deprehendendus eris que in aliis arguebas.

40 Est autem vnum per versus detractionis genus, quod non aperta voce de altero dicit malum, set quasi pietate optat ei bonum, vt sic insumet de esse quod optat. Vnde Gregorius in *Moralibus* ait: Sciendum vero est[13] quod plerumque peruersi verbotenus bona optant vt mala esse que in presentibus habentur ostendant; et quasi fouentes prospera expetunt vt benigni videantur. /171rb/Item, sunt etiam alii qui aliis detrahunt, vt sic siepiso laudent.

41 Vnde Gregorius dicit de ypocrita: Hec aliis inuidet que sibi tribui anelat; et tanto ceteros ostendere peruersos molitur, quanto videri sanctior appetit ab omnibus, vt ex eo quod alii despicabiles fiunt, ipse reuerentior semper appareat. Vnde fit vt de opinione proximi ante humana iudicia, lingue sue laqueos pretendat, vt eorum quibus placere appetit solus estimationem capiat. De ypocrite dicit Iob: 'Concepit dolorem et peperit iniquitatem; et vterus eius preparat dolos.' Dolorem quippe concipit cum peruersa cogitat. Iniquitatem parit cum explere ceperit quod cogitauit. Inuidendo dolorem concipit, derogando iniquitatem parit. Grauis quippe est iniquitas cum is qui peruersus est ostendere alios peruersos molitur, vt inde ipse quasi sanctus appareat, quod alios sanctos non ess docuerit. Vterus itaque ypocrite preparet dolos, quia tanto semper maiorem malitiam contra proximos in mente concipit, quanto solus pre omnibus videri innocentior querit.

42 Iohannes autem Crysostomus ait: Quidam sunt verbi supplantare proximos cupientes mordentes inuicem et comedentes que vtique aperte insanie est. Quid enim aliud faciunt insani et demone replete nisi membra sua morsibus lamant. Cum igitur tanta pestis sit[14] detractio merito dicit videlicet iustus DETRAHENTEM SECRETO PROXIMO SUO HUNC PERSEQUEBAR. Persequitur[15] vir iustus non hominem set vicium modum vero persecutionis.

43 Docet Salamon dicens [Prov. 25:23]: 'Ventus aquilo dissipat nubes et vultus tristis linguas detrahentium.' Super quem locum dicit Ieronimus: Sicut enim sagitta si mittatur contra duram materiam, nonnumquam immmittentem reuertitur et vulnerat vulnerantem, illudque completur. 'Facti sunt michi in archum prauum.' Et alibi:

'Qui mittit in altum lapidem, recidet[16] in caput eius.' Ita detractor cum tristem faciem viderit audientis, immo ne audientis quidem, set obturantis aures suas, ne audiat iudicium sanguinis illico contitescit pallet vultus, herent labia saliua siccatur.

44 Vnde idem videlicet sapiens: 'Cum detractoribus,' inquit, 'ne miscearis, quoniam repente veniet perditio eorum et ruinam vtriusque qui nouit? Tam scilicet eius qui loquitur quam illius qui audit loquentem' [Prv. 24:21–2]. Hoc est igitur detractorem persequi verba detractionis non audire.

45 Sequitur, SUPERBO OCULO ET INSATIALI CORDE CUM HOC NON EDEBAM. Potest hoc primo ad literam intelligi quia vt dicit Augustinus: Nos proper correctionem aliquam tenemus non aliquando etiam a fratribus nostris et non cum eis comminamur vt erubescauit et corrigantur. Sicut dicit Apostolus [II Thes. 3:14–15]: 'Si quis non obaudit verbo nostro per epistulam hunc notate et nolite commisceri cum eo et non inimicum existimetis, set corripite vt fratrem.' Hoc itaque plerumque facimus propter medicinam, et tamen similiter propter medicinam cum impiis et cum paganis multis sepe corporaliter vescamur, vt per conuictum eos ad fidem et pietatem reuocemus, sicut fecit Dominus comedens aliquotiens cum publicanus et peccatoribus [Cf. Mk. 2:16]. Hoc igitur ad omnes vniuersaliter est; hoc obseruandum vt videlicet cum nullo iniquo con/171va/uescamur, set tunc conuescendum non cum separatio hec medicinalis est[17] per confusionem sanans fatrem egrotantem.

46 Vel intelligitur esus iustitie: est autem vniuscuiusque cibus id in quo delectatur et quo habito eius appetitus pascitur. Vnde cibus superbi est propria excellentia. Cibus inuidi aliena miseria; cibus cupidi cumulus auri et argenti. Huiusmodi igitur cibum[18] non comedit iustus cum impio quia non delectatur neque pascitur cum illis de quibus delectatur et pascitur impius. Esurit enim iustus et sitit iustitiam et pascitur 'omni verbo quo procedit de ore Dei' [Matt. 4:4]. Nominat autem hic spiritualiter Psalmista duo vitia, superbiam videlicet et insatiabilem cupiditatem, quarum vna est radix et principium omnium vitiorum, scilicet superbia. Altera vero est omnium vitiorum extremum, scilicet cupiditas quia ipse est immoderatus appetitus maxime terrenorum.

47 Metalla enim de sulphure, vt dicitur, generatur. Hec est terra adusta et fetente et non est in creaturis aliqua vilior creatura et inferior terra. Illa autem cupiditas de qua dicit Apostolus ad Thimotheum [I Tim. 6:10]: 'Radix omni malorum est cupiditas.' Intelligitur generalis cupiditas qua quisque appetit aliquid aliud quam oportet propter excellentiam suam et quemdam rei proprie amorem. Ista autem cupiditas generalis eadem est essentialis cum superbia. Spiritualis autem cupiditas quam hic distinguamus a superbia est amor pecunie. Per ista igitur duo vitia extrema omnia etiam media conuenit, possunt intelligi. Superbia autem est amor sui, cupiditas amor pecunie. Rationali autem creatura nichil creatum est superius. Pecunia autem nichil est inferius, ideo hec duo vitia quasi omnium vitiorum duo extreama collecantur. Non dicitur autem simpliciter superbo, set superbo oculo forte quia superbia magis se exerit in oculo et superciliorum eleuatione. Quia enim appetitus excellentie proprie omnia sub se capit despicere quod spiritualiter agit in mente, hoc corporaliter prout potest, mutatur in corpore eleuans supercilium extollens oculum erigens crimine vt quam exalto situ reliquos contueatur. Cupiditas autem insatiabilis est quia quanto plus possidet tanto pluribus eget, et tanto magis suam sentit indigentiam et iste sensus indigentie excitat ampliorem famem pecunie.

48   Testatur autem quidam philosophus quod copia pecunie mater est maioris indigentie. Ait enim multis egent qui multa habet et magna nascitur indigentia ex magna copia. Idcirco quia multa exiguntur ad multa tuenda minus habendendum vt minus desit, et quia auarus non impletur, pecunia quantumcumque possideat, miser est. Vnde Epicurus ait: Si cui sua non videntur amplissima, licet tocius mundi dominus sit, tamen miser est. Cupiditas quoque omnia deformat et inhonestat. Vnde per oppositum de quodam ait Epicurus: Si vis Pitoclea honestum non honoribus adiciendum est, set cupiditatibus detrehendum. et sicut dicit /171vb/Seneca: Quocumque transtuleris hoc verbum, idem poterit, vt si vis Pitoclea senem facere et implere vitam non annis adiciendum, set cupiditatibus detrahendum. Est cupiditatis igitur detractio sicut est bonorum decoratio, sicut est eiusdem presentia omnius bonorum dehonestatio.

49   Item hoc habet miserie cupiditas quod naturaliter superuacuua facit necessiter. Carere enim non potest viciium eo quod nature est supercilium. Solebat Attalus ad auidos hac ymagine vti; 'vidisti aliquando carnem missa a domino frusta[19] panis aut carnis aperto ore captantem? Quicquid excepit protinus integrum deuorat et semper ad spem venturi[20] hiat. Idem euenit auidis quicquid expectantibus fortuna proiceit sine voluptate admittunt statim, ad rapinam alterius erecti et attoniti.' Hoc sapienti non enuenit plenus et; si quid obuenit, secure excipit et reponit.

50   Item, turpissimum vicium est ingratitudo et pessimum genus ingratitudinis est obliuio accepti beneficii. Hoc autem generat cupiditas. Vnde Seneca ait: Queris quid sit quod obliuionem vobis acceptorum faciat? Cupiditas accipiendorum; cogitimus non quid impetratum, set quid petendum sit. Abstrahunt a recto diuitie, honores, potentia que opinione nostra cara sunt, pretio suo vilia. Nescimus estimare res, de quibus non cum fama set cum rerum natura deliberandum est; nichil habent ista mangificentie quo mentes nostras in se trahant preter hoc, quod mirari illa consueuimus. Non enim quia concupiescenda sunt laudantur, set concupisciuntur quia laudanda sunt. In misericordia sunt hiusumodi mala que pullulant de auaritia quorum plurima referre posse nisi proloxitatem vitie vellemus.

51   Augustinus autem per COR INSATIABILE intelligit inuidiam que nascitur de superbia que cum sit appetitus aliene miserie de malis alienis semper pascitur numquam tamen saciatur. Ista fera monstruosa vt videt aliquid forma decorum fortuna aut natura aut gratia, ad auitum ingenui. Et illud: vnde gaudendum est ad superna ducit ore; pallet in acie; in corpore afficitur; putrascit in ossibus; pectora felle virent linguas. Est suffusa veneno, visus abest; nisi quem nec fectere dolores nec fruitur sompno vigilantibus excita curis, set videt ingratos intabescit que videndo successus hominum; carpitque quia et carpitur vna suppliciamque sanctum est vt autem dicit Gregorius: liuor interiores tenebras tolerat, et de radio lucis et die boni operis prximi obtenebratur. Habet autem hoc monstrum et prolem pessimam, quia de inuidia, vt dicit Gregorius, nascitur odium susurratio, detractio, exultatio in aduersis proximi, afflictio in prosperis. Iram quoque generat quia quanto interno linoris vulnere animus sauciatur, /172ra/tanto etiam mansuetudo tranquillitatis amittitur.

<100.6>

52   Sequitur *OCULI MEI AD FIDELES TERRE VT SEDEANT MECUM*. Hec primo in persona Christi dicitur cuius oculi, id est relucens misericordie et benignitatis. Sunt ad fideles terre, non quod prius fuit fideles quam aspiciantur, set quia eius aspectus fiunt fideles et facti permanent. Aspectus igitur eius facit et seruat et prouehit fideles donec perueniant tandem ex merito fidei ad primum visionis et ad celsitudinem iudicarie potestatis ut sedeant cum Christo super duodecim sedes iudicantes duodecim tribus Israel. Ostendit autem consequenter qua via peruenientur ad concessum cum illo dicens, *ABMULANS IN VIA IMMACULATA HIC MIHI MINISTRATBAT*. *VIA* igitur *IMMACULATA* ducit in eius ministerium. Ministerium autem eius ducit ad eius confessum. Ait enim [Jn. 12:26]: 'Vbi ego sum illic et minister meus erit.' *VIA* itaque *IMMACULATA* Christus est in qua via ambulatur quasi duobus pedibus, amore videlicet imitandi pro modo infirmitatis humane eius actiones et amore sufferendi eius passiones.

53   Item, *VIA IMMACULATA* sunt sacre scripture. Mandata in qua ambulatur velud duobus pedibus, actiones scilicet preceptorum et fuga prohibitorum.

54   Vel, *VIA IMMACULATA*, vt supradictum est, contemplatio est in Deum intenta. In hac via ambulatur duobus pedibus, id est duobus excessibus contemplationis, vt enim ait Bernardus: Due sunt beate contemplationis excessus: in intellectu est, alter in affectus; vnus in lumine alter in feruore; vnus in agnitione, alter in deuotione. In qualibet igitur istarum viarum ambulans ministrat Iesu Christo quia non querit que sua sunt, set que Iesu Christi; qui autem in operando querit que sua sunt non Christo, set sibi ministrat.

55   Potest etiam iste versus intelligi in persona fidelis cuius intentio directa est in fideles terre, hoc est habitantes in terra vbi habundat iniquitas et trahit illecebra et ideo ibi est gloriosior victoria. Ad hoc autem intendit iustus ad fideles vt secum sedeant, hoc est vt eiusdem glorie fiat cum eo participes. Amat enim omnis sicut seipsum et ideo desiderat omnis in participatione et fruitione bonorum sibi torquari.

56   Ambulans autem *IN VIA IMMACULATA* ministrat cuilibet alii fideli quia quicquid facit ad vtilitatem, omni facit. Vnde quilibet dicere potest de quolibet alio iusto, 'iste mihi ministrat quia quicquid facit mihi prodest'. Amor namque caritatis a quolibet iusto in quemlibet alium iustum protenditur. Et cum eo conflatur et cooperatur quemadmodum, quelibet stella celi in quamlibet aliam diffundit radios sui lucis et vnit lucem suam cum luce cuiuslibet alterius et vniuscuiusque lex luci alterius cooperatur. Ab hoc quoque loco exprimitur recta conuersatio iusti cum conciuibus suis, cuius conuersationis initium est, vt oculos intentionis dirigat et dilectionis ad omnes conciues; hoc disiderans et hoc pro posse procurans et faciens, vt omnes sint secum in bonorum participatione /*172rb*/coequales et, vt sua bona sint omnibus aliis, vt sibi ipsi vtilia, vt videlicet intendat in omni opera non sibi, set reipublice prodesse non sibi; set conciuibus et reipublice, se natum credens nichil reputans proprium bonum quod non sit commune, intelligens se esse menbrum ciuitatis et parte in toto, non totum per se separatum. Vt autem sit vtile menbrum in integritatem corporis conciuium adiungit sibi in propriam familiam solum illos qui viam videntur tenere immaculatam. Sicut enim dicit Theodoricus: Opportet nos et famulis bonis vti non vt nostram vitam exeuntes mali faciant deorsum fluere. Vnde Elizeus grezi avaritiam

captum a suo ministerio eiecit. Viam autem immaculatam, dicit, omnem abiectionem maligne et omnem in directionem iusticie. Vnde Aquila per *via immaculata*, 'via perfecta' transtulit.

57   Et animaduertandum quod malus homo non potest esse iniustus et seruus hominis iusti quia homo iustus de corpore Christi est. Vnde non seruit iusto qui capiti suo contraria est. Omnis autem malus Christo contrarius est et seruit peccato et dyabolo. Et non potest simul duobus dici[21] seruore, Christo videlicet et dyabolo. Vnde nec Christi et christiano videlicet menbro et aduersario dyabolo, preter hoc quis, nisi mente captus, seruum inimici sui assumunt in famulatum sui. Si ergo inimicus est noster dyabolus et inimicum peccatum, nisi mente capti simus, non assumimus in famulatum quos nouiumus facere mortale peccatum quia qui facit peccatum, seruus est peccati et seruus dyaboli. Sicut Dominus ad quosdam dicit [Jn. 8:44]: 'Vos ex patre dyabolo estis.' *AMBULANTES* igitur *IN VIA IMMACULATA* in ministerium sunt assumendi. Vnde et Bernardus ait: Quid me beatius, quidue securius, esset si huiusmodi circa me vite mee et custodes spectarem, simul et testes? Quibus omnia mea secreta secure committerem, communicarem consilia, quibus me totum refunderem tamquam alteri michi. Qui se vellem aliquatenus deuiare, non sinerent, frenarent precipitem, dormitantem suscitarent; quorum me reuerantia et libertas extollentem reprimeret excedentem corrigeret; quorum me constantia et fortitudo nutantem firmaret, erigeret diffidentem; quorum me fides et sanctitas ad queque sancta, ad queque honesta, ad queque pudica ad queque amabilia et bone fame prouocaret.

<100.7>

58   *NON HABITANT IN MEDIO DOMUS MEE QUI FACIT SUPERBIAM*. In persona Christi potest istud dici *IN DOMO* Christi, hoc est in ecclesia non habitat superbus. Licet participet sacramentis ecclesie, nec est de vnitate corporis Christi. Et nota quod dicit *IN MEDIO DOUMUS MEE* quia quicumque habitat in domo Dei, que est ecclesia, habitat in eius medio quia fundatur et radicatur in Christo. De quo dicit Iohannes [Jn. 1:26]: 'Medius autem vestrum stetit quem vos nescitis.'

59   Dicitur etiam in persona iusti cuius domus, vt supradictum est, cor suum et conscientia sua siue voluntas et amor eius. In hac domo non habitat superbus quia in amore iusti non collocatur /172va/nisi iustus. In corde autem cuiuslibet iusti habitat quilibet alius iustus quantumque sit corpore remotus. Sic enim consueuit amator dicere de eo quem amat, 'mecum est'; 'in corde meo habitat'. In hac igitur domo non habitat iniustus quia commanere non possunt lux et tenebra bonitas at malitia. Et signante dicit *IN MEDIO DOMUS* quia ipsum cor in quo est principium vite. Medium est tabernaculi corporis humani. Preterea in supremo domus nostre, hoc est cordis nostri et amoris nostri, habitat Deus quem diligimus plusquam nos. In vltima domus nostre habitant corpora nostra et corporales creature que diligimus minus quam nos, cum ea ordinato amore diligimus. In medio vero habitant proximi iusti quos diligimus sicut nos. In nullam istarum trium partium domus nostre habitat malus quia non illum diligimus, set odimus ex parte ea qua malus est. Diligimus tamen ipsum

hominem et malis hominis naturam non amplexantes illum in amore nostro, talem qualis est per malitiam, set desiderantes, vt moriatur malitie, suscitetur natura in vitam gratie.

60 Potest quoque et istud ad literam intelligi et continuari cum literali intellectu superioris versus, quod dicit, vir volens recte conuersari inter conciues assumpti in meum famulatum AMBULANTEM IN VIA IMMACULATA et non habitabit in medio familie mee qui facit superbiam. Omnis servus in medio familie debet habitare quia oculi servi semper ad domum suum et oculi ancille in manibus domine sue. Dominus autem, vt supra expositum est, IN MEDIO DOMUS SUE perambulat. Quapropter et seruus semper in domum intentus cum intendens in aliquid magis fit vbi est illud in quod intendit in medio domus recte dicitur conversari. Superius igitur cum superbo, hoc est cum homine proximo et pari sibi initio superbie inquinato comedere nolunt. Hic vero agit non de proximo et pari, set de seruo superbient.

61 Canendum est nobis summopere male moratos familiares habere. Nulla enim peior pestis quam adversarius familiaris. Vnde Gregorius in *Moralibus* loquens de mala persuasione coniugis. Iob ait: Ex verbis autem male suadentis coniugis vigilanter debemus aspicere quod antiquus hostis non solum per semetipsum, set per eos etiam qui nobis adherant, statum satagit nostre mentis melinare cum cor nostrum sua persuasione non subruit, adhuc nimirum per linguas adherentium repit. Hinc enim scriptum est 'a filiis tuis caue et a domesticis tuis attende'. Hinc per prophetam dicitur vnusquisque se a proximo suo custodiat et in omni fratri suo non habeat fiduciam. Huic rursum scriptum est: 'Inimici hominis domestici eius.' Callidus namque adversarius cum a bonorum cordibus repelli se conspicit eos qui ab illis valde diliguntur exquirit et per eorum verba blandiens loquitur qui plus ceteris amantur vt dum vis amoris /172vb/cor perforat facile persuasionis eius gladius ad intime rectitudinis munimina irrumpat. Post damna igitur, post funera pignorum post vulnera scissuras que membrorum antiquus hostis linguam mouit vxore. Et Bernard *ad Eugenium* ait: Collaterales et coadiutores tui hii seduli tibi, hii intimi, sunt. Quamobrem si boni sunt tibi potissimum sunt, si mali eque plus tibi. Nec te dixeris sanum, malis innitentem aut, si bonus sis, bonitas tui solius quem fructum afferre potest. Quid inquam emoluenit affert ecclesiis Dei tui unius manus hominus iustitia vbi sententai preualet aliter affectorum. Nec tuta tibi tua bonitas obsessa malis, non magis quam sanitas vicino serpente. Non est quo te subducas malo intestino. Et e regione bonum domesticum eo amplius, quo sepius iuuat. Set siue levent, siue gravent cui rectius imputandum quam tibi, qui tales aut eligisti aut admisisit. Omnis autem peccator superbiam facit quia in omnibus actibus suis propriam excellentiam intendit.

62 Moraliter vero per DOMUM intelligitur cor, vt supradictum est. Facies autem superbiam praua, cogitatio praua suggestio mali est. In domo igitur, id est conscientia viri non sinitur habitare qui facit superbiam, id est cogitatio mali, id est suggestio mali. Vir enim iustus expellit statim de domo cordis cogitationes et suggestiones rerum superbarum. Testatur autem domus quia de corde exeunt opera mala in Mat. .xv. dicens [Matt. 15:18–19]: 'Que autem procedunt de ore, de corde exeunt, et ea coniquinant hominem. De corde enim exeunt cogitationes male homicidia, adulteria, fornicationes, furta, falsa testimonia, blasfemie.' Malas igitur cogitationes superbiam

facentes non sunt iustus habitare in corde suo. Tenet enim et allidit paruulos suos ad petram.

63 Ex persona autem Christi et cuiuslibet iusti et sapientis patrisfamilias dici potest hic quod sequitur, videlicet *QUI LOQUITUR INIQUA NON DIREXIT IN CONSPECTU OCULORUM MEORUM*. Odit enim quilibet istorum loquentem iniqua nec rectus est in eorum aspectu qui iniqua loquitur. Iniqua autem locutio comprehendit sermonem otiosum, superuacuum, immundum, mendacem, detrahentem, suggerentem et persuadentem et precipientem malum. Qui itaque huiusmodi loquitur, iniqua est et non rectus quia sermone vtitur non ad finem propter quem factus est. Omne autem quod non recto fine fit peccatum est. Factus autem sermo vt illuminet audientis aspectum ad veritatem, siue accendat eius affectum ad caritatem, siue vtrumque faciat, siue vt laudes Dei resonet. Verba igitur vasa sunt veritatis, caritatis et diuine laudis, nec alium vsum sunt assumenda. Sermo autem custodiendum est mundus et sine macula quia cum certa opera que hic per carnis instrumenta facimus in celo cessabunt, locutio divine laudis in celis perpetuo permanebit. Ait enim Psalmus [Ps. 88:2]: */173ra/* 'Misercordias Domini in eternum cantabo.' Et iterum [Ps. 83:5]: 'Beati qui habitant in domo tua, Domine, in secular seculorum laudabunt te.' Iterum, ideo servandum est verbum mundum quia per verbum eternum omnia facta sunt.

64 Et quia sermo est id quod inter omnes res precipuam gerit similitudinem verbi Dei incarnati, sicut enim eternum Dei verbum assumpsit sibi carnem sensibilem in vnitatem persone, sic verbum mentis interius intelligibile assumunt sibi vnitatem persone verbi exterius sonans audibile vt sit vnus sermo ex intelligibili et audibili.

65 Item, sermo est in quo solo preeminet homo omni animali. In sermone etiam ratio interior comprehenditur quia igitur in hoc est hominis preeminentia et decus hunc debet super omnia custodiri immaculum. Sermo autem malus pessimos parit fructus quia corrumpit bonos mores auditorum colloquia praua. Et vt dicit Iacobus [Ja. 3:6]: 'Lingua ignis est, vniversitas iniquitatis. Lingua constituitur in membris nostris, que maculat totum corpus et inflammat rotam nativitatis nostre.' Linguam nullus homini domare potest inquietum malum et plena venano mortifero, vt in Ecclesiastico .xx. [Ecli. 20:15], de insipiente scriptum est quod 'apertio oris illius inflammatio est'.

66 Et Gregorius in *Moralibus* ait: Sepe verba carnalium dum se inportune nostris auribus ingerunt in corde bellum temptationis gignunt et quamuis hec etiam ratio respuat et lingua reprehendat cum labore, tamen vincitur interius quod foris cum auctoritate iudicatur. Vnde necesse est quod nec ad aures veniat quod mens cogitationis aditu vigilans repellat. Sancti igitur viri cum eternitatis desideriis anhelant in tanta altitudine vite se sulleuant, vt audire iam que mundi sunt grave sibi ac deprimens pondus credant. Valde namque insolens atque intolerabile estimant quicquid illud non sonat quod intus amant. Recte igitur et in hoc loco in persona iusti dictum est qui *LOQUITUR INIQUA NON DIREXIT IN CONSPECTU OCULORUM MEORUM*. Nobis autem qui in gradu regiminis consituti sumus valde perniciosus est etiam sermon nugacitatis ac per hoc sermo peior nugacitate magis perniciosus.

67 Vnde Bernardus ait: Inter seculares nuge nuge sunt; in ore sacerdotis blasfemie. Interdum tamen si incidant ferende fortasse referende numquam. Magis interveniendeum caute et prudenter nugacitati. Prorumpendum sane in serium quid, quod non modo

vtiliter set libenter audiant et supersedeant otiosis. Consecrasti os tuum Euangelio talibus iam aperire illicitum, assuescere sacrilegium est. 'Labia saceredotis', ait, 'custodiunt scientiam, et legem requirunt de ore eius'. Non nugas profecto vel fabulas. Verbum scurile, faceti vrbani, ne nomine colorant[22] non sufficit peregrenari ab ore; procul et ab aure relegandum. Fede ad cachinnos moneris, fedius mones. Porro detrahere aut detrahentem audire quid horum dampnabilius sit, non facile dixerim. *In conspectur* igitur nostrorum *oculorum* /173rb/precipue non dirigat qui loquatur iniqua.

<100.8>

68   Sequitur *IN MATUTINO INFERFICIEBAM <OMNES PECCATORES>*[23] *TERRE, VT DISPERDEREM DE CIVITATE DEI OMNES OPERANTES INIQUITATEM*. In persona Christi dicit esse hic Psalmista quasi aliquis quereret cum non approbes malos quare eos toleras? Et ipse responderet quia nondum venit mane set adhuc nox est in qua tolerandi sunt mali cum bonis; quia adhuc tempus est immo veniet mane, tempus videlicet iudicii quando segregabuntur hedi ab ouibus, mali videlicet a iustis. Per *MATUTINUM* igitur intelligitur hoc tempus vltimi iudicii. Totum enim tempus huius vite tamquam nox est quia sicut dicit Augustinus: Quamdiu non vides cor meum et non video cor tuum nox est. Contempni te putas ab aliquo; et forte non contemneris ut quia aliquis odit te et forte diligit et ita de nobis inivicem nondum certi sumus. Ista obscuritas nox est et in ista nocte habundant temptationem. Vnde et Psalmus ait [Ps. 103:20–21]: 'Posui<sti> teneras et facta est nox. In ipsa pertransibunt omnes bestis silve catuli leonum rugientes vt rapiant et querant a Deo escam sibi.' Catuli leonum? principes sunt et potestates tenebrarum harum. Querunt sibi escam? quando temptare, scilicet quando non accedent nisi Deus dederit eis potestatem. Ideo dictum est 'querentes a Deo escam sibi' sicut petit Sathanas Iob ad temptandum et datus est ei ad temptandum non opprimendum ad purgandum, non evertendum aut forte, nec ad purgandum, set ad probandum hanc noctem. Sequitur mane quod ostendit nobis Apostolus dicens [I Cor. 4:5]: 'Nolite ante tempus iudicare quoadusque veniet. Dominus qui[24] illuminabit adscondita tenebrarum et manifestabit consilia cordium.'

69   In isto itaque *MATUTINO INTERFECIT* Christus *OMNES PECCATORES TERRE* quia tunc separabit ventilabro verbi sui paleam a tritico hedos ab agnis, malos a bonis; et malos tanquam paleam comburet igne inextinguibile, et ita combustio mors est secunda, de qua in Apoc. [Apoc. 2:11]: 'Qui vicerit non ledetur a morte secunda.' De qua et Augustinus dicit in libro *De ciuitate Dei*: Verum in damnatione novissima, quamuis homo sentire non desinat, tamen quia sensus ipse nec voluptate suauis nec quiete salubris, set dolore penalis est non immerito mors est, potius appellata quam vita. Ideo autem secunda quia post illam primam est, qua fit coherentium cohereptio naturarum siue Dei et anime et corporis. De prima igitur morte dici potest quod bonis bona sit malis mala. Secunda vero sine dubio sicut nullorum bonorum, est ita nulli bona. Hac igitur secunda morte in matutino vltimi iudicii interficiet Dominus Iesus Christus omnes peccatores terre dicens impiis: 'Ite maledicti in ignem eternum' [Matt. 25:41], vt disperdat de ciuitate Dei omnes operantes iniquitatem, hoc est vt

segreget localiter etiam malos a bonis, qui non localiter commixti sunt, quam segregationem predixit in Math. dicens [Matt. 13:13]: 'In tempore messis dicam messoribus colligite primum zizania et alligate ea in fasciculos ad comburendum triticum autem congregate in horreum meum.'

70 Est igitur hec vox cuiuslibet fidelis et maxime eorum qui erunt iudices cum Christo qui in Christo et per Christum predictam /173va/facientis interfectionem et disp<o>sitionem. Secundum Isidorum[25] autem per hoc quod dicit IN MATUTINO INTERFICIEBAM insumatur quod Deus neque ex impetu ire neque ex ebritatis perturbatione vindicat in peccatores. Ira namque et si de hesterna exacerbauit noctis, tamen quiete mitegatur ebrietas. Similiter et si vesper multa fuerit per sompnum sufficienter subtilitur, matutinum ergo opus ex rationis motu non ex ire, aut ebrietatis impetu, solet fieri. Hec igitur et hic insumatur quod ex tranquiliatte rationis condemnaturus sit et condemnatione interfecturus peccatores.

71 Moraliter autem congruit hoc cuilibet fideli qui in matutino, id est in initio suggestionis praue interficit ipsos motus primos praue suggestionis. Intelligitur quoque per mane qualibet diuina illuminatio et doctrina. Confessio quoque et reuelatio peccati; velox quoque prom<p>titudo ad bonum in quibus omnibus velut in clara luce matutina exterminat iustus et interficit omnes malas congregationes et actiones quasi peccatores terre quia male cogitationes de corde exeunt et in corde habitant, quasi in terra habitationis sue. Hec autem interfectum fit vt disperdantur de ciuitate Dei, hoc est de anima fideli; omnes operantes iniquitatem, hoc est omnes praue cogitationes et suggestiones que monent menbra corporis ad opera iniquitatis.

72 Basilius vero exponens hunc versum distinguit inter peccatores et operantes iniquitatem. Ait enim: Oportet nos non solum passionum corporalium esse interfectores, set et cogitationum passibilium anime destructores. Peccatores enim terr corporis sunt passiones, operantes vero iniquitatem ex ciuitate Dei disperdendi anime sunt perverse cogitationes. Carnis igitur passiones et opera interficienda sunt, vt de ciuitate Dei, id est de anima. Disperdantur noxie cogitatione iniquitatum operatrices. Opera namque carnis ab scisa mortificant plerumque pravas interius cogitationes sicut quarumdam plantarum ab scisis ramis mortificatur consequenter. Et radix perfectiorum non mundatio est cum prius mortificata radice commoriuntur et rami, id est cum ex cogitatione malorum executione tolluntur mala in opere vtraque tamen ordine proceditur in hominis iustificatione.

73 Possimus etiam et aliter distinguere inter peccatores et operantes iniquitatem, vt videlicet per PECCATORES intelligamus culpas; per operationes vero iniquitatis, concupiscentias carnis pronitatis ad peccatum, natas expectandi consuetudinis que interfectis peccatis per penitentiam solent adhuc in carne remanere et eam ad peccandum stimulare. Interfecit igitur iustus per confessionem et contritionem culpas, vt etiam disperdat de ciuitate Domini, hoc est de sua natura humana; omnes fomites et concupiscentias et pronitates ad peccandum que operantur etiam iniusto iniquitatem, hoc est ipsum concupiscere de quo opere diciti Apostolus ad Ro. [Rom. 7:15]: 'Non quod volo bonum, hoc ago, set quod odi[26] malum, hoc facio. Non vult enim iustus et tamen concupiscunt /173vb/continue cum ipsum concupiscere imminuit et disperdit donec tamdem aut omnino non sit aut debile sit.'

74 Iste quoque versus spiritualiter congruit prelatis et omni etiam recte conuersanti inter conciues vt in matutino, hoc est velociter cum omni studio in luce discretionis et diuine legis. Interficiat gladio verbi Dei et potestate iudicaria et modis aliis quibus potest omnes peccatores, non, vt supradictum est, homines, set ipsos peccatores vt sint homines non peccatores vt omnes, videlicet de ciuitate Dei, hoc est de ecclesia et de societate hominum sub vna Dei lege vniente. Disperdat omnes operantes iniquitatem, licet enim nullus possit hoc adimplere, vt videlicet omnes mali ex parte ea qua mali sunt, auferantur de ecclesia et societate bonorum, vel correcta nichil iuste condemnati tamen quilibet prelatus et quilibet potestas a Deo ordinata, et quibus fidelis proportione sua, hoc debet intendere et ad hoc conari pro toto posse vt omnes peccatores interficiantur et disperdantur. Sicut intendit agricola omnes tarduos sarculo prestandere de medio crescent tritici, nec tamen efficiet vt omnes ominio purgentur, nec ideo cessat et purgando triticum a carduis, licet sciat quod numquam plene purgabitur.

75 In hoc igitur Psalmo decem proposite sunt affirmationes et sex negationes attribuendo viro perfecto. Hee autem sunt affectiones: prima vt sit misericors sibi et in se omnibus miserando; secunda vt seipsum discutiat veraci iudicio; tertio vt psallat confessione et bono opere; quarta vt intelligat contemplatione; quinta vt servet innocentiam ad propriam familiam; sexta licet non sexto loco dicta vt diligit continues tamquam se non querens quod suum est set quod reipublice. Septima vt de bonis inuentis matrimonio conciuum incorporet corpori familie sue; octaue vt odiat malum; nona vt persequitur malum; decima vt interficia malum pro posse suo, vt penitus non sit, vt tollat de terra, quantum in se est, malorum memoriam.

76 Negationes autem sunt iste: persona enim per se absque illectu moneri ad malum; secunda non moneri ab illiciente; tertia non approbare in altero recessum ipsius a recto; quarta non communicare cum eo in opere qui a recto recessit; quinta non incoporare familie sue aliquem operantem malum; sexta non incorporare familie sue etiam aliquem assuetum loqui malum.

77 In hiis ataque affectionbius informantibus ad iustitiam et in hiis negationibus purgantibus ab iniusca consistit conversatio perfecta.

Notes

1   Add. E.
2   Ro. .13. B.
3   immirosus B.
4   Corr. ex E, quoniam B.
5   E, non leg. B.
6   E, non leg. B.
7   E, non leg. B.
8   Corr. ex E, interfectio B.
9   ructu B.
10 Corr. ex E, Ideo B.
11 persona qui corr. ex E, ? B.
12 omisceris B.

13 Add E.
14 Corr. ex E, erit B.
15 Corr. ex E, sequitur B.
16 Om. B.
17 Add. E.
18 cibus B.
19 frustam B.
20 Corr. ex E, ventitur B.
21 dicimus B.
22 solorat B.
23 Add. E.
24 quia B.
25 Isodorum B.
26 volo B.

Bibliography

Primary Sources

Manuscripts

Bologna, Biblioteca dell'Archiginnasio MS 983
Cambridge, Gonville and Caius College MS 439
Durham Cathedral, Dean and Chapter Library MS A.III.12.
London, British Library MS Royal 6.E.v.
London, British Library MS Royal 7.E.ii.
Modena, Biblioteca Estense MS lat. 54.

Published Sources

Alan of Lille. *Summa de arte praedicandi.* PL 210.110–98.
Alexander of Hales. *Quaestiones disputatae antequam esset frater.* Ed. PP. Collegii S. Bonaventurae. 3 vols. Bibliotheca Franciscana Scholastica Medii Aevi, 19–21. Quaracchi: College of St Bonaventure, 1960.
———. *Glossa In Quatuor Libros Sententiarum Petri Lombardi.* Ed. PP. Collegii S. Bonaventurae. 4 vols. Quaracchi: College of S. Bonaventure, 1951–57.
Anselm of Canterbury. *Opera Omnia.* Ed. F.S. Schmitt. 6 vols. Edinburgh: T. Nelson, 1961.
Augustine. *Adnotationes in Iob.* PL 34.825–86.
———. *De Doctrina Christiana.* Ed. J. Martin. CCL, 32. Turnhout: Brepols, 1962.
———. *De Genesi ad litteram.* PL 34.245–486.
———. *De trinitate libri XV*, ed. W.J. Mountain. 2 vols. CCL, 50–50A. Turnhout: Brepols, 1968. ET: *The Trinity.* Trans. E. Hill. New York: New City Press, 2002.
———. *De vera religione.* Ed. J. Martin. CCL, 32. Turnhout: Brepols, 1962.
———. *Ennarationes in Psalmos.* Ed. D.E. Dekkers and J. Fraipont. 3 vols. CCL, 38–40. Turnhout: Brepols, 1956.
———. *Sermones.* PL 38.
———. *Soliloquiorum libri duo.* PL 32.867–904.
Avicebron. *Fons vitae.* Ed. C. Beumker. Beiträge zur Geschichte der Philosophie des Mittelalters, 1, Heft 1–4. Münster: Aschendorff, 1895.
Avicenna. *De anima.* Ed. S. Van Riet. Editions orientalistes. 2 vols. Leiden: Brill, 1972.
———. *Liber De philosophia prima sive Scientia divina.* Ed. S. van Reit. Louvain: Peeters, 1977–83.

Boethius. *De persona et duabus naturis*. PL 64.1337–54.
Bonaventure. *Opera Omnia*. Ed. PP. Collegii S. Bonaventurae. 8 vols. Quaracchi: College of S. Bonaventure, 1882–1902.
Brett, M.; Brooke, C.N.L.; Cheney, C.R.; Powicke, F.M. and Whitelock, D. eds. *Councils and Synods, with Other Documents Relating to the English Church*. 2 vols. Oxford: Clarendon Press, 1964.
Chronicon de Lanercost. Ed. J. Stevenson. Edinburgh: Maitland Club, 1839.
Claudius of Turin. *In Genesim*. PL 50. 893–1043.
Decrees of the Ecumenical Councils. Ed. N. Tanner. 2 vols. London: Sheed and Ward, 1990.
Desiderius Erasmus. *Expositions of the Psalms*. Ed. Dominic Baker-Smith. Trans. Michael J. Heath. Collected Works of Erasmus, 63. Toronto: University of Toronto Press, 1997.
Dionysiaca. Ed. P. Chevallier. 2 vols. Paris: Descleé de Brouwer, 1937.
Five Texts on the Mediaeval Problem of Universals : Porphyry, Boethius, Abelard, Duns Scotus, Ockham. Trans. P.V. Spade. Indianapolis: Hackett, 1994.
Fulgentius Ruspensis. *De trinitate liber unus*. PL 65.497–508.
Gregory the Great. *Moralia in Iob*. Ed. M. Adriaen. 3 vols. CCL, 143. Turnhout: Brepols, 1979.
Guy of Orchelles. *Tractatus de sacramentis ex eius Summa de sacramentis et officiis ecclesiae*. Ed. D. Van den Eynde and P. Van den Eynde. Franciscan Institute Publications, Text Series, 4. Louvain: E. Nauwelaerts, 1953.
Hincmar of Rheims. *De una et non trina deitate*. PL 125.473–620.
Hugh of St-Victor. *De sacramentis christianae fidei*. PL 176.173–618. ET: Hugh of St-Victor. *On the Sacraments of the Christian Faith*. Trans. R. Deferrari. Cambridge: Mediaeval Academy of America, 1957.
——. *De tribus maximis circumstantiis gestorum*. Ed. W.M. Green, 'Hugo of St-Victor *De tribus maximis circumstantiis gestorum*.' *Speculum* 18 (1943), 484–93.
——. *Didascalion*. Ed. C.H. Buttimer. Studies in Medieval and Renaissance Latin, 10. Washington: Catholic University of America, 1939.
John Damascene. *De Fide Orthodoxa: Versions of Burgundio and Cerbanus*. Ed. E.M. Buytaert. Text Series, 8. St Bonaventure: Franciscan Institute, 1955.
John Scotus Erigena. *De divisione naturae*. Ed. E. Jeauneau. 4 vols. CCCM, 161–4. Turnhout: Brepols, 1996.
Liber de spiritu et anima. PL 40.779–831.
Matthew Paris. *Chronica majora*. Ed. H. Luard. Rolls Series. 5 vols. London: Longman, 1872–83.
Nicholas Trivet. *Annales sex regum Angliae*. Ed. T. Hog. London: Sumptibus Societatis, 1845.
Paul, Suzanne. 'An Edition and Study of the Sermons Attributed to Robert Grosseteste in Durham MS A.III.12.' 2 vols. Unpublished PhD diss., University of Leeds, 2002.
Pegis, Anton. *Introduction to St Thomas Aquinas*. New York: Random House, 1945.
Peter Comester. *Historia Scholastica*. PL 198.1050–1721.
Peter Lombard. *Sententiae*. Ed. I. Brady. 2 vols. Spicilegium Bonaventurianum, 4–5. Quaracchi: College of St Bonaventure, 1971–81.

———. *Collectanea in Epistolas Sancti Pauli*. PL 191.1297–1696; 192.9–520.

———. *Glossa Super Psalterium*. PL 191.55–1296.

Peter the Chanter. *Verbum abbreviatum*. PL 205.23–370.

Philip the Chancellor. *Summa de bono*. Ed. N. Wicki. 2 vols. Berne: Franke, 1985.

Die Philosophischen Werke des Robert Grosseteste, Bischofs von Lincoln. Ed. L. Baurf. Beiträge zur Geschichte der Philosophie des Mittelalters, Texte und Untersuchungen, 9. Münster: Aschendorff, 1912.

Rabanus Maurus. *De universo*. PL 112.851–1088.

Richard of St-Victor. *De trinitate*. Ed. J. Ribaillier. Texts Philosophiqueis du Moyen Age, 6. Paris: Vrin, 1958.

———. *De verbo incarnato*. PL 196.995–1010.

Robert Grosseteste. *Dictum* 19. Ed. James R. Ginther. In 'Natural Philosophy and Theology at Oxford in the Early Thirteenth Century: An Edition and Study of Robert Grosseteste's Inception Sermon (*Dictum* 19).' *Medieval Sermon Studies* 44 (2000), 108–34.

———. *Hexaëmeron*. Ed. Richard C. Dales and Servus Gieben. Auctores Britannici Medii Aevi, 6. London: British Academy, 1982. ET: *On the Six Days of Creation*. Trans. C.F.J. Martin. Auctores Britannici Medii Aevi, 6, 1. London: British Academy, 1996.

———. *Expositio in epistolam sancti Pauli ad Galatas*. In *Opera inedita Roberti Grosseteste*. Ed. J. McEvoy. CCCM, 130, pp. 3–175. Turnhout: Brepols, 1995.

———. *Glossarum in sancti Paul epistolas fragmenta*. In *Opera inedita Roberti Grosseteste*. Ed. R.C. Dales. CCCM, 130, pp. 179–231. Turnhout: Brepols, 1995.

———. *Tabula*. In *Opera inedita Roberti Grosseteste*. Ed. P. Rosemann. CCCM, 130, pp. 235–320. Turnhout: Brepols, 1995.

———. *De Libero Arbitrio*. Ed. N. Lewis, 'The First Recension of Robert Grosseteste's *De Libero arbitrio*.' *Mediaeval Studies* 53 (1991), 1–88.

———. Grossestete. *De decem mandatis*. Ed. R.C. Dales and E.B. King. Auctores Britannici Medii Aevi, 10. London: British Academy, 1987.

———. *Lecturae in Epistolam ad Romanos V–XVI*. Ed. E. Mather, '*Lecturae in Epistolam ad Romanos V–XVI Roberto Grosseteste adscriptae*.' Unpublished PhD diss. University of Southern California, Los Angeles, 1987.

———. *De cessatione legalium*. Ed. R.C Dales and E.B. King. Auctores Britannici Medii Aevi, 7. London: British Academy, 1986.

———. *Templum Dei*. Ed. J. Goering and F.A.C. Mantello. Toronto Medieval Latin Texts, 14. Toronto: PIMS, 1984.

———. *De dotibus*. Ed. J. Goering, 'The *De dotibus* of Robert Grosseteste.' *Mediaeval Studies* 44 (1982), 83–109.

———. *Commentarius in posteriorum analyticorum libros*. Ed. P. Rossi. Florence: Olschki, 1981.

———. *Ecclesia sancta celebrat*. Ed. James McEvoy, 'Robert Grosseteste's Theory of Human Nature. With the Text of his Conference, *Ecclesia sancta celebrat*.' *Recherches de théologie ancienne et médiévale* 47 (1980), 131–87.

———. *De operationibus solis*. Ed. James McEvoy, 'The Sun as *res* and *signum*: Grosseteste's Commentary on Ecclesiasticus ch. 43, vv.1–5.' *Recherches de théologie ancienne et médiévale* 41 (1974), 38–91.

——. *Deus est*. Ed. S. Wenzel, 'Robert Grosseteste's Treatise on Confession, *Deus est.*' *Franciscan Studies* 30 (1970), 218–93.

——. *Dictum* 60. Ed. S. Gieben, 'Traces of God in Nature According to Robert Grosseteste. With the Text of the Dictum, *Omnis creatura speculum est.*' *Franciscan Studies* 24 (1964), 144–58.

Roberti Grosseteste quondam episcopi Lincolniensis Epistolae. Ed. H. Luard. Rolls Series, 25. London: Longman, 1861.

Robert of Melun. *Sententiae*, in *Oeuvres de Robert de Melun*. Ed. R. Martin. 4 vols. Spicilegium Sacrum Lovaniense. Études et documents, 13, 18, 21, 25. Louvain: Spicilegium Sacrum Lovaniense, 1932–52.

Roger of Wendover. *Flores historiarum*. Ed. H.G. Hewlett. 3 vols. Rolls Series, 84. London: Longman, 1889.

Rotuli Hugonis de Welles episcopi Lincolniensis. Ed. F.N. Davis and W.P.W. Phillimore. 3 vols. Lincoln Record Society 3,6,9. Lincoln: Morton and Sons, 1912–14.

Salimbene. *Cronica*. Ed. O. Holder-Egger. Monumenta Germaniae Historiae, Scriptores, 32. Hanover: Monumenta Germaniae Historiae, 1913.

A Scholastic Miscellany: From Anselm to Ockham. Ed. E.R. Fairweather. Library of Christian Classics. Philadelphia: Westminster Press, 1956.

Summa Fratris Alexandri. Ed. PP. Collegii S. Bonaventurae. 4 vols. Quaracchi: Collegium S. Bonaventurae, 1924–48.

Teoria della scienza teologica: Quaestio de scientia theologiae di Odo Rigaldi e altri testi inediti (1230–50). Ed. Leonardo Sileo. 2 vols. Studia Antoniana, 27. Rome: Pontificium Athenaeum Antonianum, 1984.

Thomas Aquinas. *Opuscula theologica*. Ed. R.A. Verardo et al. 2 vols. Turin: Marietta, 1954.

——. *Summa theologiae*. Leonine Edition. 3 vols. Turin: Marrietti, 1948.

Thomas of Eccleston. *De adventu fratrum minorum in Angliam*. Ed. A.G. Little. Manchester: Manchester University Press, 1951.

Three Treatises on Man: A Cistercian Anthropology. Ed. B. McGinn. Cistercian Fathers Series. 24. Kalamazoo, MI: Cistercian Publications, 1977.

Tugwell, Simon. *Albert and Thomas: Selected Writings*. Classics of Western Spirituality. New York: Paulist Press, 1988.

William of Auvergne. *Opera Omnia*. 2 vols. Paris: [n.p.],1674; rprt. Frankfurt am Main: Minerva, 1963.

——. *De Trinitate*, ed. B. Switalski, Studies and Texts, 34. Toronto: PIMS, 1976.

William of Auxerre. *Summa Aurea*. Ed. J. Ribaillier. 4 vols. Spicilegium Bonaventurianum, 16–20. Quaracchi: College of St Bonaventure, 1980–87.

William de Melitona. *Quaestiones de sacramentis*. Ed. PP. Collegii S. Bonaventurae. 2 vols. Bibliotheca Franciscana Scholastica Medii Aevi, 22–3. Quaracchi: College of St Bonaventure, 1961.

Secondary Sources

Arquillière, Henri X. *Le plus ancien traité de l'église: Jacques de Vitèrbe, De regimine Christiano (1301–1302). Etude des sources et édition critique.* Paris: Beauchesne, 1926.
Backus, Irena. 'John of Damascus, *De fide orthodoxa*: translations by Burgundio (1153/4), Grosseteste (1235/40) and Lefèvre d'Etaples (1507).' *Journal of the Warburg and Courtauld Institutes* 49 (1986), 211–17.
Bazàn, Bernardo C. and Wippel, John F. *Les questions disputées et les questions quodlibétiques dans les facultés de théologie, de droit, et de médecine.* Typologie des Sources du Moyen Âge Occidental, 44–5. Turnhout: Brepols, 1985.
Beinert, Wolfgang. *Dei Kirche, Gottes Heil in der Welt: die Lehre von der Kirche nach den Schriften des Rupert von Deutz, Honorius Augustodunensis und Gerhoch von Reichersburg. Ein Beitrag zur Ekklesiologie des 12. Jahrhunderts.* Beiträge zur Geschichte des Philosophie und Theologie des Mittelalters, neue Folge, 13. Münster: Aschendorff, 1973.
Beumer, Johannes. 'Zur Ekklesiologie der Frühscholastik.' *Scholastik* 26 (1951), 364–89; 27 (1952), 183–209.
Biographical Register of the University of Cambridge to AD 1500. Ed. A.B. Emden. Cambridge: Cambridge University Press, 1963.
Biographical Register of the University of Oxford to AD 1500. Ed. A.B. Emden. 3 vols. Oxford: Clarendon Press, 1957–59.
Bonnefoy, J.-F. 'La Question hypothétique *Utrum si Adam non peccesset* . . . au XIIIe siècle.' *Revista Espanola de Teologi* 14 (1954), 327–68.
Boyle, Leonard E. 'The Fourth Lateran Council and Manuals of Popular Theology,' in *The Popular Literature of Medieval England.* Ed. T.J. Heffernan, pp. 30–43. Knoxville: University of Tennessee Press, 1985.
——. 'Robert Grosseteste and the Pastoral Care.' *Medieval and Renaissance Studies* 8 (1979), 3–51.
Brady, I., Gurr, J.E. and Weisheipl, J.A., 'Scholasticism.' *New Catholic Encyclopedia*, 19 vols. 12.1153–70. New York: McGraw-Hill, 1967–95.
Bright, Pamela. *The Book of Rules of Tyconius. Its Purpose and Inner Logic.* Notre Dame: University of Notre Dame Press, 1988.
Burns, Robert M. 'Divine Infinity in Thomas Aquinas: I. Philosophico-Theological Background.' *Heythrop Journal* 39 (1998), 57–69.
Bynum, Carol Walter. *The Resurrection of the Body in Western Christianity, 200–1336.* New York: Columbia University Press, 1995.
Callus, D.A. 'Robert Grosseteste as Scholar.' In *Robert Grosseteste, Scholar and Bishop*, Essays in Commemoration of the Seventh Centenary of his Death. Ed. Daniel A. Callus, pp. 1–69. Oxford: Clarendon Press, 1955.
——. 'The Date of Grosseteste's Translations and Commentaries of Pseudo-Dionysius and the Nicomachean Ethics.' *Recherches de théologie ancienne et médiévale* 14 (1947), 186–209.
——. 'The Oxford Career of Robert Grosseteste.' *Oxoniensia* 10 (1945), 45–72.

——. 'Philip the Chancellor and the *De anima* ascribed to Robert Grosseteste.' *Medieval and Renaissance Studies* 1 (1941), 105–27.
Camargo, Martin. *Ars dictaminis, ars dictandi.* Typologie des Sources du Moyen Âge Occidental, 60. Turnhout: Brepols, 1991.
Cheney, C.R. *Episcopal Visitations of Monasteries in the Thirteenth Century.* Manchester: Manchester University Press, 1931.
Chenu, M.-D. *La théologie comme science au XIIIe siècle.* Third edition. Paris: Vrin, 1957.
——. 'Maîtres et bacheliers de l'université de Paris, v. 1240.' *Etudes d'histoire littéraire et doctrinale du XIIIe siècle* 1 (1932), 11–39.
Colish, Marcia. 'Early Scholastic Angelology.' *Recherches de théologie ancienne et médiévale* 62 (1995), 80–109.
Congar, Yves. *L'Eglise de Saint Augustin à l'époque moderne.* Paris: Cerf, 1970.
——. 'Aspects ecclésiologiques de la querelle entre mendiants et seculiers dans la seconde motié du XIIIe siècle et le debut de XIVe.' *Archives d'histoire doctrinale et littéraire du moyen âge* 28 (1961), 35–151.
——. 'Ecclesia ab Abel,' in *Abhandlung über Theologie und Kirche. Feschrift für Karl Adam.* Ed. M. Reding, pp. 79–108. Düsseldorf: Patmos, 1952.
Constable, Giles. *Letters and Letter Collections.* Typologie des Sources du Moyen Âge Occidental, 17. Turnhout: Brepols, 1976.
Coolman, Boyd Taylor. 'Spiritual Apprehension: the Spiritual Senses and the Knowledge of God in the Theology of William of Auxerre.' Unpublished PhD diss. University of Notre Dame, 2001.
Coté, Antoine. 'Note sur Guerric de Saint-Quentin et la question de l'infini divin.' *Recherches de théologie ancienne et médiévale* 62 (1995), 71–9.
Cross, Richard. *The Metaphysics of the Incarnation: Thomas Aquinas to Duns Scotus.* Oxford: Oxford University Press, 2002.
Dahan, Gilbert. *Les Intellectuels chrétiens et les juifs au moyen âge.* Paris: Cerfs, 1990.
Dales, Richard C. 'A Medieval View of Human Dignity.' *Journal of the History of Ideas* 38 (1977), 557–72.
David, Marian. 'Truth, Correspondence Theory of' in *Stanford Encyclopedia of Philosophy.* Ed. E.N. Zalta <http://plato.stanford.edu/entries/truth-correspondence/>.
D'Avray, David. *The Preaching of the Friars: Sermons Diffused from Paris before 1300.* Oxford: Clarendon, 1985.
Davy, M.M., *Les sermons universitaires parisiens de 1230–1231.* Etudes de philosophie médiévale, 15. Paris: Vrin, 1931.
Van Deusen, Nancy. 'Thirteenth-century motion theories and their musical applications: Robert Grosseteste and the Anonymous IV.' In *The Intellectual Climate of the Early University: Essays in Honor of Otto Gründler.* Ed. N. Deusen, pp. 101–24. Studies in Medieval Culture, 39. Kalamazoo: Medieval Institute Publications, 1997.
——. *Theology and Music at the Early University. The Case of Robert Grosseteste and Anonymous IV.* Brill's Studies in Intellectual History, 57. Leiden: Brill, 1994.

Dijk, S.J.P. Van and Walker, J. Hazeldon. *The Origins of the Modern Roman Liturgy.* London: Darton, Longman & Todd, 1960.

Dionisotti, A.C., 'On the Greek Studies of Robert Grosseteste.' In *The Uses of Greek and Latin: Historical Essays.* Ed. A.C. Dionisotti, A. Grafton and J. Kraye, pp. 19–39. London: University of London, 1988.

Dobson, E.J. *Moralities on the Gospels: A New Source of Ancrene Wisse.* Oxford: Clarendon Press, 1978.

Dondaine, H.F. 'L'objet et le *médium* de la vision béatifique chez les théologiens du XIIIe siècle.' *Recherches de théologie ancienne et médiévale* 19 (1952), 60–130.

Donneaud, Henry. 'Histoire d'une histoire: M.-D. Chenu et "La théologie comme science au XIIIe siècle".' *Mémoire Dominicaine* 4 (1994), 139–75.

Dulles, Avery. *Models of the Church.* New York: Doubleday, 1974; rprt: New York, Image Books, 1978.

Easton, Stewart. *Roger Bacon and His Search for a Universal Science: A Reconsideration of the Life and Work of Roger Bacon in the Light of his own Stated Purposes.* Oxford: Blackwell, 1952.

Evans, G.R. 'The *Conclusiones* of Robert Grosseteste's Commentary on the *Posterior Analytics.*' *Studi Medievali* 24 (1983), 729–34.

——. 'Boethian and Euclidean Axiomatic Method in the Theology of the Later Twelfth Century.' *Archives internationales d'histoire des sciences* 30 (1980), 36–52.

Ferruolo, Stephen C. *The Origins of the University: The Schools of Paris and their Critics, 1100–1215.* Stanford: Stanford University Press, 1985.

Fleming, Peter. *Family and Households in Medieval England.* Basingstoke: Palgrave, 2001.

Fontana, Maria. 'Il commento ai Salmi di Giberto della Porrée.' *Logos* 13 (1930), 283–301.

Fortman, Edmund J. *The Triune God. A Historical Study of the Doctrine of the Trinity.* Philadelphia: Westminster Press, 1972.

Friedman, L.M. *Robert Grosseteste and the Jews.* Cambridge, MA: Harvard University Press, 1934.

Fritz, G. and Michel, A. 'Scolastique.' *Dictionaire de théologie catholique,* 14, 2.1691–728.

Ghellinck, Joseph de. *Le mouvement théologique du XIIe siècle.* Second edition. Museum Lessanium, Section historique, 10. Paris: Brouwer, 1948.

Gieben, Servus. 'Robert Grosseteste and Adam Marsh on Light in a Summary Attributed to St. Bonaventure.' In *Aspectus et Affectus: Essays and Editions in Grosseteste and Medieval Intellectual Life in Honor of Richard C. Dales.* Ed. G. Freibergs, pp. 17–33. New York: AMS Press, 1993.

——. 'Robert Grosseteste at the Papal Curia, Lyons, 1250: Edition of the Documents.' *Collectanea Franciscana* 41 (1971), 340–93.

Ginther, James R. 'There is a Text in this Classroom: The Bible in the Medieval University.' In *Essays in Medieval Theology and Philosophy in Memory of Walter Principe: Fortresses and Launching Pads.* Ed. J.R. Ginther and C.N. Still, pp. 31–62. Aldershot: Ashgate Press, 2004.

———. 'Grosseteste and Universal Science.' In *Robert Grosseteste and the Beginnings of a British Theological Tradition*. Ed. M. O'Carroll, pp. 219–38. Bibliotheca Seraphico-Capuccina, 69. Rome: Istituto storico dei Capuccini, 2003.

———. 'Robert Grosseteste and the Theologian's Task.' In *Robert Grosseteste and the Beginnings of a British Theological Tradition*. Ed. M. O'Carroll, pp. 239–63. Bibliotheca Seraphico-Capuccina, 69. Rome: Istituto storico dei Cappuccini, 2003.

———. 'The *Super Psalterium* in Context.' In *Editing Robert Grosseteste*. Proceedings of the Annual Editorial Conference, held at University College, University of Toronto, 2–5 November 2000. Ed. J. Goering and E. Mackie, pp. 31–60. Toronto: University of Toronto Press, 2003.

———. 'A Scholastic Idea of the Church: Robert Grosseteste's Exposition of Psalm 86.' *Archives d'histoire doctrinale et littéraire du moyen âge* 66 (1999), 49–72.

———. 'Monastic Ideals and Episcopal Visitations: the *Sermo ad religiosos* of Robert Grosseteste, Bishop of Lincoln (1235–1253).' In *Medieval Monastic Preaching*. Ed. C.A. Meussig, pp. 231–53. Leiden: Brill, 1998.

———. 'Theological Education at the Oxford Studium in the Thirteenth Century: A Reassessment of Robert Grosseteste's Letter to the Oxford Theologians.' *Franciscan Studies* 55 (1998), 83–104.

———. 'The *Super Psalterium* of Robert Grosseteste. A Scholastic Psalms Commentary, c.a. 1170–1253.' Unpublished PhD diss. University of Toronto, 1995.

Glorieux, P. 'Les 572 questions de Douai MS 434.' *Recherches de théologie ancienne et médiévale* 10 (1938), 123–52, 255–67.

Goering, Joseph. 'Robert Grosseteste at the Papal Curia.' In *A Distinct Voice: Medieval Studies in Honor of Leonard E. Boyle, O.P.* Eds J. Brown and W.P. Stoneman, pp. 253–76. Notre Dame: University of Notre Dame Press, 1997.

———. 'When and Where did Grosseteste Study Theology?' In *Robert Grosseteste: New Perspectives on his Thought and Scholarship*. Ed. James McEvoy, pp. 17–51. Instrumenta Patristica, 18. Turnhout: Brepols, 1995.

———. *William de Montibus (c.1140–1213). The Schools and the Literature of the Pastoral Care*. Studies and Texts, 108. Toronto: PIMS, 1992.

——— and Mantello, F.A.C. 'The Early Penitential Writings of Robert Grosseteste.' *Recherches de théologie ancienne et médiévale* 54 (1987), 52–112.

——— and Mantello, F.A.C. 'The *Perambulavit Iudas . . . (Speculum confessionis)*, Attributed to Robert Grosseteste.' *Revue Bénédictine* 96 (1986), 125–68.

———. 'The *De dotibus* of Robert Grosseteste.' *Mediaeval Studies* 44 (1982), 83–109.

Grabmann, Martin. *I divieti ecclesiastici di Aristotele sotto Innocenzo III e Gregorio IX*, Miscellanea Historiae Pontificiae 5. Rome: Saler, 1941.

Grabowski, Stanislaus. *The Church: An Introduction to the Theology of St. Augustine*. London: Herder, 1957.

Gracia, J.J.E. 'Scholasticism and Scholastic Method.' *Dictionary of the Middle Ages*. Ed. J. Strayer. 13 vols., 11.55–8. New York: Scribner, 1982–89.

Grant, Edward. *God and Reason in the Middle Ages*. Cambridge: Cambridge University Press, 2001.

Gratsch, Edward J. *Where Peter Is: A Survey of Ecclesiology*. New York: Alba House, 1975.

Gross-Diaz, Theresa. *The Psalms Commentary of Gilbert of Poitiers: From* lectio divina *to the Lecture Room*, Brill's Studies in Intellectual History, 68. Leiden: Brill, 1996.

Haas, Roger M. 'Adam Marsh (de Marisco), a Thirteenth Century English Franciscan.' Unpublished PhD diss. Rutgers University, 1989.

Hanson, R.P.C. *The Search for the Christian Doctrine of God: the Arian Controversy 318–381*. Edinburgh: T&T Clark, 1988.

Harvey, E. Ruth. *The Inward Wits: Psychological Theory in the Middle Ages and the Renaissance*. London: Warburg Institute, 1975.

Hasse, Dag Nikolaus. *Avicenna's* De anima *in the Latin West*. Warburg Institute Studies and Texts, 1. London: Warburg Institute, 2000.

Haubst, Rudolf. *Vom Sinn der Menschwerdung: Cur Deus Homo*. Munich: Hueber, 1969.

Hendrix, Scott H. 'In Quest of the *Vera Ecclesia*: the Crisis of Late Medieval Ecclesiology.' *Viator* 7 (1976), 347–78.

——. *Ecclesia in Via: Ecclesiological Developments in the Medieval Psalms and the* Dictata Super Psalterium *(1513–1515) of Martin Luther*. Studies in Medieval and Reformation Thought, 10. Leiden: E.J. Brill, 1974.

Herlihy, David. *Medieval Households*. Cambridge, MA: Harvard University Press, 1985.

Hill, Kathryn. 'Robert Grosseteste and his Work of Greek translation.' In *The Orthodox Churches and the West*, Studies in Church History 13. Ed. D. Baker, pp. 213–22. Oxford: Blackwell, 1976.

Hodge, Charles. *Systematic Theology*. 3 vols. Grand Rapids: Eerdmanns, 1960.

Holmes, Stephen R. 'The Upholding of Beauty: a Reading of Anselm's *Cur Deus homo*.' *Scottish Journal of Theology* 54 (2001), 189–203.

Hopkins, Jasper. *A Companion to the Study of Saint Anselm*. Minnesota: University of Minneapolis Press, 1972.

Hotze, M.A. 'Scholastic Theology.' *New Catholic Encyclopedia*, 19 vols., 12.1153. New York: McGraw-Hill, 1967–95.

Hunt, Richard W. 'The Library of Robert Grosseteste.' In *Robert Grosseteste, Scholar and Bishop*. Essays in Commemoration of the Seventh Centenary of his Death. Ed. D.A. Callus, pp. 121–45. Oxford: Clarendon Press, 1955.

James, M.R. *A Descriptive Catalogue of the Manuscripts in the Library of Gonville and Caius College*. 2 vols. Cambridge: Cambridge University Press, 1907–8.

Jay, Eric. *The Church: Its Changing Image Through Twenty Centuries*. 2 vols. Atlanta: Knox Press, 1978.

Jenkins, John. *Knowledge and Faith in Thomas Aquinas*. Cambridge: Cambridge University Press, 1997.

De Jonge, Maike. 'Robert Grosseteste and the Testaments of the Twelve Patriarchs.' *Journal of Theological Studies* 42 (1991), 115–25.

Kantorowicz, Ernst H. *The King's Two Bodies. A Study in Mediaeval Political Theology*. Princeton: Princeton University Press, 1957.

Keck, David. *Angels and Angelology in the Middle Ages*. Oxford: Oxford University Press, 1998.

Keeler, L.W. 'The Dependence of Robert Grosseteste's *De anima* on the *Summa* of Philip the Chancellor.' *New Scholasticism* 11 (1937), 197–219.
Kemp, B.R., ed. *Reading Abbey Cartularies*. 2 vols. Camden Fourth Series 31 and 33. London: Royal Historical Society, 1986.
Kilma, Gyula 'The Medieval Problem of Universals.' In *The Stanford Encyclopedia of Philosophy*. Ed. E.N. Zalta. <http://plato.stanford.edu/entries/universals-medieval/>.
King, Edward B. 'Durham MS A.III.12 and Grosseteste's Homiletical Works.' In *Robert Grosseteste: New Perspectives on his Thought and Scholarship*. Ed. James McEvoy, pp. 277–88. Instrumenta Patristica, 18. Turnhout: Brepols, 1995.
Knowles, D. *The Evolution of Medieval Thought*. New York: Vintage Books, 1962.
Kvart, Igal. *A Theory of Counterfactuals*. Indianapolis: Hackett, 1986.
Laird, W.R. 'Robert Grosseteste on the Subalternate Sciences.' *Traditio* 43 (1987), 147–69.
Landgraf, A.M. *Introduction à l'histoire de la littérature théologique de la scolastique naissante*. Trans. A.-M. Landry and L.-B. Geiger. Publications de l'Institut d'Etudes Médiévales, 22. Montreal: Institut d'Etudes Médiévales, 1973.
——. *Dogmengeschichte der Frühscholastik*. 4 vols. Regensburg: Pusset, 1952–56.
——. 'Die Lehre von geheimnisvollen Leib Christi in dem fruhen Paulinenkommentaren und in der Frühscholastik.' *Divus Thomas* 24 (1946), 217–48, 393–428; 25 (1947) 365–94; 26 (1948) 160–80, 291–323, 395–434. Partially reprinted in Landgraf, *Dogmengeschichte*, 4.2.48–99.
——. 'Sünde und Trennung von der Kirche in der Frühscholastik.' *Scholastik* 5 (1930), 210–27.
Lawrence, C.H. 'The Letters of Adam Marsh and the Franciscan School at Oxford.' *Journal of Ecclesiastical History* 42 (1991), 218–38.
Leinsle, Ulrich G. *Einführung in dei scholastische Theologie*. Paderborn: Ferdinand Schöningh, 1995.
Lewis, David. *Counterfactuals*. Cambridge: Harvard University Press, 1973.
Lewis, Neil. 'Robert Grosseteste and the Church Fathers.' In *The Reception of the Church Fathers in the West: from the Carolingian to the Maurists*. Ed. I. Backus. 2 vols. 1.198–229. Leiden: Brill, 1997.
——. 'Time and Modality in Robert Grosseteste.' Unpublished PhD diss. University of Pittsburgh, 1988.
Little, A.G. and Douie, D.L. 'Three Sermons of Friar Jordan of Saxony, the Successor of St Dominic, Preaching in England, A.D. 1229.' *English Historical Review* 54 (1939), 1–19.
——. 'The Franciscan School at Oxford.' *Archivum Franciscanum Historicum* 19 (1926), 803–74.
Long, R. James. 'The *Sentences* Commentary of Richard Fishacre, OP.' In *Medieval Commentaries on the Sentences of Peter Lombard. Current Research*. Vol. 1. Ed. G.R. Evans, pp. 345–57. Leiden: Brill, 2002.
——. 'Of Angels and Pinhead: The Contribution of early Oxford Masters to the Doctrine of Spiritual Matter.' *Franciscan Studies* 56 (1998), 239–54.

———. 'The Question "Whether the Church Could Better Be Ruled by a Good Canonist than by a Theologian" and the Origins of Ecclesiology.' *Proceedings of the PMR Conference* 10 (1985), 99–112.

———. 'The Science of Theology according to Richard Fishacre: Edition of the Prologue to his Commentary on the Sentences.' *Mediaeval Studies* 34 (1972), 71–98.

Longère, J. *La prédication médiévale*. Paris: Etudes Augustiniennes, 1983.

De Lubac, Henri. *Corpus mysticum: L'eucharistie et l'église au moyen âge. Etude historique*. Paris: Aubier, 1944.

Luscombe, David. *The School of Peter Abelard: The Influence of Abelard's Thought in the Early Scholastic Period*. Cambridge: Cambridge University Press, 1969.

Macy, Gary. *The Theologies of the Eucharist in the Early Scholastic Period. A Study of the Salvific Function of the Sacrament according to the Theologians, c. 1080–c. 1220*. Oxford: Clarendon Press, 1984.

Marenbon, John. *From the Circle of Alcuin to the School of Auxerre: Logic, Theology, and Philosophy in the Early Middle Ages*. Cambridge: Cambridge University Press, 1981

Marrone, Stephen P. *The Light of Thy Countenance: Science and Knowledge of God in the Thirteenth Century*, Studies in the History of Christian Thought. 2 vols. Leiden: Brill, 2000.

———. *William of Auvergne and Robert Grosseteste: New Ideas of Truth in the Early Thirteenth Century*. Princeton: Princeton University Press, 1983.

McEvoy, James. 'Grossatesta: An Essay in Historiography.' In *Robert Grosseteste and the Beginnings of a British Theological Tradition*. Ed. M. O'Carroll, pp. 21–99. Bibliotheca Seraphico-Capuccina, 69. Rome: Istituto storico dei Cappuccini, 2003.

———. *Robert Grosseteste*. Oxford: Oxford University Press, 2000.

———. 'Nature as Light in Eriugena and Grosseteste.' In *Man and Nature in the Middle Ages*, Sewanee Medieval Studies 6. Ed. S.J. Ridyard and R.G. Benson, pp. 37–61. Sewanee: Sewanee University of the South Press, 1995.

———. *Robert Grosseteste, Exegete and Philosopher*. Aldershot: Variorum, 1995.

———. 'Robert Grosseteste's Use of the Argument of Saint Anselm.' In *Robert Grosseteste: New Perspectives on his Thought and Scholarship*. Ed. J. McEvoy, pp. 257–75. Instrumenta Patristica, 18. Turnhout: Brepols, 1995.

———. 'Robert Grosseteste on the Ten Commandments.' *Recherches de théologie ancienne et médiévale* 58 (1991), 167–205.

———. 'Ioannes Scottus Eriugena and Robert Grosseteste: An Ambiguous Influence.' In *Eriugena redivivus. Zur Wirkungsgeschichte seines Denkens im Mittelalter und im Übergang zur Neuzeit*. Ed. W. Beierwaltes, pp. 192–223. Heidelberg: Carl Winter Universitätsverlag, 1987.

———. *The Philosophy of Robert Grosseteste*. Oxford: Clarendon Press, 1982.

———. 'Der Brief des Robert Grosseteste an Magister Adam Rufus (Adam von Oxford, O.F.M.): ein Datierungsversuch.' *Franziskanische Studien* 63 (1981), 221–6.

———. 'The Absolute Predestination of Christ in the Theology of Robert Grosseteste.' In *Sapientiae Doctrinae: Mélanges de théologie et de littérature médiévales offerts à Dom Hildebrand Bascour O.S.B.*, pp. 212–30. Louvain: Abbaye du Mont César, 1980.

———. 'Robert Grosseteste and the Reunion of the Church.' *Collectanea Franciscana* 45 (1975), 39–84.
McGrath, Alistair. *Iustitia Dei: A History of the Christian Doctrine of Justification*. Second Edition. Cambridge: Cambridge University Press, 1998.
Meeks, Wayne A. *The First Urban Christian: the Social World of the Apostle Paul*. New Haven: Yale University Press, 1983.
Mersch, Emile. *Le Corps mystique du Christ*. 2 vols. Museum Lessianum, Section théologique, 28–9. Louvain: Museum Lessianum, 1933.
———. 'L'objet de la théologie et le *christus totus*.' *Recherches de science religieuse* 26 (1936), 129–57.
Miccoli, Lucia, 'Two thirteenth-century Theories of Light: Robert Grosseteste and St. Bonaventure.' *Semiotica* 136 (2001), 69–84.
Minnis, Alistair. *The Medieval Theory of Authorship*. Second edition. Philadelphia: University of Pennsylvania Press, 1984.
Molland, A.G. 'The Geometrical Background to the "Merton School".' *British Journal for the History of Science* 4 (1995), 110–25.
Moonan, Lawrence. *Divine Power: The Medieval Power Distinction up to its Adoption by Albert, Bonaventure and Aquinas*. Oxford: Clarendon Press, 1994.
Moorman, John. *A History of the Franciscan Order from its Origins to the Year 1517*. Oxford: Clarendon Press, 1968.
Morrison, Karl F. *The Two Kingdoms: Ecclesiology in Carolingian Political Thought*. Princeton: Princeton University Press, 1964.
Mulcahey, Michèle. *'First the Bow is Bent': Dominican Education to 1350*. Studies and Texts, 132. Toronto: PIMS, 1998.
Normore, Calvin. 'Future Contingents.' In *Cambridge History of Later Medieval Philosophy*. Ed. N. Kretzmann, A. Kenny, J. Pinborg and E. Stump, pp. 358–81. Cambridge: Cambridge University Press, 1982.
Oakley, Francis. 'Review of *Divine Power: The Medieval Power Distinction up to its Adoption by Albert, Bonaventure and Aquinas*, by L. Moonan.' *Speculum* 71 (1996), 985–7.
———. *The Western Church in the Later Middle Ages*. Ithaca: Cornell University Press, 1979.
Palma, Robert J. 'Grosseteste's Ordering of *Scientia*.' *The New Scholasticism* 50 (1976), 447–63.
Panti, Cecilia. 'L'Incorporazione della Luce secondo Roberto Grossetesta.' *Medioevo e Rinascimento* 13 (1999), 45–102.
Pelikan, J. *The Christian Tradition: a History of the Development of Doctrine*. Volume 3: The Growth of Medieval Theology (600–1300). Chicago: University of Chicago Press, 1978.
Phelan, G. 'An Unedited Text of Robert Grosseteste on the Subject-matter of Theology.' *Revue néoscolastique de philosophie* 36 (1934), 172–9.
Powicke, F.M. *Robert Grosseteste and the Nicomachean Ethics*. Proceedings of the British Academy 16. London: Milford, 1930.
Price, B. *Medieval Thought: An Introduction*. Oxford: Blackwell, 1992.

Principe, Walter H. 'Toward Defining Spirituality.' *Studies in Religion/Sciences religieuses* 12 (1983), 127–41.

——. '*Quaestiones* Concerning Christ from the First Half of the Thirteenth Century: IV. *Quaestiones* from Douai 434: Christ as Head of the Church: The Unity of the Mystical Body.' *Mediaeval Studies* 44 (1982), 1–82.

——. *Alexander of Hales's Theology of the Hypostatic Union*. Studies and Texts, 12. Toronto: PIMS, 1967.

——. *William of Auxerres's Theology of the Hypostatic Union*. Studies and Texts, 7. Toronto: PIMS, 1963.

Raedts, Peter. *Richard Rufus of Cornwall and the Tradition of Oxford Theology*. Oxford: Oxford University Press, 1987.

Rizzerio, Laura. 'Robert Grosseteste, Jean Chrysostome et l'*expositor graecus* (=Théophylacte) dans le commentaire *Super Epistolam ad Galatas*.' *Recherches de théologie ancienne et médiévale* 59 (1992), 166–209.

Robert Grosseteste, Scholar and Bishop. Essays in Commemoration of the Seventh Centenary of his Death. Ed. D.A. Callus. Oxford: Clarendon Press, 1955.

Robson, Michael, 'Saint Anselm, Robert Grosseteste and the Franciscan Tradition.' In *Robert Grosseteste: New Perspectives on His Thought and Scholarship*. Ed. J. McEvoy, pp. 233–56. Instrumenta Patristica, 18. Turnhout: Brepols, 1995.

Roese, Neal J. and Olson, James M. 'Counterfactual Thinkings: A Critical Overview.' In *What Might Have Been: the Social Psychology of Counterfactual Thinking*. Ed. N.J. Roese and J.M. Olson, pp. 1–56. Mahwah: Lawrence Erlbaum Associates, 1995.

Roest, Bert. *A History of Franciscan Education (c. 1210–1517)*. Education and Society in the Middle Ages and Renaissance, 11. Leiden: Brill, 2000.

Rossi, Pietro B. 'Robert Grosseteste and the Object of Scientific Knowledge.' In *Robert Grosseteste: New Perspectives on his Thought and Scholarship*. Ed. J. McEvoy, pp. 53–75. Instrumenta Patristica, 18. Turnhout: Brepols, 1995.

Rouse, Richard and Rouse, Mary. 'Concordances et index.' In *Du livre manuscrit. Mise en page et mise en texte*. Ed. H.J. Martin and J. Vezin, pp. 218–28. Paris: Promodis, 1990.

——. '*Statim invenire*: Schools, Preachers and New Attitudes to the Page.' In *Renaissance and Renewal in the Twelfth Century*. Ed. R.L. Benson, G.Constable and C.D. Lanham, pp. 201–25. Oxford: Clarendon Press, 1982.

The Sermon. Ed. B. Mayne Keinzle. Typologie des Sources du Moyen Âge Occidental, 81–3. Turnhout: Brepols, 2000.

Smalley, Beryl. *The Study of the Bible in the Middle Ages*. Second edition. Notre Dame: University of Notre Dame Press, 1964.

——. 'The Biblical Scholar.' In *Robert Grosseteste, Scholar and Bishop*, Essays in Commemoration of the Seventh Centenary of his Death. Ed. D.A. Callus, pp. 70–97. Oxford: Clarendon Press, 1955.

——. 'A Collection of Paris Lectures of the Later Twelfth Century in MS Pembroke College, Cambridge 7.' *Cambridge Historical Journal* 6 (1938), 103–13.

Smith, A. Mark. 'Picturing the Mind: The Representation of Thought in the Middle Ages and Renaissance.' *Philosophical Topics* 20 (1992), 149–70.

Smith, Lesley. 'The *De decem mandatis* of Robert Grosseteste.' In *Robert Grosseteste and the Beginnings of a British Theological Tradition*. Ed. M. O'Carroll, pp. 265–88. Bibliotheca Seraphico-Capuccina, 69. Rome: Istituto Storico dei Cappuccini, 2003.

Southern, Richard W. *Scholastic Humanism and the Unification of Europe*. 2 vols. Oxford: Blackwell, 1995–2000.

——. 'Richard Dales and the Editing of Robert Grosseteste.' In *Aspectus et Affectus: Essays and Editions in Grosseteste and Medieval Intellectual Life in Honor of Richard C. Dales*. Ed. G. Freibergs, pp. 3–14. New York: AMS Press, 1993.

——. *Robert Grosseteste: the Growth of an English Mind in Medieval Europe*. Second Edition. Oxford: Clarendon Press, 1992.

——. *Saint Anselm: a Portrait in a Landscape*. Cambridge: Cambridge University Press, 1990.

——. 'From Schools to Universities.' In *The Early Oxford Schools*. The History of the University of Oxford, 1. Ed. J. Catto, pp. 1–36. Oxford: Clarendon Press, 1984.

Spiegel, Gabriel and Freedman, Paul. 'Medievalisms Old and New: the Rediscovery of Alterity in North American Medieval Studies.' *American Historical Review* 103 (1998), 677–704.

Stock, Brian. *Listening for the Text: On the Uses of the Past*. Baltimore: Johns Hopkins University Press, 1991.

Sweeney, Leo. *Divine Infinity in Greek and Medieval Thought*. New York: Peter Lang, 1992.

Teske, Roland J. 'William of Auvergne on the Relation between Faith and Reason.' *The Modern Schoolman* 75 (1998), 279–91.

Thomson, S.H. *The Writings of Robert Grosseteste*. Cambridge: Cambridge University Press, 1940.

Torrell, J.P. *Théorie de la prophétie et philosophie de la connaissance aux environs de 1230: la contribution d'Hugues de Saint-Cher*. Spicilegium Sacrum Lovaniense Etudes et Documents, 40. Louvain: Spiciliegium Sacrum Lovaniense, 1977.

Tummers, Paul M.J.E. 'Geometry and Theology in the XIIIth Century: An Example of their Interrelation as found in the Ms Admont 442: the Influence of William of Auxerre?' *Vivarium* 18 (1980), 112–42.

Ullmann, Walter. *The Growth of Papal Government in the Middle Ages. A Study of the Ideological Relation of Clerical to Lay Power*. Third Edition. London: Methuen, 1970.

Wasserstein, David J. 'Grosseteste, the Jews and Medieval Christian Hebraism.' In *Robert Grosseteste: New Perspectives on his Thought and Scholarship*. Ed. J. McEvoy, pp. 357–76. Instrumenta Patristica, 18. Turnhout: Brepols, 1995.

Watt, J.A. 'Grosseteste and the Jews: A Commentary on Letter V.' In *Robert Grosseteste and the Beginnings of a British Theological Tradition*. Ed. M. O'Carroll, pp. 201–16. Bibliotheca Seraphico-Capuccina, 69. Rome: Istituto Storico dei Cappuccini, 2003.

Weijers, Olga. *Terminologie des universités au XIIIe siècle*. Lessico Intellettuale Europeo, 39. Rome: Edizioni dell' Ateneo, 1987.

Weisheipl, James A. 'The Nature, Scope and Classification of the Sciences.' In *Science in the Middle Ages*. Ed. D.C. Lindberg, pp. 461–82. Chicago: University of Chicago Press, 1978.

Westermann, Edwin J. 'A Comparison of Some of the Sermons and the *Dicta* of Robert Grosseteste.' *Medievalia et Humanistica* 3 (1945), 49–68.

Wilks, Michael. *The Problem of Sovereignty in the Later Middle Ages. The Papal Monarchy with Augustinus Triumphus and the Publicists*. Cambridge: Cambridge University Press, 1963.

Wood, Rega. 'Early Oxford Theology.' In *Medieval Commentaries on the* Sentences *of Peter Lombard. Current Research*. Vol. 1. Ed. G.R. Evans, pp. 289–343. Leiden: Brill, 2002.

Index

Abelard, Peter 36
Adam of Oxford (=Adam Rufus) 9n, 89–91, 99
Agnellus of Pisa 3, 4, 5
Albert of Pisa 9n
Albert the Great 128
Alexander III 139
Alexander of Hales 35, 58, 73, 92, 98, 100, 121, 128
Allan of Lille 54
angels 41, 42, 46, 91–2, 95, 134, 136, 172, 173
Anselm of Canterbury 39, 41, 54, 59, 63, 73, 93, 94, 97, 98, 123, 126, 127, 128, 130, 134, 142n
Anselm of Laon 36
Aquinas, Thomas 3, 21n, 28, 35, 39, 40, 58, 67, 128
Aristotle 13, 14, 25, 26, 28, 35, 37–8, 39, 47n, 54, 55, 61, 63, 77, 106, 157, 177n, 190
aspectus/affectus mentis 54–6, 62, 103
Augustine 36, 41, 54, 59, 61, 65, 68, 73, 75, 76, 90, 93, 97, 98, 99, 102–3, 110, 115n, 128, 130, 138, 154, 165–6, 190, 194, 195, 196, 197, 198, 199, 203, 208
Avicebron 104
Avicenna 81n, 93

Bacon, Roger 27, 189
Baker-Smith, Dominic 141n
baptism 158
Basil of Caesarea 83n, 209
Bazàn, Bernardo 16
Bede 127
Bernard of Clairveaux 63, 162, 198, 204, 205, 206, 207
Bible, *see* Scripture
Boethius 93, 95, 101, 102, 134, 157
Bonaventure 128, 192
books of nature and Scripture 25, 68–70

Callus, Daniel 4
canon law 7, 75, 164

Cassiodorus 3, 54
Chenu, Marie-Dominique 35
Christ 6, 7, 38, 40, 46, 47, 59, 64, 67, 121, 166, 194, 196, 204, 205, 206, 208, 209
  expectatio gentium 125, 127, 128
  flesh of 84n, 131, 135–6
  head of the Church 132, 140, 158
  homo assumptus 121, 130
  hypostatic union 62–3, 123, 136, 137, 138–9, 157
  necessity of the Incarnation 39–40, 59–60, 124–38, 129
  optimus hominum 124–5
  promised seed of Abraham 124
  sermo patris 96
  suffering servant 125–6
Chrysostom, John 201
church 16, 46, 47, 67, 135, 151–5, 160, 162, 168, 173, 191, 197, 205, 210
  body of Christ 46, 140, 155, 157, 158, 162, 173
  ecclesia militans/triumphans 162, 172
  the faithful 156, 162, 204, 209
  whole Christ 33, 36, 38, 39, 44, 45, 121, 191
Cicero 93, 133
circumcision 66, 122
Claudius of Turin 129
collatio 19, 23n
Comestor, Peter 66
conduct 155–8, 160, 161
confession, *see* penance
Constantine the African 142n
contemplation 157, 159
counterfactuals 128–9, 144n
creation 6, 33–4, 130, 131, 136–7, 141, 156, 160, 168
credibilia 34, 44
Cyril of Alexandria 155, 193

Damascene, John 14, 74, 130, 131
decalogue 19, 110, 159, 167, 168, 170–72, 197
deification 33, 45, 137, 161, 166, 200

229

Diogenes of Sinope 25
discernment 155, 156
disputation 16–18, 77
distinctio 70
Dominicans 27

Epicurus 25, 203
Erasmus of Rotterdam 141n
Eriugena, John Scotus 89, 137
Eucharist, *see* liturgy
Euclid 63–4, 68
Eusebius of Caesaria 200
exegesis
  allegorical 197
  anagogical 69
  literal 65–8, 71, 202
  prosopological 67, 156, 189
  spiritual 65, 66, 70–72, 123
  tropological 71, 178, 198, 206, 209

faith 28, 34, 44, 45, 69
  articles of 43–4, 59
  and knowledge 41–5
  and love 69, 158–9, 194
fideism 28
Fishacre, Richard 27, 107, 128, 192
form 41, 89, 90, 91, 106, 107
Franciscans 1, 3, 4, 16, 17, 19, 72
free will/choice 92, 98, 169
future contingents 92, 93–4

Gascoigne, Thomas 16
geometry 25, 63–4, 81n
Gilbert of Poitiers 36
glory 128
glossa ordinaria, *see* Scripture
God 6, 39, 40, 42, 47, 57, 70, 89, 92, 97
  agency 107
  Creator 34, 156, 160, 166
  first form 89–91, 189
  the form of all things 91–2, 189
  goodness 103–4, 130, 171
  Holy spirit 76, 77, 140, 166
  knowledge 92–4, 97, 190
  nature 3, 53, 96, 98, 111
  power 94–8, 103, 106–7
  transcendence 90, 91, 94
  Trinity 33, 45, 46, 62, 89, 97, 98–106, 109, 110, 134, 136, 139, 173, 190, 191
  ubiquity 91–2
  vestiges of in creation 100, 103, 104–6
Goering, Joseph 16, 18

grace 98, 128, 156, 165, 169
Gregory the Great 43, 59, 73, 128, 162, 201, 203, 206, 207
Grosseteste, Robert
  archdeacon of Leicester 19, 163
  bishop of Lincoln 1, 3, 4, 7–8, 13, 57, 74, 191
  deacon 163
  knowledge of Greek 66, 74
  master of the sacred page, 1, 3–5, 61, 72, 164, 191–2
  priest 3, 163–5
  theological method 53, 56–7, 90–92, 123–4
Writings:
  Commentarius in libros posteriorum analyticorum 37–38, 39, 43, 55–6, 64
  De cessatione legalium 16, 18, 20, 58–9, 64–5, 66, 70–72, 74, 75–7, 108, 121–41
  De decem mandatis 19, 110, 170
  Dicta 14, 18–19
  Dictum 2: 50n, 57, 78n, 79n; **3:** 133–4, 145n, 146n; **8:** 79n, 111, 119n; **15:** 50n; **19:** 1, 3, 14, 18, 71, 79n; **21:** 148n; **33:** 49n, 117n; **35:** 179n; **38:** 79n, 143n; **41:** 153, 174n; **60:** 104–5; **70:** 133, 145n; **74:** 133, 145n; **90:** 165, 167–72, 182n, 183n, 184n; **91:** 165–7, 180n, 181n, 182n; **101:** 168, 175n, 182n, 184n, 185n; **118:** 25–6, 28, 77; **129:** 43–4, 51n
  De dotibus 16, 18, 136, 173
  Epistolae 14, 19, 19–20, 23n, 75, 89–92, 163, 164, 179n
  Expositio... ad Galatas 20, 74, 75
  Hexaëmeron 16, 33–35, 43, 44, 46, 74, 89, 98–104, 111, 137
  De liberalibus artibus 55
  De libero arbitrio 17, 18, 89, 92–8
  De luce 107–8, 109
  De operationibus solis 16
  De ordine emanandi causatorum a Deo 17, 18
  De potentia et actu 17
  Regule libri priorum 29n
  De scala paupertatis 19
  De sciencia Dei 93
  sermons 14, 19, 107
  Speculum confessionis 19, 164–5
  De statu causarum 17

Super psalterium 3, 15, 16, 19, 20, 65–6, 72, 74, 81n, 82n, 107, 116n, 117n, 144n, 154–62, 175n, 176n, 177n, 178n, 182n, 183n, 184n, 186n, 193–210
Tabula distinctionum 5–7, 46, 74, 89, 107, 109, 121, 151–2
Templum Dei 13, 164
Testament of the Twelve Patriarchs 14
De veritate 17, 18, 58, 96
De veritate proposicionis 17
Spurious:
De anima 17–18
Lecturae in epistolam ad Romanos 16
Moralitates super evangelia 16
Gueric of St-Quentin 128
Guy of Orchelles 58

Henry of Coventry 9n
Henry of Ghent 81n
Hill, Edmund 115n
Hodge, Charles 83n
Honorius III 89
Hugh of Lincoln 7
Hugh of St-Cher 58, 73, 98
Hugh of St-Victor 36, 66, 190
humanism 77
humanity 92, 98, 99
  fall of 131, 135
  glorified body 173
  image of God 99, 100, 111
  prelapsarian state 111, 129, 134, 136
Hunt, Richard 16

illumination 56, 57
imagination 25–6, 30n, 34, 42, 56, 61–4, 91, 127
incarnation, *see* Christ
infinity 97, 104–5, 106–9, 190, 194
innocence 159, 160, 163, 197, 198
Innocent IV 13, 27
intellectus 42, 130
intelligentia 42, 56
Isaac Israeli 142n

Jacques de Vitry 38
Jerome 65, 75, 76
Jews 121, 122, 123, 127, 142n
Joachim of Fiore 102
Jordan of Saxony 5, 163
justice 90, 132, 133–4, 156, 157, 161, 195, 202
justification 128, 131, 132, 133

knowledge
  human 41, 42, 54, 55, 156
  of God 53–4, 109–11

Lateran IV (Council of) 13, 102, 168
lecturing 15–16, 77
Legatine Ordinance 3, 4
Lewis, Neil 95
Liber de spiritu et anima 42, 99, 135
light 57, 101, 102, 104, 124
Lincoln Cathedral 4
liturgy 72, 126, 169
logic 25, 59, 63, 68, 69, 11, 132
Lombard, Peter 5, 27, 54, 65, 73, 75, 102, 107, 115n, 121, 130, 137–8, 189
love 69, 108, 118n, 165, 166, 170, 196, 197, 206, 207; *see also* faith
Luther, Martin 128

marriage gifts 156
McEvoy, James 104, 112n, 137
Marsh, Adam 4, 9n, 19–20, 164, 192
mathematics 42, 104
mercy 155, 156, 169, 194, 195
metaphysics 13, 40, 41, 42, 106, 130, 170
Minnis, Alistair 66
moral philosophy 157
Mosaic law 18, 64, 76, 108, 122, 123, 127
music 76

natural philosophy 14, 38, 40, 41, 65, 67, 68, 69
necessity 39–41, 46, 94, 95, 97, 124

Oxford University 1, 3, 4, 8, 14, 16, 27, 73, 121, 136, 163, 164, 172

papacy 152, 153
Paris, University of 4, 16, 27, 73
Paschasius Radbertus 54
pastoral care 13, 14, 26, 155, 163, 165–72, 191
Pegge, Samuel 141n
Pegis, Anton 49n
penance 156, 159, 167–8, 178n
Peter of Ramsey 4
Peter the Chanter 21n, 168
Philip the Chancellor 17–18, 35, 73, 114n
Plato 41
de potentia absoluta/de potentia ordinata 97–8, 114n
preaching 18–19, 56–7, 77, 168–9
Ps-Dionysius the Areopogite 13–14, 41, 74, 104, 107, 108

quadrivium 67

Rabanus Maurus 129
ratio 42, 54
redemption, *see* salvation
remoto Christo 123
reportatio/nes 17, 22n
resurrection 136
Richard of St-Victor 129
Robert of Melun 36
Roger of Wesham 4
Roland of Cremona 98
Rufus, Richard 128, 192

Sabbath 66, 122
sacra doctrina 45
sacraments 152
salvation 123, 129, 132
   Christus victor 126–7
   satisfaction 126
sanctification 132, 141
scibilia 34, 44
sciencia 25–6, 34, 35, 41–2
Scotus, John Duns 128
Scripture 1, 2, 6, 7, 26, 27, 34, 38, 43, 44, 45, 59, 64–5, 66, 68, 70, 71, 72, 76, 93, 95, 100, 105, 122, 123, 125, 127, 138, 153, 154, 168, 169, 189, 191, 204
   creation narrative 34–5, 61, 69, 98–9
   glossa ordinaria 75
   'Paris' Bible 16
Seneca 203
sensation 35, 42, 135, 198, 202
Sentences, *see* Lombard, Peter

Septuagint 66
similitude 27
singulars 135
soul 42, 55, 91–2, 130, 135, 155, 158, 158, 166
Southern, Ricard 4, 26, 31n, 60, 63, 72
spirituality 46, 109, 154, 165, 170, 172
Stock, Brian 170
Summa 'fratris Alexandri' 28, 54, 58, 78n
Sweeney, Leo 107

Theodoret 204
theology
   natural 29, 105
   scholastic 2, 5, 28–9, 45, 74, 109, 189
   speculative 29, 54, 57–60
   subject matter of 33–5, 39, 53
Thomas of Eccleston 3, 191
trivium 38, 68
Tyconius 154

universals 62, 91
upright heart 160–62, 168

Vincent of Coventry 9n
virtue 46, 160, 163

Wallensis, Thomas 4, 9n
Willermus 47n
William of Auvergne 73, 98, 101, 109
William of Auxerre 35, 53, 58, 73, 75–6, 92, 98, 112n, 116n, 121, 138–40, 148n
wisdom 34, 41–3, 56